RELIABILITY OF SOFTWARE INTENSIVE SYSTEMS

RELIABILITY OF SOFTWARE INTENSIVE SYSTEMS

by

Michael A. Friedman
Phuong Y. Tran
Peter L. Goddard

Hughes Aircraft Company

Advanced Computing
and
Telecommunications Series

NOYES DATA CORPORATION
Park Ridge, New Jersey, U.S.A.

Transferred to Digital Printing, 2011

Printed and bound in Great Britain by
CPI Antony Rowe, Chippenham and Eastbourne

Library of Congress Cataloging-in-Publication Data

Friedman, Michael A.
        Reliability of software intensive systems / Michael A. Friedman,
Phuong Y. Tran, Peter L. Goddard
            p.   cm. -- (Advanced computing and telecommunications series)
        Reprint. Originally published in 2 v.: Griffiss Air Force Base,
N.Y. : Rome Laboratory Air Force Systems Command, 1991-92.
        Includes bibliographical references
        ISBN 0-8155-1361-5
        1. Computer software--Reliability. 2. Electronic digital
computers--Reliability. I. Tran, Phuong Y. II. Goddard, Peter L.
III. Title,   V. Series.
QA76.76.R44F75   1994
005--dc20   94-23431
                                                       CIP

Preface

Many modern military and commercial systems and products contain both hardware and executable software elements. The hardware comprises the physical, tangible elements of the system. Executable software is a logical element of the system, consisting of sequences of instructions (programs).

High reliability is an important need in commercial systems. High reliability is also a crucial need of complex military systems, which can inflict or prevent death. As hardware becomes more and more reliable as the result of technological advances, software is assuming an increasing role in achieving system reliability requirements. System reliability considerations have in many cases made a transition from hardware to software.

Methods for the prediction and measurement of hardware reliability are considerably older and more mature than those for software. Over the past fifteen years, the field of software reliability has made significant progress. Major achievements have taken place in understanding software reliability, including modeling, prediction, estimation, its relationship to software quality metrics, and its relationship to mission environment. These results are scattered throughout the industrial and academic literature. This study is intended to bring this research together, and build on it, adding new theoretical and empirical results to create a comprehensive methodology for software reliability assessment.

The methodology resulting from this study covers the entire life cycle, and is aligned with existing hardware reliability standards and practice, so that it can be applied in a unified, integrated approach to total systems reliability.

This book provides a reliability assurance methodology to predict and estimate the reliability of systems that employ both hardware and software subsystems. Since the methods used to predict the reliability of hardware systems are well known, this book concentrates on the methods to predict and estimate the reliability of software configuration items and methods for combining hardware and software reliability figures of merit into an overall system parameter.

Notice

Part I is the final report on research into *Reliability Techniques for Combined Hardware/Software Systems,* performed by Hughes Aircraft Company for the U.S. Air Force under the contractual auspices of Rome Air Development Center, Griffiss Air Force Base, Rome, New York.

Part II is a draft military handbook prepared for Rome Laboratory entitled: *Hardware/Software Reliability, Assurance, and Control.* Although written for military applications, it is also pertinent to industrial and commercial systems.

To the best of our knowledge the information in this publication is accurate; however, the authors and the Publisher do not assume any responsibility or liability for the accuracy or completeness of, or consequences arising from use of such information. Mention of trade names or commercial products does not constitute endorsement or recommendation for use by the authors or the Publisher.

Final determination of the suitability of any information or product for use contemplated by any user, and the manner of that use, is the sole responsibility of the user. We recommend that anyone intending to rely on any recommendation of materials or procedures in this publication should satisfy himself as to such suitability.

Contents and Subject Index

PART II
HARDWARE/SOFTWARE RELIABILITY ASSURANCE AND CONTROL

Part I

Reliability Techniques
for Combined
Hardware and Software Systems

Michael A. Friedman
Phuong Y. Tran
Peter L. Goddard

Hughes Aircraft Company

1. Introduction

1.1 Scope

This document constitutes the final report on research into "Reliability Techniques for Combined Hardware/Software Systems," performed for the U.S. Air Force under the contractual auspices of Rome Air Development Center, Griffiss Air Force Base, Rome, New York. This report fully satisfies the requirements of CLIN 0002, ELIN A004, of contract F30602-89-C-0111, Reliability Techniques for Combined Hardware and Software Systems.

1.2 Research Problem Background

Many modern military and commercial systems and products contain both hardware and executable software elements. The hardware comprises the physical, tangible elements of the system. Executable software is a logical element of the system, consisting of sequences of instructions (programs). As speed, capacity, and cost-effectiveness advance, an ever-increasing number of applications are being found for computers. Society and its institutions are becoming more and more dependent upon computers. Microprocessors are being embedded into all manner of devices and systems to add "intelligence." Computers lie at the heart of real-time applications that control critical and vital functions, where system failure can have catastrophic results. High reliability is a crucial need of complex military systems, which can inflict or prevent death. As hardware becomes more and more reliable as the result of technological advances, software is assuming an increasing role in achieving system reliability requirements. System reliability considerations have in many cases made a transition from hardware to software.

Methods for the prediction and measurement of hardware reliability are considerably older and more mature than those for software. The hardware methods have become standardized and institutionalized throughout the defense and related industries through military standards and handbooks. Over the past fifteen years, the field of software reliability has made significant progress. Major achievements have taken place in understanding software reliability, including modeling, prediction, estimation, its relationship to software quality metrics, and its relationship to mission environment. These results are scattered throughout the industrial and academic literature. This study is intended to bring this research together, and build on it, adding new theoretical and empirical results to create a comprehensive methodology for software reliability assessment.

The methodology resulting from this study covers the entire life cycle, is compatible with the military standard for defense system software development--DOD-STD-2167A--and is aligned with existing hardware reliability standards and practice, so that it can be applied in a unified, integrated approach to total systems reliability. To the end of moving software reliability engineering towards standardization and institutionalization, a draft military handbook on combined hardware/software system reliability prediction and estimation is being written as part of this study effort (ELIN A003).

1.3   Approach

The study team began the research project by establishing a software error/failure database for use in developing techniques for system decomposition and reliability allocation, reliability prediction and modeling, reliability growth testing, and reliability demonstration. The team populated this database with error data, test failure data, and product/development process metrics from eight projects. The projects were selected to encompass a wide variety of size, product, and development process characteristics. Two of the projects were ongoing projects whose data was set aside to be used solely for the validation of the techniques.

Since the database required data from several life cycle phases of each project, the data could not be collected all at once. The data collection was spread out over several months. The prediction task, which required the most data, was the last task to be completed. While the database was being populated, work began on the allocation, prediction, growth, and demonstration tasks.

System decomposition consists of allocating functional requirements to hardware and software subsystems and lower indenture levels. Reliability allocation consists of apportioning overall system reliability requirements to those items. For software the indenture levels are Computer Software Configuration Items (CSCIs), Computer Software Components (CSCs), Computer Software Units (CSUs), and modules. The approach that was taken was to allocate software reliability to processes (also called tasks), which generally correspond to the CSCI level.

A Markov (combinations) approach for repairable systems and a combinatorial approach for non-repairable systems were used for reliability modeling. Reliability combination (i.e, calculation of the reliability of assemblages of hardware and software components) was studied as a prerequisite to researching allocation.

Reliability prediction was approached by defining the problem as predicting the parameters of a suitable software reliability growth model. Predictive relationships based on regression analysis of the product/process metrics and error/failure data were developed.

For growth testing, criteria for selecting a software reliability growth model, goodness-of-fit techniques, and recalibration techniques were developed. Special attention was paid to statistically valid ways to perform the testing, including acceleration by means of multiple copies.

For demonstration testing, an appropriate model for testing frozen code was selected. The types of tests developed based on that model were fixed-length tests, failure-free execution interval tests, and sequential tests. Additional types of tests were developed for the cases of demonstration test during growth testing and for using multiple copies.

Each of the techniques developed for prediction, decomposition and allocation, growth testing, and demonstration testing were validated on ongoing projects. The techniques were organized into a reliability methodology covering the entire life cycle. The methodology forms the basis for the draft MIL-HDBK delivered under contract as ELIN A003.

1.4 Report Organization

This report is organized to provide full detailed results for all items in the SOW of contract F30602-89-C-0111 which are not supplied under separate CLIN or ELINs. Coverage of the study results for reliability modeling (SOW Task 2), allocation (SOW Task 3), prediction (SOW Task 4), growth testing (SOW Task 5), demonstration testing (SOW Task 6), and validation (SOW Task 7) are provided in the main body of the report. The appendices provide study activity reporting for reliability data base establishment (SOW Task 1) and provide supplementary, detailed, material for the other tasks in the SOW where appropriate. Reporting on Reliability Technique Application Software (SOW Task 7) and Handbook Guidelines (SOW Task 8) is not provided. SOW tasks 7 and 8 are deliverable under CLIN 0001 and CLIN 0002, ELIN A003 respectively.

1.5 Introductory Concepts

1.5.1 Software Failure

Software and hardware differ in several respects. Software does not wear out; almost all hardware goes through a wearout phase. All copies of software are perfectly identical; each manufactured copy of a piece of hardware differs to some extent. Once a fault is removed from software it is gone forever; many hardware faults can recur. When viewed at the appropriate level of abstraction, however, hardware and software reliability are very similar. Both a running program and an operating hardware item can be seen as "black boxes." Every once in a while the black box fails. The failure-inducing stress is time. For software, time brings with it a succession of input states. The more time that goes by, the higher the quantity of, and the more variety of, input states the program encounters. Eventually, because of the presence of faults, an input state will trigger a failure. With hardware, time carries with it random stresses (such as friction, shock, corrosion) which gradually or suddenly cause failure. Thus both hardware and software reliability can be modeled as random or stochastic processes.

An interesting trend is that some types of hardware are taking on the characteristics of software. A VLSI chip cannot be exhaustively tested; like software there are too many input states and too many paths. Hermetically sealed integrated circuit chips are claimed to have no wearout failure mode. Firmware has both hardware and software failure modes. While a particular version of a program does not wear out, program maintenance is an entropy-increasing process, so that a program will, in time, deteriorate.

A software failure occurs when the program produces output (display, hardcopy, command, control, etc.) that deviates from what the requirements specify. A failure can be one of conformance, in which the program does not produce the right answer, or one of performance, in which the program does not perform a required function in a timely or resource-efficient manner. Performance failures include crashes, hangs, and software that does not meet its response or throughput time requirements. Real-time systems need to respond to events in the outside world as those events are happening.

Software failures can be classified along several different dimensions. One classification is by the number of discrepancies that comprise the failure. A discrepancy is a deviation of the value of a single output variable from the required value. Another way failures can be classified is by the severity of their consequences: The impact of a failure could be as innocuous as a misspelling or as catastrophic as loss of life or limb.

Software reliability is one measure of software quality. "Software quality" refers to those attributes that a program is required to possess at all times. Examples include security, robustness, maintainability, safety, availability, and portability. Quantitatively, software reliability is defined as the probability of failure-free operation of the software for a specified period of time, in a specified environment. An alternative figure of merit is the software's failure rate, the instantaneous rate of software failures per unit time. By "time" is meant execution time. The failure-inducing stress is execution time, since software that is not running cannot fail. When combining software failure rates with one another and with hardware, the failure rate is re-expressed with respect to system

operating time.   The level at which software reliability should
be expressed needs to be a high one, such as Computer Software
Configuration Item (CSCI), so that the interfaces between lower
level items will be included.

Software failures arise from a population of software faults. A
software fault (often called "bug") is missing, extra, or
defective code that has caused or can potentially cause a
failure.   Every time a fault is traversed during execution, a
failure does not necessarily ensue; it depends on the machine
state (values of intermediate variables).   The extent to which a
source program contains faults is indicated by its fault density,
expressed in faults per thousand lines of executable source code
(KLOC).   The fault density does not translate directly into a
failure rate because different parts of the program are executed
with different frequencies.   Instructions inside loops will tend
to be executed more often than instructions outside loops.
Conditionally executed instructions tend to get executed less
than unconditional ones.   How many loop iterations occur and
which branches take place depend on the machine state, which in
turn depends on the input state.

The origin of software faults lies in human fallibility.
Compounding factors are the lagging of software engineering
technology behind the increasing capabilities of computers, the
large number of discrete states in programs, the novelty of
problems and solutions, and lack of standard off-the-shelf
software "parts" and designs. Software is very flexible because
there are no physical constraints such as power, weight, quantity
of parts, manufacturability, etc., so software engineers take on
tasks of sometimes enormous size and complexity.

1.5.2   Software Design Approaches To Reliability

High levels of software reliability are accomplished through a
triad of activities: fault avoidance, fault elimination, and
fault tolerance.

Fault avoidance consists of applying sound software engineering
practices, including standards (documentation, structured design
and programming, control), quality assurance (formal reviews,
audits; evaluation of personnel, methods), and verification and
validation.   These methods can go a long way in keeping down the
number of faults but, historically, many faults will remain.

Fault elimination is accomplished through testing, code reading,
and walkthroughs.   The only way to uncover and remove all faults
in the code is through exhaustive testing.   Exhaustive testing of
non-trivial programs is impossible from a practical point of view
because the number of inputs states is astronomically large.
Formal proof of correctness, given the current state of the art,
is likewise impractical for real-world software.   In a program

correctness proof, the program is treated as a static mathematical object. The correctness proof is a formal mathematical demonstration that a program is consistent with its specification. Such proofs are of great size and complexity, although mechanical verifier systems help. A formal specification of the program is required, and it is impossible to demonstrate whether the specification captures the intentions of the customer. Even if exhaustive testing or a formal proof of correctness could be accomplished, the results of the activity are as vulnerable to human fallibility as programming is.

Fault tolerance is achieved through special programming techniques that enable the software to detect and recover from failure incidents. Software fault tolerance is a controversial topic. The method requires "redundant" software elements that provide alternative means of fulfilling the same function. The different versions must be such that they will not all fail in response to the same circumstances. Some have suggested that diverse software versions developed using different specifications, designs, programming teams, programming languages, etc., might fail in a statistically independent manner. Empirical evidence questions that hypothesis. However, almost all software fault-tolerance experiments have reported some degree of reliability improvement. Despite advances in software fault avoidance, elimination, and tolerance, large-scale software will have faults and it will occasionally fail. There is a need to specify, predict, measure, allocate, model, and demonstrate software reliability. Software reliability figures need to be meaningfully combined with hardware reliability figures to yield system reliability figures.

1.5.3 Software Reliability Growth

For the results of growth model parameter estimation and software reliability growth testing to be valid, it is important that the environment during test be the same as the actual field use environment. The hardware platform (actual or emulated) and the system software (such as the operating system version) must be the same. A very important part of the environment is the program's operational profile. An operational profile associates each point (input state) in the program's input space with a probability of occurrence. The operational profiles during testing and field use must be identical. Since the input space of most programs is quite large, fully specifying the operational profile is impractical. An operational profile can usually be expressed as the relative frequencies of end-user functions, resulting in a "functional profile." For real-time systems, ordering and timing of inputs may also enter into a description of the environment.

Just because faults lurk in the code, however, does not mean that the program will provide unreliable service to end-users. Each user's individual operational profile will result in a different rate at which faults are encountered. The operational profile determines the probability of each input state and hence each path through the program. The input state determines the machine state (values of all intermediate variables) the computer will be in when the fault is encountered. In certain machine states the fault will cause a failure.

During a hardware item's useful life (between burn-in and wearout) a constant failure rate model is generally employed. For a program whose code is frozen, subjected to input randomly selected from a fixed operational profile, a constant failure rate model is a reasonable one (see Appendix B). During system test, as the code is altered as the result of fault correction activity, the failure rate will vary as a function of cumulative execution time.

The failure rate of a piece of software is a function of the number and location of faults in the code, how fast the program is being executed, and the operational profile. Faults cannot be directly observed, if only for the reason that any faults whose whereabouts are known would presumably have already been removed. The way to find faults is to execute the software starting from various input states. When a failure occurs the symptoms are recorded. Fault-correction personnel analyze the symptoms and look at the code to try and locate the fault that caused the failure. If the fault is not obvious, the personnel will try to reproduce the failure, this time running with a debugging tool or having inserted additional output statements into the program. A debugging tool typically allows the user to execute the program a step at the time and lets him or her examine and deposit variable values. Usually, the programmer finds the fault and removes it. At times the repair activity introduces new faults into the code.

While repair activity is imperfect, the hoped-for and generally observed result is that the times between failures tend to grow longer and longer as the process of testing and fault correction goes on. A software reliability growth model mathematically summarizes a set of assumptions about the phenomenon of software failure. The model provides a general form for the failure rate as a function of time and contains unknown parameters that are determined either by prediction or estimation.

Growth testing and modeling is used to estimate the time and effort needed to reach intermediate or required reliability goals and to track the progress the software is making toward those reliability goals. If the software is falling short, management can re-allocate resources or take other corrective action. Growth testing thus provides visibility to management about where the software reliability is currently and where it is expected to be at a given milestone.

A software reliability growth model makes assumptions about the nature of the distribution that fits the failure data. Since there is usually no prior statistical information about the failure behavior of a specific program, a goodness-of-fit procedure can be applied to assess how well the model is fitting the data. If the fit is not good, an alternate model or statistical estimation technique can be employed or a recalibration technique can be applied to the model to improve the results.

1.5.4 Basic Reliability Concepts

Quantitatively, the reliability of an item is expressed by its reliability function R(t). To be meaningful, the environment in which the item operates must be specified. The reliability function gives the probability that the item will fail by time t. The reliability of an item is usually specified for mission oriented systems. An alternative way of expressing an item's relative reliability is by its failure rate $\lambda(t)$, which is the rate of failures per unit time at the instant t. In situations where the failure rate is a constant, λ, the reliability function and failure rate are related by the equation $R(t) = \exp[-\lambda t]$. MTBF, the reciprocal of failure rate or availability are the most common reliability figures of merit for systems which are continuously operated and undergo repair when failures occur.

2. System and Software Modeling/Combination

Reliability modeling of combined hardware and software systems is analogous to reliability modeling of purely hardware systems. The failure rates for both hardware and software are treated as constant (see Appendix B). Reliability block diagrams of system elements are developed and employed. Individual hardware platforms and the software assigned to those platforms are independent of other hardware/software platforms. State diagrams that accurately portray the interrelationship between the hardware platforms and the software executing on the platforms are developed and used in estimating reliability figures of merit.

This section provides a summary overview of the techniques applicable to the reliability modeling of combined hardware and software systems. An abbreviated overview of the system modeling process is provided. This overview is used to help the analyst identify those system properties which are unique to combined hardware and software systems. The majority of this section is dedicated to describing the development of software failure rates that are a composite of the multiple processes that may be executing during any time period. A major treatment of reliability modeling of HW/SW systems was provided in [James et al. (1982)]. This report provides modest clarification to the major work on reliability modeling that has been previously done. Specifically, some discussion of the reliability modeling detail as it relates to active redundancy is provided.

Modeling methods used to model combined HW/SW systems for the purposes of reliability estimation and allocation need to accurately assess the interdependence between individual software elements, the hardware platforms on which these software elements execute, and the services provided by the system being analyzed. Additionally, the methods used need to be based on and compatible with modern system engineering methods.

Reliability modeling is based on system FMEA (Failure Modes and Effects Analysis), a traditional, bottom up, reliability analysis technique that provides a mapping between failures and their impact on system services. These FMEAs need not always be a formal analysis since the results are expressed in the reliability model block diagrams. Both fault tree analysis and FMEA were critically examined for use in combined HW/SW system reliability model development. Either fault tree analysis or FMEA can produce the needed analysis of the dependencies between system hardware elements and system services. However, fault tree analysis of the loss of each system service, while accurate and complete, creates a large amount of duplication of information. FMEA techniques tend to result in a more compact display of the needed data. However, traditional FMEAs that are entered on multiple pages of FMEA forms create a large amount of data that is poorly organized for reliability model development. The use of a system level adaptation of Matrix FMEA techniques [Barbour (1977), Goddard (1984)] results in a compact readily usable display of the needed FMEA information.

The modeling of combined HW/SW systems, whether for reliability allocation or estimating purposes, is best approached on a functional service basis using a matrix FMEA approach. The resultant FMEA can then be used to develop a HW/SW system reliability block diagram of independent elements. The individual series/parallel elements of the reliability block diagram can then be modeled. Non-redundant systems can be modeled as series strings of hardware and HW/SW system elements. Complex, redundant systems and system elements are modeled using Markov state diagrams to accurately portray the possible operational and non-operational states. In general, these state diagrams will be complex enough to require access to automated tools for solution. They are not, strictly speaking, intractable. However, the labor required to manually determine a specific closed form solution for a state diagram that has been developed to model a specific design being analyzed is usually prohibitive. Automated solutions of these state diagrams are possible both analytically and through simulation. Tools for analytic and simulation solutions of Markov state diagrams are available to government offices and their contractors through Rome Labs and NASA at nominal costs. The user of these tools will need to determine whether or not the numerical accuracy needed for their specific situation is supported. Analytic solutions to these diagrams often require the solution of a transition matrix with potentially significant losses in numerical accuracy due to the multiple arithmetic operations compounded by the accuracy limitations of the processing platform being used. Monte Carlo solutions to Markov chains can result in both numerical inaccuracy due to the methods employed and may involve substantial cost for multiple program runs. The costs associated with Monte Carlo solutions rise dramatically as the degree of accuracy demanded increases.

Estimation of system reliability characteristics is based on the reliability block diagrams and Markov state diagrams developed from the system services FMEA and the individual hardware and software component reliability. Estimation techniques for hardware reliability and maintainability characteristics are well known and can be applied to the hardware portions of combined HW/SW systems. Software reliability characteristics can be estimated using the methods described in this report. For redundant, fault tolerant systems, software recovery characteristics are system design and implementation dependent. These recovery characteristics will need to be estimated on a case by case basis in conjunction with performance modeling and estimation.

Software maintainability, the time required to isolate and correct a fault in the design, is not used in the reliability modeling and allocation discussed in this section. Software maintenance is expected to proceed in parallel with ongoing system operation following a software failure. Thus, the time required to reestablish system operation following a software failure is used as the repair or recovery rate in the modeling of software elements of combined HW/SW elements. Software maintenance will result in a software failure rate that is not constant over time due to the software corrections being implemented. However, for the purposes of modeling and allocation of combined hardware and software systems, an assumption of constant software failure rate at any operational period (i.e., between software fixes) is justified. Estimations of the software failure rate and of software reliability growth rates are discussed elsewhere within this report.

2.1 Development of the System Model

The development of an accurate and representative system reliability model for use in reliability estimation and allocation is dependent on a thorough understanding of the system being modeled. First a FMEA is developed for the system design which relates the services provided by the system to the various hardware and software components. This FMEA is then translated into a system model.

2.1.1 Developing the System FMEA

Development of a reliability model for use in reliability estimation and allocation begins with the use of the functional decomposition that has been developed as a part of the system engineering process. For small or relatively simple system structures, system functional analysis may have been omitted as a formal procedure. If the system level functional decomposition is not available, the reliability engineer may find it necessary to recreate this analysis using either Data Flow Diagrams [DeMarco (1978)] or using the Real Time System Specification Strategies of Hatley and Pirbhai [Hatley (1987)]. The functional decomposition of the system is used to identify the hardware configuration items (HWCIs), the computer software configuration items (CSCIs) along with the processing provided by these CSCIs, and the allocation of CSCIs to various HWCIs within the system. The analyst can then begin to create the system level FMEA that will support reliability modeling of the combined HW and SW system.

The system level FMEA, shown diagrammatically in Figure 2-1, is a mapping of the hardware and software components of the system onto the system services provided. To create the FMEA, the analyst first constructs a matrix with each of the hardware CIs and their associated software CSCIs or CSCs as appropriate along the vertical axis.   The horizontal axis is formed by the system services or outputs of the system grouped in convenient ways that support the desired analysis.   A grouping of system services by system operating mode often supports development of the various models required by the system specification.   The HWCIs and CSCIs (CSCs) are then mapped onto the system services or outputs based on the impact on system services caused by the failure of each hardware and software element.   In performing this mapping, the analyst will need to assess the impact of failure of both hardware platforms and software elements.   The failure impact of software elements will need to be examined in depth based on the data flow that has been established for the system design. Similarly, the failure of hardware platforms will need to be examined for its impact on software-provided services using the data flow diagrams for the system software resident on the hardware platform.

Once the system level FMEA has been completed, the analyst can examine the hardware and software that is required for any particular mode or set of system services.   A reliability model for these services can then be developed.

2.1.2   System Model Development

2.1.2.1   Reliability Block Diagram Development

The reliability block diagram for combined HW/SW systems is developed based on the system FMEA, using a procedure that is analogous to that used for purely hardware systems.   The FMEA results are used to determine which hardware and software elements are required to provide a set of system services of interest.   The analyst then proceeds to develop a reliability block diagram that consists of a set of series blocks for each of the independent HW/SW subsystems or elements that must be operational to provide the services being modeled.   In general, the analyst should only separate software elements from the hardware elements on which they execute as a final step in the reliability block diagram modeling.   Distinct separation of hardware platforms and the software that executes on those platforms is based on system application specific information that is used in developing a state diagram(s) that accurately represents the interaction between the hardware platform and the software executing on it.

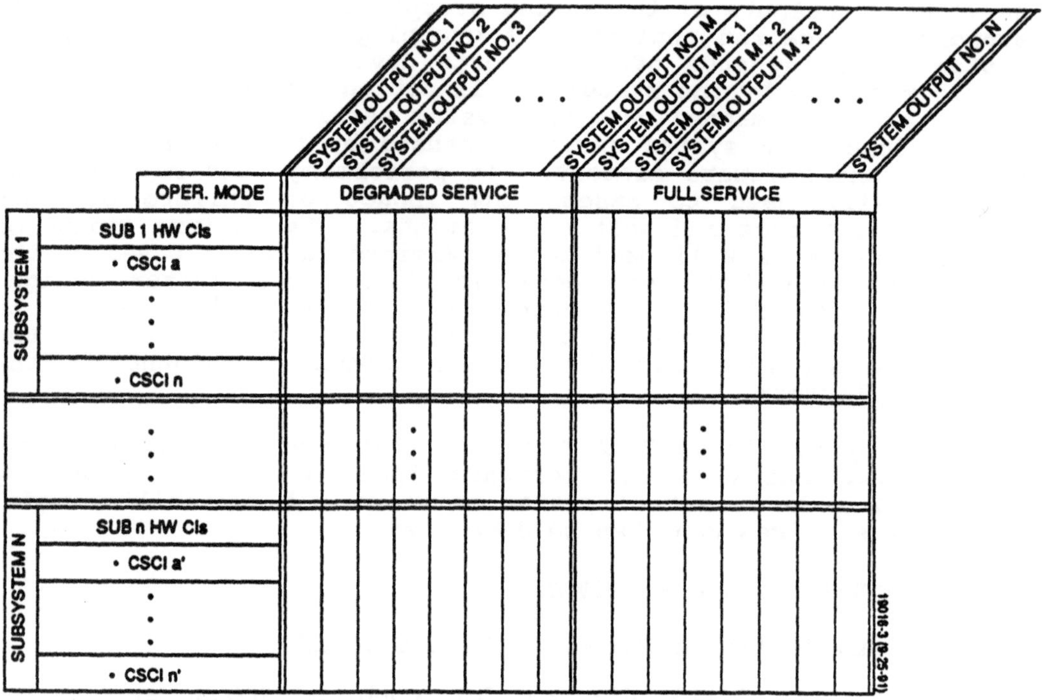

Figure 2-1. Example of System Level Functional FMEA

2.1.2.2 State Diagram Development

The development of one or more state diagrams that accurately represent the hardware and software interactions for all system processing elements, both series and redundant, is the next step in developing reliability models of combined HW/SW systems. The notation that will be used for the presentation and discussion of state diagrams in this section of the report is given in Figure 2-2. The reader should review that figure for notation prior to proceeding with the remainder of this section.

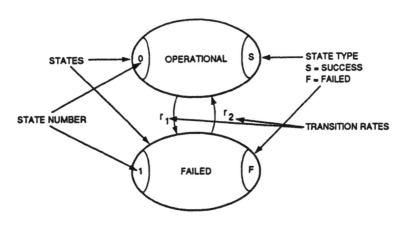

TEXT NOTATION

STATE N : [N]
STATE TRANSITION M TO N : (M, N)

DEFINITIONS

λ HW - HARDWARE FAILURE RATE

λ SW - SOFTWARE FAILURE RATE

TR - TIME REQUIRED FOR MANUAL RECOVERY

μ HW - HARDWARE REPAIR RATE

μ SW - SOFTWARE REPAIR RATE

C_d - FAULT DETECTION COVERAGE

C_i - FAULT ISOLATION COVERAGE

C_r - FAULT RECOVERY COVERAGE

Figure 2-2. Notation Used in State Diagrams and Text

Software restart, which is used in the state diagrams discussed below, is the time required to restart the failed software without changing the software itself. As discussed previously, software repair rates are not used in the state diagrams discussed in this section. Instead, the software recovery rate is adjusted to include those cases where software must be "patched" prior to successful restart. Software failures are assumed to be dependent on the state of the software execution environment at the time of failure. Thus, the failed software can often be restarted, without any change to the software itself, and will resume operation as long as the environment that was in existence at the time of the software failure has changed sufficiently. Successful restart after failure is a reasonable assumption for software with moderate maturity. The software that has failed may have operated successfully for tens to hundreds of hours prior to being presented with a specific processing system state and set of inputs that were sufficient to cause the failure to be manifested. However, successful restart of the failed software will depend on the persistence of the set of execution conditions that caused the original failure. If the persistence of the failure is sufficiently long, repair of the software may be required prior to any restart. For the purpose of reliability modeling of HW/SW systems, a long persistence failure is one that will continue to cause software failure when restart is attempted. Any set of execution conditions that persists long enough to cause a failure upon attempted restart is expected to result in system shutdown for most non-redundant systems and effective loss of redundancy in cases of software failure for redundant systems. The relative fractions of long persistence to short persistence failures for mature software are not known. James et al. (1982) reported an average of 60 percent short persistence failures for immature software undergoing factory test.

The time required to restart software with a short persistence failure may vary widely and may exceed the repair time required for hardware failures in some cases. Long restart times are expected to occur for failures that "crash" the operating system leaving system resources in an indeterminate state that must be determined and corrected (if needed) manually. Software failures that leave large data stores inconsistent are also expected to require long restart times due to the difficulty in restoring the data to a known acceptable state. For example, failures that cause a data base to lose integrity may require restoration from a backup tape with subsequent update using journal files. However, the average time required for software restart is expected to be less than the average hardware repair time since restart of all system software is included in the hardware maintenance time and at least some hardware failures may leave system resources and/or data stores in an inconsistent state.

2.1.2.2.1 Series Elements

The state diagrams used to represent series HW/SW elements are simple state models as shown in Figure 2-3. The hardware and software elements can be treated as independent paths that can lead to failure since both hardware and software must be fully operational for the system to be in a success state. The three possible state models are shown in the figure as (a) for systems undergoing a continuous operation and repair cycle, (b) non-repairable systems that are not self healing in the case of software failure (i.e., single shot systems), and (c) non-repairable systems with self-healing for software failures.

As shown in part "a" of the figure, repairable systems experience hardware and software failures and recover independently through either hardware repair or software restart. The recovery time for software in this model includes the impact of any long persistence software failures (i.e., those which cannot be repaired through restart). At any time that either the hardware or software has failed and not yet been repaired or restarted, the system is considered to be in a failed state. It is possible to transition from state 2 (software failure) to state 1 (hardware failure) if a hardware failure occurs prior to successful software restart. Since the hardware remains operational after a software failure, there is a continuous exposure to the possibility of hardware failure. The transition (2,1) can usually be safely ignored without undue loss of accuracy since (2,1)<<(2,0) in most cases. The reliability metrics of interest for repairable systems (e.g., availability, MTBF) can be derived from the closed form semi-Markov process shown.

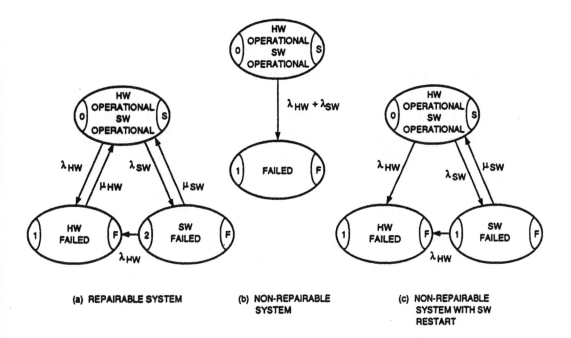

Figure 2-3. State Diagrams for Simple Series HW/SW Elements

Series non-repairable system elements are modeled as shown in part "b" of the figure. The system element is considered fully operational as long as both the hardware and software remain operational. If a failure of either hardware or software occurs, the system transitions from state 0 to state 1, which is an absorbing failed state. The state diagram shown allows the calculation of relevant reliability metrics of interest (MTTF, Reliability, Probability of Success) through evaluation of the probability of the transition (0,1) occurring during any given time period t1 to t2. In practice, completely non-repairable systems are relatively rare. This type of system would be expected to be found in systems where the critical duration of operation is too short to allow software restart to be attempted. Most critical real time military systems of interest are expected to include the ability to restart software.

Series non-repairable elements with software restart are modeled using the state diagram shown in part "c" of the figure. Transitions from successful operation (state 0) to either hardware failure (state 1) or software failure (state 2) occur at the respective failure rates shown. Hardware failures cause the system to enter a permanent failed state (state 1) that is absorbing. Software failures cause the system to enter a software failed state (state 2). The element then restarts the software in an attempt to resume operation. This type of system operation is commonly found in aircraft avionics that have software (firmware) embedded into the equipment. Typically, upon failure of a hardware or software element, the equipment removes itself from any active operation, flags the pilot that an error has occurred, and enters a self test mode. Following successful completion of the self test, a restart is attempted. If the failure was induced into hardware by the environment or was a short persistence software failure, an equipment restart will be successful, allowing the equipment to resume operation.

2.1.2.2.2 Redundant Elements

Reliability models of redundant HW/SW elements are significantly more complex than reliability models of series elements. The addition of redundancy introduces complexity associated with the ability of the HW and SW to correctly respond to failure events. Reliability modeling of redundant HW/SW elements with hot standby and automatic switchover capability significantly increases the number of states required to properly account for system behavior.

2.1.2.2.2.1 Hardware Systems

A general model for hardware redundancy using identical equipment is shown in Figure 2-4. As shown in the figure, redundant system elements transition to the next higher state upon the occurrence of any HW failure. Hardware repairs transition the system element model to the next lower (numerically) state. The system is a closed form semi-Markov process that can be solved for the appropriate reliability measures using conventional methods. Closed form solutions for the reliability measures of interest for this type of model under most common repair restrictions, types of standby, etc, are available in the literature [Kozlov and Ushakov (1970)].

The model shown in Figure 2-4 provides an upper bound on the reliability of redundant hardware systems. Estimation of the expected reliability of hardware systems requires that the fault tolerance employed in the redundancy be included in the model. For cold standby system, where backup elements are not powered and thus immune to failure occurrence, the model of Figure 2-4 provides a reasonable estimate if the transition rates shown from each success state to the next higher number state are adjusted to account for the constant number of elements in operation (m units). However, for hot standby systems with automatic switchover, the model of Figure 2-4 significantly overstates the reliability achieved by the redundant hardware elements. Failures in the fault detection mechanisms that may lead to latent faults in backup equipment, as well as failures in fault detection, fault isolation, and fault recovery mechanisms that may lead to an inability to activate redundant system elements and resume system services in response to primary element failures, are not included in the model shown in the figure.

Figure 2-5 is a simplified reliability model for a hardware system employing hot standby, and automatic switchover with one of two identical elements required. The model accounts for failures in the fault detection, isolation, and recovery mechanisms. The concept of three types of "coverage" is introduced as a part of the model. Fault detection coverage (Cd) is the probability of detecting a fault given that a fault has occurred. Fault Isolation coverage (Ci) is the probability that a fault will be correctly isolated to the recoverable interface (level at which redundancy is available) given that a fault has occurred and been detected. Fault recovery coverage is the probability that the redundant structure will recover system services given that a fault has occurred, been detected, and correctly isolated. The model shown in Figure 2-5 is a simplified model since it does not separately consider the possible impact of transient failures. The model also assumes that fault detection coverage (Cd) is the same for both the primary element and the backup element. In practice, there may be different levels of fault detection coverage between primary and backup equipments due to a difference in test exposure intensity.

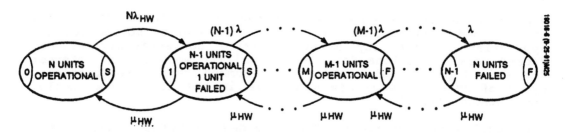

Figure 2-4. General Hardware Redundancy Model: M Required of N Supplied Identical Elements

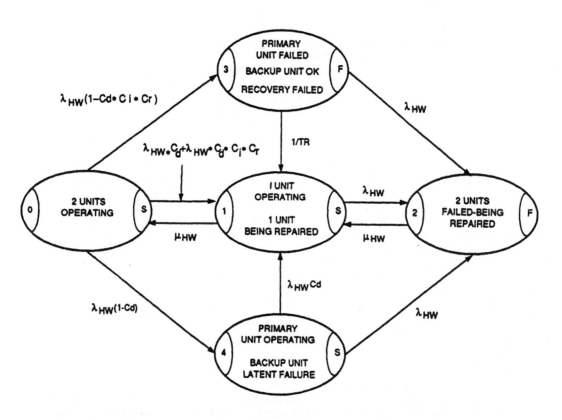

Figure 2-5. Hardware Reliability Model for 1:2 Identical Elements Hot Standby with Automatic Switchover

As shown in the reliability model, the structure can transition from the full up state (1) to one of three states. The structure transitions to state 1 whenever a hardware failure occurs in the primary element that is correctly detected, isolated, and recovered from. Similarly, a detected failure in the backup element results in a transition from state 0 to state 1. The structure transitions from state 0 to state 4 when a failure occurs in the backup equipment which is not detectable. Failures in the primary hardware element that cannot be correctly detected, isolated, or recovered from result in a transition from state 0 to state 3. State 3 is a system state to account for the failure time accrued during manual intervention by the system operator to restore lost system services. Transitions from states 1, 3, and 4 to state 2 are caused by a hardware failure occurring prior to repair of the first failure which occurred in the system structure.

In actual practice, the model to be used will need to be based on the specific fault tolerant characteristics of the design being analyzed. Models that incorporate system fault behavior, such as shown in Figure 2-5, do not specifically include SW as a part of the model. However, the system control processing, a software based functionality, determines the model structure to account for system behavior under fault conditions.

The reliability estimates which result from the use of system reliability models that account for fault detection, isolation, and recovery are less optimistic than estimates from reliability models based only on the quantity of hardware supplied and required. The reliability of the system structure being modeled is usually very sensitive to the total fault coverage provided by the system design. System designs that feature well-designed fault detection and isolation coupled with rapid and effective recovery of system services avoid most sudden losses of system services due to undetected latent failures in backup equipment or due to the inability of backup equipment to successfully restore system services when failures to the primary equipment occurs. Similarly, models of HW/SW systems that include SW as well as the fault tolerance characteristics of the system design are sensitive to the overall effectiveness of the fault detection, isolation, and recovery provided by the hardware and software designs.

2.1.2.2.2.2 HW/SW Systems

Inclusion of software into hardware reliability redundancy models further increases the complexity of the models. As in the hardware-only reliability models, accurate modeling of system behavior requires that fault coverage (Cd, Ci, Cr) be included into the model. Similarly, software fault coverage and the impact of long persistence faults must be included in the system models where appropriate. This results in each model of redundant HW/SW elements being uniquely tailored to the design being analyzed.

The examples of specific models given below are presented to allow a skilled analyst to determine the system attributes that need to be considered in deriving a reliability model for a set of redundant elements. There is no attempt to fully develop all of the possible modeling situations that may apply to a HW/SW system. Most of the reliability models that will be needed to evaluate the reliability of HW/SW systems will be specific to the exact hardware and software design being evaluated. Only a minimal level of generalization is possible.

2.1.2.2.2.1 Cold Standby Systems

Redundant hardware/software systems that use cold standby techniques to provide fault tolerance can be modeled without undue difficulty as long as automatic switchover and startup schemes are not used in the design. In general, only the hardware and software failure rates for the HW/SW elements need to be considered in developing the reliability model. For designs that use manual restoration of system services through the activation of an unpowered backup unit, an adaptation of the reliability model shown in Figure 2-6 can be used to estimate the reliability of the redundant structure. The models shown in the figure are based on the earlier work of James et al. (1982). As shown in the figure, structure state transitions are caused by either hardware or software failures. Hardware failures cause a transition to a state with one less hardware element and commencement of repair actions on the failed element if repair is allowed. The reliability model of Figure 2-6 does not allow latent failures in the backup element to be modeled. The model assumes that failures of unpowered elements are impossible. Similarly, problems in recovering system services are not modeled since the recovery of system services must be directly managed by the system operator. Software failures result in system recovery using the same processing hardware and a restart of the failed software. Both repairable and non-repairable systems are allowed to have software restarted to enable recovery from software failures. Inclusion of the transition path allowing recovery from software failures is optional for non-repairable systems. The existence or lack of this transition path will depend on how the equipment is operationally employed.

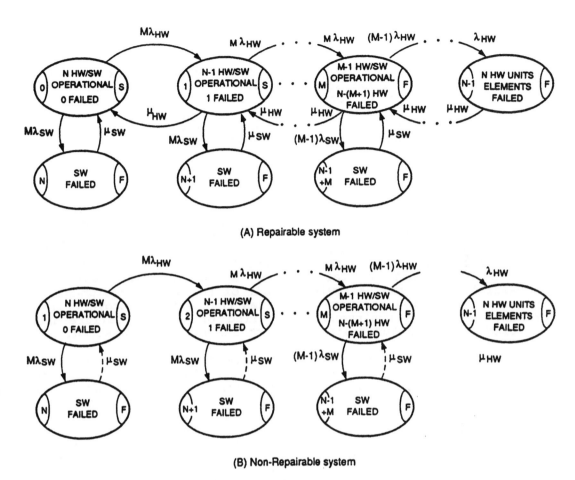

(A) Repairable system

(B) Non-Repairable system

Figure 2-6. HW/SW Reliability Model: M Required of N Supplied Identical Elements, Cold Standby

2.1.2.2.2.2   Hot Standby Systems

Reliability modeling of hot standby HW/SW systems requires consideration of hardware failure rates, software failure rates, hardware fault detection, isolation, and recovery coverage, software failure detection, isolation, and recovery coverage, hardware repair rates and software restart/recovery rates. The effect of long persistence software failures on the reliability achieved by hot standby redundant structures is included in the software fault coverage estimates for recovery coverage (Cr). Depending on the system design being modeled, all or most of these parameters will be used to help identify states and/or transition rates between structure states. The exact state diagrams that result from an FMEA of the HW/SW system will depend on the design being evaluated. An example of a reliability model for a very simple system structure is discussed below.

Figure 2-7 presents a simplified state diagram for a HW/SW structure with one of two identical elements required. The model shown is for a hot standby system with automatic switchover. This type of structure is very common in air traffic control, command and control, and air defense systems where a high probability of continuous system services is required.   In modeling this structure, five parameters of interest are recognized. The model states depend on primary HW platform state (operational or failed), primary SW state (operational or failed), backup hardware platform state, backup software state, and recovery status.   Recovery status is defined to have two states, successful or failed.   A successful recovery indicates that the structure has successfully transitioned from primary equipment to the backup equipment after failure of either the primary hardware or software. Alternatively, successful recovery can indicate that a failure in a backup equipment was successfully detected, allowing·repair of the backup equipment to commence.   A failed recovery indicates that either recovery from primary to backup equipment has failed or that a failure has occurred in the backup equipment which has not been detected.

Since there are five parameters of interest, each of which has two possible values, a total of 32 possible states would be expected.   However, some of the 32 possible states cannot exist in practice.   Also, some of the states that can exist are functional duplicates that can be merged.   For example, a state with a hardware failure in the primary equipment and operational software in the primary equipment can by shown to be one of the 32 possible states.   However, the state is impossible because software cannot be operational on a failed hardware platform. The two states that can exist for (1) a failed backup equipment with successful recovery and (2) a failed primary equipment with successful recovery can be shown to be functionally equivalent since successful recovery implies that whichever hardware remains operational has been assigned to primary processing as a part of the recovery process.

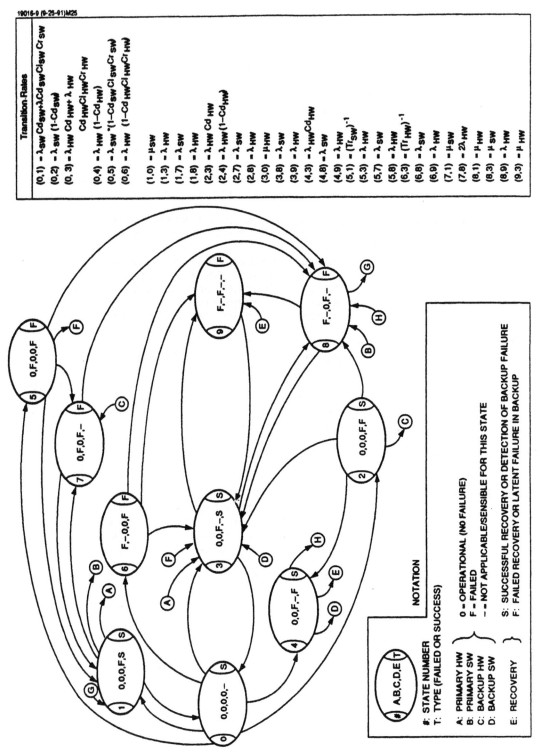

Figure 2-7. Simplified State Diagram for 1:2, Hot Standby, HW/SW System

For the model of Figure 2-7, a total of ten states result, with the following definitions:

State 0: Success State - Fully Operational State

State 1: Success State - Backup has a detected SW failure which is being recovered from.

State 2: Success State - System is operational with a latent SW failure in the backup element.

State 3: Success State - System is operational with a detected hardware failure in the backup element.

State 4: Success State - System operational with a latent HW failure in the backup element.

State 5: Failed State - Primary SW has failed, recovery to the backup HW and SW has not been successful. System operations intervention will be required to restore system operation on either HW platform.

State 6: Failed State - Primary HW has failed. The recovery process has failed. Either incorrect detection, isolation, or incomplete recovery has occurred. Manual intervention by the system operator will be required to restore system services on the backup equipment.

State 7: Failed State - Software failures have occurred on both primary and backup system elements.

State 8: Failed State - The primary HW and backup SW have failed. Both elements are down, recovery is not possible without manual intervention by the system operator and/or maintenance personnel.

State 9: Failed State - Both hardware elements have failed.

As shown in the figure, transitions between states occur due to either failures in the hardware or software or due to the status of the recovery process. Using state diagrams that model the impact of hardware, software, and fault coverage for both hardware and software failures results in more accurate approximations of the potential reliability of redundant systems. Also, accurate models that reflect the system design decisions which have been made provide a basis for evaluating the reliability demands of candidate architectural approaches early in the design process [Goddard (1989)].

2.1.3 System Model Evaluation

State diagrams that have been developed to model the reliability of combined HW/SW structures tend to be relatively complex. Manual solutions are possible, but not considered practical. Numerous programs are currently available in the commercial marketplace that can aid in the solution of closed form semi-Markov state diagrams. Additionally, government procurement offices and their contractors have access to both simulation and analytic tools which allow solutions to these reliability models through appropriate Rome Laboratory and NASA offices. Acquisition of one or more of these tools should be considered before attempting to accurately model HW/SW systems.

2.1.4 Estimation of Model Parameters

Reliability models of HW/SW systems are based on hardware failure rates, hardware repair rates, software failure rates, software recovery times, and the probability of fault detection, isolation, and recovery for both hardware and software (hardware and software coverage). Values for each of the model parameters will need to be derived as a part of the reliability estimating process.

2.1.4.1 Hardware Failure Rate Estimation

Hardware failure rates for use in combined HW/SW models should be obtained from the same sources as those traditionally used for hardware only reliability models. In service, field, reliability records are the best estimators of expected hardware failure rates. When field reliability records are not available, reliability test results are the next best estimator of expected hardware reliability performance. When neither field nor test reliability records are available, MIL-HDBK-217 is the preferred reference for obtaining component level failure rates that can be used to predict hardware reliability performance. When MIL-HDBK-217 predictions cannot be applied due to lack of equipment definition, the reliability performance of the previous generation of similar equipment can be used as an estimate of the lower bound for the expected reliability of current generation equipment.

2.1.4.2   Hardware Repair Rate Estimation

Hardware repair rates for use in combined HW/SW models should be obtained from the same sources as those traditionally used for hardware only reliability models. In order of preference, field repair time data, maintainability demonstration test data, MIL-HDBK-472 predictions, and prior generation of equipment maintainability performance should be used to estimate the equipment repair time required.

2.1.4.3   Hardware and Software Coverage Estimation

Fault coverage estimates for use in combined HW/SW models can be obtained from a combination of FMEA to assess hardware built-in test (BIT) effectiveness, and fault tree analysis (FTA) to assess the result of software failure. Assessing the likelihood for a failure to be detected and to leave the system in a state where fault isolation and recovery are possible will require an in depth understanding of at least the part of the software design dedicated to system control and to the handling of faults. The determination of software fault coverage and software BIT effectiveness is an area where further research will be required to detail adequate and accurate methods of estimation.

2.1.4.4   Software Recovery Time

Software recovery time estimates for use in combined HW/SW models can be derived using the methods of system performance analysis. Accurate estimation of these times will depend on the hardware available for processing, the loading on the system, and the impact of the failure on system resources (eg. files). The results of FMEAs and FTAs performed to support estimation of hardware and software coverage should provide an estimation of the amount of system resource damage that may be attributable to a given software failure. Estimation of software recovery time during early design phases, before test data is available, will need to be based on performance analysis results.   Further research to develop methodologies for estimating system performance metrics under various failure and recovery conditions is needed.

2.1.4.5   Software Failure Rates

Software failure rates to be used in modeling combined hardware and software systems, although constant, differ from hardware failure rates in their dependency on operational profile and workload. For purposes of illustration, a computer, containing one or more individual processors, which is part of a system, is used along with its software to provide one or more system functions. The rate at which these assigned system functions are unavailable is dependent on the failure rate of the hardware and the failure rate of the software. Calculating failure rates for hardware elements was discussed in 2.1.4.2 above. The software failure rate can be decomposed into three parts: the operating system or executive failure rate, the failure rate associated with any re-used software, and the failure rate for any newly developed software. These software failure rates, once converted to a common time frame of reference are additive. A reliability block diagram for a hypothetical processor is shown in Figure 2-8, below.

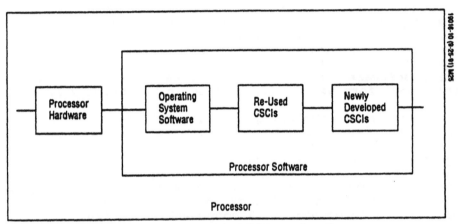

Figure 2-8. Reliability Block Diagram for a Processor

Failure rates for operating systems or executives can usually be obtained from the supplier of the operating system or executive. Failure rates obtained from the operating system supplier are usually quoted in the number of outages caused over some period of time (e.g., a year). Failure rates for operating systems are generally quoted with respect to system operating time because the operating system is active at all times when the computer is powered and ready for processing. The reliability analyst will need to convert the failure rate given to failures per hour for compatibility with hardware failure rates. Operating system failure rates can be substantial and should not be ignored. Operating systems for mainframe computers can be several million lines of code in size and are often very complex and difficult to completely debug. Smaller computers, including single board processor applications, sometimes use real-time executives which can still contribute substantially to the overall software failure rate. Failure rates for re-used code can be obtained from applications where the code was previously used. These failure rates should generally be much lower than the failure rates for newly developed code. The availability of this data depends on the completeness of organizational record keeping and the amount of code modification that has been necessary to allow the code re-use.   If the failure rate for re-used code is available in terms compatible with conversion to failures per system operating hour, the failure rate can generally be used directly in the reliability modeling.   If the failure rate for re-used code is known in failures per CPU operating period (second, minute, hour, etc), the failure rate will have to be converted to failures per system operating hour using the methods discussed in paragraph 2.1.4.5.3 below.

Estimates of the failure rate for newly developed software are obtained using the research results discussed in section 4 of this report.   The failure rate estimates produced by these methods is provided in failures per CPU operating second for each software element being developed. These failure rates must then be combined as discussed in paragraph 2.1.4.5.4 to account for the specific software topology and timing.   Additionally, the resultant software failure rate must be converted to a system operating hour form as discussed below in paragraph 2.1.4.5.3.

For the purposes of developing software failure rates, a software system can be viewed as a hierarchy.   The hierarchy consists of modules, computer software components (CSCs), computer software configuration items, and so on, as described in DOD-STD-2167A. Because of the different names for items at different levels, two generic names will be used to represent software items at adjacent levels in the discussion that follows.   The first generic name is "component." A component is an item at any level in the system hierarchy.   The second name is "aggregate."   An aggregate is an item composed of an interrelated set of components. An aggregate lies at the next level up in the system hierarchy from its components.   For example, an aggregate of CSCIs can be a software subsystem.   The software components that comprise an aggregate will be related to one another in two ways: a particular timing configuration and a particular reliability topology.

Timing configuration describes the time intervals during which the various components are active and inactive during a period of interest.   Reliability topology is concerned with the number of components in the aggregate that can fail before the aggregate fails.

2.1.4.5.1 Timing Configurations

Several different timing configurations are possible.   The major timing relationships between software components are concurrent and sequential. Components will be termed concurrent if they are active simultaneously. The components are sequential if they are active one after the other.   A single component alternated between active and inactive periods will be termed intermittent, and several components alternating their activity will be termed interleaved. Hybrid timing configurations, for instance concurrent/sequential, may also occur.

Some common examples of timing configurations: In most electronic equipment, all hardware components are energized and operating all the time. The components are therefore in a concurrent timing configuration. Software components (in computer science called "processes" or "tasks") execute in an interleaved manner on a single central processing unit (CPU). The software and the computer that hosts it are active concurrently. In a multiprocessing system with three processors, the three programs running on those processors are active concurrently. In a distributed system, the local and remote hardware and the local and remote software are active concurrently. In a batch-oriented computer system, the programs execute sequentially.

Software reliability topology can be expressed in the form "k-out-of-n," where n is the number of components and k is the number that must succeed. There are two distinguished cases: An n-out-of-n configuration is the most common and is called a series configuration; a 1-out-of-n configuration is called a parallel configuration.

2.1.4.5.2 Notation

Capital letters will be used to refer to the aggregate item and lowercase letters to refer to the component item. The aggregate reliability function will be denoted R(t) and the aggregate failure rate will be denoted $\Lambda(t)$ or Λ. The corresponding component reliability figures of merit are: the component reliability function, denoted $r(t) = \exp[-\lambda t]$, and the component failure rate, denoted λ.

One reason that aggregate failure rate $\Lambda(t)$ can be a function of time is that an aggregate of redundant constant-failure-rate components will have a time-dependent failure rate; as the redundant components fail, the aggregate "ages." Another reason is that a component might not be active during the entire period of interest. When the component changes state from active to inactive or vice versa, the failure rate of the aggregate will change.

2.1.4.5.3 Failure Rate Adjustment

A computer program's failure rate can be expressed with respect to three different time frames of reference: execution (CPU) time, system operating time, and calendar time.

A program can only fail when it is running. The failures uncover faults, and the removal of the faults results in reliability growth.   Thus, software reliability growth curves are based on cumulative execution time and express a single program's failure rate in terms of execution time.   Such a failure rate is sensitive to processor speed: The execution-time failure rate is always linearly proportional to the processor speed.   If the failure rate λ for a software component was measured on or predicted for a processor with average instruction rate g_1 (e.g., instructions per second), and the target machine's processor has average instruction rate g_2, then the failure rate should be adjusted [Musa et al. (1987)] to

$$\lambda^* = \frac{g_2}{g_1} \lambda \qquad (1)$$

During the operation of a system, programs may not operate continuously. For example, some of the programs might time-share a single CPU.   Also, multiple CPUs may be present, allowing program executions to overlap.   In order to combine the failure rates of the various programs with one another to arrive at an overall software failure rate, it is first necessary to translate all the program failure rates into a common time frame of reference.   This frame of reference is system operating time.

To convert an execution-time failure rate to a system-operating-time failure rate, the program's utilization u_{es} needs to be determined.   This is the ratio of execution time to system operating time.   The utilization can exceed 100% if the same program executes on more than one CPU (each CPU reading a different input stream).

The formula for converting a program's execution-time failure rate λ_e to the system-operating-time failure rate λ_s is

$$\lambda_s = \lambda_e \cdot u_{es} \qquad (2)$$

Conversely, the execution-time failure rate can be recovered as

$$\lambda_e = \frac{\lambda_s}{u_{es}} \qquad (3)$$

If the programs are in a series configuration, then the (average) failure rate is simply the sum of the system-operating-time failure rates of the individual programs.   This result can be derived as follows. Suppose there are N software components that run during the time period T.   Let λi be the execution-time failure rate for the i-th software component.   Let $\mu(T)$ be the expected number of failures during that period.   The expected number of failures contributed by the i-th software component is $\lambda_i(u_iT)$. Thus

$$\mu(T) = \sum \lambda_i(u_iT) \qquad (4)$$

The overall failure rate is

$$\Lambda = \frac{\mu(T)}{T} = \sum \lambda_i u_i \qquad (5)$$

The sum $\Sigma\lambda_i u_i$ is seen to be the sum of the programs' system-operating-time failure rates.

2.1.4.5.4 Reliability Combination Models

This section is organized by type of aggregate. The type of aggregate is a conjunction of timing configuration and reliability topology. Table 2-1 shows the various combinations and designates each model by a letter. The material presented discusses both the software reliability calculation and cumulative failure rate model for the timing configuration and reliability topology being discussed. The cumulative failure rate discussion is presented for use in calculation of software failure rates for use in much of the system modeling previously discussed.

Table 2-1. Reliability Combination Models

Model Des-ignation	Reliability	Timing	Special Name
A	Series	General	
B	Series	Indeterminate	Mission Model
C	Series	Sequential	
D	Series	Random	Semi-Markov
E	Series	Concurrent	
F	Parallel	Concurrent	
G	k-out-of-n	Concurrent	
H	Parallel	Concurrent	N-Modular Redundancy
I	Parallel	Sequential	Standby Redundancy

The failure rate and reliability function of a software aggregate can in many cases be expressed as a closed-form function of the component failure rates and/or reliability functions. The following discussion focuses on those cases.

2.1.4.5.4.1 Model (A) General Series Model

The most common reliability topology for a software aggregate is the series configuration. In this configuration, the aggregate fails if and when any one of its components fails. The failure rate of the aggregate is the sum of the failure rates of the active components. Suppose the components are numbered 1, 2, ..., k. Let the function $a_i(t)$ evaluate to unity if component i is active at time t, and let it evaluate to zero otherwise. Then the aggregate failure rate $\Lambda(t)$ is

$$\Lambda(t) = \sum_{i=1}^{k} \lambda_i a_i(t) \qquad (6)$$

where λ_i is the failure rate of the i-th component.

The failure rate is useful when aggregating to higher levels and is a reliability figure of merit in its own right. If the result is a constant failure rate, or can be approximated by a constant failure rate, then the rules given here can be applied to the aggregate failure rates to find the failure rates and reliability of even higher-level aggregates.

2.1.4.5.4.2 Model (B) Mission Reliability Model

A mission-oriented system is described by means of a mission profile and consists of N consecutive time periods, called phases. During each phase the mission has to accomplish a specified task. An example of a space vehicle's mission phases is ground operation, launch, and orbit. Furthermore, at any point in time the system is in one of M possible operational modes. The effective operating time X_j for the j-th operational mode is given by

$$X_j = \sum_{i=1}^{N} t_i z_{ij} , \qquad j=1,2,...,M \qquad (7)$$

where t_i is the duration of the i-th mission phase and z_{ij} is the fraction of time the j-th mode is utilized during that phase.

Suppose there are S components in the software aggregate. Let u_{jk} be the utilization ("duty cycle") of component k during operating mode j.   Then the amount of time component k is active during the mission is

$$\tau_k' = \sum_{j=1}^{N} X_j u_{jk} , \quad k=1,2,\dots,M \tag{8}$$

In matrix notation, the foregoing equations are

$$X = TZ; \quad T' = XU \tag{9}$$

(Note that T' is merely the uppercase of active time τ'; the prime does not mean matrix transpose.)   Let λ_k be the failure rate of the k-th component.   Assuming that all components form a series configuration, the expected number of failures from the k-th component is

$$\mu_k = \lambda_k \tau_k' , \quad k=1,2,\dots,S \tag{10}$$

and the expected number of failures for a given   mission is

$$\mu(t_m) = \sum_{k=1}^{S} \mu_k \tag{11}$$

Note that in practical situations these μ values will all be fractional.

Because it is unknown which components are active at any moment, it is not possible to determine the instantaneous failure rate $\Lambda(t)$.   However, the average failure rate can be computed as

$$\Lambda_{ave} = \frac{M(t_m)}{t_m} \tag{12}$$

In situations where the activation/inactivation times are known, it will be possible to determine $\Lambda(t)$ for all t.   Paragraphs 2.1.4.5.4.3 through 2.1.4.5.4.5 discuss some common timing situations in series configurations.

2.1.4.5.4.3   Model (C) Series Sequential

In this situation, components 1 through k are active one after the other. For software, this arrangement is commonly seen in batch-oriented systems. The time t_i is the point at which component i finishes and component (i+1) is activated.

For $t \in [t_i, t_{i+1}]$ the failure rate of the aggregate is

$$\Lambda(t) = \lambda_{i+1} \tag{13}$$

Sometimes the components are not active consecutively; a time period during which no component is active can be represented by a pseudocomponent whose failure rate is zero. If a component is active intermittently, that is, for several piecewise continuous periods, then a pseudocomponent (with the same failure rate) can be created for each such period.

2.1.4.5.4.4   Model (D) Semi-Markov

If the software system consists of k components that follow one another sequentially according to known probabilities, then a semi-Markov technique [Littlewood (1979b), Cheung (1980), Siegrist (1988)] can be employed to obtain an overall failure rate for the aggregate.

A Markov process is a stochastic process in which the future development is completely determined by the present state. It does not matter at all the way in which the current state arose. A Markov chain is a Markov process that has a discrete state space. A semi-Markov process [Lévy (1954), Smith (1958)] is a Markov chain in which the amount of time spent in each state before a transition occurs (the "sojourn time") is random.

Let p_{ij} be the probability of the operation of component j following the operation of component i. For software, this transition consists of software component i passing control to software component j. The equilibrium probabilities (also called "limiting" or "steady-state" probabilities) are the probabilities of being in each of the states when the aggregate is operated for a long time. The equilibrium probabilities π_i are found by solving the system of equations

$$\pi_i = \sum_{j=1}^{k} \pi_j p_{ji} , \quad i=1,2,\dots,k \tag{14}$$

together with $\Sigma \pi_i = 1$.

Let m_{ij} be the mean time that component i is active before it finishes and is followed by component j (the "sojourn time"). Then the failure rate of the aggregate is approximated by

$$\Lambda = \frac{\sum_{i=1}^{k}\sum_{j=1}^{k} \pi_i p_{ij} m_{ij} \lambda_i}{\sum_{i=1}^{k}\sum_{j=1}^{k} \pi_i p_{ij} m_{ij}} \tag{15}$$

Failures can also occur during the transition from one component to another. If r_{ij}, the reliability of the transition from component i to component j is considered, then the $m_{ij}\lambda_i$ in the numerator can be replaced by $m_{ij}\lambda_i + (1-r_{ij})$ to take transition failure into account.

2.1.4.5.4.5 Model (E) Series Concurrent

If throughout a time interval $[0,t_a]$, components 1, ..., k are active, then the failure rate at time $t \epsilon [0,t_a]$ is

$$\Lambda(t) = \sum_{i=1}^{k} \lambda_i \tag{16}$$

If all k components have the same failure rate λ, the aggregate failure rate will be

$$\Lambda = \sum_{i=1}^{k} \lambda = k\lambda \tag{17}$$

2.1.4.5.4.6 Redundant Software Configurations

Redundancy is the provision of additional software components beyond the minimum needed to perform the functions of the software aggregate. The purpose of this redundancy is to increase the reliability of the aggregate. Unlike hardware, all copies of a computer program are identical and will all fail under the same circumstances, so simple duplication of the software is of limited benefit due to the potential for long persistence software failures which were discussed previously.

Software redundancy is accomplished by providing multiple distinct versions of the software developed to the same requirements specification.   The goal is for it to be very unlikely that multiple versions will fail on the same inputs.   By having each version independently developed by a different programming team, the hope is that the versions will turn out differently enough that they will not often fail on the same inputs.

Multiversion programming is a controversial topic.   Knight and Leveson (1986) showed through a large-scale experiment that independently developed versions do not necessarily fail completely independently of one another.   In fact, the number of coincident failures was "surprisingly high."   Eckhardt and Lee (1985) developed a detailed statistical model of multiversion programming.   "Independently developed programs" are modeled as programs randomly selected from the universe of possible program versions that purport to solve the problem at hand.   The independence criterion is enforced by requiring the joint probability of selecting the programs to equal the product of the marginal probabilities of selecting each one.

Eckhardt and Lee, who concentrated on modeling N-version programming, express the reliability of the N-version aggregate as

$$R = 1 - \int \sum_{\ell=m}^{N} \binom{N}{\ell} [\theta(x)]^{\ell} [1-\theta(x)]^{N-\ell} \, dQ \qquad (18)$$

where m=(N+1)/2, a majority of the N versions.   The aggregate fails whenever at least m versions fail. $\theta(x)$ is the proportion of versions failing when executing on input state x.   Q(A) is the usage distribution, the probability that the subset of input states A is selected.

One of Eckhardt and Lee's major results was that independently developed versions do not necessarily fail independently.   Up until the Eckhardt and Lee model came out, practitioners of multiversion programming had set independent development as their goal.   Eckhardt and Lee show that the departure from independent behavior is governed by Var(θ), where $\theta=\theta(X)$, where X is a randomly chosen input.   If this probability θ is identical for all the programs, then Var(θ)=0 and the independently developed programs fail independently; otherwise the reliability will be overstated by Var(θ).   The best candidates for multiversion programming are those problems for which Var(θ) is low. Intuitively, Var(θ) is the variation in difficulty in processing different inputs.   Different independently developed versions will tend to fail on the same "hard" input cases, even though the different versions use different solutions.   The independently developed versions do not necessarily fail via similar faults or output, but they will nevertheless tend to fail on the same inputs.

Littlewood and Miller (1989) built on the Eckhardt and Lee model to show that forced diversity can improve reliability to a point where it is superior to independent failure behavior. Diversity is modeled by design decisions that induce a partition on the universe of possible programs. Much more research needs to be done in how to practically inject diversity and how to quantify the reliability benefits of such diversity. Since chance alone does not guarantee the independence of the multiple versions, diversity must somehow be deliberately built into the software; this is also a topic for research.

2.1.4.5.4.6.1 Model (F) Parallel Concurrent

In an active parallel aggregate, all components operate simultaneously and all must fail for the system to fail. This reliability-related use of the word "parallel" should not be confused with its use in the computer science term "parallel processing."

The parallel configuration is useful when the components continuously perform some "chore." It is not useful in situations where the components produce an "answer." Software and some types of hardware produce information. If the components differ in the answer produced, there is no provision in a parallel system for reconciling the different answers. Other techniques such as recovery blocks and N-modular redundancy, do provide a means of deciding which, if any, answer to consider correct.

If k components are active simultaneously and all components must fail for the system to fail, then the aggregate reliability is

$$R(t) = 1 - \prod_{i=1}^{k} (1 - \exp[-\lambda_i t]) = 1 - \prod_{i=1}^{k} [1 - r_i(t)] \qquad (19)$$

The failure rate [Nieuwhof (1975)] is

$$\Lambda(t) = \frac{\sum_{i=1}^{k} \lambda_i (\alpha_i - 1)}{\left(\prod_{i=1}^{k} \alpha_i \right) - 1} \qquad (20)$$

where

$$\alpha_i = \frac{1}{1-r_i(t)}, \quad i=1,2,\ldots,k \tag{21}$$

In the case of the same failure rate λ for each component, then

$$R(t) = 1 - (1-\exp[-\lambda t])^k = 1 - [r(t)]^k \tag{22}$$

and [Grosh (1982)]

$$\Lambda(t) = k\lambda B_k(t) \tag{23}$$

where

$$B_k(t) = \frac{\exp[-\lambda t](1-\exp[-\lambda t])^k}{1-(1-\exp[-\lambda t]^k} \tag{24}$$

Note that the failure rate of the aggregate is not constant but increases monotonically through time and converges to λ. Intuitively, the reason is that, as time goes on, the redundant components will eventually succumb one-by-one to random failure, causing the level of redundancy to degrade. However, this assumes that individual software components are not restarted upon failure

The effective aggregate failure rate [RADC (1988)] is a constant approximation based on time to first failure:

$$\Lambda = \frac{1}{\displaystyle\sum_{i=1}^{k}(i\lambda)^{-1}} \tag{25}$$

2.1.4.5.4.6.2   Model (G) k-out-of-n Configuration

A k-out-of-n aggregate consists of n components such that the aggregate succeeds if and only if k of its components succeed. When the components have differing failure rates, computation of the reliability function is more an algorithm than a formula. The best way to calculate the reliability function of such a system is through a computer program such as described and listed in Sarje and Prasad (1989). The most common situation, where the components have equal failure rates, will be considered here.

If k out of n components with the same failure rate must succeed for the aggregate to succeed, the reliability is

$$R(t) = \sum_{i=k}^{n} \binom{n}{i} [r(t)]^i [1-r(t)]^{n-i} \tag{26}$$

After R(t) is computed, the failure rate can be obtained as [Rau (1970)]

$$\Lambda(t) = \frac{\lambda \dfrac{n!}{(n-k)!(k-1)!} \exp[-k\lambda t](1-\exp[-\lambda t])^{n-k}}{R(t)} \tag{27}$$

The effective aggregate failure rate [RADC (1988)] is a constant approximation based on time to first failure:

$$\Lambda = \frac{\lambda}{\displaystyle\sum_{i=k}^{n} \frac{1}{i}} \tag{28}$$

2.1.4.5.4.6.3 Model (H) N-Modular Redundancy

In an aggregate with N-modular redundancy, N=2n+1 redundant components are active concurrently. A voter compares the results from the N components and chooses the results of the aggregate as the output of a majority of the components. If there is no majority, the aggregate fails. Furthermore, for the aggregate to succeed, the majority must have the correct output. The aggregate reliability is the same as that of an (n+1)-out-of-N aggregate:

$$R(t) = \sum_{j=n+1}^{N} \binom{N}{j} [r(t)]^j [1-r(t)]^{N-j} \tag{29}$$

The effective failure rate [RADC (1988)] is a constant approximation based on time to first failure:

$$\Lambda = \frac{\lambda}{\sum_{i=n+1}^{N} \frac{1}{i}} \tag{30}$$

An important caveat is that N-modular redundancy can result in worse reliability than the component alone [Dhillon and Singh (1981)]. For example, for N=3--triple modular redundancy (TMR)-- the reliability of the aggregate is

$$R(t) = [r(t)]^2 [3 - 2r(t)] \tag{31}$$

Solving R(t)=r(t) yields a crossover point of λt=0.693. Before the crossover point, TMR will have superior reliability; after that point the simplex component will be better. In a mission-oriented system the mission time should be such that λ<0.693.

The use of N-modular redundancy for software fault tolerance is called N-version programming [Avizienis (1980)]. The reader is referred to the Eckhardt and Lee (1985) model for insights into the limitations of multiversion programming. The formulas given in this section apply when it can be justified that the multiple versions fail independently.

2.1.4.5.4.6.4 Model (I) Standby Redundancy

Software standby redundancy is a scheme in which k redundant components are tried in sequence until one succeeds or all components have been exhausted. The aggregate only fails if and when all components have failed.

The reliability [Grosh (1989)] of the aggregate is

$$R(t) = \sum_{i=1}^{k} \exp[-\lambda_i t] \prod_{\substack{j=1 \\ j \neq i}}^{k} \frac{\lambda_j}{\lambda_j - \lambda_i} \tag{32}$$

The effective failure rate is a constant approximation based on time to first failure:

$$\Lambda = \frac{1}{\sum\limits_{1}^{k} \frac{1}{\lambda_i}} \tag{33}$$

In the usual case of all components having the same reliability,

$$R(t) = \exp[-\lambda t] \sum_{i=0}^{n-1} \frac{(\lambda t)^i}{i!} \tag{34}$$

The formula, based on the Erlang distribution, assumes perfect sensing and switching, and no idle failure rate. If the reliability of the switcher is R_{sw}, then all terms in the summation except the first must be weighted by R_{sw}:

$$R(t) = \exp[-\lambda t] \left[1 + R_{sw}\lambda t + \frac{R_{sw}(\lambda t)^2}{2} + \cdots + \frac{R_{sw}(\lambda t)^k}{k!} \right] \tag{35}$$

The failure rate of the aggregate [Becker and Jensen (1977)] is

$$\Lambda(t) = \frac{\lambda}{(k-1)! \sum\limits_{i=0}^{k-1} (\lambda t)^{i+1-k}/i!} \tag{36}$$

The failure rate increases over time and slowly approaches the constant failure rate λ. The effective failure rate [RADC (1988)] is a constant approximation based on time to first failure:

$$\Lambda = \frac{\lambda}{k} \tag{37}$$

Software, standby redundancy is implemented through the technique of recovery blocks [Randell (1975)]. The results of each component version are checked through an acceptance test. The acceptance test may itself be susceptible to failure. The aggregate now can fail in three circumstances [Scott et al. (1987)]: (E_1) An incorrect result is accepted; (E_2) A correct result is not accepted; and (E_3) An incorrect result is not accepted.   Suppose that the acceptance test has reliability r_T and therefore failure probability $q_T=1-r_T$.   Each component has failure probability $q=1-r$.

The formulas given here apply when it can be justified that the multiple versions fail independently.   To simplify the equations, let $X=q_T-2q_Tq+q$.   If the reliability of the acceptance test is R_T, the probability of the first type of aggregate failure occurring is

$$Pr\{E_1,\ n\}\ =\ \frac{q_T \cdot q \cdot (1-X^n)}{1-X} \qquad (38)$$

The probability of the second type of aggregate failure occurring is

$$Pr\{E_2, n\}\ =\ (q_T-q_T \cdot q)\ \cdot\ X^{n-1} \qquad (39)$$

and for the third type of aggregate failure it is

$$Pr\{E_3,\ n\}\ =\ (q-q_T \cdot q)\ \cdot\ X^{n-1} \qquad (40)$$

The reliability of the aggregate is then calculated as

$$R_n\ =\ 1-\sum_{i=1}^{3} Pr\{E_i,\ n\} \qquad (41)$$

If the recovery software is imperfect and exhibits reliability r_R, an error type E_4 of unsuccessful recovery can occur.   For the case of $n=1$ independent versions of the software, $Pr\{E_4,1\}=0$; for $n=2$ the probability is

$$Pr\{E_4,2\}\ =\ r \cdot (1-r_T) \cdot r_R\ +\ (1-r) \cdot r_T \cdot r_R \qquad (42)$$

For $n \geq 3$, the recurrence relationship is

$$Pr\{E_4,n\}\ =\ Pr\{E_4,n-1\}+Pr\{E_4,n-2\}\,r \cdot [r \cdot (1-r_T)+(1-r) \cdot r_T] \qquad (43)$$

The reliability of the aggregate is then obtained as

$$R_n = 1 - \sum_{i=1}^{4} \text{Pr}\{E_i, n\} \tag{44}$$

2.1.4.5.4.7 Combination Concurrent-Sequential Configuration

To handle an aggregate that contains both concurrent and sequential components, divide the time-line into time segments such that one or more components are concurrently active throughout each such time segment.   For each time segment, replace the components with a pseudocomponent.   Let the failure rate of the pseudocomponent be the sum of the failure rates of the concurrently active components in that time segment.   Once this "collapsing" of time segments is completed for all time segments, the aggregate can be treated as purely sequential.

2.1.4.5.4.8 Combination Series-Parallel Configuration

If a system consists of series-connected parallel configurations, first reduce each parallel configuration to a single pseudocomponent, and handle as a series system.   If a system consists of parallel-connected series configurations, first reduce each series configuration to one pseudocomponent, and handle as a parallel system.   These strategies can be applied recursively to lower levels, until the component level is reached.

3. Reliability Decomposition and Allocation

Reliability allocation is a planning technique for guiding design and implementation toward meeting specified reliability requirements. It is especially useful when different teams or subcontractors work on different parts of a system. In system functional decomposition, the functional requirements of the system are allocated to subsystems and lower-level items. In reliability allocation, the overall system reliability requirements are apportioned to those same items.

In fulfillment of SOW Task 2, techniques were developed for decomposing hardware/software systems and allocating quantitative reliability requirements to the hardware and software subsystems and to lower indenture levels.

3.1. Approach

Reliability allocation, in its simplest form, consists of finding an achievable combination of failure rates and repair rates that supports achievement of a system's or subsystem's specified reliability requirements. One needs to start with a model, such as obtained from the modeling techniques of Section 2, and "solve" for the unknown failure rates and repair rates. The failure rates and repair rates cannot have just any values; the values are constrained by the range of values that are realistically achievable. The reliability engineer begins the allocation process by determining what the achievable range is for each rate. An acceptable allocation is one in which all rates lie within their achievable ranges and the overall subsystem or system reliability meets or exceeds the specified reliability requirement. The reliability model is evaluated to assess whether the allocated values meet or exceed the specified requirements. The process of finding the failure rates and repair rates involves a systematic trial-and-error exploration of alternatives. The reliability engineer makes an initial cut by choosing rates from the achievable ranges. The values can be chosen arbitrarily but ideally would be chosen based on intuition and on experience with similar and previous-generation items. Next, the reliability is evaluated through the reliability model. If the allocated values (MTBF, MTTR, etc) ensure that the system requirements are met, the allocation is complete and any "excess" can be either allocated to another part of the system, or reserved as a means of mitigating risk.

For software components, timing relationships, relative execution frequency, complexity, and criticality are important considerations. Several techniques were developed for apportioning reliability requirements and goals through the levels of a software hierarchy. One of these, "Allocation Based On Achievable Failure Rate" is a bottom-up methodology. The other allocation methods presented are top-down methodologies.

3.2. Results

The trade-off between implementing functionality in hardware or software often depends on cost considerations: Software development costs can be amortized over each unit produced, but hardware has a per-unit manufacturing cost.   Once the system functionality is partitioned into hardware and software subsystems, the levels of software hierarchy are established through DOD-STD-2167A and a software design methodology (such as data structure-oriented design, data flow-oriented design, or object-oriented design).   The levels of software decomposition, such as computer software components (CSCs) and computer software configuration items (CSCIs), refer to parts of the static program as it is viewed for the purposes of configuration management. When executing the software subsystem will exhibit a dynamic structure--the timing relationships and reliability topologies of different threads of execution.   Reliability allocation should take place at the level at which individual threads of execution ("processes" or "tasks") exist.   Generally, this level corresponds to the CSCI level.   This level is also appropriate for allocation because the interfaces among modules are included.

3.2.1. Software Reliability Allocation

If the utilization factors for each CSCI being allocated to are known or can be estimated, the bottom-up method "Allocation Based On Achievable Failure Rate" can be used. When utilization factors for the CSCIs cannot be estimated, one of the top-down allocations methods should be used. When using these top-down allocation methods, several iterations may be required to ensure that the allocations to the individual components are achievable and fully support the system requirements.

3.2.2 Notation for Software Reliability Allocation Models

The term "aggregate" refers to an interrelated collection of software "components." In systems, the aggregate is a software subsystem as a whole, and a component is a CSCI within that subsystem.   In a distributed system, the aggregates of one computer system can serve as the components of the overall distributed system, and so the allocation would be performed twice, once to allocate from the distributed system as a whole to the individual computer systems, and once to allocate from the individual computer systems to their respective processes (generally, CSCIs).

Λ_G: Failure rate goal for a software aggregate.

$R_G(t)$: Reliability goal for a software aggregate. Note that
$\Lambda_G=[-\ln R_G(t)]/t$ and $R_G(t)=\exp[-\Lambda_G t]$.

λ_G: Failure rate objective for a software component.

$r_G(t)$:   Reliability objective for a software component.

Let R_G be the reliability goal for a mission. The purpose of reliability allocation is to set reliability objectives $(r_G)_1$, $(r_G)_2$, ..., $(r_G)_n$ for components 1, 2, ..., n so that

$$f((r_G)_1, (r_G)_2, ..., (r_G)_n) \geq R_G \qquad \textbf{(45)}$$

where f is defined by the rules of reliability combination covered previously. An infinite number of different allocations can satisfy the above inequality. A good allocation not only meets or exceeds the overall system reliability requirements but optimizes or "balances" the allocation in some way.

3.2.3 Allocation Techniques

The allocation techniques that are presented here are Allocation Based on Achievable Failure Rates, Equal Apportionment, Proportional Allocation, Weighted Allocation, Constrained Allocation, and Re-allocation. Appendix C covers the "Dynamic Allocation" class of re-allocation techniques.

The bottom-up allocation method, "Allocation Based on Achievable Failure Rates" requires the ability to estimate CSCI utilization rates and the test time available for each CSCI. This method provides a set of failure rate allocations to each CSCI which are achievable within the planned program test schedule and which accurately reflect the planned usage and the execution time available for achieving reliability growth. If failure rate allocations provided by this method do not support achievement of the system or subsystem specified reliability figures of merit, it is an indication that there may be a problem with the specification requirements or one or more higher level allocations with respect to the program schedule.

In "Equal Apportionment," the components of an aggregate are allocated equal failure rates or equal failure probabilities in such a way that the aggregate meets its reliability goal.

"Proportional Allocation" takes into account the length of time each component is active. The longer a component is active, the more exposure it has to the possibility of failure. The premise of proportional allocation is that higher reliability should be demanded of components that are active for a greater share of the time relative to the other components.

In "Weighted Allocation," the failure rate allocated to a component is based on the criticality of the component and/or feasibility of its meeting a reliability objective.   The criticality of the component includes the consequences of the failure to mission success and safety. The feasibility [Fuqua (1986)] of a reliability objective is dependent on the complexity (number of parts for hardware, program size [or other measure] for software), the state-of-the-art, and the skills and tools available for the development process.

In "Constrained Allocation," the allocation is optimized with respect to additional considerations such as cost.

In "Re-allocation," a previous allocation is revised because one or more components could not meet their reliability objectives. Dynamic allocation (Appendix C) is a technique for re-allocation with minimized effort. Table 3-1 summarizes the allocation models.

Table 3-1. Allocation Models

Class	Model	Type of Allocation	Topology	Timing
Bottom Up	A	Achievable Failure Rate	All	All
Top Down	B	Equal Apportionment	Series	Sequential
Top Down	C	Equal Apportionment	Series	Concurrent
Top Down	D	Equal Apportionment	Parallel	Concurrent
Top Down	E	Equal Apportionment	Parallel	Sequential
Top Down	F	Equal Apportionment	NMR	Concurrent
Top Down	G	Proportional Allocation	Series	Sequential
Top Down	H	Proportional Allocation	Parallel	Concurrent
Top Down	I	Importance Factors	Series	Concurrent
Top Down	J	Weighted Allocation	Series	Concurrent
Top Down	K	Constrained Allocation	Series	Concurrent
Top Down	L	Re-Allocation	Series	Concurrent

Dynamic allocation models appear in Appendix C.

3.2.3.1 Model (A) Allocation Based On Achievable Failure Rate

Allocation Based on Achievable Failure Rates uses each CSCI's utilization (see paragraph 2.1.4.5.3). The utilization governs the growth rate a CSCI will experience during system test. All things being equal, the greater a CSCI's utilization, the faster its reliability will grow during system test.

A forecast is made of each CSCI's initial failure rate by using predicted size and processor speed and assuming industry average figures for fault density and other prediction model quantities (see Chapter 4). Then the software reliability growth model parameters are predicted to determine the growth curve formula. An achievable failure rate figure is obtained from the growth curve. The relative distribution of achievable failure rates is used to apportion the aggregate's failure rate goal Λ_G to the CSCIs.

Note that changing to a faster processor does not change the system-operating-time failure rate; the reduction in u_i is offset by a proportionate increase in the execution-time failure rate. Therefore, a CSCI's allocated system-operating-time failure rate does not need to be changed if the hardware platform changes to a faster processor.

The software aggregate's failure rate goal Λ_G is assumed to be expressed with respect to system operating time.

The allocation scheme is based on first determining an achievable distribution of failure rates among the CSCIs, considering their predicted initial failure rates and how much reliability growth they can each expect to experience during system test. The distribution of failure rates is then used to allocate the software aggregate's failure rate goal Λ_G to the constituent CSCIs.

A CSCI's achievable failure at release is determined by predicting an initial failure rate λ_0 and applying a software reliability growth curve to forecast CSCI's failure rate at release.

The i-th CSCI's initial failure rate is the failure rate at the start of system test ($t_i=0$). Using the Proposal/Pre-Contractual stage prediction model (see section 4.), a CSCI's initial failure rate with respect to execution time is

$$\lambda_0 = r \cdot K \cdot \omega_0 / I \qquad (46)$$

where r is the processor speed (average number of instructions executed per unit of time), K is the fault exposure ratio (4.20×10^{-7} industry average), ω_0 is the CSCI's fault content (developed KLOC x 6 industry average), and I is the CSCI's number of object instructions). The number of object instructions is found by multiplying the number of predicted source instructions by the programming language's code expansion ratio (see paragraph 4.2.2 and Table 4-2). For example, the code expansion ratio for Ada is 4.5. Note that the initial failure rate is primarily determined by fault density and processor speed, as opposed to size.

It is thus assumed that each CSCI is developed by a mature, reproducible software development process that produces code with the industry-average of 6 faults per developed KLOC (developed excludes reused code).

The growth curve relates failure rate decline to cumulative wall-clock time expended in system test:

$$\lambda_i(t_i) = \lambda_0 \cdot \exp[-\beta \cdot t_i \cdot u_i] \cdot u_i \qquad (47)$$

where β is the decrement in failure rate per failure experienced:

$$\beta = B \cdot \frac{\lambda_0}{\omega_0} \qquad (48)$$

An industry-average value of 0.955 is recommended for B. B is the fault reduction factor, the average net number of faults removed per failure. The cumulative wall-clock time expended in system test t_i may differ from CSCI to CSCI if the software is incremented in a series of successive "builds." If the software is incremented all at once, then the t_i's will be equal.

It is assumed that the CSCIs are in series, so the CSCI failure rates with respect to system operating time must add up to the overall software failure rate Λ_G. Once the achievable failure rates $\lambda_1(t)$, $\lambda_2(t)$, ..., $\lambda_n(t)$ are determined, each CSCI is assigned a relative weight

$$w_i = \frac{\lambda_i(t_i)}{\sum \lambda_i(t_i)} \qquad (49)$$

These relative weights add up to one. The failure rate Λ_{Ai}, with respect to system operating time, to be allocated to the i-th CSCI is

$$\lambda_{Ai} = \Lambda_G \cdot w_i \qquad (50)$$

The allocation is acceptable since the CSCI failure rates add up to the goal:

$$\sum w_i \Lambda_G = \Lambda_G \sum w_i = \Lambda_G \cdot 1 = \Lambda_G \qquad (51)$$

To change a CSCI's allocated system-operating-time failure rate to execution time, the allocated failure rate is divided by the CSCI's utilization u_i.

3.2.3.2   Equal Apportionment

Let the failure rate goal of the aggregate be

$$\Lambda_G = \frac{-\ln R_G(t)}{t} \tag{52}$$

The strategy of equal apportionment is for the system never to be exposed to an instantaneous failure rate exceeding Λ_G. This results in an overall reliability of at least $\exp[-\Lambda_G t] = R_G$. The formulas for equal apportionment are obtained by solving the corresponding reliability combination formulas for component failure rate or reliability.

3.2.3.2.1   Model (B) Sequential Series

Each sequentially active component is allowed a failure rate of $\lambda_G = \Lambda_G$, so that a constant, satisfactory failure rate is maintained at all times regardless of which component is active.

3.2.3.2.2   Model (C) Concurrent Series

Each of k concurrently active components is allocated a failure rate objective of $\lambda_G = \Lambda_G / k$. This results in an overall reliability of at least

$$\exp\left[-t \sum_{i=1}^{k} \frac{\Lambda_G}{k}\right] = R_G(t) \tag{53}$$

The reliability of each component is

$$r(t) = \sqrt[k]{R_G(t)} \tag{54}$$

Alternatively, consider the failure probability (unreliability)

$$Q_G(t) = 1 - R_G(t) \tag{55}$$

Each component can be allocated an equal portion of the failure probability for a reliability objective of

$$r_G(t) = 1 - \frac{Q_G(t)}{k} \tag{56}$$

3.2.3.2.3 Model (D) Concurrent Parallel

If k components are connected in parallel, the failure rate λ_G to be allocated to each component is

$$\lambda_G = \Lambda_G \cdot \sum_{i=1}^{k} \frac{1}{i} \tag{57}$$

A similar problem is to determine how many components with reliability r are needed to meet an aggregate reliability goal of R_G. The solution is

$$k = \frac{\ln(1-R_G)}{\ln(1-r)} \tag{58}$$

3.2.3.2.4 Model (E) Standby Redundancy

For recovery blocks (under the assumption that the multiple versions fail independently) with k components, the reliability allocation is

$$r_G(t) \approx 1 - \sqrt[k]{[1-R_G(t)]\,k!} \tag{59}$$

3.2.3.2.5 Model (F) N-Modular Redundancy

For N-version programming (under the assumption that the multiple versions fail independently), the failure rate allocation is

$$\lambda_G = \frac{\sum_{i=n+1}^{N} \frac{1}{i}}{\Lambda_G} \tag{60}$$

3.2.3.3 Proportional Allocation

Let the expected-number-of-failures objective be

$$M_G = -\ln[R_G(t)] \tag{61}$$

The strategy of proportional allocation is for each component of the aggregate to contribute the same expected number of failures. The expected number of failures is a function of the failure rates and the time exposures of the components that comprise the aggregate.

3.2.3.3.1 Model (G) Sequential Series

For each of the k components, let the expected-number-of-failures allocation be

$$\mu = \frac{M_G}{k} \tag{62}$$

and allow each component i a failure rate of

$$(\lambda_i)_G = \frac{\mu}{t_i'} \quad , \; i=1,2,\ldots,k \tag{63}$$

where t_i' is the amount of time component i is active. This results in an overall reliability of at least

$$\exp\left[-\sum_{i=1}^{k} \lambda_i t_i'\right] = R_G \tag{64}$$

The reliability objective for component i is

$$r_i(t) = \exp[-(\lambda_i)_G \, t] \quad , \; i=1,2,\ldots,k \tag{65}$$

Thus the longer the time exposure of the component the lower its failure rate must be. This criterion is appropriate for hardware and for software that is run repetitively.

3.2.3.3.2 Model (H) Concurrent Parallel

For proportional allocation of k components connected in parallel, the reliability objective to be allocated to each component is [Dennis (1974)]

$$r_G(t) = 1 - \sqrt[k]{1-R_G(t)} \tag{66}$$

and the failure rate objective is

$$(\lambda_G)_i = \frac{-\ln\left[1-\sqrt[k]{1-R_G(t)}\right]}{t_i'} \quad , \; i=1,2,\ldots,k \qquad (67)$$

3.2.3.4 Model (I) Importance Factors

Let k be the number of subsystems; n_i, the number of items in each subsystem i; R, the desired mission reliability; and t_i', the mission time for subsystem i. Let

$$N = \sum_{i=1}^{k} n_i \qquad (68)$$

be the total number of components in the system. Assign each subsystem i an importance index w_i that is the probability that the mission will fail if the i-th subsystem fails. The failure rate objective to be allocated to the i-th subsystem [AGREE (1957)] is

$$(\lambda_i)_G = \frac{\ln\left[1-1/w_i(1-R_G^{n_i/N})\right]}{-t_i'} \qquad (69)$$

Software fault tree analysis [Leveson and Stolzy (1983)] is useful for pinpointing safety- and reliability-critical sections of computer programs. However, software fault tree analysis examines the software at too low a level to provide quantitative criticality figures which can be used in developing importance indices. Regular fault tree analysis, which stops at the interfaces to the software components, is capable of providing quantitative criticality figures.

3.2.3.5 Model (J) Weighted Allocation

If the mission reliability goal is R_g, then the unreliability (1-R_g) can be allocated proportionally to each phase in the mission according to the distinct conditions at each stage [Amstadter (1971)]. If the weighting of phase i is ω_i, with

$$\sum_i \omega_i = 1 \qquad (70)$$

then the reliability objective for that phase is

$$(R_G)_i = 1 - [(1-R_G)\,\omega_i] \tag{71}$$

and the failure rate objective is

$$(\lambda_G)_i = \Lambda_G \cdot \omega_i \tag{72}$$

3.2.3.6   Model (K) Constrained Allocation

A software system consists of n serial stages. A reliability of

$$(R_G)_i = \sqrt[n]{R_G} \tag{73}$$

is allocated to each of the n stages. The minimum number of redundant components at each stage i [Sandler (1963)] is

$$n_i = \left\lceil \frac{\ln\,(1-R_G)}{\ln\,(1-r_i)} \right\rceil \tag{74}$$

If c_i is the cost of components for the i-th stage, the least-cost allocation is given by [Moscovitz and McLean (1956)]

$$n_i = \left\lceil \frac{\ln\,(1-R_G^{a_i})}{\ln\,(1-r_i)} \right\rceil \tag{75}$$

where

$$a_i = \frac{\dfrac{c_i}{\ln\,[1-r_i]}}{\displaystyle\sum_{j=1}^{n}\left(\frac{c_j}{\ln\,(1-r_j)}\right)} \tag{76}$$

3.2.3.7 Model (L) Re-Allocation

Suppose Λ_R is the failure rate goal and Λ_t is the current reliability of the component. Then if Λ_R is less than Λ_t, a suitable reliability goal λ_i^* for each component [von Alven (1964)] is

$$\lambda_i^* = \lambda_i \cdot \frac{\Lambda_R}{\Lambda_t} \tag{77}$$

It is most effective to raise the reliability of the least reliable component in a series configuration, and the most reliable component in a parallel configuration.

Appendix C develops and presents "dynamic allocation" techniques for minimizing the effort required for reallocation.

4. Software Reliability Prediction

Reliability prediction has several important uses. Early in the acquisition cycle it can be employed to determine the feasibility of the system reliability requirements. It can highlight which components in a design can be anticipated to contribute most to the system unreliability. It enables schedule and cost forecasts to be made. It allows tradeoffs to be made between reliability and other factors (such as maintainability). Often, absolute prediction values are not as important as relative values, especially when comparing alternative configurations or designs.

In fulfillment of SOW Task 4, a technique for modeling and predicting the reliability of hardware/software systems was developed. Emphasis was placed on reliability prediction for the software part of the system, because hardware reliability prediction techniques are already well established.

4.1 Approach

The goal of the prediction research was the development of a method for the prediction of software reliability that could be used in conjunction with MIL-HDBK-217 and other published failure rate data to obtain a reliability prediction for the overall system. Hardware reliability prediction provides a failure rate for the inherent reliability, which, in theory, is the best reliability achievable as the development and manufacturing processes are perfected.

Software does not have the same kind of inherent reliability limitation. The reliability of software will generally improve over time as faults are uncovered through testing and are fixed. There are two conditions that limit the attainable reliability for software: (1) There reaches a point at which a program that has poor maintainability becomes a victim of entropy--the code has been modified so much that it has become a patchwork quilt and an attempt to fix one fault results in the introduction of at least as many new faults. (2) The software achieves a high level of reliability, so that the times between failures are excruciatingly long, with the result that further testing becomes impractical. As discussed in the section of this report on Reliability Growth, the simultaneous execution of multiple identical copies of the software can be helpful in postponing that point in time.

When software reliability or combined hardware/software reliability is predicted, that prediction must be related to a point in time. The earliest point in time for which it makes sense to predict reliability is when the system is fully integrated and is operating in an environment that emulates field use. This point in time is the beginning of "system test" and is denoted by cumulative operating time $\tau=0$. The software reliability prediction methods developed in this section will forecast the reliability the software can be expected to exhibit at that point. Also forecast will be the parameters of the time domain software reliability growth model described in Section 5 of this report, so that software reliability can be predicted for points in time later during system test. It is assumed that when the software code has been frozen and is being subjected to a stationary operational profile (probability distribution of input states--see Section 5), it will exhibit a constant failure rate (see Appendix B).

The study team applied multivariate regression (SOW para. 4.1.3.2.3) and related statistical analysis to the data collected in the reliability database (SOW para. 4.1.1.1).   The team explored which product (requirements, documentation, code) and software development process characteristics are significantly correlated with fault content (SOW para. 4.1.3.3, 4.1.3.2.3).

The technique for software reliability prediction uses metrics derived from characteristics of the software development process and of the products. Also provided are techniques for taking into account the influence of two additional factors on the reliability figures: the program structure and the operational profile.

The study team first investigated techniques for predicting program size during the early stages of software development, before the code has been written (SOW para. 4.1.3.1).   Program size is important for relating fault content to fault density, and is a product metric in its own right.

4.1.1   Prediction of Software Size (SOW para. 4.1.3.1)

Halstead's (1977) software science was the first technique the study team evaluated.   Software science is an information-theoretic approach to properties of representations of algorithms.   By invoking these properties, one can obtain predictions of various quantities of interest such as program size, complexity, and fault density. Surprisingly little data is required for the predictions.

Using software science, the size of a program can be predicted if the number of distinct operators (verbs) and the number of distinct operands (nouns) in the program are known. Software science defines the length of the program as

$$LENGTH = \eta_1 \log_2 \eta_1 + \eta_2 \log_2 \eta_2 \qquad (78)$$

where η_1 is the total number of distinct operators and η_2 is the total number of distinct operands. The phenomenon that the size of a program is a function of the size of its lexicon has parallels in other fields. The linguist George Zipf (1965) observed this phenomenon in natural languages such as English, and B. Mandelbrot, the father of fractals, saw the phenomenon in unordered random symbols [Jones (1986)].

The number of executable source instructions is obtained as

$$I_s = \frac{LENGTH}{Q} \tag{79}$$

where Q=7 for higher-order languages (HOLs) and Q=4.5 for assembly language. From no additional data, the fault density can also be obtained. The software science "volume" metric is defined as

$$VOLUME = LENGTH \times \log_2(\eta_1 + \eta_2) \tag{80}$$

The volume is roughly defined as the number of characters that it takes to encode the program. The number of faults is predicted by

$$\omega_0 = \frac{VOLUME}{3000} \tag{81}$$

and the fault density by

$$\omega_I = \frac{\omega_0}{I_s} \tag{82}$$

The number of distinct operators and the number of distinct operands are available after coding but can usually be estimated at the end of detailed design. However, software science provides a means of making the same predictions based on data obtainable even earlier, during preliminary design.

The early prediction method is based on the number of input and output parameters and the "language level." Since module interfaces are established during preliminary design, the number of input and output parameters for each module will be available.

Let η_2^* be the number of input/output parameters of a module. Let ℓ be the language level. Then the total number of distinct operators, η_1 and the total number of distinct operands, η_2, can be determined by simultaneously solving

$$\eta_2 = \eta_2^* \log_2[(2+\eta_2^*)/2](\eta_1 - 2)/(2+\eta_2^*) + \eta_2^* \tag{83}$$

and

$$[(2+\eta_2^*)\ \log_2\ (2+\eta_2^*)]^2 = \ell\,(\eta_1 \log_2 \eta_1 + \eta_2 \log_2 \eta_2)\ \log_2\ (\eta_1 + \eta_2) \quad \textbf{(84)}$$

A drawback to this method is that, while Halstead theorized that language level is a function of the programming language, it appears that it is also a function of the individual programmer [Pressman (1982)].   If historical data is available on the programmer who is expected to implement the module, an estimate of the language level can be found from taking a sample of his code and computing

$$\ell = \left(\frac{2\eta_2}{\eta_1 N_2}\right)^2 (\eta_1 \log_2 \eta_1 + \eta_2 \log_2 \eta_2)\ [\log_2 (\eta_1 + \eta_2)] \quad \textbf{(85)}$$

where N_2 is the total number of operand appearances in the code.

The study team was skeptical of software science because of research articles critical of the theoretical and empirical bases of Halstead's work [Coulter (1983), Hamer and Frewin (1982, 1985), Shen et al. (1983)].   The size of already written programs was "predicted" using mean language level figures.   The results were mixed.   Trying out the software science relationships on already-written   software,   calculating   language   level historically, to see if those relationships hold is recommended.

The next program size method the team investigated was function point analysis [Albrecht (1979), Albrecht and Gaffney (1983)]. This   method   allows   program   size   to   be   predicted   after requirements analysis, which is even earlier than predictions can be made using software science.   A function point is one end-user function.   The requirements statements are examined to determine the number of logical end-user functions required, namely inputs, outputs, inquiries, master files, and interfaces.   Dreger (1989) discusses the manner in which these functions should be counted. The counts are multiplied by the empirically obtained factors given in Table 4-1.

Table 4-1.   Function Point Factors

Function Point	Factor
Inputs	4
Outputs	5
Inquiries	4
Master Files	10
Interfaces	7

The products of the counts and the factors are totaled and adjusted ±25% based on the estimated processing complexity of the program. The following characteristics are considered to increase processing complexity: data communications, distributed data or processing, performance objectives, heavily-used configuration, transaction rate, on-line data entry, end user efficiency, on-line update, complex processing, reusability, conversion and installation ease, operational ease, multiple site use, and facilitation of change. Dreger (1989) provides guidelines for quantifying the complexity added by each of the characteristics.

The translation of the number of function points to the number of lines of code depends on the programming language. For Ada, Jones (1986) has determined that there are approximately 71 source statements per function point. For JOVIAL, the number is 106; for basic assembler, 320; for macro assembler, 213; for FORTRAN and COBOL, 105; and for C, 128.

The use of function point analysis in software engineering is expanding, especially as a measure of productivity. The drawback to function point analysis is that it is currently geared to business applications areas. Methods applicable to a wider variety of application areas were sought.

People in the defense industry involved in making sizing predictions were interviewed and a comprehensive comparative evaluation of software sizing models [AFCCE (1987)] was reviewed. The sizing method that emerged at the top of the AFCCE assessment is that implemented by an increasingly popular commercial product called Software Sizing Model (SSM) [Bozoki (1987)]. This method was developed by Dr. George Bozoki of Lockheed. SSM has also been incorporated into RCA's computerized cost-estimating software, PRICE. The method uses psychological scaling methods to convert qualitative sizing information (relative sizes of modules) to absolute sizes.

The exact inner workings of SSM are not published, but the study team has devised similar methods based on the scholarly literature. An example of a psychological scaling method is the technique of paired comparisons: one or more "experts", persons familiar with the type of application and who have worked on similar projects within the same organization, are presented with random pairings of module names and asked to judge, for each pairing, which module they would expect to be bigger. If at least two of these modules are "reference modules" of known size, then it is possible to compute predictions of the absolute sizes of every module. Appendix D discusses some psychometric methods that have been adapted for the purpose of program size prediction.

4.1.2 Predicting Fault Density and Content (SOW para. 4.1.3.2)

A software failure is a discrepancy between the program's output and that dictated by requirements [Musa et al. (1987)].   A software fault is a missing, extra, or defective statement or set of statements that is the cause of, or can potentially cause, a software failure [Musa et al. (1987)].   Taking a snapshot of the program at the start of system test, the inherent fault density of a program is the fault content (number of inherent faults) divided by the number of executable lines of code.   The term "inherent faults" will be used to contrast with faults that are inadvertently introduced during repair activity.

An industry average figure for fault density is 6 faults per kiloline of executable source code [Musa et al. (1987)].   This figure may be useful in forming very early predictions of software reliability, for example, in a proposal.   For the regression analysis, the team sought methods for determining the number of faults in a program.   Unfortunately, the faults in a program are not directly observable.   Any faults that have been identified have presumably already been removed.   What is observable during system test are software failures.   Each software failure, by definition, is caused by a single fault.

The occurrence of a software failure is conclusive evidence that a fault exists.   But counting the number or rate of failures over time does not by itself say anything about the number of faults that remain.   The only way to count all the faults in the program is to keep testing until all faults have been exposed and removed.   This feat would require exhaustive testing of all possible input states, which, for most programs, would take an astronomical amount of time to complete.   (One round of exhaustive testing would not even be enough, because of the possibility that repair activity will introduce new faults.)

One proposed method for estimating the number of faults is called "fault seeding."   It is based on the same idea as "capture-recapture" studies used in estimating the size of animal populations.   Such a study proceeds as follows: First comes the "capture" phase. A group of animals, say, zebras, are caught, counted, tagged, and released back into the wild.   Next comes the "recapture" phase. After a period of time the researchers go out and capture a group of zebras.   The numbers of tagged and untagged zebras in this new group are noted. The proportion p of tagged zebras in the group is calculated. The number of untagged zebras in the entire population is estimated by dividing p into the number of untagged zebras in the second group.

In software fault seeding, originally discussed by Mills (1972), a number of artificially created faults are injected into the code. Testing proceeds and, at some point, the number of seeded faults and indigenous faults found are noted. An estimate of the number of indigenous faults in the program is obtained from the assumption that the proportion of indigenous faults found out of the population of indigenous faults is the same as the proportion of seeded faults found.

For software, let y be the number of faults injected initially; u, the number of indigenous faults found so far; v, the number of seeded faults found to date.   Then the maximum likelihood estimator of the number of indigenous faults x is

$$x = \left\lfloor \frac{y}{v} \cdot u \right\rfloor$$

(86)

[Feller (1957)].

The problem that fault seeding encounters in practice is that the seeded faults are easier (usually much easier [Musa et al. (1987)]) to find than the indigenous faults. To carry the animal analogy further, suppose that the zebras that are originally captured are "tagged" by having one leg amputated. Then the three-legged zebras are released into the wild. Later, for the recapture phase, a group of zebras is caught and the number of three-legged zebras noted.   Obviously the method is flawed because the three-legged zebras are much easier to catch than the untagged (four-legged) zebras.

Variations on fault seeding have been proposed. Myers (1976) suggests having two independent teams test the software. The faults that the two teams find in common are treated as if they had been tagged. The formula is [Shooman (1983)]

$$\omega_0 = \frac{B_2}{b_c} B_1$$

(87)

where B_1 is the number of faults that tester #1 found, B_2 is the number of faults that tester #2 found, and b_c is the number of faults found in common. This variation has the advantage that no artificial faults have to be created.   However, several conditions need to be met. First, the faults found during the test period must be representative of the total population of faults.   Second, the independent testing and debugging must result in similar program versions, and third, the common faults must be representative of the total fault population. (It could be argued that the faults found in common will tend to be the easiest ones to find.)

Ideally, the dependent variable in the multivariate regression is fault density. The study team concluded that the state of the art in fault seeding is not advanced enough to provide good estimates of fault content.   Since neither software science nor fault seeding can currently provide accurate fault content figures, the study team decided to choose an observable quantity, the Basic Execution Time Model initial failure rate parameter, λ_0, as the dependent variable for the regression analysis.   Additional methods provide the parameters B and K.   Established parametric relationships (SOW para. 4.1.3.3) are then employed to derive fault density, fault content, and growth rate predictions. Because processor speed varied from project to project, the observed failure rates were standardized to an instruction execution rate of 3 million instructions per second (MIPS).

Automated support for the multivariate regression was provided by the SAS (Statistical Analysis System) package.   Custom software to pre- and postprocess the data and perform additional calculations was also written.

In predicting fault density, the two product characteristics that immediately came to mind were size and complexity.   The two most commonly employed complexity measures are McCabe's (1976) "cyclomatic complexity" and Halstead's (1977) "E".

To calculate McCabe's metric a program graph is drawn to depict flow of control.   The metric V(G) is computed as the number of enclosed areas on the plane of the graph.   The metric can be obtained after the detailed design is complete.

Halstead "E", which denotes "effort", is given by

$$E = \frac{(\eta_1 \log_2 \eta_1 + \eta_2 \log_2 \eta_2)[\log_2(\eta_1 + \eta_2)]}{\dfrac{2\eta_2}{\eta_1 N_2}} \tag{88}$$

where N_1 is the total number of distinct operators and N_2 is the total number of distinct operands.   Because of the presence of the quantity N_2, this metric can only be obtained after coding.

Halstead even provides the following formula to obtain the number of faults from the effort:

$$\omega_0 = \frac{E^{2/3}}{3000} \tag{89}$$

Several studies have shown that complexity correlates with program size [Shen et al. (1983), Sunohara et al. (1981), Basili and Hutchens (1983), Gremillion (1984)].   For this reason the study team decided not to collect a separate complexity metric.

4.1.3 Prediction of Software Failure Rate (SOW para. 4.1.3.2)

As detailed in Appendix A, this study has hypothesized 24 characteristics that affect the software failure rate as shown below broken down by software life cycle phase.

Requirements Analysis:

- x_1: Errors in requirements specification (SRS)
- x_2: Requirements statements in the SRS
- x_3: Pages in the SRS
- x_4: Man-months for requirements analysis
- x_5: Requirements changes after baseline

Preliminary Design:

- x_6: Errors in preliminary design documents
- x_7: Number of computer software components (CSCs)
- x_8: Units (or Ada packages) in design structure
- x_9: Pages in design documents
- x_{10}: Man-months for preliminary design

Detailed Design:

- x_{11}: Errors in design documents
- x_{12}: Man-months for detail design
- x_{13}: Design flaws identified after baseline
- x_{14}: Design flaws identified after an internal review

Coding:

- x_{15}: Number of executable lines of code (LOC)
- x_{16}: Faults found through code reviews
- x_{17}: Programmer skill level (average years of experience)
- x_{18}: Number of units undergoing review
- x_{19}: Average number of source LOC per unit

Unit Test:

- x_{20}: Average number of branches in a unit
- x_{21}: Percent of branches covered
- x_{22}: Nesting depth average
- x_{23}: Number of times a unit is unit-tested
- x_{24}: Man-months for coding and unit test

$x_{25} = x_{13} + x_{14} + x_{16}$ (Defects identified from walkthroughs and reviews)

Some of the independent variables were normalized based on kilo lines of executable code (KLOC). The normalized independent variables are $x_1, \ldots, x_{14}, x_{16}, x_{24}, x_{25}$. The formula to normalize x_i where $i \in \{1, 2, \ldots, 14, 16, 24, 25\}$ is

$$x_i = (x_i \ / \ x_{15}) \cdot 1000 \qquad\qquad (80)$$

Recall that x_{15} is the number of LOC in each observation.

For each phase of the software development process, a new regression model was formed which involves Y (software failure rate as the dependent variable) and x_i, i= 1,2,...,k where k ≤ n, and contains more software characteristics as they become available. Therefore, several regression models were formulated for each software development phase (such as Requirements Analysis, Preliminary Design, Detailed Design, Coding and Unit Test).

Scatter plots of Y (software failure rate) versus x_i (software characteristic), i = 1,2,...,n, based on the collected data from Appendix A, were drawn. These scatter diagrams suggest that the regression models can be linear in terms of all the variables except x_6, x_{11}, x_{13}, x_{14}, x_{16}, x_{23}. However, both linear and nonlinear regression models involving software failure rate (dependent variables) and the software characteristics (independent variables) described above were developed for each phase of software development.

The general linear regression model is of the form

$$Y = a_0 + a_1 x_1 + a_2 x_2 + \ldots + a_k x_k \qquad\qquad (81)$$

where k assumes different values depending on the software development phase. Similarly, the non-linear regression model for each phase of the software development is a sum of the linear combination of items in a subset of $\{x_1, \ldots, x_5, x_7, \ldots, x_{10}, x_{12}, x_{17}, \ldots, x_{22}, x_{24}, x_{25}\}$ and the linear combination of items in the subset of $\{1/x_6, \ 1/x_{11}, \ 1/x_{13}, \ 1/x_{14}, \ 1/x_{16}, \ 1/x_{23}\}$; the sizes of these subsets depend on the phase of the software development. Notice that x_{15} is not used in any of the regression models, except to normalize appropriate independent variables, since the software failure rate Y should not depend on the size (x_{15}) of the software.

Due to the fact that the number of metrics exceeded the number of observations in all software development phases, except for the Requirements Analysis phase, full regression models cannot be formulated. Advanced statistical techniques were applied to reduce the number of independent variables which can participate in the regression model after each phase of software development. The reduction was accomplished in two alternative ways. One way was to work with only the subset of metrics that was determined to most influence the reliability of the software. This was done by using the stepwise selection method. The other approach taken was to work not with the metrics themselves but with aggregates of the metrics. Principal component analysis was employed to achieve this goal.

The regression models that were formulated after each software development phase were compared to one another in the Validation Task. The comparisons were done based on the values of their statistical characteristics (such as: R^2, p-values, 95% confidence limits, etc.), and on how well they can predict the failure rates of known software. A model was chosen to be used to describe the relationship between software failure rate and software characteristics.

The following is the discussion of the "stepwise selection" method and principal components analysis.

a. Stepwise Selection Method

Since it would have been impractical to try all subsets of independent variables, the stepwise selection method was used to effectively eliminate some independent variables which have a small contribution to the regression model.

Stepwise regression is a composite of two different procedures: forward selection and backward elimination.

The forward selection technique begins with no variables in the model. Then it selects the independent variable that is most highly correlated with the dependent variable. For each of the independent variables, forward selection calculates F-statistics that reflect the variable's contribution to the model if it is included. The F-statistic is the ratio of the explained variance to the unexplained variance. The p-values for these F-statistics are compared to a predetermined value, f. If no F-statistic has a significance level smaller than f, forward selection terminates. Otherwise, forward selection adds to the model the remaining independent variable that has the largest F-statistic (accomplishes the greatest reduction in unexplained variance). Forward selection then calculates F-statistics again for the variables still remaining outside the model, and the evaluation process is repeated. Thus, variables are added one by one to the model until no remaining variable produces a significant F-statistic. Once a variable is added to the model, it stays there.

The backward elimination technique begins by calculating statistics for a model, including all of the independent variables. Then the variables are deleted from the model one by one until all the variables remaining in the model produce F-statistics significant at a pre-specified level, b. At each step, the variable showing the smallest contribution to the model is deleted.

The stepwise method is a cross between forward selection and backward elimination. The variables already in the stepwise model do not necessarily stay there; the decision is reversible. As in forward selection, variables are added one by one to the model, and the F-statistic for a variable to be added must be the largest among the outside variables and it must be at the f significance level. After a variable is added, however, the stepwise procedure looks at all the variables already included in the model and deletes any variable that does not produce an F-statistic significant at the b significance level. Only after this check is made and the necessary deletions are accomplished can another variable be added to the model. The process ends only when none of the outside variables has the F statistic significant at the f level, and none of the inside variables has the F statistic significant at the b level.

Moreover, the value of R^2 (the coefficient of multiple determination) is also taken into consideration, when the Stepwise regression analysis is performed. The R^2 quantifies the degree of association that exists among the variables. C_p, Mallow's statistic, is another factor which is used in generating a stepwise regression model. C_p was introduced by Mallows (1964) as a criterion for evaluating the adequacy of multiple regression functions of differing orders. It is a measure of total squared error, defined as

$$C_p = (SSE_p / s^2) - (N - 2*p)$$ (82)

where s^2 is the mean square error (MSE) for the full model, and SSE_p is the sum-of-squares error for a model with p parameters including the intercept, if any. If C_p is plotted against p, Mallows recommends the model where C_p first approaches p. When the correct model is chosen, the parameter estimates are unbiased, and this is reflected in C_p near p. If the full model is not available due to lack of a "reasonable" number of observations, only the value of R^2 is taken into the decision-making process.

The main advantages of the stepwise procedure are that it is fast, easy to compute, and available in statistical packages for most computers. Also, the cost of the computation rises slowly as the number of variables increases. Another advantage of the stepwise procedure is that it possesses order independence, (i.e., the order which the independent variables are fed into the regression model does not affect the final outcome of the analysis). Unfortunately, there are some drawbacks to the use of stepwise regression. The model chosen by stepwise regression need not be the best by criterion of interest; indeed, because of the nature of the one-at-a-time philosophy of the stepwise method, there is no guarantee that the model chosen will in fact include any of the variables that would be in the best subset. The stepwise procedure is best when the independent variables are nearly uncorrelated, but this is a condition that is seldom satisfied in practice.

b. Principal Component Analysis

An alternative approach to alleviate the difficulty of having fewer data points than the number of regressors is the principal components analysis (PCA) Method.   The technique uses as few principal components of the original independent variables as possible in the regression model.

Principal components P_1, P_2,...,P_n are linear combinations of the original independent variables, say x_1, x_2,..., x_n (in the study's case n=25). P_1, P_2,..., P_n have special properties in terms of variances; for example, the first principal component P_1 is the normalized linear combination with maximum variance.   The coefficients in the linear combinations for the principal components turn out to be the normalized eigenvectors of the variance-covariance matrix of $x_1,x_2,...,x_n,y$, called Σ.   Since Σ is a non-negative definite matrix, it has non-negative real eigenvalues $\lambda_1 \geq \lambda_2 \geq ... \geq \lambda_n$ and associated eigenvectors α_1, $\alpha_2,...,$ α_n.

Suppose α_1, $\alpha_2,...,$ α_n are normalized; i.e., $\alpha_i'\alpha_i = 1$, where ' means "transpose." Let $Z_i = \alpha_i'X$, where $X = [x_1, x_2,...,x_n]'$ and i = 1,2,...,n; then Z_i is the ith principal component.   It can be shown that the variance of Z_i is the eigenvalue λ_i, where i = 1,2,...,n.   The idea of the principal components method is to use the first k principal components as the independent variables in the regression model, where k satisfies

$$\frac{\sum_{i=1}^{k} \lambda_i}{\sum_{i=1}^{n} \lambda_i} \geq C \; ; \qquad \text{where } C = 0.90 , 0.95 \qquad (83)$$

since it can be proven that the first k principal components can explain at least C*100% of the total variation of the sampled standardized software failure rates.

Often, k is much less than n. Therefore, the new regression model has many fewer independent variables than the old model, but it still contains all the original characteristics, since these independent variables are linear combinations of the original variables.

The major advantages of the principal components method are that it works well if the original data is highly correlated, and that all the information pertinent to the model is reserved. Also, as in the stepwise procedure, principal components analysis is order independent. One of the disadvantages of the principal components method is that the results may be unstable since there is too much data contributing to the model (a small perturbation of the data may result in a significant change in the result). Another drawback of this technique is that the eigenvalues and eigenvectors of Σ must be calculated, but Σ is usually large and may be ill-conditioned; therefore, this task can be troublesome in some cases.

4.2 Results

4.2.1 Results of Prediction of Software Failure Rate

Several regression models were formulated to describe the relationship between the software failure rate and the software characteristics. Comparisons were done to select an appropriate regression model to be used to predict software failure rate for each phase of the software development.

The comparisons were done based on several statistical values of the regression models (such as: R^2, p-values of hypothesis tests (I) and (II), standard errors of the parameter estimates, etc.), and on how well the models predict known software failure rates. In addition to these criteria, the following ground rules were applied:

1. The model with the best correlation to the observed software failure rate was chosen whenever there were any significant differences in correlation between the two models.

2. When two models produced essentially identical correlation between the predicted software failure rate and the failure rate observed on the projects, the model which accounted for the largest number of metrics (most recent information) was selected.

The need to select the model which provided a software failure rate with the best statistical correlation to the observed failure rate is obvious. The study team's preference for a prediction model which used the largest number of metrics is based on two areas of concern with respect to the data collected during the study period. The data collected to support development and validation of the prediction models was all collected after all system integration testing on the program was complete. In most cases, the software was in use at the customers facility. As a result, the metric data collected on the projects was essentially complete. Thus, the data available to the study team was much more accurate and complete than the data which would normally be available at the end of a given program phase (eg requirements analysis). This may have resulted in much better accuracy for the early program phase models than would normally be expected. Also, the metric data collected during the project was limited to one company (Hughes Aircraft) and thus potentially valuable variations in values of the metric data which would occur between companies was omitted, possibly yielding better stability and accuracy for the early prediction models than would ordinarily result.

A complete discussion of the regression analyses is provided in Appendix E. Also, details of the comparisons among the developed regression models are included in the Validation section of this report.

Three regression models were chosen for use through the software development phases to predict software failure rate. These models are:

- Model M3:

    $Y = 18.04 + 0.05\ P_1$ (Y is restricted to be non-negative)

    $P_1 = 0.009x_1 + 0.99x_2 + 0.10x_3 - 0.0001x_4 + 0.0005x_5$

- Model M6:

    $Y = 17.90 + 0.04\ P_1$ (Y is restricted to be non-negative)

    $P_1 = 0.007x_1 + 0.796x_2 + 0.08x_3 - 0.0003x_4 + 0.0003x_5 +$
    $\quad\quad 0.00009x_6 + 0.0043x_7 + 0.013x_8 + 0.6x_9 + 0.003x_{10}$

- Model M10:

    $Y = 17.88 + 0.04\ P_A$ (Y is restricted to be non-negative)

    $P_A = 0.007x_1 + 0.80x_2 + 0.08x_3 + 0.01x_8 + 0.6x_9 + 0.008x_{23} +$
    $\quad\quad 0.03x_{25}$

M3 is used to predict the software failure rate during the Preliminary Design phase. M6 can then be used during the Detailed Design phase and the Code and Unit Test phase. Model M10 can be used after Code and Unit Test phase has passed.

4.2.2 Predicting Hazard Rate/Fault and Related Quantities (SOW para. 4.1.3.3)

The relationship between software fault content and the software failure rate is as follows: Let ϕ_i be the hazard rate of the ith software fault in a program. Then the overall program failure rate is

$$\lambda_0 = \sum_{i=1}^{\omega_0} \phi_i \tag{84}$$

The Basic Execution Time Model, discussed more fully in Section 5 of this report, asserts that every fault hazard rate ϕ_i is equal to a constant, the per-fault hazard rate ϕ. In this case the overall program failure rate is

$$\lambda_0 = \sum_{i=1}^{\omega_0} \phi = \phi\omega_0 \tag{85}$$

The multiple regression models predict a standardized failure rate that corresponds to the Basic Execution Time Model's λ_0 parameter. To obtain the same two Basic Execution Time Model parameters that are supplied by estimation during growth testing (see Section 5), v_0 and β, the following formulas are employed. For total failures,

$$v_0 = \frac{\lambda_0}{f \cdot K \cdot B} \tag{86}$$

and for β,

$$\beta = B \cdot \phi = B \cdot f \cdot K \tag{87}$$

where the linear execution frequency f is

$$f = \frac{r}{I} \tag{88}$$

The linear execution frequency is the number of program passages there would be in unit execution time if the program's instructions were executed in linear sequence. I is the number of object instructions and is obtained by multiplying the number of source instructions by a code expansion ratio. Table 4-2 provides the code expansion ratios for selected programming languages [Jones (1986)].

Table 4-2.   Code Expansion Ratios

Programming Language	Expansion Ratio
Assembler	1
Macro Assembler	1.5
C	2.5
COBOL	3
FORTRAN	3
JOVIAL	3
Ada	4.5

A method of relating fault content (obtained from applicable product/process related metrics) to failure rate, based on program structure and operational profile was developed. In the framework of the Basic Execution Time Model, fault content is related to failure rate through the fault exposure ratio, K. Specifically, if there are ω_0 faults in the program, then the failure rate is

$$\lambda_0 = f \cdot K \cdot \omega_0 \tag{89}$$

With regard to faults, the failure rate depends primarily on fault density, not on fault content. The initial failure rate, λ_0, and the inherent faults, ω_0, are the failure rate and fault content at the start of system test, but in actuality any point during system test could be arbitrarily designated the "official start" of system test, so the relationship holds throughout system test and during field use.

Zeroing in on a single, "typical" fault, the Basic Execution Time Model defines the per-fault hazard rate as

$$\phi = f \cdot K \tag{90}$$

The per-fault hazard rate is the equal contribution each fault makes to the overall program failure rate. The method developed also handles the situation in which a program departs from that assumption. In that situation, faults will fall into various hazard rate classifications (hazard rate profile) (SOW para. 4.1.3.3.1).

Musa introduced the factor K to account for two distinct phenomena, the dynamic structure of the program and the varying machine state. The dynamic structure of the program is the looping and conditional and unconditional branching that takes place during execution. The machine state is the values of all program variables. The machine state can change upon execution of each instruction. When a fault is encountered during execution, a failure may or may not occur during a particular encounter; it depends on the machine state. When K=1,

$$\phi = f \tag{91}$$

This occurs only when the program is executed linearly and all faults cause failures regardless of the machine state.

The study team separated K into two factors

$$K = S \cdot M \tag{92}$$

where S is a structure factor and M is a machine state factor. In relation to a single fault, S and M are defined as

$$M = \frac{\text{failure-causing machine states}}{\text{total machine states}} \tag{93}$$

and

$$S = \frac{\text{actual encounters}}{\text{linear encounters}} \tag{94}$$

Both M and S are multiplicative factors because doubling either of them doubles the failure rate. So now

$$\phi = f \cdot S \cdot M \tag{95}$$

The product f·S is the frequency with which a fault is encountered. Once the fault is encountered, the probability of a failure ensuing is M. Stochastically, S is the probability of an arbitrary fault being encountered during one program passage (of which there are f per unit time). M is the probability of a failure ensuing (because of an unfavorable machine state), given that a fault is encountered.

If, as in the Basic Execution Time Model, K is assumed to be constant for a particular program, what about S and M? Since K = S · M is a constant, there are two possibilities: (1) S and M are themselves constant; or (2) S and M countervail each other so as always to equal a constant. Alternative 2 is the suggestion that when S is large, M=K/S is small, and when M is large S=K/M is small.

Since S is a function of the structure (loops, branches) of the program, and M is a function of the arithmetic and logic within the fault, it is reasonable to assume that S and M are independent quantities. Hence, since K=S·M is a constant, and S and M vary independently, it can be concluded that S and M are each by itself a constant for a particular program, which is alternative 1. The ramification of K being separable into S and M is that the two quantities can be studied individually. If K is affected by the structure of the program, then the effect should be seen in S and not M.

S is the rate at which a particular fault is encountered during a single program passage. One way to estimate S would be to inject a program with a single fault and see how often that fault is encountered. By injecting several faults, a more accurate and quicker estimate would be obtained. But as discussed earlier in this section, it is difficult to fabricate faults that are representative of a program's indigenous faults.

But why inject a fault? A fault is in essence just a place in the program. The major issue is how often an arbitrary place in the program is reached per program passage. S can be estimated by observing how often one or more randomly chosen places in a program are encountered during execution. The assumption that is being made here is that a fault can occur anywhere in a program, and every place in the program is as likely as any other to have a fault. That is, the fault density of a program (faults/kilolines of executable code) is uniform. This assumption has been borne out through empirical studies [Basili and Hutchens (1983), Takahashi and Kamayachi (1985)].

Here, then, is the method developed for estimating S and using that estimate to refine K to better reflect program structure and operational profile.

1. An array of counters is declared. In Ada, the declaration would be

$$\text{counter: array}(1..n) \text{ of integer}:=(0,0,0,...,0); \qquad (96)$$

2. A random sample is taken of n "places" within the program. These places must lie in between existing program statements. At each place a counter iteration statement is inserted. For example, the following statement is inserted into the program at the i-th such place:

$$\text{counter}(i) := \text{counter}(i) + 1; \qquad (97)$$

3. The program is executed for w time units. During the period of execution the operational profile should, ideally, be stationary and representative of field use. When the execution

period is complete, the values of elements of the COUNTER array are examined, and the sample values for S are calculated from

$$s_i = \frac{COUNTER(i)}{f \cdot w} \quad , \quad i=1,2,\dots,n \qquad (98)$$

Note that $f \cdot w$ is the number of program passages that take place during the w time units. If S is a constant for a particular program, as implied by the Basic Execution Time Model, then any variability in the observed values $\{s_i\}$ can be attributed to "sampling fluctuations." The best estimator for S will be the sample mean

$$\bar{S} = \frac{\sum_{i=1}^{n} s_i}{n} \qquad (99)$$

Under the assumption that K is constant, the Gaussian law of errors applies. The sample standard deviation is

$$\hat{\sigma} = \sqrt{\sum_{i=1}^{n} (s_i - \bar{S})^2 / (n-1)} \qquad (100)$$

A $100(1-\alpha)\%$ confidence interval for S has endpoints

$$\bar{S} \pm t_{n-1,1-\alpha/2} \frac{\hat{\sigma}}{\sqrt{n}} \qquad (101)$$

where $t_{n-1,1-\alpha/2}$ is that value of the t-distribution with n-1 degrees of freedom that has $1-\alpha/2$ to the left. The t-distribution is tabulated in many statistics textbooks. A numerical method suitable for programmable calculators and computers is given in [Volk (1982)]. For n>30, $t_{n-1,1-\alpha/2}$ can be replaced by the standard normal deviate $\kappa_{1-\alpha/2}$.

If no information is available about K for this program, the industry average value of 4.20×10^{-7} is recommended [Musa et al. (1987)]. If the same or a similar program has gone through growth testing, then the value can be obtained from the following parametric relationship:

$$K = \frac{1}{Bf} \cdot \frac{\lambda_0}{v_0} \tag{102}$$

In any case, the value of M can then be recovered as

$$M_{tested} = \frac{K}{S} \tag{103}$$

Here is a summary of the dimensions of the various quantities involved in predicting the parameters of the Basic Execution Time Model:

$$f: \frac{\text{program passages}}{\text{execution time}} \tag{104}$$

$$S: \frac{\text{encounters}}{\dfrac{\text{faults}}{\text{program passages}}} \tag{105}$$

$$M: \frac{\text{failures}}{\text{encounters}} \tag{106}$$

$$K: \frac{\text{failures}}{\dfrac{\text{faults}}{\text{program passages}}} \tag{107}$$

$$\omega_0: \text{faults} \tag{108}$$

$$\lambda_0: \frac{\text{failures}}{\text{execution time}} \tag{109}$$

If the s_i values are highly variable or skewed, then the assumption of a constant per-fault hazard rate should be questioned. Skewness--the degree of symmetry in the shape of the distribution--can be measured by

$$Sk = \frac{3(\bar{S} - Md)}{\hat{\partial}} \qquad (110)$$

where Md is the median of the $\{s_i\}$. A large positive score indicates that the distribution is skewed to the right, and a large negative score indicates that it is skewed to the left. For the purposes of prediction, a skewed distribution suggests that the Basic Execution Time Model may not be appropriate.

If the $\{s_i\}$ are highly skewed or highly variable, then the hazard rate for each counter should be computed individually as

$$\phi_i = s_i \cdot M \cdot f \qquad (111)$$

The distribution of hazard rates can be expressed through a "hazard rate profile." The range of fault hazard rate values is partitioned into n subranges, which will be termed classes. Adams (1984) researched a similar situation and devised a classification scheme. Adapted here to the purposes of fault hazard rate classification, the first step is to find the highest fault hazard rate, ϕ_{high}, and the lowest fault hazard rate, ϕ_{low}. Starting from ϕ_{high}, the class boundaries are formed by successively multiplying ϕ_{high} by $10^{-\frac{1}{2}} \approx 0.31623$:

$$\phi_{high}, \phi_{high}(10^{-\frac{1}{2}}), \phi_{high}(10^{-\frac{1}{2}})^2, \phi_{high}(10^{-\frac{1}{2}})^3, \dots, \phi_{low} \qquad (112)$$

Denote the proportion of fault hazard rates falling into the classes as

$$p_1, p_2, \dots, p_n \qquad (113)$$

with

$$\sum_{j=1}^{n} p_j = 1 \qquad (114)$$

Let the mean hazard rate value in each class j be denoted m_j. Class j as a whole contributes $\omega_0 p_i m_i$ to the overall program failure rate, which will be

$$\lambda_0 = \omega_0 \sum_{j=1}^{n} p_j m_j \qquad (115)$$

If a similar program is predicted to have a fault content of ω_0, and it is presumed that the hazard rate profile is the same, then the program failure rate is

$$\lambda_0' = \omega_0' \sum_{j=1}^{n} p_j m_j \tag{116}$$

4.2.3   Fault Reduction Factor

Another quantity that appears in the Basic Execution Time Model is the fault reduction factor, B. The fault reduction factor is the net number of faults removed per failure occurrence. B is not generally equal to unity because of imperfect debugging. Repair activity can fail to find the causative fault, can find and remove several related faults, or can inadvertently generate new faults. The fault reduction factor can be computed [Musa (1984)] from

$$B = D(1+A)(1-G) \tag{117}$$

where D is the "detectability ratio"--the proportion of faults whose causative failures can be found. The quantity A is the "associability ratio"--the ratio of faults discovered by code reading to faults discovered by testing. G is the "fault growth ratio"--the increase in faults per fault corrected. Generally, D is close to 1, A is close to 0, and G ranges from 0 to 0.91 [Miyamoto (1975), Musa (1980)].

If data from growth testing on a similar project is available, then B can be obtained from the relationship

$$B = \frac{\beta}{f \cdot K} \tag{118}$$

where β is a parameter of the Basic Execution Time Model (see Section 5).

Another option, when no information is available, is to use the industry average figure 0.955 [Musa et al. (1987)].

4.2.4   Summary of Prediction Technique

a. With no prior information, use

$$\omega_I = \frac{6 \text{ faults}}{1000 \text{ source instructions}} \tag{119}$$

Predict the number of developed source instructions ΔI_s (omitting reused code). Then compute the inherent fault density as

$$\omega_0 = \omega_I \cdot \Delta I_s \tag{120}$$

Use 0.955 for B, or obtain it from historical data, and obtain the total failures as

$$v_0 = \frac{\omega_0}{B} \qquad (121)$$

Using the appropriate code expansion ratio, compute the number of object instructions I.   From manufacturer's specifications or benchmarking, find out the average instruction execution rate r. Obtain the linear execution frequency as

$$f = \frac{r}{I} \qquad (122)$$

Use 4.20×10^{-7} as the value for K, or obtain K from historical information on a similar project.   Predict the initial program failure rate as

$$\lambda_0 = fK\omega_0 \qquad (123)$$

and the time-dependent failure rate as

$$\lambda(\tau) = \lambda_0 \exp\left[-\frac{\lambda_0}{v_0}\tau\right] \qquad (124)$$

where τ is cumulative execution time since the start of system test.

b.   As product/process metrics come in during requirements analysis, preliminary design, detailed design, and coding and unit test, use the regression model to obtain a better prediction of λ_0.

c.   Once system test begins, use actual failure data to estimate the software reliability model parameters, as described in Section 5.

5. Reliability Growth Testing

Reliability growth is the positive improvement in reliability over time. For hardware, reliability growth occurs over a period of time due to improvements in the product design or manufacturing process. For software, reliability growth occurs through systematic testing and debugging resulting in effective removal of software faults.

Growth management is part of the system engineering process, and complements other basic reliability program activities such as prediction, allocation, and demonstration testing. Growth management consists of planning the achievement of reliability as a function of time and other resources.

The rate of software reliability growth depends on how fast the test-debug-test loop can be accomplished. The rate is constrained by the failure rate of the software, the amount of computer time available, and the availability of failure identification personnel (testers) and failure resolution personnel (debuggers). The rate is controlled by reallocation of resources and other forms of intervention, based on comparisons between planned and assessed reliability values.

In fulfillment of SOW Task 4, a standard methodology for reliability growth testing, measurement, and management was developed. The techniques are built around a time domain software reliability model. Methods were developed for selecting random test cases from an operational profile that emulates field use, and established procedures for data collection, parameter estimation, determination of the calendar time/execution time ratio, assessment of model goodness-of-fit, recalibration, and use of multiple copies.

5.1 Approach

First, criteria were identified for selecting an appropriate time domain software reliability model around which to build the growth, testing methodology (SOW para. 4.1.4.1). An important consideration was that the model had to be compatible with existing hardware reliability standards, concepts, and procedures. The model should be mathematically tractable, so that the formulas can be easily invertible to find out various quantities of interest (such as forecasting when a future reliability objective will be met). The parameters of the model needed to have simple interpretations that are meaningful to software engineers.

Another important consideration is the predictive validity of the model. Ideally, the model should be one that has been validated on a broad selection of software development projects. Because no software reliability model has been completely validated on all types of applications across different organizations, it was decided that the growth testing methodology should include a goodness-of-fit technique and a recalibration technique. A goodness-of-fit technique would allow a user to gauge how well the software reliability model is working on a given program. If the fit is poor, the user can switch to an alternative model or parameter estimation technique. In many cases, the reason for poor fit will turn out to be a systematic bias (consistent optimism or pessimism) or noisiness in the estimations. These problems can be corrected by recalibration. The study team sought to develop a new type of recalibration technique that is numerical, as opposed to the existing graphical techniques. A numerical technique is more accurate and has the advantage of being easily implemented on a programmable calculator or computer.

The team paid special attention to the procedures for conducting growth testing. The prevailing objective of testing in recent years has been to aggressively seek faults by testing at high workload and at boundary values of the input variables. This type of testing should be completed prior to growth testing. During growth testing, the input states must be chosen "statistically," which is to say that the input states must be randomly selected from a stationary operational profile (probabilities of input states). The operational profile during growth testing should be close to the operational profile the program will experience during field use. Statistical testing is effective in contributing to improved reliability, because it finds the faults that the user will tend to encounter most. On the other hand, stress testing or coverage testing might find many faults, but because the user will rarely encounter those faults, their removal may not significantly improve the failure rate.

5.2 Results

The team chose a variation of the Basic Execution Time Model [Musa et al. (1987)] as the time domain software reliability model on which to base the growth testing methodology. This model has a wide following among software practitioners in large corporations. Much practical knowledge and many auxiliary techniques have come out of the model's real-world experience, which enable the model to be adapted to a wide variety of software development technologies and project situations.

The Basic Execution Time Model has simple parameters that are easy for software engineers and project managers to understand and to which they can relate. The model is fully compatible with existing hardware reliability assessment methods and is mathematically tractable. The data needed to estimate the model parameters is minimal and relatively easy to collect. Another reason for choosing the Basic Execution Time model is that it represents a synthesis of many of the advances that have taken place in almost 20 years of research in the field of software reliability modeling.

5.2.1 Major Time Domain Software Reliability Models

Jelinski and Moranda (1972) developed the first reliability growth model created specifically for software. The model assumes that the failure rate is linearly proportional to the number of faults in the software. When a failure occurs it is assumes that the fault that caused it is removed instantaneously, without spawning any new faults. The failure rate remains piecewise constant between failures, and drops by a constant amount at each failure. The interfailure times are independent exponentially distributed random variables. Around the same time, Shooman (1973) presented a similar model but introduced additional concepts: The failure rate is not only a function of the number of faults in the program, it is also a function of the instruction processing rate, the program size, and the program structure. Fault correction occurs at a different time than failure occurrence and is affected by the nature of the project and the number of available personnel.

Musa (1975) developed a model that built on the Jelinski-Moranda and Shooman models and included several new concepts. Execution (CPU) time, not calendar time, is the failure-inducing stress placed on a program. During field operation the failure rate remains constant; only during periods of fault correction activity does the failure rate change. Musa accounts for the dissimilarity between the testing and operational environments by means of a testing compression factor.

Goel and Okumoto (1979) presented a model based on a nonhomogeneous Poisson process (NHPP). This model assumed that the number of faults in the program at the start of testing is not fixed but is a Poisson random variable. In earlier models each interfailure period is governed by a distinct (homogeneous) Poisson process, whereas now the entire system test phase is governed by a single nonhomogeneous Poisson process. At the expense of conformance to an intuitive desire for a piecewise continuous failure rate, Goel and Okumoto achieve the analytical simplicity of a smooth failure rate curve. New concepts included the idea that repair of the underlying fault occurs at some variable time after failure occurrence. Other concepts included were that a program can be "perfect" and have no faults and that the effectiveness of repair actions is imperfect.

The concept of imperfect debugging is an important one. Evidence strongly suggests that most faults originate in the requirements and design phases [Lipow (1979)]. A fault caused by a requirements misunderstanding or design deficiency may require extensive reworking of the program, and this reiteration of the original development process will likely spawn new faults.

Musa and Okumoto created a model called the Basic Execution Time Model [Musa et al. (1987)] that embodies all of the foregoing concepts.

One concept championed by Littlewood (1978) was that different faults in the program make different contributions to the overall failure rate. The most frequently encountered faults (those that contribute most to the overall program failure rate) are detected and corrected first. Because some programs are subjected to a highly nonuniform operation profile, Musa and Okumoto developed a model, called the Logarithmic Poisson Model, that considers the hazard rates of the faults in the program to form a geometric progression, an idea similar to Littlewood's. The Logarithmic Poisson Model should be tried if the goodness-of-fit procedure is showing a poor fit with the Basic Execution Time Model.

The Basic Execution Time Model (as well as the Logarithmic Poisson Model) is a nonhomogeneous Poisson process (NHPP) model. The NHPP framework is the most commonly used for modeling reliability growth. An NHPP conforms to four axioms. The failure counting process $\{N(\tau), \tau \geq 0\}$, which gives the cumulative number of failures in the execution time interval $[0, \tau]$, is an NHPP with intensity function (time-dependent failure rate) $\lambda(\tau)$, if

(i) $N(0) = 0$;

(ii) $\{N(\tau), \tau \geq 0\}$ has independent increments;

(iii) $Pr\{N(\tau + \Delta\tau) - N(\tau) \geq 2\} = o(\Delta\tau)$;

(iv) $Pr\{N(\tau + \Delta\tau) - N(\tau) = 1\} = \lambda(\tau)\Delta\tau + o(\Delta\tau)$

where the function $o(\Delta\tau)$ is defined by

$$\lim_{\Delta\tau \to 0} \frac{o(\Delta\tau)}{\Delta\tau} = 0 \qquad (125)$$

The mean value function of the NHPP is the expected number of failures occurring in the execution time interval $[0, \tau]$ and is defined by

$$\mu(\tau) = \int_0^\tau \lambda(s)\, ds \qquad (126)$$

Yamada and Osaki (1983) surveyed the NHPP applied to growth modeling. One of the most prominent models is the power law model or the Duane model. It was developed empirically by Duane (1964) and is often called the Duane model. Duane based his model on the observation that the plot of cumulative failure rate versus cumulative test time closely follows a straight line on log-log paper. Crow (1974) represented his postulate stochastically as an NHPP with a Weibull failure rate curve and a mean value function of

$$\mu(t) = \lambda t^{\xi} \qquad\qquad (127)$$

where ξ is a growth rate parameter, generally between 0.1 and 0.65. This model is also known as the AMSAA model.

Since the Basic Execution Time Model, which has been selected is also an NHPP model, the failure rate projections of the AMSAA and Basic Execution Time models can be combined to project the system reliability of concurrent-sequential hardware/software systems.

5.2.2 Selected Software Growth Model

5.2.2.1 Failure Component

A software failure is a departure in program output (hardcopies, displays, commands, control, etc.) from that specified by the requirements. The "departure" from requirements consists of an output variable that differs from its correct value. Each incorrect output variable is counted as a software failure in its own right if it arose from a separate fault. This definition of software failure differs slightly from that used in demonstration testing, where the simultaneous appearance of several incorrect output variables would count as a single failure. In growth testing, if several output variables have incorrect values and the discrepancies were caused by multiple faults, then fault correction activity will address all those faults and the failure rate will improve by several decrements, just as if the discrepancies had occurred over the course of several runs.

As a program is debugged, the amount of execution time that elapses between failures tends to increase. In the Basic Execution Time Model, it is postulated that each failure results in fault correction activity that causes the failure rate to drop by a fixed amount. When the program is released, the code is frozen and, as long as the operational profile is stationary, the software will exhibit a constant failure rate (see Appendix B).

Let ν_0 be the (expected) total failures. This is the number of failures that need to occur to expose and remove all faults. This parameter can be predicted (see Section 4) or can be estimated from observed failure data. Exposing and removing all faults can conceivably take an infinite amount of time. Let λ_0 be the initial failure rate, at the start of system test ($\tau=0$). This parameter can also be predicted (see Section 4) or can be estimated from observed failure data. Any stress testing should take place prior to $\tau=0$. If μ is the mean cumulative number of failures experienced at some point after the start of system test, the failure rate as a function of μ is

$$\lambda(\mu) = \lambda_0 \left(1 - \frac{\mu}{\nu_0}\right) \tag{128}$$

Thus the failure rate $\lambda(\mu)$ is a linear function of mean failures experienced μ. Note that the failure rate $\lambda(\mu)$ is a smooth function. In early software reliability models, the failure rate drops discontinuously at each failure; in the Basic Execution Model the failure rate glides smoothly down to reflect the uncertainty in the times that the faults are actually removed. The slope of failure rate is

$$\frac{d\lambda}{d\mu} = -\frac{\lambda_0}{\nu_0} \tag{129}$$

The decrement of failure rate per failure as $\beta \equiv \lambda_0/\nu_0$.

Another way to express the failure rate is as the product of β and the number of failures remaining:

$$\lambda(\mu) = \beta(\nu_0-\mu) \tag{130}$$

or, since the mean failures experienced is a function of execution time τ:

$$\lambda(\tau) = \beta[\nu_0-\mu(\tau)] \tag{131}$$

The function $\mu(\tau)$ is called the mean value function. The time derivative of the mean value function is the time-dependent failure rate $\lambda(\tau)$. Thus one can form the differential equation

$$\frac{d\mu(\tau)}{d\tau} + \beta\mu(\tau) = \beta\nu_0 \tag{132}$$

the solution to which is

$$\mu(\tau) = \nu_0(1-\exp[-\beta\tau]) \tag{133}$$

Differentiating, one obtains the failure rate

$$\lambda(\tau) = \nu_0\beta\exp[-\beta\tau] \tag{134}$$

The initial failure rate is found by setting $\tau=0$:

$$\lambda_0 = \nu_0\beta \tag{135}$$

The model is thus completely determined by two parameters: β and the total failures ν_0.

5.2.2.2 Fault Component

A software fault is an extra, missing, or defective instruction or set of instructions that has caused, or can potentially cause, a software failure. When a fault is encountered during execution, a software failure may or may not ensue, depending on the machine state (values of program variables). The growth that is being modeled is in the reliability (decrease in failure rate). The number and location of faults affects the reliability only indirectly.

The model contains additional elements to describe the role of software faults. The number of failures experienced and the number of faults removed are related by a quantity called the fault reduction factor, denoted B. The fault reduction factor is the net number of faults removed per failure. B accounts for imperfect debugging. Ordinarily, the causative fault behind a failure is found and removed. But sometimes the causative fault will not be found, resulting in zero faults removed. Other times, the failure will result in the discovery--by code reading--and removal of several related faults. Sometimes fault correction activity will introduce additional faults into the program. The average number of faults removed per failure is B. Since the occurrence of one failure results in the failure rate declining by the quantity β, the amount that each fault contributes to the overall program failure rate must be

$$\phi = \frac{\beta}{B} \qquad (136)$$

which will be termed the per-fault hazard rate. It is called a hazard rate (force of mortality [FOM]) because a fault has a lifetime. When the fault is removed it is gone for good. The overall program has a failure rate (rate of occurrence of failures [ROCOF]) because it is "repairable" via restart.

Let the number of inherent faults be denoted ω_0. This is the number of faults present at the start of system test and does not include any faults introduced later as the inadvertent result of repair activity. The initial failure rate can then be expressed as the product of the per-fault hazard rate and the number of inherent faults.

$$\lambda_0 = \phi\omega_0 \qquad (137)$$

The per-fault hazard rate ϕ can be further broken apart into

$$\phi = f \cdot K \qquad (138)$$

The quantity K is called the fault exposure ratio and is discussed below. The quantity f is the linear execution frequency of the program, i.e., how many times the program would be executed per unit time if its instructions were executed in a linear sequence. The linear execution frequency can be calculated by dividing the average instruction execution rate r by the number of machine-level instructions I:

$$f = \frac{r}{I} \qquad (139)$$

The average instruction execution rate is the number of instructions executed per unit time. It is frequently expressed in terms of MIPS (millions of instructions per second). The "MIPS rating" of a computer is often available from the vendor and can be refined by customer benchmarking to reflect the instruction mix of the customer's own applications. To get the number of machine-level instructions, it is easiest to multiply the number of source-level instructions I_s by an average expansion ratio for the programming language, such as tabulated by Jones (1986).

In general, programs are not executed linearly. They contain looping constructs and unconditional and conditional branches, so the number of times an individual fault is encountered per unit time can be greater or less than the linear execution frequency f. Every time a fault is encountered a failure will not necessarily happen; a failure might only occur during certain machine states. The fault exposure ratio K is meant to account for both the structure of the program (loops and branches) and the varying machine state. The value of K can be determined from historical data. On the same project or one that is similar, failure data is collected and used to statistically estimate the value of β. Then K is obtained as

$$K = \frac{\beta}{Bf} \qquad\qquad (140)$$

When no information is available, the industry average value of $K=4.20\times10^{-7}$ [Musa et al. (1987)] is recommended. The section in this report on Prediction discusses the quantities K, S, and M in detail. K is broken down into two independent factors:

$$K = S \cdot M \qquad\qquad (141)$$

where S accounts for structure and M accounts for machine state.

5.2.2.3 Estimation

Growth testing takes place during system test, once the software has been fully integrated and stress testing has been completed. Upon the occurrence of each software failure, the failure identification personnel (testers) must record the cumulative execution time from the start of growth testing. Musa et al. (1987) furnish auxiliary techniques for evolving software (integrated in successive builds) and for situations in which grouped failure data or calendar time failure data is the only data available. Failure data is said to be grouped when the only information available is the number of failures that occurred in disjoint time intervals.

The Basic Execution Time Model provides general forms for the time-dependent failure rate and the mean value function. As derived earlier, the formulas are

$$\lambda(\tau) = \frac{\beta}{v_0} \exp[-\beta\tau] \qquad (142)$$

and

$$\mu(\tau) = v_0 (1 - \exp[-\beta\tau]) \qquad (143)$$

The unknown parameters are β and v_0. (It is also possible to parameterize the model in terms of other quantities.) Let the observed failure times be denoted

$$\tau_1, \tau_2, ..., \tau_n \qquad (144)$$

where n is the number of observed failures. Let $\tau_e \geq \tau_n$ be the time at which the test ends. In statistical quality control terminology, this type of test is called a "time-truncated test." All times are measured in cumulative execution time from the start of system test.

A number of statistical estimation methods can be employed to estimate the values of β and v_0 from the failure times. One of the best general methods for statistical estimation—and by far the most popular—is the method of maximum likelihood. The maximum likelihood estimators are the values of β and v_0 that maximize the probability of the observed outcome $\tau_1, \tau_2, ..., \tau_n$. Maximum likelihood estimators exhibit many favorable large-sample properties. They are consistent (variance tends to zero and expectation tends to the true population parameter as the number of observations increases), efficient (lowest variance), and asymptotically normal (so that confidence intervals can be easily established). Another property of maximum likelihood estimators is invariance, which means that the maximum likelihood estimator of a function of an estimator can often be obtained by substitution. As an example, if the maximum likelihood estimator of w is $\hat{w}$, the maximum likelihood estimator of w^3 is $\hat{w}^3$.

Musa et al. (1987) derive the maximum likelihood estimation equation for β as

$$\frac{n}{\beta} - \frac{n\tau_e}{\exp[\beta\tau_e]-1} - \sum_{i=1}^{n} \tau_i = 0 \qquad (145)$$

The estimate for β is obtained by solving the equation for β. The maximum likelihood estimator for v_0 is

$$v_0 = \frac{n}{1-\exp[-\beta\tau_e]} \qquad (146)$$

In that equation there is nothing to solve; the estimate for β (already obtained) is simply inserted into the equation to obtain v_0.

The two equations above provide point estimates--single values-- for the parameters. It is often more informative to provide an interval estimation. Interval estimation provides a range of values within which the true value is asserted to lie. The probability that a correct interval estimate is obtained is the confidence coefficient $1-\alpha$. The interval is bounded by lower and upper confidence limits. A confidence interval that has an associated confidence interval of $1-\alpha$ is called a $100(1-\alpha)\%$ confidence interval. The lower and upper $100(1-\alpha)\%$ confidence limits for β are denoted β_{low} and β_{high} respectively. The "Fisher information" [Fisher (1922)] is a measure of the amount of information supplied by an unknown parameter. It is the reciprocal of the variance of the estimator.

The Fisher information for β's estimator is

$$I(\beta) = n\left[\frac{1}{\beta^2} - \frac{\tau_e^2\exp[\beta\tau_e]}{(\exp[\beta\tau_e]-1)^2}\right] \qquad (147)$$

Then the lower and upper confidence limits are obtained as

$$\beta_{low} = \beta - \frac{\kappa_{(1-\alpha)/2}}{\sqrt{I(\beta)}} \qquad (148)$$

and

$$\beta_{high} = \beta + \frac{\kappa_{(1-\alpha)/2}}{\sqrt{I(\beta)}} \qquad (149)$$

where $\kappa_{(1-\alpha)/2}$ is the corresponding normal deviate. The normal deviate is found as follows: The cumulative distribution function for the standard normal distribution is

$$F(x) = \int_{-\infty}^{x} \frac{1}{\sqrt{2\pi}} \exp\left[-\frac{t^2}{2}\right] dt \qquad (150)$$

where $\pi = 3.14159\ldots$ and $-\infty < x < \infty$. The standard normal deviate $\kappa_{(1-\alpha)/2}$ is that value of x for which

$$F(x) = (1-\alpha/2) \qquad (151)$$

Tables of $F(x)$ can be found in most statistics textbooks. Table 5-1 provides some common values for $\kappa_{(1-\alpha)/2}$:

Table 5-1.   Standard Normal Deviates

α	$\kappa_{(1-\alpha)/2}$
0.2	1.282
0.1	1.645
0.05	1.960
0.02	2.326
0.01	2.576
0.002	3.090

On a programmable calculator or computer, the value of $F(x)$ can be computed to the four significant figures usually found in tables, using the approximation formula

$$F(x) = 1-W(x)\,(a_1 u + a_2 u^2 + a_3 u^3) \qquad (152)$$

where

$$W(x) = \frac{1}{\sqrt{2\pi}} \exp\left[-\frac{x^2}{2}\right] \qquad (153)$$

and

$$u = \frac{1}{1 + a_0 x} \tag{154}$$

The constants a_0, a_1, a_2, and a_3 are provided in Table 5-2.

Table 5-2. Normal Approximation Constants

Constant	Value
a_0	0.33267
a_1	0.4361836
a_2	-0.1201676
a_3	0.9372980

Because of the invariance property of maximum likelihood estimators, the corresponding confidence intervals for v_0 can be established by successively substituting β_{low} and β_{high} into the estimation equation for v_0:

$$(v_0)_{low} = \frac{n}{1 - \exp[-\beta_{low}\tau_e]} \tag{155}$$

$$(v_0)_{high} = \frac{n}{1 - \exp[-\beta_{high}\tau_e]} \tag{156}$$

5.2.2.4 Goodness of Fit

It was concluded that Littlewood's (1979a) prequential likelihood statistic and u-plot are helpful during growth modeling to determine the model's "goodness of fit."   When the tester uses the Basic Execution Time Model or some other time domain software reliability model, it is not enough to blindly apply the model. The tester should monitor how well the model is fitting the failure data. If the model is not fitting well, then the user should switch to an alternative model, such as the Logarithmic Poisson Model.

A u-plot is constructed according to the following scheme. During growth testing, the user employs a statistical inference procedure, such as maximum likelihood, to estimate the parameters of the Basic Execution Time Model.

The estimated cumulative distribution function (Cdf) is

$$\hat{F}_i(\tau') = 1 - \exp[-\lambda(\tau_m)\tau'] \qquad \textbf{(157)}$$

where τ_m is the cumulative execution time, $\lambda(\tau_m)$ is the failure rate at that time, and τ' is execution time measured from the present. When the interfailure time τ'_i is later observed, the probability integral transform

$$u_i = \hat{F}_i(\tau_i) \qquad \textbf{(158)}$$

is recorded. Each failure results in another u_i. The probability integral transform implies that the u_i's should look like a random sample from a uniform distribution over the interval $(0,1)$, if the sequence of predictions was good. The accuracy of the model with respect to the particular program can be gauged by drawing a u-plot. In a u-plot the sample cumulative distribution function of the u_i's is compared with the cumulative distribution function of the uniform distribution over $(0,1)$, visually or through use of numerical goodness-of-fit measures such as the Kolmogorov distance. The specific points plotted to form the cumulative distribution function are

$$(u_{(1)}, 1/(r+1))$$
$$(u_{(2)}, 2/(r+2))$$
$$\cdots \qquad \textbf{(159)}$$
$$(u_{(r)}, r/(r+1))$$

where $u_{(1)}$, $u_{(2)}$, $\ldots$, $u_{(r+1)}$ are the u_i's rearranged in ascending order.

5.2.2.5 Recalibration

Brocklehurst et al. (1990) show how the u-plot can be employed to perform a kind of "adaptive modeling." The u-plot shows how well the model is fitting the failure data. The information in the u-plot can be used as a feedback mechanism to modify and improve the model, to "recalibrate" it. The recalibrated model corrects for systematic bias or noisiness that the model is experiencing when being used on a particular program. The recalibration takes place by applying a function $G^*(\cdot)$ to the estimated Cdf. The Brocklehurst paper only describes $G^*(\cdot)$ graphically. The study team has developed a recalibration formula based on the same principles as the graphical technique.

The function $G^*(\cdot)$ is expressed as

$$G_i^*[\hat{F}_i(t)] = \frac{\hat{F}_i(t) + j(u_{(j+1)} + u_{(j)}) - u_{(j)}}{(r+1)(u_{(j+1)} + u_{(j)})}, \quad u_{(j)} \le t \le u_{(j+1)} \qquad (160)$$

where $u_{(j)}$ is the j-th value when the u_i's are put in ascending order of magnitude, and r is the number of u_i's, with $u_{(0)} = 0$ and $u_{(r+1)} = 1$.

To perform the recalibration the user applies the transformation

$$\hat{F}_i^*(\tau) = G_i^*[\hat{F}_i(\tau)] \qquad (161)$$

The accuracy of recalibrated models has been shown [Brocklehurst et al. (1990)] to be generally better than that of the original model.
The study team has developed a computer program to automatically create a u-plot and perform recalibration of the model.

5.2.2.6 Operational Profile

During growth testing, the environment in which the program executes must be controlled. The environment includes the hardware platform, the system generation parameters, and the workload. An important part of a program's execution environment is the operational profile.

An input state is a set of input variable values for a particular run. Each input variable has a declared data type--a range and ordering of permissible values. The set of all possible input states for a program is the input space. Each input state is a point in the input space. An operational profile is a function $p(\cdot)$ that associates a probability $p(i)$ with each point i in an input space I. Since the points in the input space are mutually exclusive and exhaustive, all the probabilities must add up to one:

$$\sum_{i \in I} p(i) = 1 \qquad (162)$$

To illustrate these definitions, consider a program with three input variables. They are each of data type Boolean, meaning that they have two possible values: TRUE and FALSE. The input space has eight points: (FALSE,FALSE,FALSE), (FALSE,FALSE,TRUE), (FALSE,TRUE,FALSE),   (FALSE,TRUE,TRUE),   (TRUE,FALSE,FALSE),

(TRUE,FALSE,TRUE), (TRUE,TRUE,FALSE), (TRUE,TRUE,TRUE).   Letting T stand for TRUE and F for FALSE, an operational profile for the program might look like:

$$p(FFF) = 0.1$$
$$p(FFT) = 0.2$$
$$p(FTF) = 0.1$$
$$p(FTT) = 0.3$$
$$p(TFF) = 0.025$$
$$p(TFT) = 0.02$$
$$p(TTF) = 0.025$$
$$p(TTT) = 0.05$$

(163)

The distribution of input states is thus established by the operational profile.

The concept of operational profile formalizes what is meant by a consistent input environment.

During growth (and demonstration) testing must be kept stationary: The p(i)'s must not change. The input states chosen for test cases must form a random sample from the input state in accordance with the distribution of input states that the operational profile specifies.

The concept of a stationary operational profile is a crucial assumption in building software reliability models such as the constant failure rate model for frozen code (see Appendix B) and the Coincident Failures model for multiversion software (see section on Reliability Allocation).

It is generally not practical to fully express or specify an operational profile, because the number of input states for even a simple program can be enormous. As an example, if a program has three input variables, each of which is a 32-bit integer, the number of distinct input states is

$$2^{32} \cdot 2^{32} \cdot 2^{32} = 2^{96} \approx 7.9 \times 10^{28}$$

(164)

At best, the customer will express or specify software usage in terms of end-user-oriented functions. For example, the customer might state that the usage of the software is 40% user function A, 45% user function B, and 15% user function C. To convert that statement into an operational profile, let u be the input variable corresponding to user function selection. Thus, u can take on the values A, B, or C. The input space can be partitioned into three classes defined as follows:

$$CLASS_A = \{i \in I \mid i_u = A\}$$
$$CLASS_B = \{i \in I \mid i_u = B\} \tag{165}$$
$$CLASS_C = \{i \in I \mid i_u = C\}$$

where i_u is the value of the input variable u in input state i. The probability of each individual input state in class A is

$$p(i) = .40 \times \frac{1}{|CLASS\_A|} \tag{166}$$

For class B it is

$$p(i) = .45 \times \frac{1}{|CLASS\_B|} \tag{167}$$

and for class C it is

$$p(i) = .15 \times \frac{1}{|CLASS\_C|} \tag{168}$$

where the vertical lines mean "number of elements."

Once the operational profile is established, a procedure for selecting a random sample of input states is required, so that test cases can be generated for growth testing and demonstration testing. The following procedure for selecting the input states is recommended.

5.2.2.7 Random Input-State Selection

The strategy employed is to associate each input state i with a subinterval of the real interval [0,1] whose size is equal to the input state's probability of selection p(i). As an example, suppose that there are only three possible input states and the operational profile says that state #1 occurs 28% of the time, state #2 occurs 11% of the time, and state #3 occurs 61% of the time. State #1 should be associated with the real interval [0,0.28]; state #2 should be associated with the real interval

[0.28,0.39]; and state #3 should be associated with the real interval [0.39,1.0].

The next step is, for each test case needed, to generate a random number in the interval [0,1]. In the example, if that random number falls in the interval [0,0.28], input state #1 is selected; if it falls in the interval [0.28,0.39], input state #2 is selected; and, if it falls in the interval [0.39,1], input state #3 is selected.

To generalize and formalize this procedure, suppose that the input space contains k input states. Further suppose that the probabilities associated with the input states are

$$p_1, \ p_2, \ ..., \ p_k \tag{169}$$

Let

$$START_1 = 0 \tag{170}$$

and

$$START_j = \sum_{i=1}^{j-1} p_i \ , \ j=2,3,...,k \tag{171}$$

and let

$$END_j = START_{j+1} \ , j=1,k-1 \tag{172}$$

and

$$END_k = 1 \tag{173}$$

Each input state is now associated with a subinterval [START$_j$,END$_j$] of the interval [0,1]. The length of the subinterval is equal to the input state's probability of selection.

Now a random number uniformly distributed in the interval (0,1) is generated. The random number will fall into exactly one of the intervals [START$_j$,END$_j$].   The input state so selected is input state j.

The cardinal rule for increasing the efficiency of growth and demonstration testing is not to repeat the same test case more than once.   ("Regression testing" after a program change is another matter.)   This rule per se is not that helpful because the large number of input states that most programs have means that the repetition of a randomly selected test case is a rare event.   However, the nonrepetition rule combined with the technique of equivalence partitioning can indeed increase testing efficiency.   Equivalence partitioning was first described by Myers (1979).

Imagine a "test oracle" e(i) that evaluates to 1 if a run starting from input state i will result in software failure (crash, hang, or erroneous output) and evaluates to 0 if the run will result in success.   Consider a set W of input states defined as follows:

$$W = \{i \in I \mid [\forall i\ e(i)=0] \lor [\forall i\ e(i)=1]\}$$ (174)

That is, W is a subset of the input space such that all input states in the subset fail alike: If any input state would cause the program to fail, then so would any other input state in the subset.   If the program starting from any input state in the subset would succeed, then the program would also succeed starting from any other input state in the subset.   Such a subset is called an equivalence class, of which there may be many.

Testing personnel can determine equivalence classes from an understanding of the program structure and logic.   Once an equivalence class is identified, only one representative input state from the class needs to be tested; if a run starting from the representative input state results in success, then it can be concluded that runs starting from all members of the class would result in success.   If a run starting from the representative input state results in failure, then it can be concluded that runs starting from all members of the class would fail.

The input states that are members of an equivalence class are removed from the operational profile and replaced by their one representative input state.   The probability associated with the representative input state is assigned the sum of the probabilities of the members of the equivalence class.

Since the probability of selection of the representative of an equivalence class is a sum, it can be relatively large compared to individual input states, and consequently the representative will likely be selected more than once during testing.   The second and subsequent times the representative is selected, the test does not have to be re-run, only the results from the original run recounted.

5.2.2.8 Software Reliability Growth Management

The demonstrated reliability is an assessment of the current reliability of the software.   It is obtained by recording the cumulative execution times at which failures have occurred so far during system test.   The operational profile from which the random test cases were selected has to have been stationary during the testing and representative of the program's field use. The statistical estimation technique presented previously is employed to obtain estimates of the Basic Execution Time Model's β and ν_0 parameters.   Then a number of derived quantities [Musa (1987)] can be obtained to support reliability growth management. The demonstrated reliability is then given by

$$R(t) = \exp[-\lambda(\tau_e)\tau] \qquad (175)$$

where τ_e is the point in cumulative execution time at which the assessment is made. The projected reliability for $\Delta\tau_e$ execution time units from now is

$$R(\tau) = \exp[-\lambda(\tau_e + \Delta\tau_e)\tau] \qquad (176)$$

The additional execution time required to reach a failure rate objective λ_F can be computed from

$$\Delta\tau_e = \beta\, \ln\frac{\lambda(\tau_e)}{\lambda_F} \qquad (177)$$

The additional number of expected failures to reach the objective is given by

$$\Delta\mu = \beta\,[\lambda(\tau_e) - \lambda_F] \qquad (178)$$

During system test, project management should expect that certain levels of reliability will be attained at certain milestones, to assure that reliability growth is progressing at a sufficient rate to meet the ultimate reliability requirement.

Since the time-dependent failure rate is

$$\lambda(\tau) = \frac{\beta}{\nu_0} \exp[-\beta\tau] \qquad (179)$$

the reliability growth curve can be plotted as a straight line on semi-log paper as

$$\ln\lambda = \ln\frac{\beta}{\nu_0} - \beta\tau \qquad (180)$$

The next section discusses how to relate execution time to calendar time.

5.2.2.9 Calendar Time Modeling

Early software reliability models used calendar time (or did not specify what type of time was being measured). Musa introduced the idea of execution time as the failure-inducing stress on a program. Software can only fail when it is executing. This simple primal idea resulted in increased accuracy in software reliability modeling [Trachtenberg (1985), Musa and Okumoto (1984), Hecht (1981)]. Concentrating on execution time, though, left a void. Project management and even software engineers usually think in terms of calendar time. Project deadlines and milestones are all expressed in terms of calendar time. Project personnel are paid for calendar time. To fill this void, Musa added a "calendar time component" to his Basic Execution Time Model. The calendar time component provides the ratio between calendar time and execution time. The model takes into account the constraints involved in applying personnel and computer resources to the software development project during system test.

The available quantities of failure identification (testing) personnel, failure resolution (debugging) personnel, and computer time are considered to be constant during system test because of the long lead times usually required for training and procurement.

At any point in time during system test, one of the three resources will be limiting and will determine the execution time/calendar time ratio. Typically, system test consists of three consecutive resource-limited segments: (1) a failure resolution personnel limited segment, (2) a failure identification personnel segment, and (3) a computer limited segment [Musa et al. (1987)].

Segment #1 is limited by the number of failure resolution personnel, because they cannot keep up with the large number of failures that occur in a short period of time when $\lambda(\tau)$ is high. In segment #2, the failure identification personnel become the bottleneck as they become fully occupied in testing and analysis of the results.   In segment #3, the interfailure times grow longer and longer and the bottleneck is the availability of computer time.

Various quantities in the model have an index subscript r appended to identify the resource referenced:

   r=F: failure identification personnel (people who find the causative faults behind the software failures)

   r=I: failure identification personnel (people who run test cases and watch for failures)

   r=C: computer time

The usage χ_r of resource r is a function of cumulative execution time τ and the expected number of failures experienced $\mu(\tau)$:

$$\chi_r = \theta_r\tau + \mu_r\mu(\tau) \tag{181}$$

Each resource r has an execution time coefficient θ_r:

   θ_F: average failure identification work expended per unit execution time (=0)

   θ_I: average failure identification work expended per unit execution time

   θ_C: average chargeable computer time expended per hour of test execution time

Each resource k has a failure coefficient μ_r:

   μ_F: average failure resolution work required per failure
   μ_I: average failure identification work required per failure
   μ_C: average chargeable computer time required per failure

Work is typically measured in person-hours and computer time in hours.   Hours would ordinarily be divided into eight hours segments to allow conversion to standard shifts and workdays.

The change in resource usage per unit of execution time is given by differentiating χ_r with respect to execution time:

$$\frac{d\chi_r}{d\tau} = \theta_r + \mu_r \lambda(\tau) \tag{182}$$

The calendar time/execution time ratio in each resource-limited segment is given by the maximum rate among the three resources in that segment:

$$\frac{dt}{d\tau} = \max_r \left(\frac{dt_r}{d\tau} \right) = \max_r \left\{ \frac{1}{P_r \rho_r} [\theta_r + \mu_r \lambda(\tau)] \right\} \tag{183}$$

where P_r is the amount of resource r available:

P_F: number of available failure resolution personnel
P_I: number of available failure identification personnel
P_C: available computer time (number of prescribed work
        periods, e.g., 40-hour weeks)

and ρ_r is the resource utilization factor:

ρ_F: failure resolution personnel utilization factor
$\rho_I = 1$
ρ_C: computer utilization factor

The boundaries of the resource-limited segments, in terms of failure rate values, are given by the following formula.   It provides potential transition points, which must be individually checked for plausibility.

$$\lambda_{rs} = \frac{P_s \rho_s \theta_r - P_r \rho_r \theta_s}{P_r \rho_r \mu_s - P_s \rho_s \mu_r} \quad , \quad r \neq s \tag{184}$$

If τ_1 and τ_2 are two points of cumulative execution time with a resource-limited segment limited by resource r, the increment of calendar time between the two points is given by

$$\Delta t_r = \frac{1}{P_r \rho_r \beta} \left\{ \theta_r \ln \left[\frac{\lambda(\tau_1)}{\lambda(\tau_2)} \right] + \mu_r [\lambda(\tau_1) - \lambda(\tau_2)] \right\} \tag{185}$$

If the interval $[\tau_1, \tau_2]$ spans more than one segment, the increment of calendar time should be calculated separately for each subinterval that lies in a different segment and the results added together.

For growth management, project management can influence the resource quantities P_C, P_F, and P_I to stimulate software growth. Because of long lead times for training and procurement, the resource quantities are usually constant during system test, except perhaps for personnel overtime. Overtime is only effective for a limiting resource.

6. Reliability Demonstration

In fulfillment of SOW Task 5, techniques for formally demonstrating the achievement of specified reliability requirements for software products and combined hardware/ software systems were developed.

6.1 Approach

A reliability demonstration test is an experiment conducted to determine whether an item has achieved a specified level of reliability. One problem with such a test is that the results are subject to chance variation. Occasionally the test results will turn out especially "lucky," allowing a bad item to be accepted, or especially "unlucky," allowing a good item to be rejected. By designing the test using sound statistical principles, the risks of accepting a bad item or rejecting a good item can be quantified and contained.

To design reliability demonstration tests, it is necessary to determine an appropriate time domain reliability model for software products and combined hardware/software systems. In particular, the applicability of the exponential (constant failure rate) model was investigated (SOW para. 4.1.5.2).

Three types of MIL-STD-781-like reliability demonstration tests were developed: fixed-length test, minimum failure-free execution period test, and sequential test. Since software reliability demonstration tests sometimes have to be performed concurrently with growth testing, how to adapt those same tests for periods during which the software is subject to repair activity is discussed.

Statistical random testing procedures for use during software reliability demonstration testing are the same as those described in the section of this report on Reliability Growth Testing (Section 4). The test cases must be selected randomly in accordance with a stationary operational profile that represents anticipated field usage. (SOW para. 4.1.5.3) An operational profile is the probability distribution of the various possible input states. When a combined hardware/software system is tested, the environmental specification is generally derived from the specified mission profile. The operating conditions will normally include thermal stress, electrical stress, vibration, and humidity. MIL-HDBK-781 addresses test sample size and burn-in requirements for hardware.

106

6.2 Results

6.2.1 Test Procedures

The test environment must be stipulated or agreed on. The environment for software includes the hardware platform, the operating system, system generation parameter settings, and the operational profile. The operational profile associates each point in the input space with a probability of occurrence. The system workload must also be specified. The important thing about the environment is that it must be representative of the conditions the software will experience in field use, if the test is to have any validity.

Let the true failure rate of the software be denoted λ. A demonstration test plan has two failure rate parameters:

The "upper test failure rate" λ_0 is typically the failure rate the customer "wants" or requires. If the producer produces a product that just barely meets the failure rate λ_0, then the producer is taking a big risk that chance variation will result in the demonstration test failing. To reduce that risk the producer must produce a product with a lower failure rate, λ_1, called the "lower test failure rate." It should be mentioned that MIL-STD-781 uses mean time between failures (MTBF)--the reciprocal of failure rate--and so the upper and lower points are reversed. MTBF is a problematical concept in software reliability because if there is a nonzero probability, however slight, of a particular program having zero faults, the program's MTBF will be infinite [Littlewood (1975)]. Consequently, in this section, only failure rates are used.

The producer's risk α is the probability of rejecting a software product or hardware/software system whose true failure rate is equal to λ_0. The consumer's risk β is the probability of accepting software whose true failure rate is equal to λ_1. (SOW para. 4.1.5.3).

A statistical test that answers a yes/no question is called a "test of hypothesis." Specifically, a reliability demonstration test tests the simple null hypothesis

$$H_0: \lambda = \lambda_0 \tag{186}$$

(accept the item) against the alternative hypothesis

$$H_1: \lambda = \lambda_1 \tag{187}$$

(reject the item). In terms of these hypotheses,

$$\alpha = \Pr\{H_1 \text{ accepted} | H_0 \text{ true}\} \tag{188}$$

and

$$\beta = \Pr\{H_0 \text{ accepted} | H_1 \text{ true}\} \tag{189}$$

To develop demonstration tests, it is necessary to choose appropriate time domain reliability models for software products and combined hardware/software systems.

During a software reliability demonstration test, the code is frozen, that is, it is not modified to remove faults or for any other reason. The reason is that any modification can introduce new faults. Frozen code, subjected to a stationary operational profile, can reasonably be modeled as having a constant failure rate. (See Appendix B). Multiple discrepancies appearing at the same time need to be counted as a single failure, because the random variable of interest is time to first failure.

For a combined hardware/software system, the model is also a constant failure rate, based on the following reasoning. MIL-STD-781 applies to demonstrating the reliability of simple series systems as well as "complex maintained electronic equipment" [O'Connor (1985)], so the hardware during its "useful life" period is already modeled by a constant failure rate. According to Appendix B, software whose code is frozen, being subjected to a stationary operational profile, can reasonably be modeled as having a constant failure rate. According to the section in this report on Reliability Combination, if the software executes concurrently and in series with the hardware, then the combined hardware/software system can be modeled by a constant failure rate that is the sum of the hardware failure rate and the software failure rate. Therefore, the demonstration test plans developed in this section apply to both software products and most combined hardware/software systems (SOW para. 4.1.5.2).

Under the constant failure rate model, the number of failures during a time interval $[0, \tau]$ obeys Poisson's law, which states that the probability of exactly i failures occurring in a time interval of length τ is

$$P_i = \exp[-\lambda\tau] \frac{(\lambda\tau)^i}{i!} \tag{190}$$

The probability of n or fewer failures occurring during that same period is given by the Poisson cumulative distribution function (Cdf)

$$F(n;\lambda,\tau) = \sum_{i=0}^{n} \frac{(\lambda\tau)^i \exp[-\lambda\tau]}{i!}$$

(191)

6.2.2 Fixed-Length Test

A fixed length software reliability demonstration test plan [Singpurwalla (1985a)] provides a predetermined test duration and an acceptable number of failures the software is allowed to accumulate during that test time. The test is terminated with a decision to accept or reject. The statistical basis of the fixed-length test derives from Epstein and Sobel (1953). Suppose that the acceptance criterion is x or fewer failures in time τ. If the true failure rate is λ_0 then $F(a;\lambda_0,\tau)$ is the fraction of time that x or fewer failures will occur. However, in $[1-F(x;\lambda_0,\tau)]$ fraction of the time, greater than x failures will occur. When greater than x failures occur during the test, the test will reject the software even though the true failure rate is λ_0. To limit the probability of rejecting good software, therefore, x and τ must be chosen such that

$$1-F(x;\lambda_0,\tau) \leq \alpha$$

(192)

Likewise, if the true failure rate is λ_1, then $F(x,\lambda_1,\tau)$ is the fraction of time that the software will be accepted, even though the true failure rate is λ_1. To limit the probability of accepting bad software, x and τ must be chosen such that

$$F(x;\lambda_1,\tau) \leq \beta$$

(193)

Thus, x and τ must simultaneously satisfy both Equations 7 and Equation 8.

A test plan provides x and τ values as a function of failure rates λ_0 and λ_1, and risk levels α and β. Since time units are arbitrary, a test plan can be made more general by replacing λ_0 and λ_1 by their ratio $d=\lambda_1/\lambda_0$, called the discrimination ratio. Then, for example, the same test plan will be valid for the combination $\lambda_0=0.000006$ and $\lambda_1=0.000002$, and the combination $\lambda_0=0.0045$ and $\lambda_1=0.0015$. For this scheme to work, the time unit is chosen so that $\lambda_0=1$. Hence, $\lambda_1=d$. As a typical example, if the original time unit was seconds, then the new time unit will be λ_0^{-1} seconds. The test time τ is multiplied by λ_0^{-1} to convert to seconds.

A test plan provides an accept number x. If x or fewer failures are observed during the test period, the software is accepted. The reject number is r=x+1. If r or more failures are observed, the software is rejected. To design the test, the smallest x and τ values need to be found such that simultaneously

$$\exp[-\tau] \sum_{i=0}^{x} \frac{\tau^i}{i!} \geq 1 - \alpha \qquad (194)$$

(because $\lambda_0=1$) and

$$\exp[-\tau d] \sum_{i=0}^{x} \frac{(\tau d)^i}{i!} \leq \beta \qquad (195)$$

(because $\lambda_1=d$).

For determining the reject number r, one can exploit the relationship between the Poisson and chi-square distributions. The cumulative distribution function of the chi-square distribution is

$$P(\chi^2|\nu) = \left[2^{\nu/2}\Gamma\left(\frac{\nu}{2}\right)\right]^{-1} \int_0^{\chi^2} (t)^{\frac{\nu}{2}-1} \exp\left[-\frac{t}{2}\right] dt , \quad (0 \leq \chi^2 < \infty) \qquad (196)$$

where for an integer argument n, $\Gamma(n+1)=n!$. The parameter ν is the number of degrees of freedom (i.e., the number of free variables entering into the statistic). The values of the chi-square Cdf are tabulated in many statistics textbooks.

On a programmable calculator or computer a series expansion [Abramowitz and Stegun (1970)] can be utilized:

$$P(\chi^2|v) = \left(\frac{1}{2}\chi^2\right)^{v/2} \frac{\exp[-\chi^2/2]}{\Gamma\left(\frac{v+2}{2}\right)}$$

$$\left[1 + \sum_{r=1}^{\infty} \frac{\chi^{2r}}{(v+2)(v+4)\cdots(v+2r)}\right]$$

(197)

The relationship between the Poisson and chi-square distributions is

$$1 - P(\chi^2|v) = \sum_{j=0}^{c-1} \exp[-m]\frac{m^j}{j!} \quad , \quad c = \frac{v}{2}, m = \chi^2/2, v \text{ even}$$

(198)

So to determine r one finds the smallest integer r such that

$$d \geq \frac{\chi^2_{2r,\beta}}{\chi^2_{2r,1-\alpha}}$$

(199)

where $\chi^2_{y,z}$ is that χ_2 value which solves the equation

$$z = P(\chi^2|y)$$

(200)

Then x=r-1 is inserted into the equation

$$\exp[-\tau] \sum_{i=0}^{a} \frac{t^i}{x!} = 1 - \alpha$$

(201)

Equation 16 is then solved for τ. Call this solution τ_a. Then x is inserted into

$$\exp[-\tau d] \sum_{i=0}^{a} \frac{(\tau d)^i}{i!}$$

(202)

which is also solved for τ.   Call this solution τ_b.   Because of the discrete nature of the distribution, τ_a and τ_b can be expected to differ slightly.   Taking τ to be the average $\tau = (\tau_a + \tau_b)/2$ is a reasonable compromise.   The α and β risk levels will change slightly.   Inserting x and τ back into Equation 16 and 17 and solving for α and β will provide the actual risk levels.   The original α and β used to construct the test are called the nominal risk levels.

The probability of the fixed-length test accepting the software is given by

$$P_{0-x}(\lambda) = \exp[-\lambda\tau] \sum_{i=1}^{x} \frac{(\lambda\tau)^i}{i!} \tag{203}$$

This yields a family of operating characteristic (OC) curves. The OC is a plot of the probability of acceptance versus the failure rate: The steeper the slope of the OC curve, the greater the efficiency of the test in discriminating between items of differing reliability.

6.2.3   Minimum Failure-Free Execution Period Test (SOW para. 4.1.5.3)

A special case of the fixed-length test is the one in which the acceptable number of failures x=0.   The probability of zero failures in a test of duration τ is

$$P_{0-0} = \exp[-\lambda\tau] \sum_{i=0}^{0} \frac{(\lambda\tau)^i}{i!} = \exp[-\lambda\tau] \tag{204}$$

Solving

$$\exp[-\lambda_0\tau] \geq 1 - \alpha \tag{205}$$

and

$$\exp[-\lambda_1\tau] \leq \beta \tag{206}$$

gives

$$\lambda_0 \tau = -\ln(1-\alpha); \; \lambda_1 \tau = -\ln\beta \qquad (207)$$

In terms of the decision risks, the discrimination ratio is

$$\frac{\lambda_1}{\lambda_0} = \frac{\lambda_1 \tau}{\lambda_0 \tau} = \frac{\ln\beta}{\ln(1-\alpha)} \equiv d_{max} \qquad (208)$$

This discrimination ratio can be quite large. For instance, in the case $\alpha=0.15$, $\beta=0.15$, the producer is saddled with a discrimination ratio of 11.67. This discrimination ratio is high; it is usual to design to a discrimination ratio on the order of 1.5 to 3. A less stringent type of failure-free test will now be described, in which the required discrimination ratios are lower.

In a minimum failure-free period life test [Angus et al. (1985)], the item is given a time limit of T time units to achieve a failure free interval of t time units. The null hypothesis is H_0: $\lambda=\lambda_0$, and the alternative hypothesis is H_1: $\lambda=\lambda_1$. Note that the null and alternative hypotheses are reversed from those of the fixed-length test. A test plan can be designed for any discrimination ratio $d<d_{max}$. Let the function F_{vt} be the cumulative distribution function of the waiting time to completion of the failure-free period. Renewal theory [Feller (1966)] provides

$$F_{W_t}(w; \lambda, t) = \begin{cases} \exp[-\lambda] \sum_{n=1}^{\infty} \dfrac{(\lambda w)^{n-1}}{(n-1)!} g(n), & w \geq t > 0 \\[2mm] 0, & w < t \end{cases} \qquad (209)$$

where

$$g(n) = \sum_{k=0}^{n} (-1)^k \binom{n}{k} \left(1 - k\frac{t}{w}\right)_+^{n-1} \qquad (210)$$

and

$$u_+^0 = 1, \ u > 0; \ u_+^0 = 0, \ u \leq 0; \ u_+^b = [\max(u,0)]^b \qquad \textbf{(211)}$$

The function g(n) represents the probability that (n-1) points, chosen randomly in the interval (0,w), partition the interval into parts all of which are of length less than or equal to t.

Test plans can be constructed by fixing the ratio t/T and iteratively finding $\lambda_0 t$ and $\lambda_1 t$ so that

$$1 - \alpha = F_{N_t}(T; \lambda_0, t); \qquad \textbf{(212)}$$

and

$$\beta = F_{N_t}(T; \lambda_1, t) \qquad \textbf{(213)}$$

6.2.4 Sequential Test

In a fixed-length test, a failed test can be stopped just as soon as the reject number r is reached. In a failure-free execution period test, a successful test can be stopped once the failure-free interval is achieved.

A sequential test can be stopped early when the test reveals its true character [Wald (1947), Epstein (1954), Singpurwalla (1985b)]. The item is operated and the cumulative number of failures and time on test are continuously monitored.

Let the null hypothesis be

$$H_0 : \lambda = \lambda_0 \qquad \textbf{(214)}$$

and let the alternative hypothesis be

$$H_1 : \lambda = \lambda_1 \qquad \textbf{(215)}$$

Let

$$A \approx \frac{1-\beta}{\alpha} \qquad \textbf{(216)}$$

and

$$B \approx \frac{\beta}{1-\alpha} \tag{217}$$

Let p_0 be the probability of a software failures in time τ if $\lambda = \lambda_0$, and p_1 be the probability of a failures in time τ if $\lambda = \lambda_1$. Then the sequential probability ratio is

$$\frac{p_1}{p_0} = \frac{\exp[-\lambda_1 \tau](\lambda_1 \tau)^x}{x!} \Big/ \frac{\exp[-\lambda_0 \tau](\lambda_0 \tau)^x}{x!} \tag{218}$$

$$= d^x \exp[(\lambda_0 - \lambda_1)\tau] \tag{219}$$

where x is the total number of failures observed by time τ. Testing continues as long as the inequality

$$B < \frac{p_1}{p_0} < A \tag{220}$$

holds. Then, when $p_1/p_0 \leq B$ for the first time, testing stops and H_0 is accepted. When $p_1/p_0 \geq A$ occurs for the first time, testing stops and H_0 is rejected.

Graphically, the "continue test" region is bounded by two straight lines with common slope s and intercepts $-h_1$ and h_0. The x-axis is the cumulative number of failures k, and the y-axis is the time on test τ.

Solving for τ gives

$$-h_1 + ks < \tau < h_0 + ks \tag{221}$$

where

$$s = \frac{\ln d}{\lambda_1 - \lambda_0} \tag{222}$$

$$h_0 = \frac{-\ln B}{\lambda_1 - \lambda_0}$$
(223)

and

$$h_1 = \frac{\ln A}{\lambda_1 - \lambda_0}$$
(224)

The acceptance time line is $\tau = h_0 + ks$. The moment the plot of failures k versus time τ crosses this line, the software can be accepted. The rejection time line is $-h_1 + ks$. The moment the plot of failures k versus time τ crosses that line, the software can be rejected. As long as the staircase plot of failures k versus time τ stays between the two lines, the test continues.

In terms of x, the rule is

$$\frac{\tau(\lambda_0 - \lambda_1) - \ln A}{-\ln d} < x < \frac{\tau(\lambda_0 - \lambda_1) - \ln B}{-\ln d}$$
(225)

Because a sequential test can theoretically go on indefinitely, it is desirable to stop ("truncate") the test at some point to provide a reasonable maximum test time. Truncation will tend to increase the decision risks α and β, but research [Epstein (1954)] has shown that the risks are not increased significantly if the test is truncated at

$$r_0 = 3r$$
(226)

where r_0 denotes truncation number of failures and r is the reject number for the corresponding fixed-length test. Recall that r is the smallest integer such that

$$d \geq \frac{\chi^2_{2r,\beta}}{\chi^2_{2r,1-\alpha}}$$
(227)

The truncation operating time r_0 is then

$$\tau_0 = s \cdot r_0 \tag{228}$$

where, as before, s is the common slope of the decision lines

$$s = \frac{\ln d}{\lambda_1 - \lambda_0} \tag{229}$$

The demonstration test can be terminated and the software accepted if $k < r_0$ and

$$\tau \geq \min(h_0 + ks, \tau_0) \tag{230}$$

The test can be terminated just as soon as

$$\tau \leq -h_1 + ks \tag{231}$$

or $k = r_0$ and

$$\tau < \tau_0 \tag{232}$$

6.2.5 Demonstration Testing during Growth Testing

Consider the counting process $\{N(\tau), \tau \geq 0\}$, where $N(\tau)$ is the number of software failures that occur by cumulative execution time τ. In Musa et al.'s (1987) software reliability growth models (the Basic Execution Time Model and the Logarithmic Poisson Model), software failures are generated according to a nonhomogeneous Poisson process (NHPP). The probability of k failures occurring by time τ is

$$P_k(\tau) = \Pr\{N(\tau) = k\} = \exp[-\mu(\tau)] \frac{[\mu(\tau)]^k}{k!}, \quad k \geq 0 \tag{233}$$

where

$$\mu(\tau) = E\{N(\tau)\} = \int_0^\tau \lambda(x)\,dx \qquad (234)$$

is the "mean value function" and $\lambda(\tau)$ is the time-dependent failure rate. In particular, the Basic Execution Time Model is characterized by the mean value function

$$\mu(\tau) = v_0(1-\exp[-\beta\tau]) \qquad (235)$$

and failure rate

$$\lambda(\tau) = \frac{d\mu(\tau)}{d\tau} = \beta v_0 \exp[-\beta\tau] \qquad (236)$$

where β and v_0 are the parameters of the model.

The techniques for reliability demonstration described in this section are based on the assumption of a constant failure rate, which implies a homogeneous Poisson process (HPP). When software is subject to repair, one expects that the software will exhibit a decreasing failure rate. Barlow and Proschan (1967) showed that, in a constant failure rate fixed-length test, a decreasing failure rate favors the consumer. Fortunately, a transformation of the time scale reduces an NHPP to an HPP, as shown below. Then, the methods for fixed-length, failure-free execution period, and sequential test design can be used without change.

Let the new time variable be denoted u, and define it by

$$u = \mu(\tau) \qquad (237)$$

That is, transform time τ into the mean value function evaluated at time τ.

Consider the stochastic process

$$\{M(u), u \geq 0\} \qquad (238)$$

where

$$M(u) = N(\mu^{-1}(u)), \quad u \geq 0 \tag{239}$$

The mean value function is

$$E\{M(u)\} = E\{N(\mu^{-1}(u))\} = \mu(\mu^{-1}(u)) = u \tag{240}$$

and the failure rate is

$$\lambda(u) = \frac{du}{du} = 1 \tag{241}$$

Since the rate parameter is a constant, M is an HPP. Thus

$$P_k(u) = \Pr\{M(u) = k\} = \exp[-u] \frac{u^k}{k!} \tag{242}$$

To transform a time on the u scale back to the original τ scale, the inverse relationship

$$\tau = \mu^{-1}(u) \tag{243}$$

is employed. For the Basic Execution Time Model,

$$\mu^{-1}(u) = \frac{\ln\left(1 - \dfrac{u}{v_0}\right)}{-\beta}, \quad \beta, v_0 > 0 \tag{244}$$

The exponential/HPP model of frozen code is completely specified by the failure rate parameter λ. The NHPP model of code under repair requires two parameters, β and v_0. (It is also possible to parameterize the model in terms of other quantities such as λ_0, ω_0, but two parameters will always be needed.)

In summary, the values of β and v are obtained through the parameter estimation techniques described in the section of this report on Reliability Growth Testing. Next an appropriate fixed-length, failure-free execution interval, or sequential test is selected. Then each failure time experienced τ_i is transformed into $u_i = \mu(\tau_i)$ in determining the results of the test.

6.2.6 Multiple Copies

Demonstration testing of highly reliable software can be time-consuming (the fixed-length test time for given set of α, β, and d parameters is proportional to λ_0^{-1}). Another time-consuming situation is when λ_0 and λ_1 are close together. One solution is to test multiple copies of the software simultaneously. Each copy must be identical and must be subjected to test cases randomly selected from the same operational profile. The test cases for each copy must be selected independently. The total time on test V(t) is the sum of the individual times on test of each copy. When a copy fails, it is restarted (that is, this is a test with replacement). Wherever time on test τ appears in the formulas for fixed-length, minimum failure-free execution period, and sequential tests, it can be replaced with V(t), where

$$V(t) = \sum_{i=1}^{N} x_i(t) \qquad\qquad (245)$$

is the total time on test up to (wall clock) time t, N is the number of copies, and $x_i(t)$ is the time on test of copy i up to (wall clock) time t.

7. Validation

In fulfillment of SOW Task 6, the models and techniques for software reliability prediction, growth, and demonstration were validated on actual projects.

7.1 Approach

The techniques are based on several models for software not subject to repair, a model for software subject to repair, and a set of models for software reliability prediction. When software is not subject to repair, the study employs a constant failure rate model (discussed in Appendix B). When software is subject to repair, the study employs a nonhomogeneous Poisson process, the Basic Execution Time Model. For software reliability prediction, the study uses models that were developed based on regression analysis of measurable product/process characteristics (metrics).

The techniques based on these models were used on ongoing projects to assess workability and accuracy. The feedback from the projects' personnel was exploited to refine the techniques and the presentation of the techniques in the draft military handbook. Since the models and techniques were validated in one organization, it is recommended that the validation be repeated in a wide variety of organizations.

7.2 Results

The first model, which will be designated Model A, is developed axiomatically in Appendix B and assumes a constant failure rate for frozen code subjected to a stationary operationally profile. This model forms that basis for software and hardware/software relibility demonstration tests.

The second model, which will be designated Model B, is the Basic Execution Time Model for software going through system test.

7.2.1 Model A (Frozen Code)

The study team first tested the validity of the assumption that the underlying time-to-failure distribution is exponential. The assumption of an exponential distribution of failure times is equivalent to an assumption of constant failure rate or the assumption that failures are generated by a Poisson process. The cumulative distribution function (Cdf) of the exponential distribution is given by

$$F(\tau) = 0, \qquad\qquad \tau < 0$$
$$ = 1 - \exp[-\lambda\tau], \quad \tau \geq 0 \qquad\qquad \textbf{(246)}$$

Suppose that the interfailure times are

$$\tau_1', \ \tau_2', \ ..., \ \tau_n' \tag{247}$$

A graphical procedure [Epstein (1960)] for testing the validity of the exponential asumption is to put the interfailure times into ascending order

$$\tau_{(1)} \leq \tau_{(2)} \leq \cdots \leq \tau_{(n)} \tag{248}$$

Form the empirical Cdf

$$F(\tau_{(i)}) = \frac{i}{n+1} \tag{249}$$

and plot the points

$$(\tau_{(i)}, \ln[1/(1-F(\tau_{(i)}))]), \quad i=1,2,...,n \tag{250}$$

If the exponential assumption holds, then the plotted points will form a straight line passing through the origin. The slope of the line will be the failure rate λ. The graphical procedure was found to be a "quick and dirty" method that could be useful as a check after a reliability demonstration test but was too inexact and subjective for final validation of the exponential assumption. A numerical procedure that would allow a formal test of hypothesis was sought.

The most well-known test for goodness of fit is the chi-square test. To use this test the time axis is divided into a number of intervals. Each of the k intervals forms a "class." Denote the class boundaries by

$$t_1 \leq t_2 \leq \cdots t_{k-1} \tag{251}$$

The failure rate parameter is estimated by the reciprocal of the sample mean:

$$\hat{\lambda} = \frac{n}{\sum_{i=1}^{n} \tau_i} \tag{252}$$

One computes the statistic

$$\chi^2 = \sum_{i=1}^{k} \frac{(o_i - e_i)^2}{e_i} \qquad (253)$$

where o_i is the number of observed interfailure times that fall into class i and e_i is the expected (theoretical) number of interfailure times that would fall into class i. The expected number of interfailure times falling into class i is

$$e_i = n[F(t_i) - F(t_{i-1})] \qquad (254)$$

The statistic χ^2 is distributed as chi-square with (k-1) degrees of freedom. The test is very sensitive to the number, size, and position of the chosen intervals. The sensitivity problem would only go away with larger sample sizes (number of observed interfailure times) than were available.

A number of studies [see Moran (1951), Bartholomew (1957)] have shown that an increasingly popular method called Bartlett's test is the most powerful available test for discriminating among increasing, constant, and decreasing failure rates. The test statistic is

$$B_r = \frac{2n\left[\ln\left(\frac{\tau_n}{n}\right) - \frac{1}{n}\left(\sum_{i=1}^{n} \ln\tau_i\right)\right]}{1 + (n+1)/6n} \qquad (255)$$

Under the null hypothesis of exponentially distributed interfailure times, the statistic B_r is chi-square distributed with (n-1) degrees of freedom. A two-tailed test is used. Let the level of significance be denoted α. The critical values for the two-tailed test are

$$\chi^2_{1-\alpha/2, n-1} \text{ and } \chi^2_{\alpha/2, n-1} \qquad (256)$$

If the statistic falls between those two values, the test does not contradict the null hypothesis that the exponential model applies to the failure data. Table 7-1 provides some percentage points of the chi-square distribution [AMCP (1968)].

Table 7-1.   Percentage Points of the Chi-Square
Distribution for $\alpha=.01$ Two-Tailed Test

Degrees of Freedom	$\chi^2_{.995}$	$\chi^2_{.005}$
2	.0100	10.597
3	.0717	12.838
4	.207	14.860
5	.412	16.750
6	.676	18.548
7	.989	20.278
8	1.344	21.955
9	1.735	23.589
10	2.156	25.188
11	2.603	26.757
12	3.074	28.300
13	3.565	29.819
14	4.075	31.319
15	4.601	32.801
16	5.142	34.267
17	5.679	35.718

Table 7-1 (con't).   Percentage Points of the Chi-Square
Distribution for α=.01 Two-Tailed Test

Degrees of Freedom	$\chi^2_{.995}$	$\chi^2_{.005}$
18	6.265	37.156
19	6.844	38.582
20	7.434	39.997
21	8.034	41.401
22	8.643	42.796
23	9.260	44.181
24	9.886	45.558
25	10.520	46.928
26	11.160	48.290
27	11.808	49.645
28	12.461	50.993
29	13.121	52.336
30	13.787	53.672
35	17.156	60.304
40	20.674	66.792

It is important that the data be from one series of runs and not
"pooled," because this could cause misleading results [Kapur and
Lamberson (1977), Cox and Smith (1954)].

Failure data set A-1 consists of the following collection of 14
interfailure times (in CPU minutes):   136, 304, 231, 13, 136,
145, 13, 306, 231, 47, 462, 326, 33, and 142.   The computed value
of Bartlett's statistic is 17.526.   Since at 13 degrees of
freedom, lies between $\chi^2_{.095}$=3.565 and $\chi^2_{.005}$=29.819, the null
hypothesis that the interfailure times are exponentially
distributed is accepted.

Failure Data Set A-2 consists of the following collection of 17
interfailure times (in CPU minutes): 9, 110, 9, 32, 3, 19, 18,
12, 65, 58, 9, 16, 20, 42, 2, 15, and 86.   The computed value of
Bartlett's statistic is 14.519.   Since at 15 degrees of freedom,
14.159 lies between $\chi^2_{.995}$=5.142 and $\chi^2_{.005}$=34.267, the null
hypothesis that the interfailure times are exponentially
distributed is accepted.

Failure Data Set A-3 consists of the following collection of 17 interfailure times (in CPU minutes): 22, 10, 9, 130, 69, 26, 15, 34, 55, 31, 139, 181, 41, 259, 43, 201, and 261. The computed value of Bartlett's statistic is 15.532. Since at 17 degrees of freedom, 15.532 lies between $\chi^{2.995}=5.697$ and $\chi^{20.005}=35.718$, the null hypothesis that the interfailure times are exponentially distributed is accepted.

Failure Data Set A-4 consists of the following collection of 9 interfailure times (in CPU minutes): 1, 63, 107, 23, 71, 62, 212, 39, and 246. The computed value of Bartlett's statistic is 9.763. Since at 8 degrees of freedom, 9.763 lies between $\chi^2_{.995}=1.344$ and $\chi^2_{.005}=34.267$, the null hypothesis that interfailure times are exponentially distributed is accepted.

7.2.2   Model B (System Test)

The Basic Execution Time Model [Musa et al. (1987)] is based on the nonhomogeneous Poisson process (NHPP). An NHPP is completely characterized by its intensity function (failure rate) $\lambda(\tau)$ or its mean value function $\mu(\tau)$. The intensity function of the Basic Execution Time Model is not a new innovation; Parzen (1962) described the intensity function form

$$\lambda(\tau) = a \exp[-b\tau] \tag{257}$$

where a and b are empirically determined positive constants, as "frequently chosen" for events that have a decreasing intensity of occurrence. In the case of the Basic Execution Time Model, the constant a is interpreted the initial failure rate λ_0, and b is interpreted as β, the decrement of failure rate per mean failure experienced.

As discussed in the chapter on Demonstration Testing, an NHPP can be turned into a homogeneous Poisson process via a transformation of the time scale. Each observed failure time epoch τ_i is transformed to

$$U_i = \mu(\tau_i) \tag{258}$$

Now that a homogeneous Poisson process is obtained, Bartlett's test can be performed as above.

To determine the mean value function $\mu(\tau)$, it is necessary to obtain estimates for the Basic Execution Time Model parameters β and ν_0. Then is the transformed failure time epoch is

$$U_i = \mu(\tau_i) = \nu_0(1-\exp[-\beta\tau_i]), \quad i=1,2,\dots,k \tag{259}$$

The interfailure times are calculated as

$$U_i' = U_i - U_{i-1}, \quad i=2,3,\ldots,k \tag{260}$$

with

$$U_1' = U_1 \tag{261}$$

For failure data set B-1 (Table 7-2), $B_r=19.056111$, which lies between the critical values $\chi^2_{.995}=5.142$ and $\chi^2_{.005}=34.267$. So for B-1, the null hypothesis is accepted. For failure data set B-2 (Table 7-3), $B_r=3.9958$, which lies between the critical values $\chi^2_{.995}=1.344$ and $\chi^2_{.005}=21.955$. So for B-2, the null hypothesis is accepted. For failure data set B-3 (Table 7-4), $B_r=14.828652$, which lies between the critical values $\chi^2_{.995}=3.074$ and $\chi^2_{.005}=28.300$. So for B-3, the null hypothesis is accepted. For failure data set B-4 (Table 7-5), $B_r=16.073745$, which lies between the critical values $\chi^2_{.995}=4.601$ and $\chi^2_{.005}=32.801$. So for B-4, the null hypothesis is accepted.

Table 7-2.   Data Set B-1

B-1 Failure #	Time (CPU min)	Time (μ)	Interfailure
1	11	0.359	
2	24	0.773	0.414
3	31	0.992	0.219
4	48	1.513	0.521
5	50	1.573	0.060
6	89	2.705	1.132
7	98	2.954	0.249
8	128	3.758	0.804
9	136	3.965	0.207
10	156	4.469	0.504
11	178	5.003	0.534
12	249	6.586	1.583
13	574	11.702	5.116
14	587	11.850	0.148
15	1023	15.230	3.380
16	1391	16.587	1.350
17	2240	17.701	1.114
18	2449	17.796	0.095

Table 7-3.   Data Set B-2

B-2 Failure #	Time (CPU min)	Time (μ)	Interfailure
1	35	2.878	
2	37	3.018	0.140
3	55	4.171	1.153
4	58	4.346	0.175
5	71	5.005	0.659
6	85	5.735	0.730
7	93	6.087	0.352
8	127	7.341	1.254
9	135	7.586	0.245
10	170	8.480	0.894

Table 7-4.   Data Set B-3

B-3 Failure #	Time (CPU min)	Time (μ)	Interfailure
1	4	0.355	
2	19	1.608	1.253
3	25	2.077	0.469
4	55	4.167	2.090
5	57	4.292	0.125
6	63	4.659	0.367
7	93	6.296	1.637
8	130	7.926	1.630
9	135	8.118	0.192
10	138	8.230	0.112
11	139	8.268	0.038
12	166	9.180	0.912
13	441	13.176	3.996
14	576	13.654	0.478

Table 7-5.   Data Set B-4

B-4 Failure #	Time (CPU min)	Time (μ)	Interfailure
1	11	0.550	
2	18	0.892	0.342
3	50	2.381	1.489
4	71	3.295	0.914
5	80	3.672	0.377
6	107	4.752	1.080
7	144	6.117	1.365
8	153	6.430	0.313
9	205	8.107	1.677
10	342	11.597	3.490
11	350	11.766	0.169
12	351	11.786	0.020
13	358	11.931	0.145
14	364	12.052	0.121
15	494	14.284	2.232
16	558	15.140	0.856
17	620	15.847	0.707

Next, growth techniques were applied to ongoing development projects. Demonstration testing techniques served to validate the results of the growth testing. The team chose a "short run high risk test plan" because the test duration is short and so could be repeated many times. The Growth Data Sets are shown in Table 7-6. The failure rate $\lambda(\tau_{30})$ is assigned to the lower test failure rate λ_0. The decision risks are 30%. The demonstration test test has a discrimination ration of 3, so λ_1 is set to $\lambda_0 \times$ 3. The test duration is $1.1 \times \Pi_1^{-1}$. The test rejects if 1 or more failures occur. The test accepts only if 0 failures occur.

Table 7-6.   Growth Data Sets

Failure Number	Failure Times			
	C-1	C-2	C-3	C-4
1	7	11	1	7
2	18	18	4	18
3	21	109	7	21
4	22	128	10	22
5	52	133	16	52
6	66	172	16	66
7	96	192	18	96
8	107	209	28	107
9	129	290	29	129
10	135	325	31	135
11	158	660	65	158
12	166	761	73	166
13	173	985	89	173
14	203	1060	97	203
15	303	1444	165	303
16	321	1504	169	321
17	407	1515	211	407
18	416	1615	253	416
19	438	1632	308	438
20	446	1730	312	446
21	456	1746	415	456
22	462	1813	433	462
23	480	1845	479	480
24	525	1892	488	525
25	562	1992	492	562
26	578	2293	492	578
27	601	2614	587	601
28	635	3430	604	635
29	701	3452	648	701
30	993	3520	727	993

For Data Set C-4, the growth model provided a failure rate estimation, at the 30th failure, of 0.0011365. The test duration is computed to be 28.24. The demonstration test was repeated 13 times. The software passed 9 tests and failed 4 tests. If the true failure rate is that given by the growth model and set to λ_0, then the demonstration test should falsely reject the software 30% of the time. Since this in fact happened

$$\frac{3}{13} = 0.3076923 \qquad\qquad (262)$$

fraction of the time, the agreement with this data set is quite close. On the other data sets, the raw growth model provided an overly optimistic failure rate, with the result that the software could not pass the demonstration test. When the model was recalibrated (as described in Section 5), the optimism was corrected. The recalibration technique, however, does not alter the failure rate, only the probabilities of failure. A future topic of research would be to set λ_0 based on the results of a recalibrated model.

7.2.3   Validation of Software Failure Rate Regression Models

In response to SOW paragraph 4.1.6.4, the software reliability prediction techniques were applied to actual projects. The results were tne compared to the actual reliability measured during growth testing.

7.2.3.1 Approach

In Appendix E, several regresssion models that describe the relationship between software failure rate (Y) and software characteristics $(x_1, \ldots, x_{25})$ are described. In this section, only the linear regression models that are developed for each phase (including the model that was chosen for the previous phase) of the software development are compared to one another, since it was discovered that the nonlinear regression models possess the same statistical characteristics as those of the linear models. Finally, only one regression model is chosen to predict the software failure rate after each phase of the software development.

As a selection criteria for the prediction model for each phase, the following ground rules were applied:

1. The model with the best correlation to the observed software failure rate was chosen whenever there were any significant differences in correlation between the two models.

2. When two models produced essentially identical correlation between the predicted software failure rate and the failure rate observed on the projects, the model which accounted for the largest number of metrics (most recent information) was selected.

The need to select the model which provided a software failure rate with the best statistical correlation to the observed failure rate is obvious. The study team's preference for a prediction model which used the largest number of metrics is based on two areas of concern with respect to the data collected during the study period. The data collected to support development and validation of the prediction models was all collected after all system integration testing on the program was complete. In most cases, the software was in use at the customers facility. As a result, the metric data collected on the projects was essentially complete. Thus, the data available to the study team was much more accurate and complete than the data which would normally be available at the end of a given program phase (eg requirements analysis). This may have resulted in much better accuracy for the early program phase models than would normally be expected. Also, the metric data collected during the project was limited to one company (Hughes Aircraft) and thus potentially valuable variations in values of the metric data which would occur between companies was ommitted, possibly yielding better stability and accuracy for the early prediction models than would ordinarily result.

Two more observations, besides the nine observations that were used to derive the regression models in Appendix E, were available to validate these models. These two observations are identified as obs.10 and obs.11.

The following statistics will be used for comparison:

- Relative error of the predicted failure rate of each observation (obs.10 or obs.11) in the regression model
- R^2
- Residuals plots
- Prob > F
- Prob > |T|
- Standard errors of the parameter estimates
- The length of the 95% confidence limits for a mean predicted values for each observation (obs.10 or obs.11), with the lower limit being 0, if its calculated value is negative.

The linear regression models which are derived in Appendix E are of the form

$$Y = \beta_0 + \beta^T x + \varepsilon \qquad\qquad (263)$$

where

Y: software failure rate
β_0: the y-intercept
β^T: an 1 x m vector of real numbers
x: an 1 x m vector of independent variables
ε: error variable of the regression model
m ≤ 24

these regression models are formulated based on the following assumptions:

i) $E(\varepsilon) = 0$ (i.e., the expected value of ε is 0)
ii) The variance of ε is the same for all value of x
iii) The values of ε are independent
iv) ε is a normally distributed random variable.

The validity of these assumptions in each regression model is determined based on its residuals plot.

7.2.3.2 Results

The regression models which were developed for each phase of the software development (Appendix E), were compared to one another. Then, the chosen model was compared to the model that had been selected for the previous phase. One regression model was selected for each software development phase to describe the relationship between software failure rate and software characteristics.

(1) Requirements Analysis Phase

Three regression models were formulated for the requirements analysis phase by using the least squares method, stepwise regression and principal components analysis.

Only five software characteristics can be identified after the Requirements Analysis phase. Therefore, only five independent variables are involved in these regression models.

A complete output of these models is provided at the end of Appendix E. A summary of these regression models (least squares model, stepwise model, and principal components model) is given below.

- **Least squares model (M1):**

$Y = 5.13 + 15.72x_1 - 0.17x_2 + 0.52x_3 + 0.39x_4 - 0.23x_5$

Y is restricted to be non-negative.

- **Stepwise model (M2):**

$Y = 11.46 + 12.58x_1 - 0.08x_2$ (Y is restricted to be non-negative)

- **Principal components regression model (M3):**

$Y = 18.04 + 0.05 P_1$ (Y is restricted to be non-negative)

$P_1 = 0.009x_1 + 0.99x_2 + 0.10x_3 - 0.0001x_4 + 0.0005x_5$

Table 7-7 provides a summary of the values of statistical characteristics of models M1, M2 and M3.

Although the value of R^2, in model M1, is high (> 0.80, i.e., more than 80% of the total variation in the failure rates sampled is explained by the regression model M1), the value of Prob > F = 0.18, which is bigger than 0.15 (the predetermined significance level), suggested that the null hypothesis in the hypothesis test (I), described below, should be accepted. Thus, M1 is not an adequate model to describe the relationship between Y and the independent variables $x_1, ..., x_5$.

Hypothesis test (I):

H_0: all coefficients of the independent variables in the regression model are 0.
H_1: there exists at least one coefficient, that is not equal to 0, of an independent variable.

Other reasons to reject M1 are that the values of the relative error of the predicted Y in obs.10 are too high, and the length of the 95% confidence limits of the predicted value for obs.10 is extremely large (≈ 592).

Table 7-7.   Summary of Statistical Values of Models M1, M2 and M3

			Model		
			M1	M2	M3
R^2			.8419	.8137	.4064
Prob > F			.1839	.0065	.0648
Standard Error	y-intercept		13.38	4.35	6.54
	x_1		8.32	3.48	0.02
	x_2		0.14	0.04	n/a
	x_3		0.85	n/a	n/a
	x_4		2.54	n/a	n/a
	x_5		2.44	n/a	n/a
Prob > |T|	y-intercept		0.72	0.04	0.03
	x_1		0.16	0.01	0.06
	x_2		0.29	0.08	n/a
	x_3		0.58	n/a	n/a
	x_4		0.89	n/a	n/a
	x_5		0.93	n/a	n/a
SW Failure Rate	Predicted	Obs. 10	234.4	182.9	18.5
		Obs. 11	21.97	24.98	21.03
	Actual	Obs. 10	36	36	36
		Obs. 11	15	15	15
	Abs. Error	Obs. 10	198.4	146.9	17.5
		Obs. 11	6.97	9.98	6.03
	Rel. Error	Obs. 10	5.51	4.08	0.486
		Obs. 11	0.46	0.66	0.402
	95% Conf. Limits	Obs. 10	0-592.1	68-297	0-62.9
		Obs. 11	0-72.7	0-52.7	0-65.2

Model M2 is better than model M1, since it yields smaller values of relative errors and smaller lengths of the 95% confidence limits for the predicted values of obs.10 and obs.11 compared to those of M1.   But, because $x_1, \ldots, x_5$ are highly correlated, stepwise regression analysis is not reliable for producing a valid regression model. In fact, even though, M2 is better than M1, the predicted failure rates of obs.10 are still too high compared to the actual value, and the 95% confidence interval of the predicted value for obs.10 does not contain the actual failure rate.

Compared to models M1 and M2, model M3 is preferable, even though the value of R^2 of M3 is much smaller than that of M1 and M2 (in model M3, only 41% of the total variation of the failure rate samples is explained by the regression model). The p-value of hypothesis test (I) and the p-value of hypothesis test (II) (which is defined on page E-21) of each parameter estimate are smaller than 0.15 (the predetermined significance level). This means P_1 (independent variable) is relevant in predicting the software failure rate (the dependent variable) in M3.

Other reasons for choosing M3, instead of M1 and M2, are that the relative errors of the predicted failure rate in obs.10 and obs.11 are reduced substantially from those of M1 and M2, and that these relative errors are similar to each other (i.e., M3 yields consistent errors in predicting failure rates for different software). Furthermore, based on the residuals plot of M3 (P_1 versus residuals), on page E-36, it is observed that all assumptions listed above hold (i.e., the residuals are of constant variance, and independent). Therefore, M3 is a good model to use for predicting software failure rate based on the software characteristics that can be obtained after the requirements analysis phase.

(2) <u>Preliminary Design Phase</u>

Similar to the requirements analysis phase, there are three regression models that are developed for use to predict the software failure rate after the preliminary design phase. These models were formulated by using stepwise regression and principal components analysis. Specifically, two of the models are developed by using principal components analysis. All of these models can be summarized as below.

- <u>Stepwise model (M4):</u>

Y = 11.92 + 14.12x_1 - 0.14x_9 (Y is restricted to be non-negative)

- **Principal components regression model M5:**

Y = 17.90 + 0.04 P_1 + 0.01 P_2 (Y is restricted to be non-negative)

P_1 = 0.007x_1 + 0.796x_2 + 0.08x_3 - 0.0003x_4 + 0.0003x_5 + 0.00009x_6 + 0.0043x_7 + 0.013x_8 + 0.6x_9 + 0.003x_{10}

P_2 = 0.03x_1 + 0.45x_2 + 0.56x_3 + 0.11x_4 + 0.08x_5 - 0.005x_6 + 0.07x_7 + 0.01x_8 - 0.67x_9 + 0.08x_{10}

- **Principal Components regression model M6:**

Y = 17.90 + 0.04 P_1 (Y is restricted to be non-negative)

P_1 : same as above

Table 7-8 provides the summary of the statistical values associated with the above models.

Model M6 is derived in order to eliminate P_2 in M5, since the p-value of the hypothesis test (II) for variable P_2 is too high compared to 0.15 (the predetermined significance level). Therefore, only models M4 and M6 and the previously chosen model (M3) will be compared to one another.

Model M4 is inferior M6 in describing the relationship between software failure rate (the dependent variable) and software characteristics (the independent variables) which can be identified after the preliminary design phase. The reason for this is that, even though the value of R^2 is high and the p-values of hypothesis tests (I) and (II) are low for M4, the absolute error (hence, the relative error) of the predicted software failure rate of obs.10 is quite large. Also, the 95% confidence limits interval of the predicted failure rate in obs.10 does not contain the actual value, and the length of the entire interval is too large. Again, it is not surprising that the stepwise regression model is not good in predicting software failure rate in this case, since there is a high correlation between the independent variables $x_1, \ldots, x_{10}$.

Table 7-8. Summary of Statistical Values of Models M4, M5 and M6

			Model		
			M4	M5	M6
R^2			0.6584	0.4016	0.40
Prob > F			0.0024	0.21	0.07
Standard Error	y-intercept		3.64	7.13	6.60
	x_1		3.07	0.02	0.02
	x_2		0.05	0.42	0.03
Prob > $\|T\|$	y-intercept		0.02	0.05	0.07
	x_1		0.003	0.09	18.66
	x_2		0.03	0.98	21.58
SW Failure Rate	Predicted	Obs. 10	202.2	18.75	18.66
		Obs. 11	22.68	21.39	21.58
	Actual	Obs. 10	36	36	36
		Obs. 11	15	15	15
	Abs. Error	Obs. 10	166.2	17.25	17.34
		Obs. 11	7.68	6.39	6.58
	Rel. Error	Obs. 10	4.62	0.48	0.48
		Obs. 11	0.51	0.43	0.44
	95% Conf. Limits	Obs. 10	101-303	0-69.58	0-63.3
		Obs. 11	0-46.14	0-74.52	0-65.9

Models M3 and M6 were compared to each other.   Notice that although model M6 has similar residuals plot as that of M3, model M6 has better values for all statistics compared to M3. Therefore, M6 was chosen to be the regression model that describes the relationship between software failure rate and software characteristics that are available after the preliminary design phase.

(3) Detailed Design Phase

A summary of the regression models that were developed for the detailed design phase is provided below:

- Stepwise model (M7):

$$Y = 28.97 + 15.63x_1 + 0.25x_6 - 2.39x_8 - 0.08x_9 - 1.2x_{11}$$
(Y is restricted to be non-negative)

- Principal components regression model (M8):

$$Y = 36.62 + 0.13 P_1 - 2.47 P_2 - 0.64 P_3$$ (Y is restricted to be non-negative)

$P_1 = 0.007x_1 + 0.80x_2 + 0.08x_3 - 0.0003x_4 + 0.0003x_5 + 0.0001x_6 + 0.004x_7 + 0.01x_8 + 0.6x_9 + 0.003x_{10} + 0.11x_{11} + 0.002x_{12} + 0.004x_{13} - 0.003x_{14}$

$P_2 = 0.01x_1 + 0.40x_2 + 0.49x_3 + 0.13x_4 + 0.08x_5 + 0.02x_6 + 0.08x_7 + 0.01x_8 - 0.6x_9 + 0.09x_{10} - 0.26x_{11} + 0.11x_{12} + 0.09x_{13} - 0.35x_{14}$

$P_3 = -0.25x_1 + 0.02x_2 - 0.26x_3 + 0.20x_4 - 0.07x_5 + 0.63x_6 + 0.10x_7 - 0.12x_8 + 0.01x_9 + 0.11x_{10} + 0.35x_{11} + 0.11x_{12} - 0.10x_{13} - 0.49x_{14}$

Table 7-9 provides a summary of the statistical values associated with these models (M7 and M8).

Similar to reasons given above for rejection of stepwise regression model M4, stepwise model M7 should also be discarded. Even though the values of all statistics of this model are reasonably good, when it is used to predict the software failure rates of obs.10, the absolute error (hence, the relative error) of the predicted value is too high.   Also, based on the relative

Table 7-9.   Summary of Statistical Values of Models M7 and M8

			Model	
			M7	M8
R^2			0.9972	0.7988
Prob > F			0.0005	0.0342
Standard Error	y-intercept		3.06	7.49
	x_1		0.83	0.03
	x_2		0.11	0.79
	x_3		0.53	0.33
	x_4		0.02	n/a
	x_5		0.11	n/a
Prob > |T|	y-intercept		0.003	0.0045
	x_1		0.0003	0.0089
	x_2		0.11	0.256
	x_3		0.02	0.1073
	x_4		0.02	n/a
	x_5		0.002	n/a
SW Failure Rate	Predicted	Obs. 10	212.8	21.64
		Obs. 11	15.19	26.90
	Actual	Obs. 10	36	36
		Obs. 11	15	15
	Abs. Error	Obs. 10	176.8	14.36
		Obs. 11	0.19	11.90
	Rel. Error	Obs. 10	4.91	0.40
		Obs. 11	0.01	0.79
	95% Conf. Limits	Obs. 10	178-247	0-55.4
		Obs. 11	5.95-24.4	0-62.1

errors of the predicted values of obs.10 and obs.11, it can be
stated that M4 is not consistent in predicting the software
failure rate.   In one case (obs.11), it yields very good
prediction and 95% confidence limits, but in the other case
(obs.10), M4 predicts the value of the software failure rate
poorly (the predicted value is 491% of the actual value!).

Next, model M8 is compared to model M6, which was chosen as the
regression model after the preliminary design phase.

M8 seems to yield good predicted value for the software failure
rate in the case of obs.10, and the value of R^2 of M8 is high.
Also, the value of Prob > F is much smaller than that of M6. But,
M8 is inconsistent in predicting the dependent variable (Y).   For
instance, the relative error of obs.10 is only 0.4, but the
relative error of obs.11 is 0.79.   Also, even though the actual
failure rate in obs.10 is twice as much as that of obs.11, the
upper bound of the 95% confidence limits of obs.10 is smaller
than the upper bound for obs.11.   Another disturbing factor of
model M8 is that the p-value of the hypothesis test (II) of P_2 is
much higher than 0.15 (the predetermined significance level).
This suggested that P_2 is not relevant in predicting software
failure rate using M8.

Therefore, once again, M6 is chosen to be the regression model
that can be used to predict the software failure rate based on
the software characteristics available after the detailed design
phase.

(4)   Code and Unit Test Phase

It can be safely stated that stepwise regression models should
not be considered in comparsion with principal components models,
since there is substantial evidence that stepwise analysis does
not work well with correlated independent variables, whereas
principal components analysis does.   Thus, in this section, only
regression models that are developed using principal components
analysis are examined.

Two principal-components regression models were formed.   These
models can be summarized below.

- Regression model (M9):

$Y = 38.03 - 2.59 \, P_1$ (Y is restricted to be non-negative)

$P_1 = -0.00001x_1 - 0.0009x_2 - 0.0001x_3 - 0.00002x_4 - 0.00002x_5 - 0.00003x_6 - 0.000017x_7 - 0.00002x_8 - 0.0006x_9 - 0.0002x_{10} + 0.00001x_{11} - 0.00002x_{12} - 0.00001x_{17} + 0.005x_{18} - 0.0001x_{19} - 0.0001x_{20} - 0.00x_{21} + 0.000004x_{22} - 0.00001x_{23} - 0.00002x_{24} - 0.0001x_{25}$

- Regression Model (M10):

$Y = 17.88 + 0.04 \, P_A$ (Y is restricted to be non-negative)

$P_A = 0.007x_1 + 0.80x_2 + 0.08x_3 + 0.01x_8 + 0.6x_9 + 0.008x_{23} + 0.03x_{25}$

Table 7-10 provides the summary of the statistical values associated with these models (M9 and M10).

It is obvious that the regression model M9 should be rejected. Since both p-values of hypothesis tests (I) and (II) (of the independent variable P_1) are much higher than 0.15 (the predetermined significance level), P_1 is not relevant in predicting software failure rate using model M9. But, if P_1 were eliminated from the model, a new model cannot be formed. Another reason to reject model M9 is that its residuals plot indicates that assumption (ii) is violated. A surprising element was noticed in model M9: the absolute errors (hence, the relative errors) of the predicted failure rates in both obs.10 and obs.11 are much smaller than those of any of the previous models.

When model M10 was compared to model M6 (which was chosen after the detailed design phase), it was noticed that all values of the statistics obtained for M6 and M10 are very similar to each other, including the residuals plots. Therefore, theoretically, either M6 or M10 can be used to predict the software failure rate after the code and unit test phase.

Model M10 is recommended for used in predicting software failure rates after code and unit test because M10 includes a larger set of the independent variables than M6 and thus may be less succeptable to any inadvertant result variations caused by the data collection limitations of the study project.

Table 7-10.   Summary of Statistical Values of Models M9 and M10

			Model	
			M9	M10
R_2			0.0748	0.4012
Prob > F			0.4764	0.0670
Standard Error	y-intercept		19.72	6.61
	x_1		3.43	0.02
Prob > |T|	y-intercept		0.0952	0.0304
	x_1		0.4764	0.0670
SW Failure Rate	Predicted	Obs. 10	22.72	18.68
		Obs. 11	11.20	21.59
	Actual	Obs. 10	36	36
		Obs. 11	15	15
	Abs. Error	Obs. 10	13.28	17.32
		Obs. 11	3.80	6.59
	Rel. Error	Obs. 10	0.37	0.48
		Obs. 11	0.25	0.44
	95% Conf. Limits	Obs. 10	0-77.9	0-63.3
		Obs. 11	0-79.8	0-65.9

8. Conclusions and Recommendations

8.1. Conclusions

This study has developed techniques for reliability prediction, allocation, growth testing, and demonstration testing of combined hardware/software systems. The software reliability techniques are compatible with existing hardware reliability standards and procedures and are aligned with DOD-STD-2167A.

The main findings of the research are:

A. Software whose code is frozen, and that is being subjected to a stationary operational profile, can be reasonably modeled as having a constant failure rate (see Appendix B). Before this result was obtained, researchers in software reliability justified the constant failure rate model primarily on intuitive considerations. The work done here puts the model on a theoretical foundation. Because hardware components during their useful life period and maintained electronic systems are conventionally modeled by a constant failure rate, this means that certain hardware reliability techniques have analogies in software. Furthermore, hardware and software failures can be combined with each other. For example, if the hardware has a certain failure rate and operates concurrently and in series with the software, the hardware and software failure rates can be added to obtain the overall failure rate.

B. Software reliability can be predicted based on measurable characteristics of the software development process and work products. Prediction models based on metrics initially available early on in the software life cycle appear to have about the same prediction power as those models that add metrics available later, when the early metrics are revised to reflect updated work products.

C. A program's failure rate is related to the program's fault hazard rate profile. Previously, the hazard rate profile could only be determined by "fault seeding" or by retrospective failure analysis. Neither method is practical. The study developed a way of determining a program's hazard rate profile, under a particular operational profile, by adding randomly placed counters to the code. These counters provide information about the frequency with which potential faults are encountered.

D. Markov modeling can be employed for the modeling and allocation of hardware/software systems that involve hardware/software repair and hardware redundancy. Modeling and allocation of software under different reliability topologies and timing configurations can generally be handled by closed-form expressions.

E.   Software reliability growth, from the start of system test, can be modeled by the Basic Execution Time Model. If the number of observations is small (<30) or when the faults in a program have widely different hazard rates, then the model may falter. In both cases, the reliability estimations and projections can be improved through numerical recalibration.   A drawback to recalibration is that it currently works by altering the cumulative distribution function (time-dependent failure probabilities), rather than by altering the failure rate.   An estimate of the failure rate is useful in designing demonstration test plans.

During growth testing, the operational profile must be kept stationary and emulate field use.   Testers must record failure times (or, equivalently, interfailure times) in terms of execution time.   This "statistical" approach to testing is an efficient way of uncovering those faults that contribute the most to the overall program failure rate.   Current testing practice is either to stress the software by choosing inputs--such as boundary values--that are likely to trigger a failure, or to attempt to "cover" the input space or code in some way.

F.   Three types of software reliability demonstration test have been developed: fixed-length tests, failure-free execution interval tests, and sequential tests.   In addition, a method was presented for performing a demonstration test concurrently with growth testing.

G.   Both growth testing and demonstration testing can be accelerated by simultaneous execution of multiple copies of the program.   When a failure occurs,, the time recorded is the total execution time accumulated on all copies.   When the code is modified, it must be modified on all versions.   The test cases for each copy must be selected independently according to the same operational profile.

H.   The random selection of test inputs from a given operational profile can be performed or automated based on the fact that the operational profile induces a partition of the real interval (0,1).   Each input state, or class of input states, is associated with a subinterval of (0,1) whose length is its probability of occurrence.   Testing efficiency can be improved through the use of equivalence partitioning.

8.2.   Recommendations

Future research is recommended to address the following areas:

A.   The prediction models have been validated in one corporation only.   The product/process metrics and failure data should be collected from projects in many organizations so that the model can be validated more universally. Additional metrics should be hypothesized and collected, to find more that are useful for predicting software reliability.

B.   The values of the many product/process metrics will change as early work products are updated. The time or phase at which the value of a metric is sampled should be made a part of the regression analysis.

C.   The current recalibration technique alters the failure probabilities. A method should be developed for recalibrating of the failure rate, altering the failure rate from one constant value to another. One approach is to fit, in a least-squares sense, the recalibrated cumulative distribution function to, that of the exponential distribution, the constant rate parameter treated an as unknown.

D.   Theory and techniques need to be developed for quantifying the benefits and costs of multiversion programming. As a prerequisite, techniques should be developed for injecting diversity into software in such a way as to deterministically increase the reliability. Currently, there is no way of knowing if the expense of creating multiple versions is cost effective compared to additional testing and review.

E.   An automated test generator program should be developed that uses information on the operational profile, and the data types and ranges of the input variables.

F.   The effect of software engineering technologies on software reliability should be quantified through a series of controlled experiments.

G.   Automated tools should be developed for accurately recording cumulative execution time. Currently, testers use calendar time.

H.   Research should be performed on designing software to facilitate reliability prediction. As an example, consider an abridged operational profile that specifies the relative frequency of the user-oriented functions, A, B, and C. Suppose that the software is designed so that A, B, and C are implemented in separate CSCs. Let operational profile #1 specify that the relative frequency of A is 20%; for B, 30%; and for C, 50%. The failure rate measured under this operational profile A λ_A, λ_B, and λ_C. Now, suppose that operational profile #2 is A, 30%; B, 40%; and C, 30%. Without performing any testing under operational profile #2, the failure rates can be predicted by

$$\lambda_A' = \frac{30\%}{20\%} \lambda_A \tag{264}$$

$$\lambda'_B = \frac{40\%}{30\%}\lambda_B \qquad\qquad (265)$$

$$\lambda'_C = \frac{30\%}{50\%}\lambda_C \qquad\qquad (266)$$

I.   Appendix B shows that if clusters of software discrepancies (differences between actual and correct values of output variables) occur according to a Poisson process, then the number of individual discrepancies is governed by a "stuttering Poisson process." Since for many programs it may be more natural or meaningful to count discrepancies, a set of demonstration tests should be developed that are based on a stuttering Poisson model.

J.   More research should be done regarding the effect of complexity on software reliability. The complexity measures commonly used today tend to correlate with size, and so are not of use in prediction. If complexity is measured not as intricacy of structure but as the number of paths, then it would appear that it must influence fault content, since a program is only free of faults to the extent that it has been tested. The structure factor S should be studied for its relationship to complexity measures.

K.   This study provides a separate growth model for software that can be combined with an existing hardware reliability growth model for a given time τ of interest. The development of a single growth model--perhaps a mathematical merging of the AMSAA model and the Basic Execution Time Model--should be developed, so that a single growth curve can be used for the combined hardware/software system.

L.   Section 2 of this report provides an overview of the significant issues raised in modeling HW and SW systems along with limited guidance in the modeling of these systems. Research into advanced modeling techniques to support HW/SW system design is needed. This research is needed to update previous RADC research in this area [James et al. (1982)].

M.   Methods of instrumenting software code to ensure that any fault which may occur can be rapidly identified and accurately isolated to the section of the code (ie. module) which caused the problem should be investigated. Development of monitoring methods which can ensure improved software fault isolation with minimum or no operational penalty will help accelerate software reliability growth and minimize the potential for maintenance induced software faults.

Appendix A—Reliability Database

The development and validation of the techniques presented in this report required the collection of empirical data which was organized into a database. The database contains metrics on the characteristics of each project's software development process and the intermediate work products that emerged from the development process. Also data was collected on the software failures that occurred during each project's system test period. The primary use of the data was to develop a regression model for the early prediction of software reliability.

For developing the predictive equations of SOW para. 4.1.3.2, the study team sought data from a set of projects that were diverse in size, application, and development strategy, yet had produced similar kinds of well-kept documentation. These projects had to be old enough to have started system test (so that failure data was available), yet young enough that project documentation, management, and development staff were still accessible as sources of information. Six projects were chosen from which to collect the data.

Many projects at Hughes already collect metrics, similar to the 24 metrics used in this study, for the purposes of management reporting and, increasingly, for use in improving the software development process. The Software Engineering Institute (SEI) at Carnegie Mellon University is under contract to the Department of Defense to examine the quality of the software development process used by potential software development contractors. SEI conducts assessments of organizations' software engineering practices. Organizations are graded by the maturity level (1-5) that SEI determines that they have reached. To reach level 4, the organization must establish and maintain a set of product/process metrics and establish, manage, and maintain a database of those metrics. It must use the metrics to assess product quality, track progress toward meeting quantitative quality targets, and compare the metrics with historical experience on similar projects. At level 5, the metrics are automatically collected, and, in the spirit of Total Quality Management (TQM), the metrics are used to improve the organization's software development process [Humphrey (1990)].

Which metrics to collect for the purpose of software reliability prediction were based on (1) how promising the metric was for predicting software reliability, from a review of the literature and in light of the team's collective software engineering experience; and (2) the availability of the metric across the six projects. Furthermore, to be useful, each metric had to be easily collectible for a project following the draft MIL-HDBK and, ideally, represent a controllable characteristic.

Most influential was the excellent paper by Takahashi and Kamayachi (1989). This paper presented their research on ten factors that could influence fault density and concluded that the following were significant factors: frequency of changes to program specification, programmers' skill,. and volume of program design documents. The team generalized these factors to three corresponding classes of metrics: (1) volatility--how often work products change (whether because of misunderstanding, mistakes, or fickleness); (2) skill and effort brought to bear on the development task; and (3) magnitude of the task. Twenty-four metrics were then chosen from among those three categories. Ultimately, the inclusion of a particular metric was a hypothesis. The metric may or may not be useful for predicting software reliability. Conversely, there are undoubtedly other metrics that were not collected that could have been useful for prediction. Indeed, one of the risks of the study was that the set of metrics chosen would be insufficient. Fortunately the set of metrics did turn out to be useful.

The Hughes study team either personally performed or oversaw the data collection process on each project, so that consistent conventions and judgments could be made in transforming the raw data into the metrics. To encourage cooperation and candor, each project was promised anonymity.

The six Hughes Ground Systems projects selected for the collection of software development and failure data are summarized in Table A-1.

Table A-1.
SUMMARY OF PROJECTS - SOFTWARE DEVELOPMENT DATA

PROJECT #	TYPE	# CSCIs	KLOC	LANGUAGE
1	Avionics	1	140	JOVIAL
2	C^2I	3	53	Ada, C, Assembly
3	Data Comm	3	230	Ada
4	Trainer	1	40	Fortran
5	Diagnostic	1	7	Fortran
6	Radar	2	295	Fortran, ULTRA-16

For the Validation task two additional projects were used employed. These appear in Table A-2.

Table A-2.   Validation Projects

Project #	Type	# CSCIs	KLOC	Language
7	Weapon	1	18	Pascal
8	Tracking	1	120	Ada

Table A-3 summarizes the metrics that were collected from these 8 projects. The first column shows the phase the data originates in. The second column is a short identification code for the metric. The third column is a description of the metric. The fourth column is the class of metric (1, 2, or 3).

The study team was successful in collecting all 24 metrics from all CSCIs of the six projects. The team had contingency plans for dealing with missing data but did not need to invoke them.

The failure data recorded consisted of the estimated failure rate at the start of system testing, adjusted to a standardized average execution rate of three million instructions per second. Fault data was in the form of program trouble reports (PTRs) and library change requests (LCRs). Where necessary, calendar time was mapped to execution time and randomization [Musa et al. (1987)] was employed to minimize the effects of uncertainty in failure times.

Metrics were normalized, where applicable, by dividing by the number of kilo lines of code.

TABLE A-3:
PRODUCT/PROCESS METRICS

PHASE	CODE	DESCRIPTION	CLASS
Requirements	1	Errors in requirements specification (SRS)	1
	2	Requirements statements in the SRS	3
	3	Pages in the SRS	3
	4	Man-months for requirements analysis	2
	5	Requirements changes after baseline	1
Preliminary Design	6	Errors in preliminary design documents	1
	7	Computer Software Components (CSCs)	3
	8	Units (Ada packages) in design structure	3
	9	Pages in design documents (SDDs)	3
	10	Man-months for preliminary design	2
Detailed Design	11	Errors in design documents	1
	12	Man-months for detailed design	3
	13	Design flaws identified after baseline	3
	14	Design flaws after an internal review	3
Coding	15	Total executable lines of code (LOC)	3
	16	Faults found through code reviews	3
	17	Programmer skill level (avg. years of exp.)	1
	18	Number of units undergoing review	2
	19	Average number of source LOC per unit	3
Unit test	20	Average number of branches in a unit	1
	21	Percent of branches covered	2
	22	Nesting depth average	3
	23	Times a unit is unit-tested	2
	24	Man-months for coding/unit test	2
	25	Defects identified through walkthroughs and reviews	1,2

Historical failure/fault field data was collected from four projects, summarized in Table A-4.

TABLE A-4:
FIELDED PROJECTS

Project	Type	# CSCIs	KLOC	Language
9	Mobile Radar	3	150	ULTRA-16
10	Air Defense Radar	3	220	ULTRA-16
11	Target Acquisition	2	280	Fortran, ULTRA-16
12	Air Defense Radar	3	270	ULTRA-16

The hazard rate per fault was not discernable from the available data. The PTRs from the field did not contain information about how many times a particular failure recurred. Generally, the user community eventually devised and disseminated among themselves some type of work-around that avoided the problem until the next version became available. The study team pursued SOW paragraph 4.1.1.2 by adopting an approach that allows a program's fault hazard rate profile to be determined experimentally. The fielded systems were not close enough geographically to be used in the validation task (section 7), so ongoing projects were employed for the validation.

Appendix B—Constant Failure Rate Model for Software

Frozen code subjected to input randomly selected from a stationary operational profile is reasonably modeled as a homogeneous Poisson process (HPP). Such a stochastic process is characterized by a constant failure rate and exponentially distributed interfailure times. This appendix provides an axiomatic derivation of the constant failure rate model. It is shown that each axiom is reasonably satisfied by software.

Let I be the input space of a computer program. The operational profile assigns to each possible input state $i \epsilon I$ a probability $p(i)$ of being selected, with $\Sigma p(i)=1$. One can imagine a "test oracle" $e(i)$ associated with each input state i that evaluates to 1 if the program fails when executed with that input state, and evaluates to 0 if the program succeeds [Kopetz (1981), MacWilliams (1973)]. In practical situations, the values of the $e(i)$'s will not be known, but the actual values are immaterial to this discussion.

The probability of failure in a single run is given by

$$Q = \sum_{i \epsilon I} p(i) e(i) \qquad \text{(B-1)}$$

The probability of success is R=1-Q. The reliability of the program for n independent runs is R^n. The probability of k failures in n runs is governed by the binomial law

$$B(n,k) = \binom{n}{k} P^n Q^{n-k} \qquad \text{(B-2)}$$

This model is called a "data domain" software reliability model because it employs the run as the unit of exposure. A data domain model is described by Nelson (1973). Analogous hardware reliability models use kilometers, cycles, and missions as units of exposure. Most hardware and software reliability models, however, are "time domain" models; they use the continuum of time as the failure-exposing force.

In the time domain, a run starting from input state i has a duration $t(i)$. Like the $e(i)$'s, the $t(i)$'s would not in general be known a priori.

To transform the data-domain model into the time domain, five axioms are introduced. It will· be shown that the data-domain model satisfies the axioms, and that the consequence of the axioms is an HPP.

Consider the counting process $(N(t), t \geq 0)$. $N(t)$ represents cumulative number of software failures by cumulative execution time t. As shall be proved later, if the following five axioms are satisfied, the process is an HPP [Parzen (1962)]:

Axiom 1--Initialization: $N(0)=0$. The counting of failures begins at time 0.

Axiom 2--Independent increments: $N(t+\Delta)-N(t)$ is independent of $N(t)$.

Axiom 3--$0<Pr(N(t)>0)<1$, $t>0$. It is neither impossible nor certain that a failure will occur in any interval.

Axiom 4--

$$\lim_{t \to 0} \frac{Pr\{N(t+\Delta t)-N(t)>1\}}{Pr\{N(t+\Delta t)-N(t)=1\}} = 0 \tag{B-3}$$

Failures do not occur simultaneously

Axiom 5--Stationary increments: For any two times t and s and any $\Delta t>0$, it is true that

$$Pr\{N(t+\Delta t)-N(t)=n\} = Pr\{s+\Delta t)-N(s)=n\} \tag{B-4}$$

It will now be shown that the data domain model satisfies the five axioms.

Axiom 1 merely defines when the counting of failures begins.

Axiom 2 says that the number of failures in a future interval is not influenced by the number of failures in the past. Software satisfies this axiom as long as any data corruption a failure leaves is cleaned up before resuming execution.

Axiom 3 says that, in any interval, there is a positive probability that a failure will occur, but failure in the interval is not a certainty. A zero probability of failure requires perfect software. The possibility of any substantive piece of software having no faults is exceedingly remote.

Axiom 4 says that only one failure can occur at a time. ANSI-IEEE Standard 100-1988 defines software reliability as "the probability that software will not cause the failure of a system for a specified time under specified conditions." This definition implies that a software failure is a crash, hang, or bad output that causes system failure. A program run on input set i will either cause system failure $[e(i)=1]$ or it will not $[e(i)=0]$. More than one software failure cannot occur at once, because a software failure is the sum total of what the program did (or did not do) to cause one system failure.

Axiom 5 says that the distribution of failures in a time interval depends on the length of that interval, not on when the interval begins. For software, the number of failures in an interval depends on the number of runs that occur during that interval, not on when the interval begins. Different runs might take different amounts of time, but the probability of n failures in an interval depends sole on the probability of failure per run and the long-run average number of runs that occur in the time interval.

Every non-negative, integer-valued random variable X has an associated probability generating function (pgf). There is a one-to-one relationship between a random variable's pgf and probability distribution. Given one, the other is uniquely determined and vice versa. The pgf is a power series transformation of the probability mass function into a function of the (usually complex) variable z. It is defined as

$$G_X(z) = \sum_{x=0}^{\infty} \Pr\{X=x\} z^x = E\{z^X\} \qquad \text{(B-5)}$$

The dummy variable z must be restricted to a range in which the power series is convergent. The series is always absolutely and uniformly convergent for $|z| \leq 1$, and may also converge for a more extensive range. Hence, $G(z)$ is a continuous function. The probability mass function of X can be recovered by

$$\Pr\{X=x\} = \frac{G_X^{(x)}(0)}{x!} \qquad \text{(B-6)}$$

which is the x-th derivative of $G_X(z)$ evaluated at z evaluated at z=0, since $G_X(z)$ is the Taylor series expansion for $G_X(z)$ about z=0.

If X and Y are independent random variables, the pgf of their sum is the product of their pgf's:

$$G_{X+Y}(z) = G_X(z) G_Y(z) \qquad \text{(B-7)}$$

because

$$E\{z^{X+Y}\} = E\{z^X\} E\{z^Y\} \qquad \text{(B-8)}$$

The pgf for the Poisson distribution is

$$G_X(z) = E\{z^X\} = \sum_{x=0}^{\infty} \exp[-\lambda t] \frac{(\lambda t)^x}{x} z^x$$

$$= \exp[-\lambda t] \sum_{x=0}^{\infty} \frac{(\lambda t z)^x}{x!}$$

(B-9)

Since the series

$$\sum_{x=0}^{\infty} \frac{(\lambda t z)^x}{x!}$$

(B-10)

converges to λtz for all $\lambda \neq 0$, Equation B-9 becomes

$$\exp[-\lambda t] \exp[\lambda t z] = \exp[\lambda t(z-1)]$$

(B-11)

To prove that the counting process $\{N(t), t \geq 0\}$ satisfying the axioms is a HPP, it suffices to show that the pgf of $N(t)$ is that of an HPP [Parzen (1962)]:

$$\psi(z, t) = \exp[\lambda t(z-1)] , \quad |z| < 1$$

(B-12)

The proof is divided into two parts. The first part shows that the pgf is a consequence of assuming that a positive constant λ exists satisfying three key equations. The second part shows that a positive constant λ satisfying those key equations does in fact exist.

The three key equations are

$$\lim_{\Delta t \to 0} \frac{1 - Pr\{N(\Delta t) = 0\}}{\Delta t} = \lambda$$

(B-13)

$$\lim_{\Delta t \to 0} \frac{Pr\{N(\Delta t) = 1\}}{\Delta t} = \lambda$$

(B-14)

$$\lim_{\Delta t \to 0} \frac{Pr\{N(\Delta t) \geq 2\}}{\Delta t} = 0$$

(B-15)

From the independent increments axiom it follows that

$$E\{z^{N(t+\Delta t)}\} = E\{z^{N(t+\Delta t) - N(t)}\} E\{z^{N(t)}\}$$

(B-16)

From the stationary increments axiom it follows that

$$\psi(z, t+\Delta t) = \psi(z, t)\,\psi(z, \Delta t) \tag{B-17}$$

and

$$\frac{1}{\Delta t}[\psi(z, t+\Delta t) - \psi(z, t)]$$

$$= \psi(z, t)\frac{1}{\Delta t}[\psi(z, \Delta t) - 1] \tag{B-18}$$

It is now shown that

$$\lim_{\Delta t \to 0}\frac{1}{\Delta t}\{\psi(z, \Delta t) - 1\} = \lambda(z-1) \tag{B-19}$$

Expanding $\psi(z, \Delta t)$, one may write

$$\frac{1}{\Delta t}[\psi(z, \Delta t) - 1]$$

$$= \frac{1}{\Delta t}[\Pr\{N(\Delta t) = 0\} - 1\} + z\frac{1}{\Delta t}\Pr\{N(\Delta t) = 1\} \tag{B-20}$$

$$+ \frac{1}{\Delta t}\sum_{n=2}^{\infty} z^n \Pr\{N(\Delta t) = 2\}$$

But, for $|z| < 1$,

$$\sum_{n=2}^{\infty} z^n \Pr\{N(\Delta t) = n\} \le \Pr\{N(\Delta t) \ge 2\} \tag{B-21}$$

Therefore, to obtain Equation B-19

$$\lim_{\Delta t \to 0}\frac{1}{\Delta t}[\psi(z, \Delta t) - 1]$$

$$= \lim_{\Delta t \to 0}\frac{1}{\Delta t}[\Pr\{N(\Delta t) = 0\} - 1] + \lim_{\Delta t \to 0} z\frac{1}{\Delta t}\Pr\{N(\Delta t) = 1\} \tag{B-22}$$

$$+ \lim_{\Delta t \to 0}\frac{1}{\Delta t}\Pr\{N(\Delta t) \ge 2\} = -\lambda + z\lambda = \lambda(z-1)$$

Next it is shown that from Equations B-18 and B-19, Equation B-12 is obtained. Let $\Delta t \to 0$ in Equation B-18:

$$\lim_{\Delta t \to 0} \frac{1}{\Delta t} [\psi(z, t+\Delta t) - \psi(z, t)]$$

$$= \lim_{\Delta t \to 0} \psi(z, t) \frac{1}{\Delta t} [\psi(z, \Delta t) - 1] \qquad \textbf{(B-23)}$$

$$= \psi(z, t) \lambda(z-1)$$

The pgf satisfies the differential equation from Equation B-19

$$\frac{\partial}{\partial t} \psi(z, t) = \lambda(z-1) \psi(z, t) , \quad t \geq 0 \qquad \textbf{(B-24)}$$

with initial condition $\psi(z, 0) = 1$. The solution to this differential equation is

$$\psi(z, t) = \exp[\lambda t(z-1)], \quad |z| < 1 \qquad \textbf{(B-25)}$$

Let $P_j(t)$ denote $\Pr\{N(t)=j\}$. Assume that $P_0(t)$ is bounded. Since

$$\Pr\{N(t_1+t_2) = 0\}$$

$$= \Pr\{N(t_1+t_2) - N(t_1) = 0 \wedge N(t_1) = 0\} \qquad \textbf{(B-26)}$$

it follows from the axioms of stationary and independent increments that

$$P_0(t_1+t_2) = P_0(t_1) P_0(t_2) \qquad \textbf{(B-27)}$$

If for some arbitrary time t_0, $P_0(t_0)=0$, and $P_0(t)$ is bounded, it can be shown that

$$P_0(t) = \exp[-\lambda t] \qquad \textbf{(B-28)}$$

The case $\lambda = 0$ corresponds to a degenerate distribution in which no events ever occur. By Axiom 3, $0 < P_0(t) < 1$ for all t, so Equation B-28 holds with $\lambda > 0$.

a.   Next, it is shown that from Equation B-28 one obtains the first key equation

$$\lim_{\Delta t \to 0} \frac{1 - \Pr\{N(\Delta t) = 0\}}{\Delta t} = \lim_{\Delta t \to 0} \frac{1 - P_0(\Delta t)}{\Delta t}$$

$$= \lim_{\Delta t \to 0} \frac{1 - \exp[-\lambda t]}{\Delta t} \qquad \textbf{(B-29)}$$

$$= \lim_{\Delta t \to 0} \lambda \exp[-\lambda \Delta t] = \lambda$$

Now the second key equation (B-14) can be proven by using the fact that

$$\frac{1-P_0(\Delta t)}{\Delta t} = \frac{P_1(\Delta t)}{\Delta t}\left[1+\frac{Q(\Delta t)}{P_1(\Delta t)}\right] \qquad \text{(B-30)}$$

and

$$\lim_{\Delta t \to 0}\frac{Q(\Delta t)}{P_1(\Delta t)} = 0 \qquad \text{(B-31)}$$

(by Axiom 3), where $Q(t)=\Pr\{N(t)\geq 2\}$. From Equations B-30, B-31, and the first key equation (B-13), one can write

$$\lambda = \lim_{\Delta t \to 0}\frac{1-P_0(\Delta t)}{\Delta t} = \lim_{\Delta t \to 0}\frac{P_1(\Delta t)}{\Delta t}\left[1+\frac{W(\Delta t)}{P_1(\Delta t)}\right]$$

$$= \lim_{\Delta t \to 0}\frac{P_1(\Delta t)}{\Delta t}[1+0] = \lim_{\Delta t \to 0}\frac{P_1(\Delta t)}{\Delta t} \qquad \text{(B-32)}$$

From the second key equation (B-14) and from Equation B-31, the third key equation (B-15) holds, since

$$0 = \lim_{\Delta t \to 0}\frac{P_1(\Delta t)}{\Delta t}\lim_{\Delta t \to 0}\frac{Q(\Delta t)}{P_1(\Delta t)} = \lim_{\Delta t \to 0}\frac{Q(\Delta t)}{\Delta t}$$

$$= \lim_{\Delta t \to 0}\frac{\Pr\{N(\Delta t)\geq 2\}}{\Delta t} \qquad \text{(B-33)}$$

Empirical evidence [Musa (1979)] also supports the constant failure rate model for software.

It should be noted that the way failures are counted for the Basic Execution Time Model during growth testing is different than that described here. Growth testing is a completely different context. Because repair activity is going on, the failure rate is not constant but varies over time. The Basic Execution Time Model allows for multiple simultaneous "software failures," contrary to Axiom #3. During growth testing, each discrepancy (difference between the output variable value and the value dictated by the requirements) caused by a distinct fault is counted as a separate software failure. The reason is that the debugging will address all of the discrepancies. The subsequent removal of each underlying fault will cause a decrement in the program failure rate.

If each discrepancy were counted as a separate failure during demonstration testing, the result would not be an HPP. In fact, the distribution of failures is given by the "stuttering Poisson distribution" [Haight (1967)]. Axiom 4 does not hold. Let the probability of k software failures in the time interval $(t, t+\Delta t)$ be

$$\lambda \beta_k dt + o(dt) \tag{B-34}$$

The probability of zero failures in an interval is

$$b_0(t) = \exp[-\lambda t] \tag{B-35}$$

The time to first failure is thus still exponentially distributed. The probability of n+1 failures in time t is given by the recurrence relation [Adelson (1966)]

$$b_{n+1}(t) = \frac{\lambda t}{n+1} \sum_{j=0}^{n} (n-j+1) \beta_{n-j+1} b_j \tag{B-36}$$

The same stuttering Poisson distribution can also be derived by providing a finite probability π that the gap between successive failures will be zero. Then the cumulative distribution function of the gap between successive failures [Smith (1957), Smith (1958a), Smith (1958b)] is

$$F(x) = \pi + (1-\pi)(1-\exp[-\lambda x]) \tag{B-37}$$

Appendix C—Dynamic Allocation

C.1. Assumptions

The following conditions are assumed to hold:

    i) the component failures are statistically independent
    ii) the failure of any component results in failure of the
        aggregate
    iii) the component failure rates are constant

C.2. Notation

R^*: the required reliability for the aggregate for the mission
    time t.
λ^*: the required failure rate for the aggregate.
$R_i(t_i)$: the allocated reliability for the i-th component
n: the total number of components
m: the total number of time intervals
λ_i: the allocated failure rate for the i-th component
t: mission time for the aggregate
t'_j: the time at which the j-th time interval ends;
    j=0,1,2,...m.
t_i: total mission time for the i-th component; i=1,2,...,n.

Note the following relationships:

    a) $t_1+t_2+...+t_n = t$.

    b) $t_0' \le t_1' \le ... \le t_m'$.

    c) $t_m' = t$.

    d) The relationship between λ^* and R^* can be written as

$$R^*(t) = e^{-\lambda^* t}$$
$$\text{or} \quad \lambda^* = -\frac{\ln R(t)^*}{t} \tag{C-1}$$

where t is the aggregate mission time.

C.3.   Dynamic Allocation Technique

Suppose that an acceptable value of the allocated failure rate for each component i must belong to $[\lambda_i, \infty)$, $i=1,2,\ldots n$.

By using the proportional allocation technique (see Section 3 of this report), a failure rate λ_i can initially be assigned to the i-th component, $i=1,2,\ldots n$, based on the timing relationship among the components (sequential, interleaved or simultaneous processes). If one of the λ_i's does not belong to its accepted region, without loss of generality, say λ_1, then the Effort Minimization Algorithm can be used to reallocate the failure rate of each component to λ_i^*, $i=1,2,\ldots,n$.

Before discussing this algorithm, some notation needs to be introduced:

λ_i: pre-allocated failure rate for the i-th components;
$$i := 1,\ldots,n.$$
λ_i: the smallest acceptable value for the allocated failure rate of the i-th component; $i := 1,\ldots,n$.
λ_i^*: new allocated failure rate for the i-th component.
$G(\lambda_i, \lambda_i^*)$: effort function; the amount of effort needed to decrease the failure rate of the i-th component from λ_i to λ_i^* ($i := 1,\ldots,n$).

Note: The effort function $G(x,y)$, $x > y \geq 0$, is assumed to satisfy the following conditions [Kapur et al. (1977)]:

a) $G(x,y) \geq 0$.

b) $G(x,y)$ is nonincreasing in y for a fixed value of x and nondecreasing in x for a fixed value of y
$$G(x,y) \geq G(x,y+\Delta y), \quad \Delta y > 0.$$
$$G(x,y) \leq G(x+\Delta x,y), \quad \Delta x > 0.$$

c) $G(x,y)$ is additive; i.e, $G(x,y) + G(y,z) = G(x,z)$; $z<y<x$.

d) $G(y,0)$ has a derivative $h(y)$ such that $h(y)$ is strictly decreasing in y.

e) $G(x,y) = G(tx,ty)$, $\forall t > 0$.

Four different effort minimization problems will be presented in light of the timing relationship among the components (sequential, interleaved and/or simultaneous processes), and the complexity factor c_i of each component, $i=1,2,\ldots n$, with

$$\sum_{i=1}^{n} c_i = 1 \ . \tag{C-2}$$

If $\lambda_1 < \underline{\lambda}_1$, then let the new allocated failure rate of the first component be $\lambda_1^* = \underline{\lambda}_1$; so, at least one of the remaining λ_i, i=1,2,...n, must be decreased. To do this, a certain amount of effort is needed (such as: further engineering development, extra manpower, extensive testing, etc.) Let the effort function be $G(\lambda_i, \lambda_i^*)$, i=1,2,...,n; and assume this function satisfies the above conditions. Now, the new allocated failure rates λ_i^*, i=2,...,n, can be calculated by solving one of the following minimization problems.

I) Problem I:

If the aggregate has sequentially active components and the complexity factors are not taken into consideration in the objective function, then the new allocated failure rates for the components 2 to n can be computed by solving the following optimization problem:

$$(P) \quad \text{Minimize} \ \sum_{i=2}^{n} G(\lambda_i, \lambda_i^*)$$

$$\text{such that} \ \ \lambda_2^* t_2 + \ldots + \lambda_n^* t_n = \lambda^* t - \underline{\lambda}_1 t_1$$

$$\underline{\lambda}_2 \le \lambda_2^* \le \lambda_2$$
$$\vdots$$
$$\underline{\lambda}_n \le \lambda_n^* \le \lambda_n \tag{C-3}$$

Rewriting the above optimization problem (P) yields:

$$(P') \quad \text{Minimize} \ \sum_{i=2}^{n} G(\lambda_i, \lambda_i^*)$$

$$s.t. \ \ \lambda_2^* t_2 + \ldots + \lambda_n^* t_n = \lambda^* t - \underline{\lambda}_1 t_1$$

$$\lambda_2^* - \underline{\lambda}_2 \ge 0$$
$$\vdots$$
$$\lambda_n^* - \underline{\lambda}_n \ge 0$$
$$-\lambda_2^* + \lambda_2 \ge 0$$
$$\vdots$$
$$-\lambda_n^* + \lambda_n \ge 0 \tag{C-4}$$

By Kuhn-Tucker conditions [Phillips et al. (1976)] , there exist $\mu_1, \ldots, \mu_{2n-2}$ and λ such that the following relations hold:

(1) $\quad \lambda_2^* t_2 + \ldots + \lambda_n^* t_n - \lambda^* t + \lambda_1 t_1 = 0$

(2) $\qquad\qquad\qquad \lambda_2^* - \lambda_2 \geq 0$

$$\vdots$$

$$\lambda_n^* - \lambda_n \geq 0$$
$$-\lambda_2^* + \lambda_2 \geq 0$$
$$\vdots$$
$$-\lambda_n^* + \lambda_n \geq 0$$

(3) $\qquad\qquad\qquad \mu_1(\lambda_2^* - \lambda_2) = 0$

$$\vdots$$
$$\mu_{n-1}(\lambda_n^* - \lambda_n) = 0$$
$$\mu_n(-\lambda_2^* + \lambda_2) = 0$$
$$\vdots$$
$$\mu_{2n-2}(-\lambda_n^* + \lambda_n) = 0$$

(C-5)

(4) $\qquad\qquad\qquad \mu_1, \ldots, \mu_{2n-2} \geq 0$

(5) $\quad G'(\lambda_2, \lambda_2^*) + \lambda t_2 - \mu_1 + \mu_n = 0$
$$G'(\lambda_3, \lambda_3^*) + \lambda t_3 - \mu_2 + \mu_{n+1} = 0$$
$$\vdots$$
$$G'(\lambda_n, \lambda_n^*) + \lambda t_n - \mu_{n-1} + \mu_{2n-2} = 0$$

Now, multiplying each formula of Equation C-5 with the corresponding λ_k^* yields:

(6) $\lambda_k^* G'(\lambda_k, \lambda_k^*) + \lambda_k^* \lambda t_k - \lambda_k^* \mu_{k-1} + \lambda_k^* \mu_{k+n-2} = 0$ (C-6)

By Equations C-3 and C-4, one of the following cases holds:

(i) if $\mu_{k-1} > 0$ then $\lambda_k^* = \lambda_k$ and $\mu_{k+n-2} = 0$.

(ii) if $\mu_{k+n-2} > 0$ then $\lambda_k^* = \lambda_k$ and $\mu_{k-1} = 0$.

(iii) Both $\mu_{k-1} = \mu_{k+n-2} = 0$.

Thus, for the values of k such that $\mu_{k-1} = \mu_{k+n-2} = 0$, Equation C-6 can be rewritten as

$$\lambda_k^* G'(\lambda_k, \lambda_k^*) + \lambda_k^* \lambda\, t_k = 0 \qquad\qquad \text{(C-7)}$$

or

$$\lambda = -\frac{G'(\lambda_k, \lambda_k^*)}{t_k} \qquad\qquad \text{(C-8)}$$

Next, assume that

$$G(\lambda_k, \lambda_k^*) = G(t_k\lambda_k, t_k\lambda_k^*), \quad \text{for all } t_k > 0, \quad k=1,2,\ldots,n. \quad \text{(C-9)}$$

then, $\lambda = -G'(\lambda_k t_k, \lambda_k^* t_k)/t_k$ for all values of k's such that $\mu_{k+1} = \mu_{k+n-2} = 0$. Since $G'(y)$ is a strictly decreasing function $\lambda_k' = c / t_k$ is true, for all values of k's such that $\mu_{k-1} = \mu_{k+n-2} = 0$, and some constant c.

Now, without loss of generality, suppose $\lambda_1 t_1 \leq \lambda_2 t_2 \leq \ldots \leq \lambda_n t_n$. Next, assume for the first k_1 variables, and the last $n-k_2$ variables, case (i) and (ii) hold, respectively, then

$$\lambda_2^* = \lambda_2, \ldots, \lambda_{k_1}^* = \lambda_{k_1}$$
$$\text{and} \quad \lambda_{k_2}^* = \lambda_{k_2}, \ldots, \lambda_n^* = \lambda_n \qquad\qquad \text{(C-10)}$$

where $k_1 < k_2$. Under these assumptions, a pair, k_1 and k_2, needs to be found that satisfies the following relations:

a) $\lambda_2 t_2 + \ldots + \lambda_{k_1} t_{k_1} + (n-k_1-(n-k_2)-1)c + \lambda_{k_2} t_{k_2} + \ldots + \lambda_n t_n = \lambda^* t - \lambda_1 t_1$

b) $\quad c \geq 0$ (C-11)

c) $\quad \lambda_m \leq \dfrac{c}{t_m} \leq \lambda_m, \quad \forall\, k_1+1 \leq m \leq k_2-1$

From (a), it is true that

$$c = \frac{\lambda^* t - \lambda_1 t_1 - \lambda_2 t_2 - \ldots - \lambda_{k_1} t_{k_1} - \lambda_{k_2} t_{k_2} - \ldots - \lambda_n t_n}{k_2 - k_1 - 1} \qquad \text{(C-12)}$$

Substituting the above equation into (c) yields for all $k_1+1 \leq m \leq k_2-1$.

Therefore, k_1 and k_2 must be found such that $k_1 < k_2$ and (7) holds for all m, where $k_1+1 \leq m \leq k_2-1$. One choice for k_1 and k_2 is as follows:

(7) $\lambda_m t_m \leq \dfrac{\lambda^\bullet t - \lambda_1 t_1 - \lambda_2 t_2 - \ldots - \lambda_{k_1} t_{k_1} - \lambda_{k_2} t_{k_2} - \ldots - \lambda_n t_n}{k_2 - k_1 - 1} \leq \lambda_m t_{m'}$

(C-13)

1) Let k_2 be the minimum value of index ℓ such that

$$\lambda_l t_l < \lambda^\bullet t - \lambda_1 t_1 - \lambda_l t_l - \lambda_{l+1} t_{l+1} - \ldots - \lambda_n t_n \qquad \text{(C-14)}$$

2) Let k_1 be the maximum value of index j such that

$$\lambda_j t_j > \frac{\lambda^\bullet t - \lambda_1 t_1 - \lambda_2 t_2 - \ldots - \lambda_j t_j - \lambda_{k_2} t_{k_2} - \ldots - \lambda_n t_n}{k_2 - (j+1)} \qquad \text{(C-15)}$$

Hence, a solution of (P) can be written as:
If $k_2 - 1 \leq k_1$ then

$$\lambda_i^\bullet = \begin{cases} \lambda_{i'} & \text{for } 2 \leq i \leq k_1 \\ \lambda_{i'} & \text{for } k_2 \leq i \leq n \end{cases} \qquad \text{(C-16)}$$

else

$$\lambda_i^\bullet = \begin{cases} \lambda_{i'} & \text{for } 2 \leq i < k_1 \\ \lambda_{i'} & \text{for } k_2 < i \leq n \\ \left(\dfrac{\lambda^\bullet t - \lambda_1 t_1 - \lambda_2 t_2 - \ldots - \lambda_{k_1} t_{k_1} - \lambda_{k_2} t_{k_2} - \ldots \lambda_n t_n}{k_2 - (k_1 + 1)} \right) \dfrac{1}{t_i} & \text{for } k_1 \leq i \leq k_2 \end{cases} \qquad \text{(C-17)}$$

2) Problem II:

This is similar to Problem I, but this time the complexity factors of each component are incorporated into the optimization

(P) to compute the failure rates for the components 2 to n.   (P) can be rewritten as follows:

$$(P) \qquad \text{Minimize } \sum_{i=2}^{n} c_i G(\lambda_i, \lambda_i^*)$$

$$\text{such that } \lambda_2^* t_2 + \ldots + \lambda_n^* t_n = \lambda^* t - \lambda_1 t_1$$

$$\underline{\lambda}_2 \leq \lambda_2^* \leq \lambda_2$$

$$\vdots \qquad\qquad\qquad\qquad\qquad\text{(C-18)}$$

$$\underline{\lambda}_n \leq \lambda_n^* \leq \lambda_n$$

$$c_i \geq 0, \quad i := 1, 2, \ldots n$$

$$\sum_{i=1}^{n} c_i = 1$$

Using Kuhn-Tucker conditions as in the above problem, a solution for Problem II is obtained that can be written as:

Let k_2 be the minimum value of index ℓ such that

$$\frac{\lambda_\ell t_\ell}{c_\ell} < \frac{\lambda^* t - \lambda_1 t_1 - \lambda_\ell t_\ell - \cdots - \lambda_n t_n}{\min_{2 \leq i \leq n} c_i} . \qquad \text{(C-19)}$$

Let k_1 be the maximum value of index j such that

$$\frac{\lambda_j t_j}{c_j} > \frac{\lambda^* t - \lambda_1 t_1 - \lambda_2 t_2 - \cdots - \lambda_j t_j - \lambda_{k_2} t_{k_2} - \cdots - \lambda_n t_n}{c_{j+1} + \cdots + c_{k_2 - 1}} \qquad \text{(C-20)}$$

If $k_2 - 1 \leq k_1$ then

$$\lambda_i^* = \begin{cases} \underline{\lambda}_i & \text{if } 2 \leq i \leq k_2 \\ \lambda_i & \text{if } k_2 < i \leq n \end{cases} \qquad \text{(C-21)}$$

else

$$\lambda_i^* = \begin{cases} \lambda_i & \text{if } 2 \le i \le k_1 \\ \lambda_i & \text{if } k_2 \le i \le n \\ \left(\dfrac{\lambda^* t - \lambda_1 t_1 - \lambda_2 t_2 - \cdots - \lambda_{k_1} t_{k_1} - \lambda_{k_2} t_{k_2} - \cdots - \lambda_n t_n}{c_{k_1+1} + \cdots + c_{k_2-1}} \right) \dfrac{c_i}{t_i} \\ \qquad \text{if } k_1 + 1 \le m \le k_2 - 1 \end{cases} \qquad \text{(C-22)}$$

III) Problem III:

If the aggregate has concurrently active components, and complexity factors are not taken into consideration in the objective function, then the new allocated failure rates for the components 2 to n can be computed by solving the following minimization problem:

$$(P) \quad \text{Minimize} \quad \sum_{i=2}^{n} G(\lambda_i, \lambda_i^*)$$

$$\text{such that} \quad \lambda_2^* + \ldots + \lambda_n^* = \lambda^* - \lambda_1 \qquad \text{(C-23)}$$
$$\lambda_2 \le \lambda_2^* \le \lambda_2$$
$$\vdots$$
$$\lambda_n \le \lambda_n^* \le \lambda_n$$

This problem has the same objective function as that of problem I, but the first constraints in these two problems are not the same. However, the Kuhn-Tucker conditions [Phillips et al. (1976)] can still be applied to obtain a solution that can be written as:

Let k_2 be the minimum value of index ℓ such that

$$\lambda_\ell < \lambda^* - \lambda_1 - \lambda_\ell - \lambda_{\ell+1} - \ldots - \lambda_n \qquad \text{(C-24)}$$

Let k_1 be the maximum value of index j such that

$$\lambda_j > \frac{\lambda^* - \lambda_1 - \lambda_2 - \ldots - \lambda_j - \lambda_{k_2} - \lambda_{k_2+1} - \ldots - \lambda_n}{k_2 - j - 1} \tag{C-25}$$

If $k_2 - 1 \leq k_1$ then

$$\lambda_i^* = \begin{cases} \lambda_i, & 2 \leq i \leq k_2 \\ \lambda_i, & k_2 < i \leq n \end{cases} \tag{C-26}$$

else

$$\lambda_i^* = \begin{cases} \lambda_i, & 2 \leq i \leq k_1 \\ \lambda_i, & k_2 \leq i \leq n \\ \dfrac{\lambda^* - \lambda_1 - \lambda_2 - \ldots - \lambda_{k_1} - \lambda_{k_2} - \ldots - \lambda_n}{k_2 - k_1 - 1}, & k_1 + 1 \leq i \leq k_2 - 1 \end{cases} \tag{C-27}$$

IV) Problem IV:

This problem is similar to problem III, except the complexity factors of each component are incorporated into the objective function. Therefore, in this case the optimization problem can be written as

$$(P) \qquad \text{Minimize} \sum_{i=2}^{n} c_i G(\lambda_i, \lambda_i^*)$$

$$\text{such that } \lambda_2^* + \ldots + \lambda_n^* = \lambda^* - \lambda_1$$

$$\lambda_2 \leq \lambda_2^* \leq \lambda_2$$

$$\vdots \tag{C-28}$$

$$\lambda_n \leq \lambda_n^* \leq \lambda_n$$

$$c_i \geq 0, \quad i = 1, 2, \ldots n$$

$$\sum_{i=1}^{n} c_i = 1$$

Applying the Kuhn-Tucker conditions to this problem, a solution can be expressed as follows:

Let k_2 be the minimum value of index ℓ such that

$$\frac{\lambda_\ell}{c_\ell} < \frac{\lambda^* - \lambda_1 - \lambda_\ell - \cdots - \lambda_n}{\min_{2 \le i \le n} c_i} \qquad \text{(C-29)}$$

Let k_1 be the maximum value of index j such that

$$\frac{\lambda_j}{c_j} > \frac{\lambda^* - \lambda_1 - \lambda_2 - \cdots - \lambda_j - \lambda_{k_2} - \cdots - \lambda_n}{c_{j+1} + \cdots + c_{k_2-1}} \qquad \text{(C-30)}$$

If $k_2 - 1 \le k_1$ then

$$\lambda_i^* = \begin{cases} \lambda_i & \text{if } 2 \le i \le k_2 \\ \lambda_i & \text{if } k_2 < i \le n \end{cases} \qquad \text{(C-31)}$$

else

$$\lambda_i^* = \begin{cases} \lambda_i & \text{if } 2 \le i \le k_1 \\ \lambda_i & \text{if } k_2 \le i \le n \\ \left(\dfrac{\lambda^* - \lambda_1 - \lambda_2 - \cdots - \lambda_{k_1} - \lambda_{k_2} - \cdots - \lambda_n}{c_{k_1+1} + \cdots + c_{k_2-1}} \right) \dfrac{c_i}{t_i}, \\ \qquad \text{if } k_1 + 1 \le m \le k_2 - 1 \end{cases} \qquad \text{(C-32)}$$

Appendix D—Early Prediction of Program Size

This appendix discusses some of the methods for predicting the size of a software program prior to coding.

The methods outlined below in Parts D.1, D.2, and D.3 are based on the psychometric techniques pioneered by Thurstone, further developed and applied by Souder and Saaty. These methods are employed to assign a position to each module along an interval scale. Such an interval scale can then be used to compute the estimated lengths of the modules; the sum of these estimated lengths is the predicted size of the software program in hand.

In order for the methods to predict the absolute size of each module, the set of modules needs to be augmented by at least two "reference" modules. These are modules that the experts are familiar with and whose sizes are known. These reference modules would ordinarily come from other projects in the organization. One reference module must be the shortest of all the modules.

D.1 Successive Ratings Method

The Successive Ratings Method was first introduced by Souder (1980). The modules are first ordered according to their conceptual lengths (based on the experts' judgments of how long or short the modules are relative to each other). Then, the modules can be entered into the successive ratings form (Table D-1), based on their order, from the longest to the shortest.

Table D-1: Successive Ratings Method Example

Modules	Column 1 Compare to longest	Column 2 Compare to shortest	Column 3 Compare to longest and shortest
1	100	120	100
3	60	70	65
4	30	20	25
2	20	10	10

Note: In the above table, module 1 is the longest and module 2 is the shortest.

The numbers 100 and 10, underlined in the table, are pre-recorded parts of the standard successive ratings form.

In the first column each lower-ordered module is then successively compared to the highest-ordered (longest) module and a number corresponding to its relative value is assigned. For example, the number 60 for module 3 in Table D-1 indicates that the length of module 3 is 60% of the length of module 1. Similarly, module 4 is 30% as long as module 1, and module 2 is 20% as long as module 1.

When column 1 is filled in, the comparison process is reversed to obtain the data in column 2. For example, module 4 is judged to be twice as long as module 2; module 3 is seven times as long as module 2; and module 1 is twelve times as long as module 2.

Each number in column 3 should reflect the values of the modules relative to the longest and shortest modules.

The sequence of numbers in column 3 can be thought of as an interval scale for the lengths of the modules.

D.2 Pairwise Comparisons

The Pairwise Comparisons Method was developed by Saaty (1982) for solving decision making problems. A judgmental matrix of the relative lengths of the modules (in a software program) is formed, using the experts' evaluation. Then, by applying either the Geometric Mean Approach or the Power Method, an interval scale for the lengths of the modules can be calculated.

In the Pairwise Comparisons Method, the user must assign numbers to the first row of a judgmental matrix of the form

$$
A = \quad
\begin{array}{c|c|c|c|c}
 & M_1 & M_2 & M_3 & M_4 \\
\hline
M_1 & 1 & & & \\
\hline
M_2 & & 1 & & \\
\hline
M_3 & & & 1 & \\
\hline
M_4 & & & & 1 \\
\end{array}
$$

based on the following definition.

If module A is being compared to module B then

Number	Definition
1	A is equal to B
3	A is moderately longer than B
5	A is longer than B
7	A is very much longer than B
9	A is extremely longer than B
2,4,6,8	Intermediate values between two adjacent judgments
Reciprocals	If module i has one of the preceding numbers assigned to it when it is compared with module j, then module j has the reciprocal value when it is compared with module i

For instance, if M_2 and M_4 are moderately longer than M_1, and M_3 is extremely longer than M_1, then the first row of matrix A can be written as

	M_1	M_2	M_3	M_4
M_1	1	3	9	4
M_2		1		
M_3			1	
M_4				1

Now, the remaining entries in the upper triangle of the matrix A can be computed from the information of the first row. For example, from the first row we have $M_2 = 3M_1$, $M_3 = 9M_1$, $M_4 = 4M_1$; thus, $M_3 = (9/3)M_2 = 3M_2$, $M_4 = (4/3)M_2$, and $M_4 = (4/9)M_3$. Therefore, the upper triangle of matrix A can be written as

	M_1	M_2	M_3	M_4
M_1	1	3	9	4
M_2		1	3	4/3
M_3			1	4/9
M_4				1

The value of each entry in the lower triangle of matrix A is the reciprocal of the value of the symmetric element with respect to that entry in matrix A. So, A is

	M_1	M_2	M_3	M_4
M_1	1	3	9	4
M_2	1/3	1	3	4/3
M_3	1/9	1/3	1	4/9
M_4	1/4	3/4	9/4	1

Next, we will compute an interval scale for the lengths of the modules based on the judgmental matrix, by using either the Geometric Mean Approach or the Power Method.

i) Geometric Mean Approach:

For each row i of matrix A, i = 1,2,3,4, take the product of the ratios in that row and denote it by $\prod_i$. Calculate the corresponding geometric mean P_i, where $P_i = (\prod_i)^{1/4}$, i = 1,2,3,4. Let $P = \sum_i P_i$. We normalize the P_i (i.e., transform them so that their resultant sum equals unity) by forming $p_i = (P_i/P)$. Each p_i is a corresponding value assigned to module i, i = 1,2,3,4. Rearranging the p_i's in descending order gives us an interval scale for the lengths of the modules.

For example,

	M_1	M_2	M_3	M_4	$\prod_i$	$P_i=(\prod_i)^{1/4}$	$p_i=P_i/P$
M_1	1	3	9	4	108	3.2237	0.59
M_2	1/3	1	3	4/3	4/3	1.0746	0.19
M_3	1/9	1/3	1	4/9	0.01646	0.3582	0.07
M_4	1/4	3/4	9/4	1	0.42188	0.8059	0.15
						P=5.4624	

So, an interval scale of the lengths of M_1, M_2, M_3, M_4 is

Interval Scale

M_1	0.59
M_2	0.19
M_4	0.15
M_3	0.07

One deficiency of the Geometric Mean Approach to obtain an interval scale is that it can reverse the order of the lengths of the modules. To detect this phenomenon, assume the lengths of two of the modules are known. If the interval scale value of module A is longer than the interval scale value of B, but the length of module A is shorter than the length of module B, then the Geometric Mean Approach has reversed the order of the lengths of the modules. In that case, the Power Method must be used instead.

ii) Power Method:

The matrix A is multiplied repeatedly by an arbitrary vector, say $[1,1,1,1]^T$. At each step, the resultant vector is normalized by making its largest component equal to unity. This recursive procedure can be stopped when the following relation holds:

$$\max_{1 \leq i \leq 4} (abs((f_k)_i - (f_{k+1})_i)) < \varepsilon,$$

where ε can be any predetermined small number, say $\varepsilon = 0.0000001$, and $(f_k)_i$ denote the i-th component of the unnormalized f_k.

Below is the illustration of the Power Method when it is applied to matrix A.

$$
\begin{bmatrix}
1 & 3 & 9 & 4 \\
1/3 & 1 & 3 & 4/3 \\
1/9 & 1/3 & 1 & 4/9 \\
1/4 & 3/4 & 9/4 & 1
\end{bmatrix}
\begin{bmatrix}
1 \\ 1 \\ 1 \\ 1
\end{bmatrix}
=
\begin{bmatrix}
17 \\ 5.666667 \\ 1.888889 \\ 4.25
\end{bmatrix}
= 17
\begin{bmatrix}
1 \\ 0.33333 \\ 0.11111 \\ 0.25
\end{bmatrix}
$$

$$f_1$$

$$
\begin{bmatrix}
1 & 3 & 9 & 4 \\
1/3 & 1 & 3 & 4/3 \\
1/9 & 1/3 & 1 & 4/9 \\
1/4 & 3/4 & 9/4 & 1
\end{bmatrix}
\begin{bmatrix}
1 \\ 0.33333 \\ 0.11111 \\ 0.25
\end{bmatrix}
=
\begin{bmatrix}
4 \\ 1.3333 \\ 0.4444 \\ 1
\end{bmatrix}
= 4
\begin{bmatrix}
1 \\ 0.33333 \\ 0.11111 \\ 0.25
\end{bmatrix}
$$

$$f_2$$

$$\begin{bmatrix} 1 & 3 & 9 & 4 \\ 1/3 & 1 & 3 & 4/3 \\ 1/9 & 1/3 & 1 & 4/9 \\ 1/4 & 3/4 & 9/4 & 1 \end{bmatrix} \begin{bmatrix} 1 \\ 0.33333 \\ 0.11111 \\ 0.25 \end{bmatrix} = \begin{bmatrix} 4 \\ 1.3333 \\ 0.4444 \\ 1 \end{bmatrix} = 4 \begin{bmatrix} 1 \\ 0.33333 \\ 0.11111 \\ 0.25 \end{bmatrix}$$

$$f_3$$

So, $[1, 0.3333, 0.1111, 0.25]^T$ gives an interval scale for the lengths of the modules M_1, M_2, M_3, M_4 to be

Interval Scale

M_1	1
M_2	0.33333
M_4	0.25
M_3	0.11111

Notice that for the above interval scale and the one in part (II)(i), one can be converted to the other by means of a linear transformation. For example, if we multiply 0.59 with each element in the above interval scale, we will obtain the interval scale in part (II)(i).

D.3   Paired Comparisons Method

The idea of the Paired Comparisons Method was developed by Thurstone (1959). In the Paired Comparisons Method the experts are prompted with the names of two modules, selected at random, and asked to decide which one in his estimation is the larger. Several experts make their judgments on many modules.

The first step is to summarize the responses in a matrix. Below is an example of such a matrix.

		Module (k)				
M		A	B	C	D	E
o						
d	A	.50	.79	.16	.48	.67
d						
u	B	.21	.50	.03	.21	.25
l						
e	C	.84	.97	.50	.76	.81
	D	.52	.79	.24	.50	.68
(1)						
	E	.33	.75	.19	.32	.50

The value of each entry in the table above indicates the proportion of experts who judged module (k) to be larger in size than each of the other modules (1).   Note that the diagonal elements contain proportion .50 and that for each pair P_{ij} it must be the case that $P_{ij} + P_{ji} = 1.00$.

The next step is to create a new matrix by converting each proportion to a z-score.   The normal deviate is used, with all proportions over .50 yielding positive z-scores and those under yielding negative z-scores:

$$\begin{bmatrix} 0.00 & 0.80 & -.99 & -.05 & .44 \\ -0.80 & 0.00 & -1.88 & .81 & -.67 \\ .99 & 1.88 & 0.00 & .71 & .88 \\ .05 & .81 & -.71 & 0.00 & .47 \\ -.44 & .67 & -.88 & -.47 & 0.00 \end{bmatrix}$$

(e.g., in the first table of this section, 79% of the experts believe that module B is longer than module A; to find the z-score which corresponds to 0.79, a value of z needs to be calculated such that $Pr(Z \leq z) = 0.79$, where $Z \in N(0,1)$. Therefore, z (or z-score) = 0.80.)

To obtain an interval scale, the sums and arithmetic means of each column are calculated.   The column sums are

$$-.21 \quad 4.17 \quad -4.46 \quad -62 \quad 1.12$$

and the averages are

-.04 .83 -.89 -.12 .22

From any of the above methods, an interval scale can be obtained for the lengths of the modules in a software program. For example, in Part(I), an interval scale was obtained for the four modules in a software system:

Modules	Interval Scale
1	100
3	65
4	25
2	10

Now, assume the lengths of modules 3 and 2 are known, say 1000 and 500, respectively. Then, the lengths of the modules 1 and 4 can be calculated as follows:

$$\text{the length of module 4} = 500 + \left(\frac{1000-500}{65-10}\right)(25-10)$$

$$= 636,$$

$$\text{the length of module 1} = 500 + \left(\frac{1000-500}{65-10}\right)(100-10)$$

$$= 1318.$$

Below is the general formula to compute the estimated sizes of the modules in a software program:

Assume that there exist n modules, and that an interval scale for the lengths of the modules has been obtained by the Successive Ratings Method. Also, assume that the lengths of modules i,j,k,n (denoted by L_i, L_j, L_k, L_n), i<j<k<n, are known.

Interval Scale (obtained from the 4th column of the Successive Ratings Form)	LOC
I_1	L_1
$\vdots$	$\vdots$
I_i	L_i
$\vdots$	$\vdots$
I_j	L_j
$\vdots$	$\vdots$
I_k	L_k
$\vdots$	$\vdots$
I_n	L_n

Then, the length of the l-th module is

$$
L_l = \begin{cases}
L_j + \dfrac{(L_i - L_j)}{(I_i - I_j)}(I_l - I_j), & \forall\ 1 \leq l < j,\quad l \neq i \\[3mm]
L_k + \dfrac{(L_j - L_k)}{(I_j - I_k)}(I_l - I_k), & \forall\ j < l < k \\[3mm]
L_n + \dfrac{(L_k - L_n)}{(I_k - I_n)}(I_l - I_n), & \forall\ k < l < n
\end{cases}
$$

Note: Any one of the three methods in Parts I, II and III can be used for producing an interval scale for the lengths of the modules. The method to use depends on the level of familiarity of the software engineering staff with the software concerned. The Successive Ratings Method requires the most understanding of the software compared to the other two methods, while the Paired Comparisons Method requires the least.

Appendix E—Multivariate Regression Analyses

This appendix presents a detailed description of the multivariate regression models which were formulated as a part of developing prediction models for software failure rate (SOW 4.1.3.2). The appendix is organized into four sections:

1. Presentation of the notation that is used in the regression analyses.

2. A detailed discussion of the multivariate regression analyses.

3. The correlation matrix for standardized software failure rate (Y) and software characteristics $(x_1, \ldots, x_{25})$

4. Printed computer outputs of stepwise selection analyses, stepwise regression model, principal component analyses, and least squares method (using principal components) for each software development phase.

Summary results of these analyses are provided within the appropriate sections of the main body of the report.

Table E-1 contains the data set for nine observations (CSCIs) which are collected from the reliability database described in Appendix A. This data will be used in regression analyses in this section.

Some of the independent variables were normalized based on kilo lines of executable code (KLOC). The normalized independent variables are $x_1, \ldots, x_{14}, x_{16}, x_{24}, x_{25}$. The formula to normalize x_i where $i \in \{1, 2, \ldots, 14, 16, 24, 25\}$ is

$$x_i = (x_i \: / \: x_{15}) \cdot 1000$$

Recall that x_{15} is the number of LOC in each observation.

For each phase of the software development process, a new regression model was formed which involves Y (software failure rate as the dependent variable) and x_i, $i = 1, 2, \ldots, k$ where $k \leq n$, and contains more software characteristics as they become available. Therefore, several regression models were formulated for each software development phase ·(such as requirements analysis, preliminary design, detailed design, coding and unit test).

The scatter plots Y (software failure rate) versus x_i (software characteristic), $i = 1, 2, \ldots, n$, based on the collected data from

181

Appendix A, were drawn. These scatter diagrams suggest that the regression models can be linear in terms of all the variables except x_6, x_{11}, x_{13}, x_{14}, x_{16}, x_{23}. However, both linear and nonlinear regression models involving software failure rate (dependent variables) and the software characteristics (independent variables) described above were developed for each phase of software development.

The general linear regression model is of the form

$$Y = a_0 + a_1x_1 + a_2x_2 + \ldots + a_kx_k$$

where k assumes different values depending on the software development phase. Similarly, the non-linear regression model for each phase of the software development is a sum of the linear combination of items in a subset of $\{x_1, \ldots, x_5, x_7, \ldots, x_{10}, x_{12}, x_{17}, \ldots, x_{22}, x_{24}, x_{25}\}$ and the linear combination of items in the subset of $\{1/x_6, 1/x_{11}, 1/x_{13}, 1/x_{14}, 1/x_{16}, 1/x_{23}\}$; the sizes of these subsets depend on the phase of the software development. Notice that x_{15} is not used in any of the regression models, except to normalize appropriate independent variables, since, the software failure rate Y should not depend on the size (x_{15}) of the software.

Table E-1.   Data Set Observations

	Obs. #1	Obs. #2	Obs. #3	Obs. #4	Obs. #5
x_1	352	30	50	323	280
x_2	929	740	4248	680	1356
x_3	653	140	472	1367	452
x_4	7	5	8	201	55
x_5	80	37	13	141	280
x_6	11	14	30	18	2086
x_7	36	19	28	4	44
x_8	1470	120	100	842	1100
x_9	206	939	3260	500	6959
x_{10}	44	5	20	22	7.5
x_{11}	26	40	90	426	4920
x_{12}	1	4	16	82	7.5
x_{13}	23	4	32	250	29
x_{14}	65	23	20	2750	445
x_{15}	230000	40000	5091	140000	241900
x_{16}	359	85	201	424	600
x_{17}	5	6	4	5	2
x_{18}	1470	120	100	842	1100
x_{19}	150	35	50	50	60
x_{20}	8	8	10	10	5
x_{21}	0.95	1	1	1	1
x_{22}	3	3	3	2	3
x_{23}	1	1	10	1	1
x_{24}	160	11	12	156	60
x_{25}	447	112	253	3424	1074
Y	36	31	64	48	10

Table E-1.   Data Set Observations (con't)

	Obs. #6	Obs. #7	Obs. #8	Obs. #9
x_1	50	0	0	0
x_2	700	296	504	270
x_3	75	63	186	97
x_4	55	53	42	35
x_5	50	38	39	0
x_6	898	32	38	113
x_7	22	29	26	22
x_8	300	36	45	22
x_9	2565	312	274	169
x_{10}	2.5	34	31	20
x_{11}	1080	6	12	36
x_{12}	2.5	51	46	16
x_{13}	6	1	3	31
x_{14}	300	86	109	94
x_{15}	53100	4889	5769	4135
x_{16}	400	39	36	53
x_{17}	2	7	7	7
x_{18}	300	36	45	22
x_{19}	60	136	128	188
x_{20}	5	48	52	18
x_{21}	1	1	1	1
x_{22}	3	1	1	2
x_{23}	1	4.1	4.1	2.6
x_{24}	20	42	53	21
x_{25}	706	126	148	178
Y	8	6.5	6	8.8

In addition to the regression models that are developed as the software development advances, other regression models were formulated by examining the correlations of the independent variables. But, only linear relationships between Y and x_i, $i = 1,2,\ldots,n$, are examined in these models.

E.1 Multivariate Linear Regression Model Development

The correlation matrix of $x_1,\ldots,x_n$ and y, based on the collected data, can be found on pages E-21 through E-24. Most of the variables are highly correlated to one another. For example, consider the sets $\{x_1, x_2, x_3, x_8, x_9, x_{23}, x_{25}\}$, $\{x_4, x_5, x_7, x_{10}, x_{12}, x_{18}, x_{19}, x_{20}, x_{22}, x_{24}\}$, etc. The variables in each set have high correlation to one other.

Several prediction models will now be systematically presented. A different model is developed for each phase of the software development life cycle, using the metrics that are cumulatively available at that stage. Using the successive models, the user can update the prediction at each design phase when the metrics from that stage become available. After system test begins, actual failure data will become available, and the results of growth testing will supersede the prediction model.

The regression is performed by using the method of least squares. Least squares finds the "best-fitting" hyperplane, where best fitting means to find the hyperplane such that the sum of the squares of the deviations of the predicted Y values from the observed Y values is a minimum, which is the criterion of minimum variance unbiased estimation. Because the number of metrics available in latter phases exceeds the number of observations, two different approaches were taken: selecting a subset of the most significant predictors using stepwise regression, and aggregating metrics using principal components analysis. Additionally, a regression model was formulated that is based on the correlations of the independent variables.

Although more than one regression model was developed, only one was ultimately chosen by comparisons among the models in the validation task. That model is the one that will be used in the draft MIL-HDBK.

(Note that all regression analyses are done based on a 0.15 significance level.)

E.1.1   Regression Models Based On Software Development Phases:

E.1.1.1   Requirements Analysis

There are only five independent variables involved in the regression model for the requirements analysis phase.

x_1: number of errors in the requirements specification (SRS)
x_2: Requirements statements in the SRS
x_3: Pages in SRS
x_4: Man-months for requirements analysis
x_5: Requirements changes after baseline

Since the number of observations is greater than the number of independent variables in this case, an attempt has been made to produce the regression model by using the method of least squares (i.e., the surface of the regression model fits the corresponding set of data points such that the sum of the squared errors is smallest). The result of this technique is:

$$Y = 5.126 + 15.717x_1 - 0.172x_2 + 0.52x_3 + 0.39x_4 - 0.234x_5$$

with Y restricted to nonnegative values.

The complete output of the above regression model is on pages E-25 and E-26 of this appendix. Based on this output one can observe that the value of the coefficient of determination (R^2) is rather significant (≈ 0.85). This number represents the percentage of total variation in the failure rate sampled that is explained by the regression surface. But, since the p-values of hypothesis tests (I) and (II) are all higher than 0.15 (the predetermined significance level), and the values of the standard deviations of the parameter estimates are also quite high, it is suggested that all of the variables x_1, x_2,..., x_5 are too insignificant to be included in the model. This phenomenon occurred as the result of too few data points (nine observations) involved in the regression analysis (with five independent variables). Therefore, either stepwise regression or principal components analysis is preferable.

Most of the regression analyses in this section are similar to each other. The list of formulas for the items that appeared in the outputs of the regression analyses were taken from the SAS/STAT user's guide and are included in this appendix starting on page E-18.

Using the stepwise regression technique, a new regression model for the requirements analysis phase involving only x_1 and x_2 was developed. It can be written as follows:

$$Y = 11.46159363 + 12.5764363\ x_1 - 0.08453592\ x_2$$

where Y is restricted to nonnegative values.

(Note: The complete output of the stepwise regression analysis for this phase is provided on pages E-27 through E-30)

The value of R^2 of each variable involved in the final stepwise regression model for requirements analysis is substantial, and all the p-values of hypothesis tests (I) and (II) are smaller than 0.15. Note that x_1, x_2 and x_3 are highly correlated, as well as x_4 and x_5 (based on the correlation matrix on page E-21), and the values of the standard deviations of the parameter estimates are high (for y-intercept and x_1). This fact suggested that the above stepwise regression model is inferior to the model that is produced using principal components analysis. This is because stepwise regression does not work well with correlated variables, whereas principal components does.

Principal components are linear combinations of the original variables; i.e., if P_i is a principal component of $\{x_1,...,x_5\}$, for i=1,2,...,5, then P_i is of the form

$$P_i = a_{1i}x_1 + a_{2i}x_2 + ... + a_{5i}x_5$$

The coefficient a_{ki} is the kth component of the ith normalized eigenvector of the sample variance-covariance matrix. For example, in the case i=1,

$$P_1 = 0.008548x_1 + 0.99488x_2 + 0.100704x_3 - 0.000135x_4 + 0.000478x_5$$

The list of eigenvalues and normalized eigenvectors of the estimated variance-covariance matrix for the requirements analysis phase is provided on page E-31.

Since the first eigenvalue is greater than 99.7% of the sum of all eigenvalues, it is only needed to form a linear regression model involving the software failure rate (dependent variable) and P_1, the first principal component (independent variables).

The data set of P_1 was formed based on the original data set of x_1, x_2,...,x_5. The linear regression model (based on principal components analysis) can be summarized as

$$Y = 18.04246146 + 0.05053379 \ P_1$$

where

$$P_1 = 0.008548x_1 + 0.99488x_2 + 0.100704x_3 - 0.000135x_4 + 0.000478x_5$$

and Y is restricted to nonnegative values.

On page E-33, the output of the least squares regression analysis of Y and P_1 is provided. All components in the column titled "Prob > |T|" and the p-value of hypothesis test (I) are much less than the 0.15 significance level. This indicates that the y-intercept and P_1 variables are relevant to the model. The minor disadvantages of this model are that $R^2 = 0.4064$, (i.e., only 40.7% of the total variation in the failure rate sampled is explained by the regression surface), and that the standard deviation of the y-intercept is large.

Although the stepwise regression method, in this case, gives a model with better values for R^2 than principal components analysis, the fact that only x_1 and x_2 are chosen by the stepwise method (even though these two variables are highly correlated) suggests that the stepwise model should not be preferred.

E.1.1.2 Preliminary Design Phase

In addition to the variables identified in the requirements analysis phase, five more variables are involved in the regression analysis in this phase. They are:

x_6: number of errors in preliminary design documents
x_7: number of computer software components (CSCs)
x_8: number of units (or Ada packages) in the design structure
x_9: Pages in design documents (SDDs)
x_{10}: Man-months for preliminary design

It is clear that a valid least squares regression cannot be obtained here, since the number of observations is less than the number of independent variables. So, only stepwise regression and principal components analysis were performed.

The stepwise regression technique in this case chooses x_1 and x_9 to be in the final stepwise regression model. This model can be written as:

$$Y = 11.91767775 + 14.11517877 \ x_1 - 0.13589515 \ x_9$$

where Y is restricted to nonnegative values.

The output for stepwise regression analysis for the preliminary design phase can be found on pages E-35 through E-38. The value for R^2 is high, and the components in the column titled "Prob > |T|", as well as the value of "Prob > F", on page E-37 are all below the predetermined level of significance. Since the stepwise procedure only allows a variable to stay or enter the regression model if that variable meets the 0.15 significance level, the fact that variables $x_2, \ldots, x_8, x_{10}$ are not in the final stepwise model shows that they are irrelevant to the model.

Since there are 10 independent variables involved in the stepwise analysis, and only 9 observations are available, the MSE for the full model cannot be computed. Therefore, C_p, the Mallow's statistic cannot be computed; so, only R^2 is used in decision-making for the model.

From the correlation matrix, it can be detected that most of the variables in $\{x_1, \ldots, x_{10}\}$ are highly correlated to each other, especially x_1 and x_9. This indicates that the stepwise regression model may not be good in terms of predicting the software failure rate. Other factors used to examine the validity of the stepwise regression model are the standard deviations of parameter estimates. Since these values of the y-intercept and x_1 are high, it is further evidence that the stepwise regression model may not be adequate to describe the relationship between software failure rate and software characteristics which are available after the preliminary design phase.

In order to perform principal components regression analysis, the eigenvalues and eigenvectors of the estimated variance-covariance matrix of $x_1, \ldots, x_{10}$ and y were computed and are shown on page E-41. Since the sum of the first two eigenvalues is greater than 99.7% of the sum of all the eigenvalues, only P_1 and P_2 will be involved in the principal components regression model. Recall that

$$\frac{\sum_{i=1}^{2} \lambda_i}{\sum_{i=1}^{10} \lambda_i} \geq 0.998$$

means 99.8% of the total variation of the sampled software failure rate can be explained by only two principal components, P_1 and P_2.

The data set for P_1 and P_2 can be easily computed by using the following formulas:

$$P_1 = 0.006892x_1 + 0.795885x_2 + 0.07994x_3 - 0.000288x_4 + 0.000323x_5 + 0.000094x_6 + 0.004297x_7 + 0.012784x_8 + 0.59995x_9 + 0.002784x_{10}$$

$$P_2 = 0.032916x_1 + 0.448504x_2 + 0.562345x_3 + 0.115656x_4 + 0.077519x_5 - 0.004974x_6 + 0.071291x_7 + 0.014141x_8 - 0.671443x_9 + 0.077466x_{10}$$

The output of the least squares regression model for Y, P_1 and P_2 can be found on pages E-42 and E-43.

The value of R^2 (the coefficient of determination) is similar to that of the principal components regression model for the requirements analysis phase. For a 0.15 level of significance, the values of the components in the column titled "Prob > $|T|$" and the values of standard deviations of parameter estimates imply that only the y-intercept and P_1 are relevant to the regression model. Since the value of "Prob > F" is bigger than 0.15, the null hypothesis of (I) should be rejected (i.e., all coefficients of independent variables must be 0).

This phenomenon may occur as the result of achieving too large a number for the total variation of software failure rate which is explained by the regression model. Thus, a new regression model that only involves Y and P_1 was considered at this point. The complete output of this regression model is on page E-44. Below is the summary of the regression model with Y and P_1 as dependent and independent variables, respectively.

$$Y = 17.89874335 + 0.04016008 \; P_1$$

where

$$P_1 = 0.006892x_1 + 0.795885x_2 + 0.07994x_3 - 0.000288x_4 + 0.000323x_5 + 0.000094x_6 + 0.004297x_7 + 0.012784x_8 + 0.59995x_9 + 0.002784x_{10}$$

Y is restricted to nonnegative values.

This model possesses very good statistical characteristics. For example, all p-values of hypothesis tests (I) and (II) are below 0.15 and the value of the coefficient of determination R^2 is not too small. Also, the values of the standard deviations of parameter estimates are reasonable, except for that of the y-intercept.

E.1.1.3   Detailed Design Phase

Four new variables are introduced for this phase:

x_{11}: number of errors in design documents
x_{12}: Man-months for detailed design
x_{13}: Design flaws identified after baseline
x_{14}: Design flaws identified after an internal review

The stepwise regression analysis and principal components analysis were performed to obtain different regression models. Then, after the validation task is completed, one of these regression models will be chosen.

From stepwise regression analysis, a regression model can be written as follows:

$$Y = 28.96925965 + 15.63285056x_1 + 0.2540362x_6 - 2.38561282x_8 - 0.08100319x_9 - 1.1992758x_{11}$$

where Y is restricted to nonnegative values.

The output of the stepwise regression analysis for the detailed design phase can be found on pages E-46 through E-50. Similar to previous phases, the value of R^2 is high, and the values of the components in the column titled "Prob > |T|", as well as the p-value of hypothesis testing (I) are relatively small compared to 0.15. But, since high correlations exist between the variables involved in the stepwise process, and the values of the standard deviations of parameter estimates are high (except for that of x_9) the stepwise regression model is not good for predicting the software failure rate, after the detailed design phase.

The output of the computed eigenvalues and eigenvectors of the estimated variance-covariance matrix for $x_1, \ldots, x_{14}$, Y is provided on page E-53. The first three principal components of $\{x_1, \ldots, x_{14}\}$ are selected for the regression model, since the sum of the first three eigenvalues is greater than 99.7% of the sum of all the eigenvalues for the matrix.

The least squares regression analysis involving Y, $P_1, \ldots, P_3$ can be found on pages E-55 and E-56. The principal components regression model for the detailed design phase can be written as

$$Y = 36.61996444 + 0.12930799\ P_1 - 2.4687751\ P_2 - 0.64069017\ P_3$$

where

P_1 = 0.006891x_1 + 0.795821x_2 + 0.07993x_3 - 0.000289x_4 + 0.000322x_5 + 0.000097x_6 + 0.004296x_7 + 0.012793x_8 + 0.599912x_9 + 0.002783x_{10} + 0.10963x_{11} + 0.001742x_{12} + 0.003708x_{13} - 0.003289x_{14}

P_2 = 0.010031x_1 + 0.403242x_2 + 0.485487x_3 + 0.131773x_4 + 0.07455x_5 + 0.018274x_6 + 0.077214x_7 + 0.009831x_8 - 0.595055x_9 + 0.08573x_{10} - 0.261383x_{11} + 0.113134x_{12} + 0.089211x_{13} - 0.348945x_{14}

P_3 = -0.25458x_1 + 0.016768x_2 - 0.263973x_3 + 0.202666x_4 - 0.072133x_5 + 0.62971x_6 + 0.103537x_7 - 0.120209x_8 + 0.013861x_9 + 0.106051x_{10} + 0.348472x_{11} + 0.111607x_{12} - 0.104901x_{13} - 0.490828x_{14}

where Y is restricted to nonnegative values.

Notice that in this case the value of R^2 is quite high and the components of the column titled "Prob > $|T|$" (see page E-55) are relatively lower than 0.15 (level of significance); but the values of the standard deviations of y-intercept, P_2 and P_3 are high. Hence, further examination is required to validate the credibility of the above model.

E.1.1.4 Coding and Unit Test Phase

Below is the list of the additional variables that were considered in the regression analysis after the Coding and Unit Testing phase:

x_{16}: Faults found through code reviews
x_{17}: Programmer skill level (average years of experience)
x_{18}: number of units undergoing review
x_{19}: Average number of source LOC per unit
x_{20}: number of branches in a typical unit
x_{21}: Percent of branches covered
x_{22}: Nesting Depth average
x_{23}: number of times a unit is unit-tested
x_{24}: Man-months for Coding and Unit test
x_{25}: Defects identified from walkthroughs and reviews

(Note: x_{25} = x_{13} + x_{14} + x_{16}; therefore, only x_{25} was considered in the regression analysis.)

As in the previous phases, the stepwise regression and principal components analyses were also performed for the coding and unit test phase.

From stepwise regression analysis, the regression model can be described as follows:

$$Y = 23.91 + 16.4x_1 + 0.33x_6 - 2.02x_8 - 0.10x_9 - 1.46x_{11} - 1.33x_{17} - 0.004x_{18} + 12.99x_{21}$$

(In case the calculated value of Y is negative, this number should not be used as the predicted software failure rate.)

The stepwise regression analysis can be found on pages E-57 through E-61. Notice that the F values for the selected variables in Step 8 are extremely large (999999.99), which indicates that this model is not reliable in describing the relationship between software failure rate and software characteristics. Despite this, an attempt was made to perform the least squares regression analysis based on Y, x_1, x_6, x_8, x_9, x_{11}, x_{17}, x_{18}, x_{21}. The results can be found on page E-62. It is not surprising that this attempt failed for the same reason as mentioned above. A stepwise regression model cannot be formed at this point, and the model was therefore discarded.

Based on the results of eigenvalues of the estimated variance-covariance matrix of $x_1, \ldots, x_{12}, \ldots, x_{17}, \ldots, x_{25}$, only the first principal component is selected to be in the regression model (for the principal components analysis approach).

The principal components regression analysis gives

$$Y = 38.02688694 - 2.58584501P_1$$

where

$$P_1 = -0.00001x_1 - 0.000851x_2 - 0.000137x_3 - 0.000021x_4 - 0.000015x_5 - 0.000025x_6 - 0.000017x_7 - 0.00002x_8 - 0.000631x_9 - 0.00017x_{10} + 0.000014x_{11} - 0.00002x_{12} - 0.000012x_{17} + 0.005288x_{18} - 0.000125x_{19} - 0.000108x_{20} - 0.000x_{21} + 0.000004x_{22} - 0.000013x_{23} - 0.000019x_{24} - 0.000117x_{25}$$

and Y is restricted to nonnegative values.

In this case, the value of R^2 is very low (0.0748, i.e., only 7.48% of the total variation of the sampled software failure rates can be explained by the above model). Also, since the second component in the column titled "Prob > |T|" is much greater than 0.15 (level of significance), and the values of the standard deviations of parameter estimates are high, P_1 is not "relevant" to the regression model. But, P_1 cannot be deleted from the model; if it is deleted, there will be no model to consider.

E.1.2 <u>Regression Models Based on Correlations among Independent Variables</u>

Since the regressors $x_1, \ldots x_{25}$ are correlated, it is difficult to disentangle the effects of one regressor from those of another, and the parameter estimates may be highly dependent on which regressors are used in the model.   Instead of formulating new regression models based on the progress made in software development, another way to approach the task of finding the relationship between software failure rate and software characteristics was used. This method is discussed below.

Independent variables are assigned to different sets such that the elements of a set are highly correlated to one another.   In this case, based on the correlation matrix on pages E-21 through E-24, it was determined that independent variables can be divided into four disjoint sets { $x_1, x_2, x_3, x_8, x_9, x_{23}, x_{25}$ } , { $x_4, x_5, x_7, x_{10}, x_{12}, x_{18}, x_{19}, x_{20}, x_{22}, x_{24}$ } , { x_{11}, x_{17} } , { x_6 } , { x_{21} }. (Some of these independent variables have been normalized, so that the mere effect of program size is canceled out.

Next, after performing principal components analysis for each set with more than one element, regression models can be formulated using either the method of least squares or stepwise regression analysis.   It was determined that only the first principal component of each set needed to be involved in regression analyses, since the fewest number of independent variables involved in regression models as possible is desired. (Note that in case of a singleton, the element in that set is its first principal component.)

This approach was expected to yield reasonable regression models, since the independent variables involved are uncorrelated.

Notation:

$A = \{ x_1, x_2, x_3, x_8, x_9, x_{23}, x_{25} \}$
$B = \{ x_4, x_5, x_7, x_{10}, x_{12}, x_{18}, x_{19}, x_{20}, x_{22}, x_{24} \}$
$C = \{ x_{11}, x_{17} \}$
$D = \{ x_6 \}$
$E = \{ x_{21} \}$

P_A: the first principal component of A
P_B: the first principal component of B
P_C: the first principal component of C
P_D: the first principal component of D; in this case $P_D = x_6$
P_E: the first principal component of E; in this case $P_E = x_{21}$

A new data set for P_A, P_B, P_C, P_D, P_E was computed based on the original data of $x_1, \ldots, x_{25}$.

E.1.2.1 Least Squares Methods Applied to Principal Components

Below is the formula of the regression model involving Y, $P_A, \ldots, P_E$ which is produced by using the Least Squares method

$$Y = 303.72 + 0.049\ P_A + 0.015\ P_B + 0.041\ P_C - 0.647\ P_D - 290.93\ P_E$$

where

$P_A = 0.006891x_1 + 0.795466x_2 + 0.079926x_3 + 0.012782x_8 + 0.599617x_9$
$\quad + 0.008398x_{23} + 0.032006x_{25}$

$P_B = -\ 0.004142x_4 - 0.002728x_5 - 0.003202x_7 - 0.003143x_{10} -$
$\quad 0.003841x_{12} + 0.999722x_{18} - 0.013048x_{19} - 0.017678x_{20} +$
$\quad 0.00063x_{22} - 0.003551x_{24}$

$P_C = 0.981742x_{11} - 0.190218x_{17}$

$P_D = x_6$

$P_E = x_{21}$

and Y is restricted to nonnegative values.

Although the value of R^2 for this regression model is large (0.7455)--i.e., a large percentage of the total variation in the failure rate sampled can be explained by the regression surface, the p-value of the hypothesis test (I) and most of those of hypothesis test (II) are much bigger than 0.15 significance level.   This suggests that all the coefficients of the independent variables in the regression model should be 0.   Thus, the model is not adequate to describe the relationship between software failure rate and its characteristics.

Notice that all p-values of hypothesis test (II), on page E-79, are much greater than 0.15 (the predetermined significance level), except for the p-value of the hypothesis test for P_A. This indicates that another regression model which only involves Y and P_A needed to be considered.

This model can be summarized as follows:

$$Y = 17.88125956 + 0.04011814\ P_A$$

where P_A is defined previously.   (In case the calculated value of Y is negative, this number should not be used as the predicted software failure rate, in this case.)

Although the value of R^2 is smaller than that of the regression model which involved Y, $P_A, ..., P_E$, this model is preferable since the all p-values of both hypothesis tests (I) and (II) are lower than 0.15 (the predetermined significance level), also, the value of the standard deviations of parameter estimates is reasonably small.

Since P_A is a linear combination of x_1, x_2, x_3, x_8, x_9, x_{23}, x_{25}, and the complete data of these independent variables will not be available until after the Code and Unit Test phase of software development, this regression model cannot be used in the early stages of software development.

E.1.2.2 Stepwise Regression Applied to Principal Components

Another way to correctly eliminate some of the independent variables in $\{P_A, ..., P_E\}$, besides examining the p-values of hypothesis test (II), is to perform stepwise regression analysis.

As mentioned earlier, stepwise regression allows a variable to enter or leave the regression model based on the value of R^2 and Mallow's statistic C_p. The result of the stepwise regression analysis in this case is:

$$Y = 27.78996571 + 0.03884431\ P_A - 1.20635275\ P_D$$

where

$$P_A = 0.006891x_1 + 0.795466x_2 + 0.079926x_3 + 0.012782x_8 + 0.599617x_9 + 0.008398x_{23} + 0.032006x_{25}$$

and $P_D = x_6$. (In case the calculated value of Y is negative, this number should not be used as the predicted software failure rate, in this case.)

Although the values of R^2 and p-values are reasonably good, the values of the standard deviations of parameter estimates of the y-intercept and P_D are substantial. Therefore, this regression model is not adequate in term of describing the relationship between software failure rate and software characteristics.

E.2 Multivariate Nonlinear Regression Models Development

Based on the scatter plots of Y versus x_i, $i = 1, 2, ..., 25$, it was noticed that Y is inversely proportional to each of the following independent variables, x_6, x_{11}, x_{13}, x_{14}, x_{16}, x_{23}. Therefore, in this section, new regression models of software failure rate and software characteristics are formulated based on

$x_1, \ldots, x_5, x_7, \ldots, x_{10}, x_{12}, x_{15}, x_{17}, \ldots, x_{22}, x_{24}, x_{25}$ and $1/x_6$, $1/x_{11}$, $1/x_{13}$, $1/x_{14}$, $1/x_{16}$, $1/x_{23}$. (Recall that some of the independent variables were normalized based on KLOC.)

There were more than one regression model which were built for each phase of the software development by using the least squares method, stepwise regression, and principal components analysis. The number of regressors involved in the regression analysis for each software development phase, in this section, is the same as that in section E.1.

These regression models are almost identical to or possess the same characteristics as the corresponding models in the discussion on Multivariate Linear Regression Models. Therefore, creating new regression models based on the inverse proportional relationship between Y and x_i , where i belongs to {6, 11, 13 ,14, 16 ,23}, results in negligible improvements to the linear regression models. Thus, the models in this section can be ignored in the process of validation.

E.3 NOTATION

- n: number of observations
- k: number of independent variables in a regression model
- y_i: actual value of software failure rate of the i-th observation; i:= 1,2,...,n.
- $\hat{y}_i$: predicted value of software failure rate of the i-th observation; i:= 1,2,...,n.
- b_i: estimated coefficient of the i-th independent variable; i:= 0,1,2,...,n; b_0: estimated y-intercept
- s_{b_i}: estimated standard deviation of the random variable b_i; i:= 0,1,2,...,n

$$\text{Dep. Mean}: \quad \bar{y} = \frac{\sum_{i=1}^{n} y_i}{n}$$

$$\text{Sum of Squares Model} = SSR$$

$$= \sum_{i=1}^{n} (\hat{y}_i - \bar{y})^2$$

$$\text{Sum of Squares Error} = SSE$$

$$= \sum_{i=1}^{n} (y_i - \hat{y}_i)^2$$

$$\text{Sum of Squares C Total} = SST$$

$$= SSR + SSE$$

$$\text{Mean Square Model} = MSTR$$

$$= \frac{SSR}{k}$$

$$\text{Mean Square Error} = \frac{SSE}{n-(k+1)}$$

$$F - Value\ (Model) = \frac{MSTR}{MSE}\ ;$$

this is the F-statistic of the hypothesis testing with

(I) H_0: $b_0 = b_1 = \ldots = b_k = 0$
          H_1: $\exists$ at least one $b_i \ni b_i \neq 0$ where $0 \leq i \leq k$

- Prob > F (Model): p-value of the above hypothesis testing (I); this is the significance probability, or the probability of getting a greater F-statistic than that observed if the hypothesis in (I) is true.

$$Root\ MSE = \sqrt{MSE}$$

Root MSE is an estimate of the standard deviation of the error term.

- C.V: coefficient of variation; this number expresses the standard deviation of the error term in unitless value.

C.V = (100 * Root MSE) / Dep. Mean

- R^2: coefficient of determination; a measure between 0 and 1 which indicates the portion of the (corrected) total variation that is attributed to the fit rather than left to residual error.

R^2 = SSR / SST

- Adj R-sq: the adjusted R^2, this is a version of R^2 that has been adjusted for degrees of freedom.

Adj R-sq = 1 - [((n - i)(1 - R^2)) / (n - p)];

where i is equal to 1 if there is an intercept, 0 otherwise; and p is the number of parameters in the model.

The parameter estimates and associated statistics are all printed; and they include the following:

- The parameter estimates

- the Standard Error, the estimate of the standard deviation of the parameter estimate

- T for H_0 Parameter = 0 gives the T-ratio of hypothesis tests with

(II) H_0: b_i = 0
            H_1: $b_i \neq 0$;   where $0 \leq i \leq k$

$$T\text{-}ratio = \frac{b_i}{s_{b_i}}$$

- Prob > |T| column on page !!1!!! provides the p-value for each of the hypothesis test in (II). This is the two-tailed significance probability, or the probability that a t statistic would obtain a greater absolute value than that observed given that the true parameter is zero.

CORRELATION MATRIX

	X1	X2	X3	X4	X5	X6
X1	1.0000	0.9362	0.8452	-0.3536	-0.1201	-0.2176
X2	0.9362	1.0000	0.9635	-0.0651	0.1014	-0.0439
X3	0.8452	0.9635	1.0000	0.1145	0.2110	0.0347
X4	-0.3536	-0.0651	0.1145	1.0000	0.6895	0.4298
X5	-0.1201	0.1014	0.2110	0.6895	1.0000	-0.1743
X6	-0.2176	-0.0439	0.0347	0.4298	-0.1743	1.0000
X7	0.2094	0.5114	0.6461	0.8147	0.6155	0.3814
X8	0.9073	0.9670	0.9496	0.0130	0.2251	-0.0898
X9	0.9411	0.9963	0.9416	-0.0932	0.0891	-0.0360
X10	-0.0041	0.3049	0.4660	0.9189	0.7586	0.3108
X11	0.4035	0.3674	0.2585	-0.3284	-0.3100	0.4513
X12	-0.1623	0.1224	0.2788	0.9134	0.9108	0.1270
X15	-0.1006	-0.3707	-0.4807	-0.6175	-0.4669	-0.3673
X17	-0.3104	-0.1035	0.0814	0.7137	0.4612	-0.0085
X18	-0.0429	-0.3204	-0.4223	-0.6001	-0.4598	-0.4065
X19	-0.4256	-0.2358	-0.0807	0.6879	0.2103	0.4592
X20	-0.3302	-0.0665	0.1197	0.8457	0.9220	0.0152
X21	0.0368	0.1637	0.2210	0.3051	0.2667	0.3339
X22	0.4056	0.1948	-0.0149	-0.8757	-0.7942	-0.0875
X23	0.7783	0.9375	0.9648	0.2588	0.4084	0.0107
X24	-0.2630	0.0317	0.2346	0.9257	0.8501	0.2057
X25	0.5060	0.6775	0.7958	0.5172	0.2281	0.4316

CORRELATION MATRIX (con't)

	X7	X8	X9	X10	X11	X12
X1	0.2094	0.9073	0.9411	-0.0041	0.4035	-0.1623
X2	0.5114	0.9670	0.9963	0.3049	0.3674	0.1224
X3	0.6461	0.9496	0.9416	0.4660	0.2585	0.2788
X4	0.8147	0.0130	-0.0932	0.9189	-0.3284	0.9134
X5	0.6155	0.2251	0.0891	0.7586	-0.3100	0.9108
X6	0.3814	-0.0898	-0.0360	0.3108	0.4513	0.1270
X7	1.0000	0.5406	0.4829	0.9626	-0.0715	0.8360
X8	0.5406	1.0000	0.9599	0.3728	0.3060	0.2275
X9	0.4829	0.9599	1.0000	0.2732	0.4215	0.0962
X10	0.9626	0.3728	0.2732	1.0000	-0.2305	0.9476
X11	-0.0715	0.3060	0.4215	-0.2305	1.0000	-0.3468
X12	0.8360	0.2275	0.0962	0.9476	-0.3468	1.0000
X15	-0.7474	-0.3308	-0.3567	-0.7003	0.0920	-0.6153
X17	0.5725	-0.0808	-0.1668	0.6689	-0.8177	0.6621
X18	-0.7104	-0.2481	-0.3140	-0.6656	0.0002	-0.5899
X19	0.4956	-0.1399	-0.2796	0.5772	-0.3857	0.5032
X20	0.6732	0.0556	-0.1020	0.8372	-0.4753	0.9504
X21	0.3261	0.0706	0.1819	0.2933	0.3494	0.2796
X22	-0.6003	0.0643	0.2346	-0.7761	0.5157	-0.8821
X23	0.7499	0.9465	0.9234	0.6047	0.2108	0.4580
X24	0.8059	0.1392	-0.0079	0.9286	-0.3908	0.9692
X25	0.8077	0.6900	0.6493	0.6798	0.1599	0.4740

CORRELATION MATRIX

	X15	X17	X18	X19	X20	X21
X1	-0.1006	-0.3104	-0.0429	-0.4256	-0.3302	0.0368
X2	-0.3707	-0.1035	-0.3204	-0.2358	-0.0665	0.1637
X3	-0.4807	0.0814	-0.4223	-0.0807	0.1197	0.2210
X4	-0.6175	0.7137	-0.6001	0.6879	0.8457	0.3051
X5	-0.4669	0.4612	-0.4598	0.2103	0.9220	0.2667
X6	-0.3673	-0.0085	-0.4065	0.4592	0.0152	0.3339
X7	-0.7474	0.5725	-0.7104	0.4956	0.6732	0.3261
X8	-0.3308	-0.0808	-0.2481	-0.1399	0.0556	0.0706
X9	-0.3567	-0.1668	-0.3140	-0.2796	-0.1020	0.1819
X10	-0.7003	0.6689	-0.6656	0.5772	0.8372	0.2933
X11	0.0920	-0.8177	0.0002	-0.3857	-0.4753	0.3494
X12	-0.6153	0.6621	-0.5899	0.5032	0.9504	0.2796
X15	1.0000	-0.5222	0.9756	-0.1376	-0.5186	-0.5707
X17	-0.5222	1.0000	-0.4545	0.5969	0.6913	0.0000
X18	0.9756	-0.4545	1.0000	-0.0563	-0.4951	-0.7011
X19	-0.1376	0.5969	-0.0563	1.0000	0.4933	-0.3709
X20	-0.5186	0.6913	-0.4951	0.4933	1.0000	0.2078
X21	-0.5707	0.0000	-0.7011	-0.3709	0.2078	1.0000
X22	0.4671	-0.7217	0.4395	-0.5073	-0.9286	-0.2887
X23	-0.5400	0.1381	-0.4858	-0.0231	0.2782	0.2343
X24	-0.6024	0.7206	-0.5728	0.6015	0.9699	0.2492
X25	-0.6567	0.3210	-0.5954	0.2408	0.2867	0.4182

CORRELATION MATRIX (con't)

	X22	X23	X24	X25
X1	0.4056	0.7783	-0.2630	0.5060
X2	0.1948	0.9375	0.0317	0.6775
X3	-0.0149	0.9648	0.2346	0.7958
X4	-0.8757	0.2588	0.9257	0.5172
X5	-0.7942	0.4084	0.8501	0.2281
X6	-0.0875	0.0107	0.2057	0.4317
X7	-0.6003	0.7499	0.8059	0.8077
X8	0.0643	0.9465	0.1392	0.6900
X9	0.2346	0.9234	-0.0079	0.6493
X10	-0.7761	0.6047	0.9286	0.6798
X11	0.5157	0.2108	-0.3908	0.1599
X12	-0.8821	0.4580	0.9692	0.4740
X15	0.4671	-0.5400	-0.6024	-0.6567
X17	-0.7217	0.1381	0.7206	0.3210
X18	0.4395	-0.4858	-0.5728	-0.5954
X19	-0.5073	-0.0231	0.6015	0.2408
X20	-0.9286	0.2782	0.9699	0.2867
X21	-0.2887	0.2343	0.2492	0.4182
X22	1.0000	-0.1353	-0.9220	-0.3584
X23	-0.1353	1.0000	0.3734	0.7711
X24	-0.9220	0.3734	1.0000	0.4698
X25	-0.3584	0.7711	0.4698	1.0000

REQUIREMENTS ANALYSIS PHASE: Least Squares Method

DEP VARIABLE: Y

ANALYSIS OF VARIANCE

SOURCE	DF	SUM OF SQUARES	MEAN SQUARE	F VALUE	PROB>F
MODEL	5	3099.68840	619.93768	3.195	0.1839
ERROR	3	582.01382	194.00461		
C TOTAL	8	3681.70222			

ROOT MSE	13.92855	R-SQUARE	0.8419	
DEP MEAN	24.25556	ADJ R-SQ	0.5784	
C.V.	57.42418			

PARAMETER ESTIMATES

VARIABLE	DF	PARAMETER ESTIMATE	STANDARD ERROR	T FOR H0: PARAMETER=0
INTERCEP	1	5.12618938	13.38038672	0.383
X1	1	15.71786692	8.32103039	1.889
X2	1	-0.17215913	0.13550831	-1.270
X3	1	0.51992600	0.85056011	0.611
X4	1	0.38956606	2.53978622	0.153
X5	1	-0.23386176	2.43926235	-0.096

VARIABLE	DF	PROB > |T|
INTERCEP	1	0.7272
X1	1	0.1553
X2	1	0.2935
X3	1	0.5842
X4	1	0.8878
X5	1	0.9297

OBS	ID	ACTUAL	PREDICT VALUE	STD ERR PREDICT	LOWER95% MEAN
1	1.53043	36.0000	29.8926	6.8038	8.2395
2	0.75	31.0000	15.3818	8.9610	-13.1366
3	9.82125	64.0000	64.0621	13.9284	19.7350
4	2.30714	48.0000	45.9538	12.9698	4.6773
5	1.1575	10.0000	23.1440	6.8621	1.3053
6	0.94162	8.0000	18.5746	7.3890	-4.9410
7	0	6.5000	3.8082	13.8177	-40.1666
8	0	6.0000	8.1040	13.7796	-35.7495
9	0	8.8000	9.3788	13.8826	-34.8026
10	13.6698	.	234.4	111.5	-120.5
11	1.47059	.	21.9711	7.7646	-2.7396

OBS	ID	UPPER95% MEAN	LOWER95% PREDICT	UPPER95% PREDICT	RESIDUAL
1	1.53043	51.5458	-19.4409	79.2262	6.1074
2	0.75	43.9001	-37.3272	68.0907	15.6182
3	9.82125	108.4	1.3737	126.8	-0.0621
4	2.30714	87.2304	-14.6159	106.5	2.0462
5	1.1575	44.9827	-26.2713	72.5592	-13.1440
6	0.94162	42.0902	-31.6043	68.7535	-10.5746
7	0	47.7830	-58.6315	66.2480	2.6918
8	0	51.9576	-54.2503	70.4584	-2.1040
9	0	53.5603	-53.2066	71.9643	-0.5788
10	13.6698	589.4	-123.3	592.1	.
11	1.47059	46.6817	-28.7789	72.7210	.

OBS	ID	STD ERR RESIDUAL
1	1.53043	12.1537
2	0.75	10.6633
3	9.82125	0.0653
4	2.30714	5.0782
5	1.1575	12.1209
6	0.94162	11.8071
7	0	1.7539
8	0	2.0317
9	0	1.1302
10	13.6698	.
11	1.47059	.

SUM OF RESIDUALS   1.57652E-14
SUM OF SQUARED RESIDUALS   582.0138
PREDICTED RESID SS (PRESS)   8041231

REQUIREMENTS ANALYSIS PHASE: Stepwise Selections

STEPWISE REGRESSION PROCEDURE FOR DEPENDENT VARIABLE Y

WARNING: 2 OBSERVATIONS DELETED DUE TO MISSING VALUES.

NOTE: SLENTRY AND SLSTAY HAVE BEEN SET TO
      .15 FOR THE STEPWISE TECHNIQUE.

STEP 1   VARIABLE X1 ENTERED   R SQUARE = 0.67484762
                                          C(P) =   1.17054544

	DF	SUM OF SQUARES	MEAN SQUARE	F	PROB>F
REGRESSION	1	2484.58798182	2484.587982	14.53	0.0066
ERROR	7	1197.11424040	171.016320		
TOTAL	8	3681.70222222			

	B VALUE	STD ERROR	TYPE II SS	F	PROB>F
INTERCEPT	13.81140806				
X1	5.69406301	1.49387362	2484.587982	14.53	0.0066

BOUNDS ON CONDITION NUMBER: 1,   1

STEP 2   VARIABLE X2 ENTERED   R SQUARE = 0.81369325
                                          C(P) =   0.53561689

	DF	SUM OF SQUARES	MEAN SQUARE	F	PROB>F
REGRESSION	2	2995.77625834	1497.888129	13.10	0.0065
ERROR	6	685.92596389	114.320994		
TOTAL	8	3681.70222222			

	B VALUE	STD ERROR	TYPE II SS	F	PROB>F
INTERCEPT	11.46159363				
X1	12.57643630	3.47633170	1496.231406	13.09	0.0111
X2	-0.08453592	0.03997734	511.188277	4.47	0.0789

BOUNDS ON CONDITION NUMBER: 8.100769,   32.40308

NO OTHER VARIABLES MET THE 0.1500 SIGNIFICANCE LEVEL FOR ENTRY

SUMMARY OF STEPWISE REGRESSION PROCEDURE FOR DEPENDENT VARIABLE Y

	VARIABLE		NUMBER	PARTIAL	MODEL	
STEP	ENTERED	REMOVED	IN	R**2	R**2	C(P)
1	X1		1	0.6748	0.6748	1.17055
2	X2		2	0.1388	0.8137	0.53562

	VARIABLE			
STEP	ENTERED	REMOVED	F	PROB>F
1	X1		14.5284	0.0066
2	X2		4.4715	0.0789

REQUIREMENTS ANALYSIS PHASE: Stepwise Regression Analysis

DEP VARIABLE: Y

ANALYSIS OF VARIANCE

SOURCE	DF	SUM OF SQUARES	MEAN SQUARE	F VALUE	PROB>F
MODEL	2	2995.77626	1497.88813	13.102	0.0065
ERROR	6	685.92596	114.32099		
C TOTAL	8	3681.70222			

ROOT MSE	10.6921	R-SQUARE	0.8137	
DEP MEAN	24.25556	ADJ R-SQ	0.7516	
C.V.	44.08103			

PARAMETER ESTIMATES

VARIABLE	DF	PARAMETER ESTIMATE	STANDARD ERROR	T FOR H0: PARAMETER=0
INTERCEP	1	11.46159363	4.35386975	2.633
X1	1	12.57643630	3.47633170	3.618
X2	1	-0.08453592	0.03997734	-2.115

VARIABLE	DF	PROB > $|T|$
INTERCEP	1	0.0389
X1	1	0.0111
X2	1	0.0789

OBS	ID	ACTUAL	PREDICT VALUE	STD ERR PREDICT	LOWER95% MEAN
1	1.53043	36.0000	30.3676	5.1568	17.7494
2	0.75	31.0000	19.3300	3.8476	9.9152
3	9.82125	64.0000	64.4400	10.6835	38.2983
4	2.30714	48.0000	40.0666	7.1778	22.5031
5	1.1575	10.0000	25.5450	4.3932	14.7952
6	0.94162	8.0000	22.1894	3.9907	12.4245
7	0	6.5000	6.3434	5.4949	-7.1021
8	0	6.0000	4.0762	6.2383	-11.1883
9	0	8.8000	5.9417	5.6189	-7.8072
10	13.6698	.	182.9	45.6505	71.1989
11	1.47059	.	24.9837	3.8277	15.6176

OBS	ID	UPPER95% MEAN	LOWER95% PREDICT	UPPER95% PREDICT	RESIDUAL
1	1.53043	42.9857	1.3210	59.4141	5.6324
2	0.75	28.7449	-8.4751	47.1351	11.6700
3	9.82125	90.5817	27.4553	101.4	-0.4400
4	2.30714	57.6301	8.5553	71.5779	7.9334
5	1.1575	36.2947	-2.7400	53.8300	-15.5450
6	0.94162	31.9543	-5.7362	50.1150	-14.1894
7	0	19.7889	-23.0720	35.7588	0.1566
8	0	19.3408	-26.2139	34.3663	1.9238
9	0	19.6906	-23.6136	35.4970	2.8583
10	13.6698	294.6	68.1760	297.6	.
11	1.47059	34.3497	-2.8049	52.7723	.

OBS	ID	STD ERR RESIDUAL
1	1.53043	9.3664
2	0.75	9.9758
3	9.82125	0.4280
4	2.30714	7.9246
5	1.1575	9.7479
6	0.94162	9.9194
7	0	9.1721
8	0	8.6836
9	0	9.0967
10	13.6698	.
11	1.47059	.

SUM OF RESIDUALS	1.84297E-14
SUM OF SQUARED RESIDUALS	685.926
PREDICTED RESID SS (PRESS)	76527.44

REQUIREMENTS ANALYSIS PHASE: Principal Component Analysis

PRINCIPAL COMPONENT ANALYSIS

11 OBSERVATIONS
5 VARIABLES

SIMPLE STATISTICS

	X1	X2	X3	X4	X5
MEAN	2.87712	105.297	20.0766	2.83031	2.59865
ST DEV	4.52637	243.706	26.7754	3.99664	3.05383

COVARIANCES

	X1	X2	X3	X4	X5
X1	20.488	507.627	76.7436	−6.88532	4.59364
X2	507.627	59392.6	6000.55	−9.22677	26.4418
X3	76.7436	6000.55	716.922	11.1813	23.2099
X4	−6.88532	−9.22677	11.1813	15.9731	5.96383
X5	4.59364	26.4418	23.2099	5.96383	9.32588

TOTAL VARIANCE=60155.27

	EIGENVALUE	DIFFERENCE	PROPORTION
CUMULATIVE			
PRIN1	60004.3	59883.3	0.997491
0.99749			
PRIN2	121.0	98.2	0.002012
0.99950			
PRIN3	22.9	17.3	0.000380
0.99988			
PRIN4	5.6	4.2	0.000093
0.99998			
PRIN5	1.4	.	0.000024
1.00000			

EIGENVECTORS

	PRIN1	PRIN2	PRIN3	PRIN4	PRIN5
X1	0.008548	0.229267	-.593818	0.443844	0.630671
X2	0.994880	-.097623	0.003010	0.024948	0.007280
X3	0.100704	0.944222	0.020841	-.287915	-.122369
X4	-.000135	0.104725	0.782781	0.146934	0.595565
X5	0.000478	0.188107	0.184906	0.835401	-.482213

REQUIREMENTS ANALYSIS PHASE: Least Squares Method
(using Principal Components)

DEP VARIABLE: Y

ANALYSIS OF VARIANCE

SOURCE	DF	SUM OF SQUARES	MEAN SQUARE	F VALUE	PROB>F
MODEL	1	1496.13872	1496.13872	4.792	0.0648
ERROR	7	2185.56350	312.22336		
C TOTAL	8	3681.70222			

ROOT MSE	17.66984	R-SQUARE	0.4064	
DEP MEAN	24.25556	ADJ R-SQ	0.3216	
C.V.	72.84864			

PARAMETER ESTIMATES

VARIABLE	DF	PARAMETER ESTIMATE	STANDARD ERROR	T FOR H0: PARAMETER=0
INTERCEP	1	18.04246146	6.53814173	2.760
P1	1	0.05053379	0.02308493	2.189

VARIABLE	DF	PROB > |T|
INTERCEP	1	0.0281
P1	1	0.0648

OBS	ID	ACTUAL	PREDICT VALUE	STD ERR PREDICT	LOWER95% MEAN
1	4.31759	36.0000	18.2606	6.4955	2.9011
2	18.7646	31.0000	18.9907	6.3621	3.9467
3	839.563	64.0000	60.4687	17.5602	18.9451
4	5.83555	48.0000	18.3374	6.4808	3.0126
5	5.7755	10.0000	18.3343	6.4814	3.0082
6	13.2658	8.0000	18.7128	6.4111	3.5528
7	61.534	6.5000	21.1520	6.0582	6.8266
8	90.1651	6.0000	22.5988	5.9384	8.5567
9	67.323	8.8000	21.4445	6.0283	7.1898
10	9.03386	.	18.4990	6.4503	3.2462
11	59.2754	.	21.0379	6.0706	6.6831

OBS	ID	UPPER95% MEAN	LOWER95% PREDICT	UPPER95% PREDICT	RESIDUAL
1	4.31759	33.6202	-26.2559	62.7772	17.7394
2	18.7646	34.0347	-25.4180	63.3994	12.0093
3	839.563	102.0	1.5618	119.4	3.5313
4	5.83555	33.6621	-26.1672	62.8419	29.6626
5	5.7755	33.6605	-26.1707	62.8394	-8.3343
6	13.2658	33.8729	-25.7353	63.1610	-10.7128
7	61.534	35.4774	-23.0184	65.3224	-14.6520
8	90.1651	36.6410	-21.4805	66.6782	-16.5988
9	67.323	35.6993	-22.7030	65.5921	-12.6445
10	9.03386	33.7517	-25.9809	62.9788	.
11	59.2754	35.3927	-23.1421	65.2178	.

OBS	ID	STD ERR RESIDUAL
1	4.31759	16.4326
2	18.7646	16.4848
3	839.563	1.9652
4	5.83555	16.4384
5	5.7755	16.4382
6	13.2658	16.4657
7	61.534	16.5988
8	90.1651	16.6421
9	67.323	16.6097
10	9.03386	.
11	59.2754	.

SUM OF RESIDUALS   3.46390E-14
SUM OF SQUARED RESIDUALS   2185.563
PREDICTED RESID SS (PRESS)   84362.07

PRELIMINARY DESIGN PHASE: Stepwise Selections

STEPWISE REGRESSION PROCEDURE FOR DEPENDENT VARIABLE Y

WARNING: 2 OBSERVATIONS DELETED DUE TO MISSING VALUES.

NOTE: SLENTRY AND SLSTAY HAVE BEEN SET TO
      .15 FOR THE STEPWISE TECHNIQUE.

STEP 1   VARIABLE X1 ENTERED   R SQUARE = 0.67484762
                                       C(P) = .

	DF	SUM OF SQUARES	MEAN SQUARE	F	PROB>F
REGRESSION	1	2484.58798182	2484.587982	14.53	0.0066
ERROR	7	1197.11424040	171.016320		
TOTAL	8	3681.70222222			

	B VALUE	STD ERROR	TYPE II SS	F	PROB>F
INTERCEPT	13.81140806				
X1	5.69406301	1.49387362	2484.587982	14.53	0.0066

BOUNDS ON CONDITION NUMBER: 1,   1

STEP 2   VARIABLE X9 ENTERED   R SQUARE = 0.86541068
                                       C(P) = .

	DF	SUM OF SQUARES	MEAN SQUARE	F	PROB>F
REGRESSION	2	3186.18444000	1593.092220	19.29	0.0024
ERROR	6	495.51778222	82.586297		
TOTAL	8	3681.70222222			

	B VALUE	STD ERROR	TYPE II SS	F	PROB>F
INTERCEPT	11.91767775				
X1	14.11517877	3.07005978	1745.770281	21.14	0.0037
X9	-0.13589515	0.04662451	701.596458	8.50	0.0268

BOUNDS ON CONDITION NUMBER: 8.745719,   34.98288

NO OTHER VARIABLES MET THE 0.1500 SIGNIFICANCE LEVEL FOR ENTRY

SUMMARY OF STEPWISE REGRESSION PROCEDURE FOR DEPENDENT VARIABLE Y

	VARIABLE		NUMBER	PARTIAL	MODEL	
STEP	ENTERED	REMOVED	IN	R**2	R**2	C(P)
1	X1		1	0.6748	0.6748	.
2	X9		2	0.1906	0.8654	.

	VARIABLE			
STEP	ENTERED	REMOVED	F	PROB>F
1	X1		14.5284	0.0066
2	X9		8.4953	0.0268

PRELIMINARY DESIGN PHASE: Stepwise Regression Analysis

DEP VARIABLE: Y

ANALYSIS OF VARIANCE

SOURCE	DF	SUM OF SQUARES	MEAN SQUARE	F VALUE	PROB>F
MODEL	2	3186.18444	1593.09222	19.290	0.0024
ERROR	6	495.51778	82.58629704		
C TOTAL	8	3681.70222			

ROOT MSE	9.0877	R-SQUARE	0.8654	
DEP MEAN	24.25556	ADJ R-SQ	0.8205	
C.V.	37.46647			

PARAMETER ESTIMATES

VARIABLE	DF	PARAMETER ESTIMATE	STANDARD ERROR	T FOR H0: PARAMETER=0
INTERCEP	1	11.91767775	3.63650384	3.277
X1	1	14.11517877	3.07005978	4.598
X9	1	-0.13589515	0.04662451	-2.915

VARIABLE	DF	PROB > $|T|$
INTERCEP	1	0.0169
X1	1	0.0037
X9	1	0.0268

OBS	ID	ACTUAL	PREDICT VALUE	STD ERR PREDICT	LOWER95% MEAN
1	1.53043	36.0000	33.3983	4.8157	21.6148
2	0.75	31.0000	19.3139	3.2591	11.3392
3	9.82125	64.0000	63.5265	9.0808	41.3065
4	2.30714	48.0000	43.9981	6.6057	27.8345
5	1.1575	10.0000	24.3466	3.3913	16.0483
6	0.94162	8.0000	18.6444	3.1730	10.8804
7	0	6.5000	3.2453	5.0935	-9.2181
8	0	6.0000	5.4633	4.5832	-5.7513
9	0	8.8000	6.3636	4.3968	-4.3949
10	13.6698	.	202.2	39.9995	104.4
11	1.47059	.	22.6830	3.0574	15.2017

OBS	ID	UPPER95% MEAN	LOWER95% PREDICT	UPPER95% PREDICT	RESIDUAL
1	1.53043	45.1818	8.2323	58.5643	2.6017
2	0.75	27.2887	-4.3096	42.9375	11.6861
3	9.82125	85.7466	32.0908	94.9623	0.4735
4	2.30714	60.1616	16.5074	71.4887	4.0019
5	1.1575	32.6449	0.6119	48.0813	-14.3466
6	0.94162	26.4084	-4.9089	42.1976	-10.6444
7	0	15.7086	-22.2461	28.7367	3.2547
8	0	16.6779	-19.4414	30.3680	0.5367
9	0	17.1221	-18.3391	31.0662	2.4364
10	13.6698	300.1	101.9	302.6	.
11	1.47059	30.1643	-0.7786	46.1446	.

OBS	ID	STD ERR RESIDUAL
1	1.53043	7.7069
2	0.75	8.4832
3	9.82125	0.3528
4	2.30714	6.2411
5	1.1575	8.4312
6	0.94162	8.5158
7	0	7.5261
8	0	7.8473
9	0	7.9533
10	13.6698	.
11	1.47059	.

SUM OF RESIDUALS   9.99201E-15
SUM OF SQUARED RESIDUALS   495.5178
PREDICTED RESID SS (PRESS)   99409.95

PRELIMINARY DESIGN PHASE: Principal component analysis

PRINCIPAL COMPONENT ANALYSIS

11 OBSERVATIONS
10 VARIABLES

SIMPLE STATISTICS

	X1	X2	X3	X4	X5
MEAN	2.87712	105.297	20.0766	2.83031	2.59865
ST DEV	4.52637	243.706	26.7754	3.99664	3.05383

	X6	X7	X8	X9	X10
MEAN	7.11785	2.11232	8.02100	90.035	2.05379
ST DEV	8.39976	2.56330	4.62116	183.950	2.65265

COVARIANCES

	X1	X2	X3	X4	X5
X1	20.488	507.627	76.7436	-6.88532	4.59364
X2	507.627	59392.6	6000.55	-9.22677	26.4418
X3	76.7436	6000.55	716.922	11.1813	23.2099
X4	-6.88532	-9.22677	11.1813	15.9731	5.96383
X5	4.59364	26.4418	23.2099	5.96383	9.32588
X6	-13.2205	5.33685	-0.195098	15.8104	-6.66383
X7	-0.495505	327.701	41.0176	8.56419	3.46024
X8	15.039	949.037	108.598	-1.976	3.52059
X9	391.763	44639.8	4421.27	-34.1497	12.0465
X10	-2.19708	215.614	30.1225	9.80594	4.3422

	X6	X7	X8	X9	X10
X1	-13.2205	-0.495505	15.039	391.763	-2.19708
X2	5.33685	327.701	949.037	44639.8	215.614
X3	-0.195098	41.0176	108.598	4421.27	30.1225
X4	15.8104	8.56419	-1.976	-34.1497	9.80594
X5	-6.66383	3.46024	3.52059	12.0465	4.3422
X6	70.556	9.12385	-6.63936	7.76958	8.10716
X7	9.12385	6.5705	4.27394	230.478	6.54925
X8	-6.63936	4.27394	21.3551	721.786	2.82043
X9	7.76958	230.478	721.786	33837.8	144.485
X10	8.10716	6.54925	2.82043	144.485	7.03654

PRINCIPAL COMPONENT ANALYSIS

TOTAL VARIANCE=94098.56

	EIGENVALUE	DIFFERENCE	PROPORTION	CUMULATIVE
PRIN1	93667.6	93421.9	0.995421	0.99542
PRIN2	245.8	157.5	0.002612	0.99803
PRIN3	88.2	15.3	0.000938	0.99897
PRIN4	72.9	53.2	0.000775	0.99975
PRIN5	19.7	17.1	0.000209	0.99995
PRIN6	2.6	1.3	0.000027	0.99998
PRIN7	1.3	1.0	0.000014	1.00000
PRIN8	0.3	0.3	0.000004	1.00000
PRIN9	0.1	0.1	0.000001	1.00000
PRIN10	0.0	.	0.000000	1.00000

EIGENVECTORS

	PRIN1	PRIN2	PRIN3	PRIN4	PRIN5
X1	0.006892	0.032916	0.366908	0.150251	-.254943
X2	0.795885	0.448504	-.211750	-.308118	-.079096
X3	0.079940	0.562345	0.444684	0.560961	-.068881
X4	-.000288	0.115656	-.208398	0.157267	0.588020
X5	0.000323	0.077519	0.152115	0.114932	0.472312
X6	0.000094	-.004974	-.671152	0.629435	-.310480
X7	0.004297	0.071291	-.112194	0.094569	0.296663
X8	0.012784	0.014141	0.185999	0.094390	0.017227
X9	0.599950	-.671443	0.214720	0.329098	0.112776
X10	0.002784	0.077466	-.111784	0.086729	0.397160

	PRIN6	PRIN7	PRIN8	PRIN9	PRIN10
X1	-.132385	0.833557	0.225988	0.007562	-.114912
X2	0.025944	0.072973	0.113615	-.021007	-.005793
X3	-.079061	-.277114	-.276344	0.026034	0.011202
X4	0.053866	0.353501	-.348731	-.566503	0.047860
X5	-.268552	-.193451	0.777313	-.139691	0.035931
X6	0.014661	0.023119	0.233663	-.031726	-.024293
X7	-.008912	0.219785	-.048807	0.613538	0.676878
X8	0.938085	0.003176	0.244888	-.072321	0.103053
X9	-.042748	-.071209	-.121775	0.018832	0.003802
X10	0.135658	0.082206	-.045238	0.524752	-.716705

PRELIMINARY DESIGN PHASE: Least Squares Method
(using two Principal Components)

DEP VARIABLE: Y

ANALYSIS OF VARIANCE

SOURCE	DF	SUM OF SQUARES	MEAN SQUARE	F VALUE	PROB>F
MODEL	2	1478.65941	739.32971	2.014	0.2143
ERROR	6	2203.04281	367.17380		
C TOTAL	8	3681.70222			

ROOT MSE	19.16178	R-SQUARE	0.4016
DEP MEAN	24.25556	ADJ R-SQ	0.2022
C.V.	78.99955		

PARAMETER ESTIMATES

VARIABLE	DF	PARAMETER ESTIMATE	STANDARD ERROR	T FOR H0: PARAMETER=0
INTERCEP	1	17.90009142	7.12992838	2.511
P1	1	0.04015744	0.02001400	2.006
P2	1	0.01016278	0.42464199	0.024

VARIABLE	DF	PROB > |T|
INTERCEP	1	0.0459
P1	1	0.0916
P2	1	0.9817

OBS	ID	ACTUAL	PREDICT VALUE	STD ERR PREDICT	LOWER95% MEAN
1	4.07256	36.0000	18.0942	7.2177	0.4330
2	29.1337	31.0000	19.0161	7.2326	1.3186
3	1056.04	64.0000	60.2882	19.0892	13.5786
4	6.88223	48.0000	18.2343	7.4892	-0.0912
5	21.9383	10.0000	18.6229	9.5496	-4.7440
6	39.6677	8.0000	19.2342	12.7410	-11.9419
7	87.6421	6.5000	21.3631	6.9391	4.3838
8	100.738	6.0000	22.2260	13.4384	-10.6566
9	78.4684	8.8000	21.2210	9.7140	-2.5482
10	18.9421	.	18.7546	8.0228	-0.8766
11	91.6716	.	21.3924	10.2067	-3.5825

OBS	ID	UPPER95% MEAN	LOWER95% PREDICT	UPPER95% PREDICT	RESIDUAL
1	4.07256	35.7553	-32.0090	68.1973	17.9058
2	29.1337	36.7136	-31.0998	69.1321	11.9839
3	1056.04	107.0	-5.8949	126.5	3.7118
4	6.88223	36.5598	-32.1069	68.5755	29.7657
5	21.9383	41.9899	-33.7643	71.0102	-8.6229
6	39.6677	50.4102	-37.0718	75.5401	-11.2342
7	87.6421	38.3424	-28.5038	71.2300	-14.8631
8	100.738	55.1086	-35.0425	79.4945	-16.2260
9	78.4684	44.9902	-31.3469	73.7889	-12.4210
10	18.9421	38.3857	-32.0765	69.5856	.
11	91.6716	46.3674	-31.7316	74.5164	.

OBS	ID	STD ERR RESIDUAL
1	4.07256	17.7504
2	29.1337	17.7444
3	1056.04	1.6659
4	6.88223	17.6376
5	21.9383	16.6126
6	39.6677	14.3123
7	87.6421	17.8612
8	100.738	13.6595
9	78.4684	16.5170
10	18.9421	.
11	91.6716	.

```
SUM OF RESIDUALS                 9.50351E-14
SUM OF SQUARED RESIDUALS            2203.043
PREDICTED RESID SS (PRESS)          245131.3
```

PRELIMINARY DESIGN PHASE: Least Squares Method
(using one Principal Component)

DEP VARIABLE: Y

ANALYSIS OF VARIANCE

SOURCE	DF	SUM OF SQUARES	MEAN SQUARE	F VALUE	PROB>F
MODEL	1	1478.44911	1478.44911	4.697	0.0669
ERROR	7	2203.25312	314.75045		
C TOTAL	8	3681.70222			

ROOT MSE	17.74121	R-SQUARE	0.4016	
DEP MEAN	24.25556	ADJ R-SQ	0.3161	
C.V.	73.14286			

PARAMETER ESTIMATES

VARIABLE	DF	PARAMETER ESTIMATE	STANDARD ERROR	T FOR H0: PARAMETER=0
INTERCEP	1	17.89874335	6.60114006	2.711
P1	1	0.04016008	0.01852996	2.167

VARIABLE	DF	PROB > |T|
INTERCEP	1	0.0301
P1	1	0.0669

OBS	ID	ACTUAL	PREDICT VALUE	STD ERR PREDICT	LOWER95% MEAN
1	4.07256	36.0000	18.0623	6.5680	2.5314
2	29.1337	31.0000	19.0688	6.3796	3.9832
3	1056.04	64.0000	60.3093	17.6552	18.5611
4	6.88223	48.0000	18.1751	6.5455	2.6974
5	21.9383	10.0000	18.7798	6.4308	3.5732
6	39.6677	8.0000	19.4918	6.3090	4.5733
7	87.6421	6.5000	21.4185	6.0569	7.0961
8	100.738	6.0000	21.9444	6.0091	7.7350
9	78.4684	8.8000	21.0500	6.0959	6.6354
10	18.9421	.	18.6595	6.4528	3.4008
11	91.6716	.	21.5803	6.0412	7.2950

OBS	ID	UPPER95% MEAN	LOWER95% PREDICT	UPPER95% PREDICT	RESIDUAL
1	4.07256	33.5932	-26.6719	62.7965	17.9377
2	29.1337	34.1543	-25.5128	63.6503	11.9312
3	1056.04	102.1	1.1244	119.5	3.6907
4	6.88223	33.6528	-26.5406	62.8909	29.8249
5	21.9383	33.9864	-25.8429	63.4024	-8.7798
6	39.6677	34.4103	-25.0335	64.0171	-11.4918
7	87.6421	35.7408	-22.9106	65.7476	-14.9185
8	100.738	36.1538	-22.3483	66.2371	-15.9444
9	78.4684	35.4646	-23.3089	65.4090	-12.2500
10	18.9421	33.9181	-25.9810	63.2999	.
11	91.6716	35.8655	-22.7368	65.8974	.

OBS	ID	STD ERR RESIDUAL
1	4.07256	16.4807
2	29.1337	16.5545
3	1056.04	1.7449
4	6.88223	16.4896
5	21.9383	16.5347
6	39.6677	16.5815
7	87.6421	16.6753
8	100.738	16.6925
9	78.4684	16.6611
10	18.9421	.
11	91.6716	.

SUM OF RESIDUALS	5.24025E-14
SUM OF SQUARED RESIDUALS	2203.253
PREDICTED RESID SS (PRESS)	148443.6

DETAILED DESIGN PHASE: Stepwise Selections

STEPWISE REGRESSION PROCEDURE FOR DEPENDENT VARIABLE Y

WARNING: 2 OBSERVATIONS DELETED DUE TO MISSING VALUES.

NOTE: SLENTRY AND SLSTAY HAVE BEEN SET TO
      .15 FOR THE STEPWISE TECHNIQUE.

STEP 1   VARIABLE X1 ENTERED   R SQUARE = 0.67484762
                                             C(P) = .

	DF	SUM OF SQUARES	MEAN SQUARE	F	PROB>F
REGRESSION	1	2484.58798182	2484.587982	14.53	0.0066
ERROR	7	1197.11424040	171.016320		
TOTAL	8	3681.70222222			

	B VALUE	STD ERROR	TYPE II SS	F	PROB>F
INTERCEPT	13.81140806				
X1	5.69406301	1.49387362	2484.587982	14.53	0.0066

BOUNDS ON CONDITION NUMBER: 1,   1

STEP 2   VARIABLE X9 ENTERED   R SQUARE = 0.86541068
                                             C(P) = .

	DF	SUM OF SQUARES	MEAN SQUARE	F	PROB>F
REGRESSION	2	3186.18444000	1593.092220	19.29	0.0024
ERROR	6	495.51778222	82.586297		
TOTAL	8	3681.70222222			

	B VALUE	STD ERROR	TYPE II SS	F	PROB>F
INTERCEPT	11.91767775				
X1	14.11517877	3.07005978	1745.770281	21.14	0.0037
X9	-0.13589515	0.04662451	701.596458	8.50	0.0268

BOUNDS ON CONDITION NUMBER: 8.745719,   34.98288

STEP 3   VARIABLE X11 ENTERED   R SQUARE = 0.97400689
                                            C(P) = .

	DF	SUM OF SQUARES	MEAN SQUARE	F	PROB>F
REGRESSION	3	3586.00334120	1195.334447	62.45	0.0002
ERROR	5	95.69888102	19.139776		
TOTAL	8	3681.70222222			

	B VALUE	STD ERROR	TYPE II SS	F	PROB>F
INTERCEPT	17.61432258				
X1	14.26567506	1.47832193	1782.310925	93.12	0.0002
X9	-0.12192015	0.02265278	554.427691	28.97	0.0030
X11	-0.88959153	0.19463790	399.818901	20.89	0.0060

BOUNDS ON CONDITION NUMBER: 8.908018,   56.62403

STEP 4   VARIABLE X8 ENTERED   R SQUARE = 0.99235831
                                          C(P) = .

	DF	SUM OF SQUARES	MEAN SQUARE	F	PROB>F
REGRESSION	4	3653.56779471	913.3919487	129.86	0.0002
ERROR	4	28.13442751	7.0336069		
TOTAL	8	3681.70222222			

	B VALUE	STD ERROR	TYPE II SS	F	PROB>F
INTERCEPT	30.24108727				
X1	14.41817104	0.89751810	1815.147839	258.07	0.0001
X8	-2.32512285	0.75019785	67.564454	9.61	0.0362
X9	-0.06824032	0.02210312	67.042926	9.53	0.0367
X11	-1.04402729	0.12808083	467.340584	66.44	0.0012

BOUNDS ON CONDITION NUMBER: 23.07832,   193.2544

STEP 5   VARIABLE X6 ENTERED   R SQUARE = 0.99716673
                                                C(P) = .

	DF	SUM OF SQUARES	MEAN SQUARE	F	PROB>F
REGRESSION	5	3671.27097173	734.2541943	211.17	0.0005
ERROR	3	10.43125049	3.4770835		
TOTAL	8	3681.70222222			

	B VALUE	STD ERROR	TYPE II SS	F	PROB>F
INTERCEPT	28.96925965				
X1	15.63285056	0.82946548	1235.079284	355.21	0.0003
X6	0.25403620	0.11258423	17.703177	5.09	0.1093
X8	-2.38561282	0.52814664	70.942420	20.40	0.0203
X9	-0.08100319	0.01653809	83.415842	23.99	0.0163
X11	-1.19927580	0.11332964	389.373377	111.98	0.0018

BOUNDS ON CONDITION NUMBER: 26.13549,   304.9335

NO OTHER VARIABLES MET THE 0.1500 SIGNIFICANCE LEVEL FOR ENTRY

SUMMARY OF STEPWISE REGRESSION PROCEDURE FOR DEPENDENT VARIABLE Y

	VARIABLE		NUMBER	PARTIAL	MODEL	
STEP	ENTERED	REMOVED	IN	$R^{**}2$	$R^{**}2$	C(P)
1	X1		1	0.6748	0.6748	.
2	X9		2	0.1906	0.8654	.
3	X11		3	0.1086	0.9740	.
4	X8		4	0.0184	0.9924	.
5	X6		5	0.0048	0.9972	.

	VARIABLE			
STEP	ENTERED	REMOVED	F	PROB>F
1	X1		14.5284	0.0066
2	X9		8.4953	0.0268
3	X11		20.8894	0.0060
4	X8		9.6059	0.0362
5	X6		5.0914	0.1093

DETAILED DESIGN PHASE: Stepwise Regression Analysis

DEP VARIABLE: Y

ANALYSIS OF VARIANCE

SOURCE	DF	SUM OF SQUARES	MEAN SQUARE	F VALUE	PROB>F
MODEL	5	3671.27097	734.25419	211.170	0.0005
ERROR	3	10.43125049	3.47708350		
C TOTAL	8	3681.70222			

ROOT MSE	1.864694	R-SQUARE	0.9972	
DEP MEAN	24.25556	ADJ R-SQ	0.9924	
C.V.	7.687698			

PARAMETER ESTIMATES

VARIABLE	DF	PARAMETER ESTIMATE	STANDARD ERROR	T FOR H0: PARAMETER=0
INTERCEP	1	28.96925965	3.05969593	9.468
X1	1	15.63285056	0.82946548	18.847
X6	1	0.25403620	0.11258423	2.256
X8	1	-2.38561282	0.52814664	-4.517
X9	1	-0.08100319	0.01653809	-4.898
X11	1	-1.19927580	0.11332964	-10.582

VARIABLE	DF	PROB > |T|
INTERCEP	1	0.0025
X1	1	0.0003
X6	1	0.1093
X8	1	0.0203
X9	1	0.0163
X11	1	0.0018

OBS	ID	ACTUAL	PREDICT VALUE	STD ERR PREDICT	LOWER95% MEAN
1	1.53043	36.0000	37.4512	1.2162	33.5806
2	0.75	31.0000	30.5251	1.8107	24.7626
3	9.82125	64.0000	64.0698	1.8639	58.1379
4	2.30714	48.0000	46.7829	1.4536	42.1568
5	1.1575	10.0000	11.6845	1.4654	7.0209
6	0.94162	8.0000	6.2026	1.2781	2.1350
7	0	6.5000	6.4245	1.2872	2.3278
8	0	6.0000	5.6922	1.3460	1.4086
9	0	8.8000	9.4672	1.8078	3.7141
10	13.6698	.	212.8	10.7106	178.8
11	1.47059	.	15.1868	2.2232	8.1115

OBS	ID	UPPER95% MEAN	LOWER95% PREDICT	UPPER95% PREDICT	RESIDUAL
1	1.53043	41.3218	30.3661	44.5363	-1.4512
2	0.75	36.2877	22.2532	38.7971	0.4749
3	9.82125	70.0018	55.6791	72.4606	-0.0698
4	2.30714	51.4089	39.2584	54.3073	1.2171
5	1.1575	16.3480	4.1369	19.2320	-1.6845
6	0.94162	10.2702	-0.9920	13.3972	1.7974
7	0	10.5211	-0.7866	13.6355	0.0755
8	0	9.9758	-1.6267	13.0111	0.3078
9	0	15.2204	1.2019	17.7326	-0.6672
10	13.6698	246.9	178.2	247.4	.
11	1.47059	22.2620	5.9523	24.4213	.

OBS	ID	STD ERR RESIDUAL
1	1.53043	1.4135
2	0.75	0.4454
3	9.82125	0.0539
4	2.30714	1.1680
5	1.1575	1.1532
6	0.94162	1.3578
7	0	1.3491
8	0	1.2905
9	0	0.4573
10	13.6698	.
11	1.47059	.

SUM OF RESIDUALS   1.32561E-13
SUM OF SQUARED RESIDUALS   10.43125
PREDICTED RESID SS (PRESS)   7220.791

DETAILED DESIGN PHASE: Principal component analysis

PRINCIPAL COMPONENT ANALYSIS

11 OBSERVATIONS
14 VARIABLES

SIMPLE STATISTICS

	X1	X2	X3	X4	X5
MEAN	2.87712	105.297	20.0766	2.83031	2.59865
ST DEV	4.52637	243.706	26.7754	3.99664	3.05383

	X6	X7	X8	X9	X10
MEAN	7.11785	2.11232	8.02100	90.035	2.05379
ST DEV	8.39976	2.56330	4.62116	183.950	2.65265

	X11	X12	X13	X14
MEAN	7.29776	2.43642	2.65967	8.51365
ST DEV	8.21082	3.64045	4.22452	9.09573

COVARIANCES

	X1	X2	X3	X4	X5
X1	20.488	507.627	76.7436	-6.88532	4.59364
X2	507.627	59392.6	6000.55	-9.22677	26.4418
X3	76.7436	6000.55	716.922	11.1813	23.2099
X4	-6.88532	-9.22677	11.1813	15.9731	5.96383
X5	4.59364	26.4418	23.2099	5.96383	9.32588
X6	-13.2205	5.33685	-0.195098	15.8104	-6.66383
X7	-0.495505	327.701	41.0176	8.56419	3.46024
X8	15.039	949.037	108.598	-1.976	3.52059
X9	391.763	44639.8	4421.27	-34.1497	12.0465
X10	-2.19708	215.614	30.1225	9.80594	4.3422
X11	0.731235	785.26	46.8588	-6.66139	-8.98976
X12	-3.84745	139.957	25.7475	13.3912	7.72505
X13	15.3442	279.528	62.0205	-0.0315304	3.65136
X14	-16.7971	-206.739	8.92737	29.6529	6.2227

PRINCIPAL COMPONENT ANALYSIS

COVARIANCES

	X6	X7	X8	X9	X10
X1	-13.2205	-0.495505	15.039	391.763	-2.19708
X2	5.33685	327.701	949.037	44639.8	215.614
X3	-0.195098	41.0176	108.598	4421.27	30.1225
X4	15.8104	8.56419	-1.976	-34.1497	9.80594
X5	-6.66383	3.46024	3.52059	12.0465	4.3422
X6	70.556	9.12385	-6.63936	7.76958	8.10716
X7	9.12385	6.5705	4.27394	230.478	6.54925
X8	-6.63936	4.27394	21.3551	721.786	2.82043
X9	7.76958	230.478	721.786	33837.8	144.485
X10	8.10716	6.54925	2.82043	144.485	7.03654
X11	34.3681	0.495098	6.72665	662.567	-2.72536
X12	5.65109	7.941	1.76349	83.1111	9.17345
X13	4.16506	2.2108	9.27088	199.47	0.768962
X14	34.3645	13.8536	-8.64942	-239.719	16.2101

	X11	X12	X13	X14
X1	0.731235	-3.84745	15.3442	-16.7971
X2	785.26	139.957	279.528	-206.739
X3	46.8588	25.7475	62.0205	8.92737
X4	-6.66139	13.3912	-0.0315304	29.6529
X5	-8.98976	7.72505	3.65136	6.2227
X6	34.3681	5.65109	4.16506	34.3645
X7	0.495098	7.941	2.2108	13.8536
X8	6.72665	1.76349	9.27088	-8.64942
X9	662.567	83.1111	199.47	-239.719
X10	-2.72536	9.17345	0.768962	16.2101
X11	67.4176	-7.23447	-1.97936	-13.1373
X12	-7.23447	13.2529	-0.967642	21.8739
X13	-1.97936	-0.967642	17.8466	0.119597
X14	-13.1373	21.8739	0.119597	82.7322

PRINCIPAL COMPONENT ANALYSIS

TOTAL VARIANCE=94279.81

	EIGENVALUE	DIFFERENCE	PROPORTION	CUMULATIVE
PRIN1	93681.5	93378.8	0.993654	0.99365
PRIN2	302.6	170.3	0.003210	0.99686
PRIN3	132.4	45.4	0.001404	0.99827
PRIN4	87.0	42.8	0.000923	0.99919
PRIN5	44.2	28.8	0.000469	0.99966
PRIN6	15.5	3.5	0.000164	0.99982
PRIN7	12.0	8.8	0.000127	0.99995
PRIN8	3.2	2.0	0.000034	0.99999
PRIN9	1.2	1.0	0.000013	1.00000
PRIN10	0.2	0.2	0.000002	1.00000
PRIN11	0.0	0.0	0.000000	1.00000
PRIN12	0.0	0.0	0.000000	1.00000
PRIN13	0.0	0.0	0.000000	1.00000
PRIN14	0.0	.	0.000000	1.00000

EIGENVECTORS

	PRIN1	PRIN2	PRIN3	PRIN4	PRIN5
X1	0.006891	0.010031	-.254580	0.269774	-.048789
X2	0.795821	0.403242	0.016768	-.311843	-.275479
X3	0.079930	0.485487	-.263973	0.651541	-.036734
X4	-.000289	0.131773	0.202666	0.030697	0.299039
X5	0.000322	0.074550	-.072133	0.123923	0.284615
X6	0.000097	0.018274	0.629710	0.333602	-.290808
X7	0.004296	0.077214	0.103537	0.026186	0.138031
X8	0.012783	0.009831	-.120209	0.132078	0.100100
X9	0.599912	-.595055	0.013861	0.314393	0.376196
X10	0.002783	0.085730	0.106051	0.012106	0.199331
X11	0.010963	-.261383	0.348472	0.229051	-.409717
X12	0.001742	0.113134	0.111607	0.001101	0.355924
X13	0.003708	0.089211	-.104901	0.329080	-.124027
X14	-.003289	0.348945	0.490828	0.001316	0.380947

PRINCIPAL COMPONENT ANALYSIS

EIGENVECTORS

	PRIN6	PRIN7	PRIN8	PRIN9	PRIN10
X1	0.065220	-.185084	0.318798	0.339223	0.515515
X2	-.008989	0.074080	0.043256	0.131509	0.070023
X3	0.124301	0.152766	-.233068	-.344909	-.179224
X4	-.169591	0.216492	0.224524	0.232286	-.131803
X5	0.090926	0.384482	0.140738	-.019361	0.565857
X6	-.534051	-.048653	-.138761	-.085276	0.297339
X7	-.147464	0.156599	0.148703	0.084184	-.187037
X8	-.045080	-.118376	-.662186	0.681261	0.005320
X9	-.010021	-.125001	-.021633	-.155073	-.068002
X10	-.138017	0.200346	0.019376	0.158105	-.325802
X11	0.602462	0.377237	0.068697	0.251417	-.127454
X12	-.061335	0.382822	0.040467	0.139263	0.013158
X13	-.161653	-.310900	0.533749	0.288358	-.325483
X14	0.471376	-.509939	0.003508	-.032622	0.055718

	PRIN11	PRIN12	PRIN13	PRIN14
X1	0.121428	0.028732	-.209447	0.528654
X2	0.012142	0.003778	0.006262	-.028462
X3	-.055022	-.053056	-.019333	0.109401
X4	-.374842	-.601314	0.275238	0.275655
X5	0.131140	0.082213	0.421095	-.441733
X6	0.050973	0.011588	-.037910	-.024237
X7	-.314295	0.784849	0.240080	0.284081
X8	-.083031	0.043435	0.110332	-.134874
X9	-.009516	-.005255	-.005790	0.020943
X10	0.838748	0.014480	0.092226	0.196460
X11	-.015001	0.000861	0.010199	0.004646
X12	-.102931	0.074573	-.789099	-.194181
X13	0.001998	0.021967	0.004358	-.509974
X14	0.041114	0.060967	0.007364	-.017769

DETAILED DESIGN PHASE: Least Squares Method
(using Principal Components)

DEP VARIABLE: Y

ANALYSIS OF VARIANCE

SOURCE	DF	SUM OF SQUARES	MEAN SQUARE	F VALUE	PROB>F
MODEL	3	2940.81945	980.27315	6.616	0.0342
ERROR	5	740.88277	148.17655		
C TOTAL	8	3681.70222			

ROOT MSE	12.17278	R-SQUARE	0.7988	
DEP MEAN	24.25556	ADJ R-SQ	0.6780	
C.V.	50.18553			

PARAMETER ESTIMATES

VARIABLE	DF	PARAMETER ESTIMATE	STANDARD ERROR	T FOR H0: PARAMETER=0
INTERCEP	1	36.61996444	7.48811514	4.890
P1	1	0.12930799	0.03115062	4.151
P2	1	-2.46877510	0.78585547	-3.142
P3	1	-0.64069017	0.32689299	-1.960

VARIABLE	DF	PROB > |T|
INTERCEP	1	0.0045
P1	1	0.0089
P2	1	0.0256
P3	1	0.1073

OBS	ID	ACTUAL	PREDICT VALUE	STD ERR PREDICT	LOWER95% MEAN
1	4.08355	36.0000	36.1923	7.3742	17.2367
2	29.1376	31.0000	34.4870	6.6722	17.3359
3	1055.35	64.0000	62.7505	.12.1539	31.5085
4	6.94778	48.0000	30.0115	6.0234	14.5280
5	22.1509	10.0000	15.7142	6.6366	-1.3455
6	39.8681	8.0000	6.2566	9.2345	-17.4811
7	87.6266	6.5000	15.6072	4.5599	3.8857
8	100.724	6.0000	19.1111	8.3167	-2.2675
9	78.4993	8.8000	-1.8305	9.5147	-26.2884
10	19.0778	.	21.6373	4.9104	9.0149
11	91.6872	.	26.9036	6.2962	10.7190

OBS	ID	UPPER95% MEAN	LOWER95% PREDICT	UPPER95% PREDICT	RESIDUAL
1	4.08355	55.1480	-0.3921	72.7768	-0.1923
2	29.1376	51.6381	-1.1959	70.1698	-3.4870
3	1055.35	93.9926	18.5332	107.0	1.2495
4	6.94778	45.4950	-4.9005	64.9235	17.9885
5	22.1509	32.7739	-19.9248	51.3532	-5.7142
6	39.8681	29.9944	-33.0192	45.5324	1.7434
7	87.6266	27.3287	-17.8069	49.0213	-9.1072
8	100.724	40.4896	-18.7855	57.0076	-13.1111
9	78.4993	22.6275	-41.5457	37.8847	10.6305
10	19.0778	34.2598	-12.1034	55.3780	.
11	91.6872	43.0883	-8.3249	62.1322	.

OBS	ID	STD ERR RESIDUAL
1	4.08355	9.6849
2	29.1376	10.1813
3	1055.35	0.6783
4	6.94778	10.5780
5	22.1509	10.2045
6	39.8681	7.9309
7	87.6266	11.2864
8	100.724	8.8887
9	78.4993	7.5926
10	19.0778	.
11	91.6872	.

```
SUM OF RESIDUALS              1.31672E-13
SUM OF SQUARED RESIDUALS        740.8828
PREDICTED RESID SS (PRESS)     164097.7
```

CODE AND UNIT TEST PHASE: Stepwise Selections

STEPWISE REGRESSION PROCEDURE FOR DEPENDENT VARIABLE Y

WARNING: 2 OBSERVATIONS DELETED DUE TO MISSING VALUES.

NOTE: SLENTRY AND SLSTAY HAVE BEEN SET TO
      .15 FOR THE STEPWISE TECHNIQUE.

STEP 1   VARIABLE X1 ENTERED   R SQUARE = 0.67484762
                                        C(P) = .

	DF	SUM OF SQUARES	MEAN SQUARE	F	PROB>F
REGRESSION	1	2484.58798182	2484.587982	14.53	0.0066
ERROR	7	1197.11424040	171.016320		
TOTAL	8	3681.70222222			

	B VALUE	STD ERROR	TYPE II SS	F	PROB>F
INTERCEPT	13.81140806				
X1	5.69406301	1.49387362	2484.587982	14.53	0.0066

BOUNDS ON CONDITION NUMBER: 1,   1

STEP 2   VARIABLE X9 ENTERED   R SQUARE = 0.86541068
                                        C(P) = .

	DF	SUM OF SQUARES	MEAN SQUARE	F	PROB>F
REGRESSION	2	3186.18444000	1593.092220	19.29	0.0024
ERROR	6	495.51778222	82.586297		
TOTAL	8	3681.70222222			

	B VALUE	STD ERROR	TYPE II SS	F	PROB>F
INTERCEPT	11.91767775				
X1	14.11517877	3.07005978	1745.770281	21.14	0.0037
X9	-0.13589515	0.04662451	701.596458	8.50	0.0268

BOUNDS ON CONDITION NUMBER: 8.745719,   34.98288

STEP 3   VARIABLE X11 ENTERED   R SQUARE = 0.97400689
                                                C(P) = .

	DF	SUM OF SQUARES	MEAN SQUARE	F	PROB>F
REGRESSION	3	3586.00334120	1195.334447	62.45	0.0002
ERROR	5	95.69888102	19.139776		
TOTAL	8	3681.70222222			

	B VALUE	STD ERROR	TYPE II SS	F	PROB>F
INTERCEPT	17.61432258				
X1	14.26567506	1.47832193	1782.310925	93.12	0.0002
X9	-0.12192015	0.02265278	554.427691	28.97	0.0030
X11	-0.88959153	0.19463790	399.818901	20.89	0.0060

BOUNDS ON CONDITION NUMBER: 8.908018,   56.62403

STEP 4   VARIABLE X8 ENTERED   R SQUARE = 0.99235831
                                               C(P) = .

	DF	SUM OF SQUARES	MEAN SQUARE	F	PROB>F
REGRESSION	4	3653.56779471	913.3919487	129.86	0.0002
ERROR	4	28.13442751	7.0336069		
TOTAL	8	3681.70222222			

	B VALUE	STD ERROR	TYPE II SS	F	PROB>F
INTERCEPT	30.24108727				
X1	14.41817104	0.89751810	1815.147839	258.07	0.0001
X8	-2.32512285	0.75019785	67.564454	9.61	0.0362
X9	-0.06824032	0.02210312	67.042926	9.53	0.0367
X11	-1.04402729	0.12808083	467.340584	66.44	0.0012

BOUNDS ON CONDITION NUMBER: 23.07832,   193.2544

STEP 5   VARIABLE X6 ENTERED   R SQUARE = 0.99716673
                                        C(P) = .

	DF	SUM OF SQUARES	MEAN SQUARE	F	PROB>F
REGRESSION	5	3671.27097173	734.2541943	211.17	0.0005
ERROR	3	10.43125049	3.4770835		
TOTAL	8	3681.70222222			

	B VALUE	STD ERROR	TYPE II SS	F	PROB>F
INTERCEPT	28.96925965				
X1	.15.63285056	0.82946548	1235.079284	355.21	0.0003
X6	0.25403620	0.11258423	17.703177	5.09	0.1093
X8	-2.38561282	0.52814664	70.942420	20.40	0.0203
X9	-0.08100319	0.01653809	83.415842	23.99	0.0163
X11	-1.19927580	0.11332964	389.373377	111.98	0.0018

BOUNDS ON CONDITION NUMBER: 26.13549,   304.9335

STEP 6   VARIABLE X18 ENTERED   R SQUARE = 0.99965209
                                        C(P) = .

	DF	SUM OF SQUARES	MEAN SQUARE	F	PROB>F
REGRESSION	6	3680.42132510	613.4035542	957.77	0.0010
ERROR	2	1.28089712	0.6404486		
TOTAL	8	3681.70222222			

	B VALUE	STD ERROR	TYPE II SS	F	PROB>F
INTERCEPT	28.34682750				
X1	16.87615739	0.48468544	776.4463286	1212.35	0.0008
X6	0.20563632	0.04998622	10.8388523	16.92	0.0543
X8	-1.99036494	0.24962427	40.7170268	63.58	0.0154
X9	-0.11274143	0.01099462	67.3427958	105.15	0.0094
X11	-1.10981860	0.05409062	269.6151332	420.98	0.0024
X18	-0.00386060	0.00102136	9.1503534	14.29	0.0634

BOUNDS ON CONDITION NUMBER: 62.71203,   709.8545

STEP 7   VARIABLE X17 ENTERED   R SQUARE = 0.99999735
                                            C(P) = .

	DF	SUM OF SQUARES	MEAN SQUARE	F	PROB>F
REGRESSION	7	3681.69247422	525.9560677	9999.99	0.0001
ERROR	1	0.00974801	0.0097480		
TOTAL	8	3681.70222222			

	B VALUE	STD ERROR	TYPE II SS	F	PROB>F
INTERCEPT	35.34086513				
X1	16.55363291	0.06613116	610.7875117	9999.99	0.0001
X6	0.29622944	0.01004828	8.4720459	869.11	0.0216
X8	-2.00284334	0.03081597	41.1773272	4224.18	0.0098
X9	-0.10483743	0.00152282	46.2011223	4739.55	0.0092
X11	-1.38270678	0.02481132	30.2744491	3105.71	0.0114
X17	-1.08045895	0.09461672	1.2711491	130.40	0.0556
X18	-0.00423198	0.00013014	10.3087888	1057.53	0.0196

BOUNDS ON CONDITION NUMBER: 79.0415,   1475.295

STEP 8   VARIABLE X21 ENTERED   R SQUARE = 1.00000000
                                            C(P) = .

	DF	SUM OF SQUARES	MEAN SQUARE	F	PROB>F
REGRESSION	8	3681.70222222	460.2127778	9999.99	0.0001
ERROR	0	0.00000000	0.0000000		
TOTAL	8	3681.70222222			

	B VALUE	STD ERROR	TYPE II SS	F	PROB>F
INTERCEPT	23.91179944				
X1	16.40108872	0	94.85822032	9999.99	0.0001
X6	0.32541684	0	1.08333040	9999.99	0.0001
X8	-2.01511923	0	35.97475149	9999.99	0.0001
X9	-0.10108771	0	6.08156755	9999.99	0.0001
X11	-1.46447109	0	2.86348417	9999.99	0.0001
X17	-1.33068597	0	0.24119088	9999.99	0.0001
X18	-0.00380003	0	0.69167302	9999.99	0.0001
X21	12.99647065	0	0.00974801	9999.99	0.0001

BOUNDS ON CONDITION NUMBER: 558.2853,   13148.58

NO OTHER VARIABLES MET THE 0.1500 SIGNIFICANCE LEVEL FOR ENTRY

SUMMARY OF STEPWISE REGRESSION PROCEDURE FOR DEPENDENT VARIABLE Y

STEP	VARIABLE ENTERED	REMOVED	NUMBER IN	PARTIAL $R**2$	MODEL $R**2$	C(P)
1	X1		1	0.6748	0.6748	.
2	X9		2	0.1906	0.8654	.
3	X11		3	0.1086	0.9740	.
4	X8		4	0.0184	0.9924	.
5	X6		5	0.0048	0.9972	.
6	X18		6	0.0025	0.9997	.
7	X17		7	0.0003	1.0000	.
8	X21		8	0.0000	1.0000	.

STEP	VARIABLE ENTERED	REMOVED	F	PROB>F
1	X1		14.5284	0.0066
2	X9		8.4953	0.0268
3	X11		20.8894	0.0060
4	X8		9.6059	0.0362
5	X6		5.0914	0.1093
6	X18		14.2874	0.0634
7	X17		130.4009	0.0556
8	X21		9999.9999	0.0001

CODE AND UNIT TEST PHASE: Stepwise Regression Analysis

DEP VARIABLE: Y

ANALYSIS OF VARIANCE

SOURCE	DF	SUM OF SQUARES	MEAN SQUARE	F VALUE	PROB>F
MODEL	8	3681.70222	460.21278	.	.
ERROR	0	9.95121E-12	.		
C TOTAL	8	3681.70222			

ROOT MSE	.	R-SQUARE	1.0000
DEP MEAN	24.25556	ADJ R-SQ	.
C.V.	.		

PARAMETER ESTIMATES

VARIABLE	DF	PARAMETER ESTIMATE	STANDARD ERROR	T FOR H0: PARAMETER=0
INTERCEP	1	23.91179944	.	.
X1	1	16.40108872	.	.
X6	1	0.32541684	.	.
X8	1	-2.01511923	.	.
X9	1	-0.10108771	.	.
X11	1	-1.46447110	.	.
X17	1	-1.33068597	.	.
X18	1	-0.003800033	.	.
X21	1	12.99647065	.	.

VARIABLE	DF	PROB > |T|
INTERCEP	1	.
X1	1	.
X6	1	.
X8	1	.
X9	1	.
X11	1	.
X17	1	.
X18	1	.
X21	1	.

CODE AND UNIT TEST PHASE: Principal Component Analysis

PRINCIPAL COMPONENT ANALYSIS

11 OBSERVATIONS
22 VARIABLES

SIMPLE STATISTICS

	X1	X2	X3	X4	X5
MEAN	2.87712	105.297	20.0766	2.83031	2.59865
ST DEV	4.52637	243.706	26.7754	3.99664	3.05383

	X6	X7	X8	X9	X10
MEAN	7.11785	2.11232	8.02100	90.035	2.05379
ST DEV	8.39976	2.56330	4.62116	183.950	2.65265

	X11	X12	X15	X17	X18
MEAN	7.29776	2.43642	70585.5	5.45455	419.000
ST DEV	8.21082	3.64045	90661.0	2.33939	494.511

	X19	X20	X21	X22	X23
MEAN	102.455	21.1818	0.990909	2.36364	2.52727
ST DEV	55.682	17.9990	0.020226	0.80904	2.77708

	X24	X25
MEAN	2.74685	22.6800
ST DEV	3.34931	15.8044

PRINCIPAL COMPONENT ANALYSIS

COVARIANCES

	X1	X2	X3	X4	X5	X6
X1	20.488	507.627	76.7436	-6.88532	4.59364	-13.2205
X2	507.627	59392.6	6000.55	-9.22677	26.4418	5.33685
X3	76.7436	6000.55	716.922	11.1813	23.2099	-.195098
X4	-6.88532	-9.22677	11.1813	15.9731	5.96383	15.8104
X5	4.59364	26.4418	23.2099	5.96383	9.32588	-6.66383
X6	-13.2205	5.33685	-.195098	15.8104	-6.66383	70.556
X7	-.495505	327.701	41.0176	8.56419	3.46024	9.12385
X8	15.039	949.037	108.598	-1.976	3.52059	-6.63936
X9	391.763	44639.8	4421.27	-34.1497	12.0465	7.76958
X10	-2.19708	215.614	30.1225	9.80594	4.3422	8.10716
X11	0.731235	785.26	46.8588	-6.66139	-8.98976	34.3681
X12	-3.84745	139.957	25.7475	13.3912	7.72505	5.65109
X15	-85891.3	-6993472	-1125733	-173297	-121470	-208659
X17	-2.24013	-67.8237	-2.55027	3.42244	0.814652	-.740503
X18	-310.767	-34904.1	-5612.36	-1011.46	-665.931	-1412.74
X19	32.6381	-3627.07	7.38965	105.698	65.6658	123.696
X20	-7.72981	-467.318	35.1436	43.4028	37.4768	-7.76181
X21	-0.04723	1.00458	.0225336	0.02798	-.011351	.0709393
X22	1.63621	31.2285	0.970624	-2.6418	-1.18823	-.977816
X23	4.00557	630.372	67.4554	3.63113	2.43762	1.78892
X24	-3.33469	49.5614	21.6735	12.3389	7.18182	6.57276
X25	29.9385	2403.47	323.785	25.635	11.0381	46.6303

	X7	X8	X9	X10	X11	X12
X1	-.495505	15.039	391.763	-2.19708	0.731235	-3.84745
X2	327.701	949.037	44639.8	215.614	785.26	139.957
X3	41.0176	108.598	4421.27	30.1225	46.8588	25.7475
X4	8.56419	-1.976	-34.1497	9.80594	-6.66139	13.3912
X5	3.46024	3.52059	12.0465	4.3422	-8.98976	7.72505
X6	9.12385	-6.63936	7.76958	8.10716	34.3681	5.65109
X7	6.5705	4.27394	230.478	6.54925	0.495098	7.941
X8	4.27394	21.3551	721.786	2.82043	6.72665	1.76349
X9	230.478	721.786	33837.8	144.485	662.567	83.1111
X10	6.54925	2.82043	144.485	7.03654	-2.72536	9.17345
X11	0.495098	6.72665	662.567	-2.72536	67.4176	-7.23447
X12	7.941	1.76349	83.1111	9.17345	-7.23447	13.2529
X15	-139309	-161883	-5188362	-137945	115772	-165204
X17	1.54663	0.804153	-62.6251	2.38462	-12.4703	2.99725
X18	-782.588	-635.836	-26117.9	-767.761	183.637	-938.115
X19	46.1192	-1.10482	-3110.33	57.2551	-206.265	71.0751
X20	20.9603	14.0138	-413.461	30.1997	-72.7273	47.5335
X21	.0180623	-.009843	0.799326	.0186701	.0701341	.0221496
X22	-1.17045	0.360237	28.9647	-1.60379	2.74265	-2.43871
X23	5.48843	9.75502	466.099	4.68082	6.06845	5.06006
X24	6.99544	0.741977	8.56358	8.19207	-8.53385	11.7909
X25	27.366	51.4449	1758.18	24.0727	12.0449	22.1815

PRINCIPAL COMPONENT ANALYSIS

COVARIANCES

	X15	X17	X18	X19	X20	X21
X1	-85891.3	-2.24013	-310.767	32.6381	-7.72981	-0.04723
X2	-6993472	-67.8237	-34904.1	-3627.07	-467.318	1.00458
X3	-1125733	-2.55027	-5612.36	7.38965	35.1436	.0225336
X4	-173297	3.42244	-1011.46	105.698	43.4028	0.02798
X5	-121470	0.814652	-665.931	65.6658	37.4768	-.011351
X6	-208659	-.740503	-1412.74	123.696	-7.76181	.0709393
X7	-139309	1.54663	-782.588	46.1192	20.9603	.0180623
X8	-161883	0.804153	-635.836	-1.10482	14.0138	-.009843
X9·	-5188362	-62.6251	-26117.9	-3110.33	-413.461	0.799326
X10	-137945	2.38462	-767.761	57.2551	30.1997	.0186701
X11	115772	-12.4703	183.637	-206.265	-72.7273	.0701341
X12	-165204	2.99725	-938.115	71.0751	47.5335	.0221496
X15	8.2E+09	-100343	43466853	-1027794	-886584	-531.93
X17	-100343	5.47273	-421.9	47.1727	30.3091	.0045455
X18	43466853	-421.9	244541	-3143.5	-4314.1	-4.18
X19	-1027794	47.1727	-3143.5	3100.47	451.909	-.620455
X20	-886584	30.3091	-4314.1	451.909	323.964	.0318182
X21	-531.93	.0045455	-4.18	-.620455	.0318182	4.1E-04
X22	29464.8	-1.18182	153.7	-13.9818	-12.0727	-.006364
X23	-110036	-.103636	-585.29	-15.2036	7.29455	.0152727
X24	-155027	3.02282	-866.958	89.9873	45.7	.0147347
X25	-964771	11.8092	-4723.07	242.107	93.5026	.0678547

	X22	X23	X24	X25
X1	1.63621	4.00557	-3.33469	29.9385
X2	31.2285	630.372	49.5614	2403.47
X3	0.970624	67.4554	21.6735	323.785
X4	-2.6418	3.63113	12.3389	25.635
X5	-1.18823	2.43762	7.18182	11.0381
X6	-.977816	1.78892	6.57276	46.6303
X7	-1.17045	5.48843	6.99544	27.366
X8	0.360237	9.75502	0.741977	51.4449
X9	28.9647	466.099	8.56358	1758.18
X10	-1.60379	4.68082	8.19207	24.0727
X11	2.74265	6.06845	-8.53385	12.0449
X12	-2.43871	5.06006	11.7909	22.1815
X15	29464.8	-110036	-155027	-964771
X17	-1.18182	-.103636	3.02282	11.8092
X18	153.7	-585.29	-866.958	-4723.07
X19	-13.9818	-15.2036	89.9873	242.107
X20	-12.0727	7.29455	45.7	93.5026
X21	-.006364	.0152727	.0147347	.0678547
X22	0.654545	-.330909	-2.29616	-4.01265
X23	-.330909	7.71218	3.83036	29.4533
X24	-2.29616	3.83036	11.2179	21.0877
X25	-4.01265	29.4533	21.0877	249.778

PRINCIPAL COMPONENT ANALYSIS

TOTAL VARIANCE=8219758114

	EIGENVALUE	DIFFERENCE	PROPORTION	CUMULATIVE
PRIN1	8.2E+09	8.2E+09	0.999987	0.99999
PRIN2	84900	69761.1	0.000010	1.00000
PRIN3	15138.8	12949.2	0.000002	1.00000
PRIN4	2189.6	1964.14	0.000000	1.00000
PRIN5	225.454	65.7749	0.000000	1.00000
PRIN6	159.679	69.6715	0.000000	1.00000
PRIN7	90.0073	16.6248	0.000000	1.00000
PRIN8	73.3826	54.1628	0.000000	1.00000
PRIN9	19.2198	9.49877	0.000000	1.00000
PRIN10	9.72102	9.72102	0.000000	1.00000
PRIN11	0	0	0.000000	1.00000
PRIN12	0	0	0.000000	1.00000
PRIN13	0	0	0.000000	1.00000
PRIN14	0	0	0.000000	1.00000
PRIN15	0	0	0.000000	1.00000
PRIN16	0	0	0.000000	1.00000
PRIN17	0	0	0.000000	1.00000
PRIN18	0	0	0.000000	1.00000
PRIN19	0	0	0.000000	1.00000
PRIN20	0	0	0.000000	1.00000
PRIN21	0	0	0.000000	1.00000
PRIN22	0	.	0.000000	1.00000

PRINCIPAL COMPONENT ANALYSIS

EIGENVECTORS

	PRIN1	PRIN2	PRIN3	PRIN4	PRIN5	PRIN6
X1	-.000010	0.006547	0.008942	0.015709	-.056049	-.027712
X2	-.000851	0.792770	-.005018	0.125958	0.290333	-.394896
X3	-.000137	0.074101	0.013055	0.136146	0.177494	-.283701
X4	-.000021	-.002599	-.004742	0.041235	0.080102	0.033727
X5	-.000015	-.001226	-.000662	0.022608	0.095339	0.062615
X6	-.000025	-.002694	-.018707	0.063500	-.286712	0.012262
X7	-.000017	0.002939	-.002872	0.027039	0.039931	0.012168
X8	-.000020	0.012140	0.012796	0.006392	0.010191	0.068581
X9	-.000631	0.598875	-.025286	-.062719	-.394262	0.584968
X10	-.000017	0.001283	-.002044	0.026875.	0.067131	0.033779
X11	0.000014	0.013522	-.031911	-.011518	-.272706	0.155914
X12	-.000020	-.000226	-.003417	0.030181	0.127467	0.068530
X15	0.999985	0.000881	-.005163	0.001263	0.000170	0.000130
X17	-.000012	-.002327	0.007790	-.000286	0.060955	0.020186
X18	0.005288	0.032807	0.978640	-.195482	-.016331	-.011999
X19	-.000125	-.070327	0.195277	0.947814	-.146752	0.081288
X20	-.000108	-.018550	0.031153	0.074918	0.698184	0.606836
X21	-.000000	0.000008	-.000099	-.000159	0.000185	0.000162
X22	0.000004	0.000876	-.000384	-.002532	-.034071	-.012485
X23	-.000013	0.007887	-.001381	0.011288	0.038796	0.007426
X24	-.000019	-.001483	-.001897	0.034407	0.120677	0.029016
X25	-.000117	0.023148	0.023930	0.095601	-.029662	-.062825

	PRIN7	PRIN8	PRIN9	PRIN10	PRIN11	PRIN12
X1	-.293858	0.275821	-.025936	0.014946	0.048740	-.348375
X2	0.156175	-.179663	0.062062	-.093238	-.025203	0.014341
X3	-.267890	0.565052	0.420062	0.125267	-.031861	-.029553
X4	0.180554	-.109308	-.111397	0.454105	-.192343	0.075215
X5	-.135989	0.058072	0.063965	0.407151	-.150030	0.219978
X6	0.567977	-.094870	0.336352	-.094909	-.011000	-.089616
X7	0.083063	-.070265	-.049460	0.186226	-.082482	0.300076
X8	-.077519	0.151142	0.034662	-.085038	0.041736	0.409439
X9	-.200525	0.123037	-.131569	0.092745	0.037645	-.021297
X10	0.094753	-.076646	-.049870	0.215596	-.098653	-.019585
X11	0.237169	0.146081	0.614340	0.052314	-.040643	0.012401
X12	0.084185	-.097099	-.033303	0.452755	-.194558	-.285452
X15	-.000084	0.000099	-.000199	-.000126	0.000011	0.000013
X17	0.057001	-.035248	-.174552	-.320315	0.110811	-.133557
X18	0.025319	-.005396	0.033735	0.024263	-.001820	-.003126
X19	-.099915	-.108883	-.045596	-.042101	0.001505	0.004463
X20	0.141469	0.093127	0.161746	-.225223	-.048940	-.025880
X21	0.001300	-.000066	-.000282	-.000126	-.000093	0.334952
X22	-.040800	0.002275	0.013730	-.052786	0.026725	0.546899
X23	0.022714	-.030572	0.013111	0.137401	-.060137	-.210299
X24	0.081935	-.061950	0.063160	0.333376	0.926134	-.000054
X25	0.524962	0.664756	-.472468	0.034461	0.020334	0.035530

PRINCIPAL COMPONENT ANALYSIS

EIGENVECTORS

	PRIN13	PRIN14	PRIN15	PRIN16	PRIN17	PRIN18
X1	0.199128	-.359479	0.391893	-.136960	0.390616	-.196401
X2	0.005427	-.199781	-.003183	-.016528	0.027346	-.014632
X3	-.008700	0.490104	0.008092	0.067065	-.027554	0.041603
X4	-.022381	0.180401	-.260259	-.007030	0.735978	0.000068
X5	-.095413	-.248823	0.111701	-.681884	-.243781	0.148275
X6	0.041258	0.287062	0.507988	-.286705	0.118915	0.007171
X7	-.173016	0.181651	0.076335	0.003010	-.240268	-.697337
X8	-.297886	-.030281	0.284005	0.299489	0.195084	0.109361
X9	-.004497	0.214741	0.004291	0.004041	-.030021	0.017103
X10	0.037686	0.083519	0.084083	0.105474	-.164224	0.633405
X11	0.007912	-.401870	-.377370	0.191306	-.057342	-.031783
X12	0.228759	-.087482	0.364731	0.492725	-.251713	-.094534
X15	-.000013	-.000004	0.000016	0.000001	0.000002	0.000008
X17	0.044917	0.246077	0.002049	-.055759	-.088485	0.066265
X18	0.003053	0.005759	0.000606	-.002667	0.000074	-.001606
X19	-.008090	-.040399	-.045695	0.018790	-.018198	0.003918
X20	0.047828	-.025298	0.026223	-.057862	0.065408	-.047505
X21	-.268063	-.077573	0.275962	0.175039	0.048879	0.135981
X22	0.829799	0.039323	0.022126	0.011990	0.023361	0.005436
X23	0.106060	0.262388	-.229525	-.106444	-.121024	-.050686
X24	0.000030	0.000775	0.000021	0.000048	-.000068	0.000024
X25	0.019472	-.135545	-.083447	-.010290	-.101755	0.003187

	PRIN19	PRIN20	PRIN21	PRIN22
X1	0.312574	0.192387	0.164207	0.120852
X2	0.013817	0.033314	-.010028	0.052385
X3	-.042890	-.019354	0.032367	-.167744
X4	-.088692	0.142406	0.058971	-.103824
X5	-.257313	0.163611	-.030508	0.008069
X6	-.022146	-.084717	-.069407	0.018173
X7	0.424621	0.228990	0.049723	-.060920
X8	-.112328	0.282543	-.425997	0.451916
X9	-.019425	-.054921	0.011163	-.071648
X10	0.649457	0.205211	0.003963	-.031687
X11	0.024771	0.277025	0.134527	0.011138
X12	-.350791	0.050171	-.036486	-.034579
X15	-.000016	-.000024	-.000027	0.000020
X17	-.274292	0.764548	0.286583	-.091256
X18	0.002874	0.003550	0.005124	-.005044
X19	-.011927	-.008882	0.000199	0.002506
X20	0.063823	-.103640	0.010887	-.017095
X21	-.083387	-.217809	0.791683	0.033157
X22	-.008422	0.006488	0.040242	0.034118
X23	0.012418	-.058269	0.220111	0.846512
X24	-.000033	0.000167	0.000161	-.000250
X25	-.017378	-.066171	-.006465	0.021055

CODE AND UNIT TEST PHASE: Least Squares Method
(using Principal Components)

DEP VARIABLE: Y

ANALYSIS OF VARIANCE

SOURCE	DF	SUM OF SQUARES	MEAN SQUARE	F VALUE	PROB>F
MODEL	1	275.45981	275.45981	0.566	0.4764
ERROR	7	3406.24241	486.60606		
C TOTAL	8	3681.70222			

ROOT MSE	22.05915	R-SQUARE	0.0748	
DEP MEAN	24.25556	ADJ R-SQ	-0.0574	
C.V.	90.94473			

PARAMETER ESTIMATES

VARIABLE	DF	PARAMETER ESTIMATE	STANDARD ERROR	T FOR H0: PARAMETER=0
INTERCEP	1	38.02688694	19.72530460	1.928
P1	1	-2.58584501	3.43686223	-0.752

VARIABLE	DF	PROB > $\lvert T \rvert$
INTERCEP	1	0.0952
P1	1	0.4764

OBS	ID	ACTUAL	PREDICT VALUE	STD ERR PREDICT	LOWER95% MEAN
1	5.76979	36.0000	23.1071	7.5098	5.3491
2	6.15126	31.0000	22.1207	7.8815	3.4836
3	3.13332	64.0000	29.9246	10.5281	5.0295
4	5.2445	48.0000	24.4654	7.3583	7.0656
5	2.27999	10.0000	32.1312	12.7921	1.8825
6	2.27047	8.0000	32.1558	12.8189	1.8438
7	7.61732	6.5000	18.3297	10.7750	-7.1493
8	7.55941	6.0000	18.4794	10.6304	-6.6577
9	7.90488	8.8000	17.5861	11.5172	-9.6479
10	5.91787	.	22.7242	7.6295	4.6830
11	10.373	.	11.2038	18.8412	-33.3490

OBS		ID	UPPER95% MEAN	LOWER95% PREDICT	UPPER95% PREDICT	RESIDUAL
	1	5.76979	40.8651	-31.9948	78.2090	12.8929
	2	6.15126	40.7577	-33.2708	77.5121	8.8793
	3	3.13332	54.8198	-27.8737	87.7229	34.0754
	4	5.2445	41.8653	-30.5221	79.4530	23.5346
	5	2.27999	62.3798	-28.1669	92.4292	-22.1312
	6	2.27047	62.4679	-28.1741	92.4857	-24.1558
	7	7.61732	43.8087	-39.7225	76.3819	-11.8297
	8	7.55941	43.6165	-39.4235	76.3823	-12.4794
	9	7.90488	44.8201	-41.2575	76.4297	-8.7861
	10	5.91787	40.7653	-32.4696	77.9180	.
	11	10.373	55.7566	-57.3952	79.8028	.

OBS		ID	STD ERR RESIDUAL
	1	5.76979	20.7415
	2	6.15126	20.6031
	3	3.13332	19.3847
	4	5.2445	20.7957
	5	2.27999	17.9714
	6	2.27047	17.9522
	7	7.61732	19.2485
	8	7.55941	19.3288
	9	7.90488	18.8138
	10	5.91787	.
	11	10.373	.

SUM OF RESIDUALS	9.14824E-14
SUM OF SQUARED RESIDUALS	3406.242
PREDICTED RESID SS (PRESS)	6058.221

Regression Models Using Principal Components Analysis
for Highly Correlated Variables

PRINCIPAL COMPONENT ANALYSIS

11 OBSERVATIONS
7 VARIABLES

SIMPLE STATISTICS

	X1	X2	X3	X8
MEAN	2.87712	105.297	20.0766	8.02100
ST DEV	4.52637	243.706	26.7754	4.62116

	X9	X23	X25
MEAN	90.035	2.52727	22.6800
ST DEV	183.950	2.77708	15.8044

COVARIANCES

	X1	X2	X3	X8
X1	20.48802	507.6274	76.7436	15.03902
X2	507.6274	59392.56	6000.551	949.0371
X3	76.7436	6000.551	716.922	108.5977
X8	15.03902	949.0371	108.5977	21.35512
X9	391.7628	44639.85	4421.269	721.7865
X23	4.005569	630.3725	67.45542	9.755015
X25	29.93848	2403.468	323.7854	51.44488

	X9	X23	X25
X1	391.7628	4.005569	29.93848
X2	44639.85	630.3725	2403.468
X3	4421.269	67.45542	323.7854
X8	721.7865	9.755015	51.44488
X9	33837.77	466.0989	1758.177
X23	466.0989	7.712182	29.45329
X25	1758.177	29.45329	249.7776

PRINCIPAL COMPONENT ANALYSIS

TOTAL VARIANCE=94246.59

	EIGENVALUE	DIFFERENCE	PROPORTION
CUMULATIVE			
PRIN1	93767.7	93474.0	0.994919
0.99492			
PRIN2	293.6	163.8	0.003116
0.99803			
PRIN3	129.8	81.3	0.001377
0.99941			
PRIN4	48.5	43.9	0.000515
0.99993			
PRIN5	4.6	2.5	0.000049
0.99998			
PRIN6	2.1	1.8	0.000022
1.00000			
PRIN7	0.3	.	0.000003
1.00000			

EIGENVECTORS

	PRIN1	PRIN2	PRIN3	PRIN4
X1	0.006891	0.053822	0.138704	0.458959
X2	0.795466	0.322656	-.460802	-.164212
X3	0.079926	0.560871	0.141991	0.674916
X8	0.012782	0.040068	0.121577	0.146618
X9	0.599617	-.533522	0.553546	0.147258
X23	0.008398	0.031659	-.015624	-.029001
X25	0.032006	0.539598	0.653317	-.512696

	PRIN5	PRIN6	PRIN7
X1	0.658582	-.466968	0.339683
X2	0.151586	-.020767	0.020326
X3	-.421264	0.072819	-.143518
X8	0.500471	0.840668	-.068991
X9	-.164496	0.006469	-.024806
X23	-.280461	0.248635	0.925940
X25	0.098187	-.087309	0.029412

PRINCIPAL COMPONENT ANALYSIS

11 OBSERVATIONS
10 VARIABLES

SIMPLE STATISTICS

	X4	X5	X7	X10	X12
MEAN	2.83031	2.59865	2.11232	2.05379	2.43642
ST DEV	3.99664	3.05383	2.56330	2.65265	3.64045

	X18	X19	X20	X22	X24
MEAN	419.000	102.455	21.1818	2.36364	2.74685
ST DEV	494.511	55.682	17.9990	0.80904	3.34931

COVARIANCES

	X4	X5	X7	X10	X12
X4	15.9731	5.96383	8.56419	9.80594	13.3912
X5	5.96383	9.32588	3.46024	4.3422	7.72505
X7	8.56419	3.46024	6.5705	6.54925	7.941
X10	9.80594	4.3422	6.54925	7.03654	9.17345
X12	13.3912	7.72505	7.941	9.17345	13.2529
X18	-1011.46	-665.931	-782.588	-767.761	-938.115
X19	105.698	65.6658	46.1192	57.2551	71.0751
X20	43.4028	37.4768	20.9603	30.1997	47.5335
X22	-2.6418	-1.18823	-1.17045	-1.60379	-2.43871
X24	12.3389	7.18182	6.99544	8.19207	11.7909

	X18	X19	X20	X22	X24
X4	-1011.46	105.698	43.4028	-2.6418	12.3389
X5	-665.931	65.6658	37.4768	-1.18823	7.18182
X7	-782.588	46.1192	20.9603	-1.17045	6.99544
X10	-767.761	57.2551	30.1997	-1.60379	8.19207
X12	-938.115	71.0751	47.5335	-2.43871	11.7909
X18	244541	-3143.5	-4314.1	153.7	-866.958
X19	-3143.5	3100.47	451.909	-13.9818	89.9873
X20	-4314.1	451.909	323.964	-12.0727	45.7
X22	153.7	-13.9818	-12.0727	0.654545	-2.29616
X24	-866.958	89.9873	45.7	-2.29616	11.2179

PRINCIPAL COMPONENT ANALYSIS

TOTAL VARIANCE=248029.9

	EIGENVALUE	DIFFERENCE	PROPORTION	CUMULATIVE
PRIN1	244676	241553	0.986480	0.98648
PRIN2	3123	2921	0.012591	0.99907
PRIN3	202	180	0.000813	0.99988
PRIN4	22	17	0.000088	0.99997
PRIN5	5	4	0.000020	0.99999
PRIN6	1	1	0.000006	1.00000
PRIN7	0	0	0.000001	1.00000
PRIN8	0	0	0.000000	1.00000
PRIN9	0	0	0.000000	1.00000
PRIN10	0	.	0.000000	1.00000

EIGENVECTORS

	PRIN1	PRIN2	PRIN3	PRIN4	PRIN5
X4	-.004142	0.030741	0.074788	0.557404	-.255778
X5	-.002728	0.019341	0.093433	0.086419	0.933384
X7	-.003202	0.011849	0.017808	0.359227	-.076413
X10	-.003143	0.015895	0.057780	0.362158	-.098286
X12	-.003841	0.020303	0.124832	0.480359	0.144420
X18	0.999722	0.015776	0.016865	0.004420	0.000214
X19	-.013048	0.988986	-.145044	-.023291	-.000806
X20	-.017678	0.137151	0.965536	-.190685	-.090993
X22	0.000630	-.004264	-.039851	-.062573	0.079428
X24	-.003551	0.026534	0.106152	0.387360	0.111473

	PRIN6	PRIN7	PRIN8	PRIN9	PRIN10
X4	-.580518	0.358151	-.282895	0.259850	-.067073
X5	-.059107	0.189811	-.259442	0.043326	0.059209
X7	0.679620	0.062402	-.365802	0.049403	-.512465
X10	0.392905	0.100794	-.033061	0.024990	0.830259
X12	0.022076	0.164348	0.739272	-.348577	-.191995
X18	0.000998	0.000412	-.000880	0.000605	-.000169
X19	0.003909	-.000096	0.008653	-.008030	-.000077
X20	0.033509	0.026429	-.018878	0.038192	-.018449
X22	0.152950	0.083966	0.412597	0.885806	-.053252
X24	-.135011	-.887066	-.023766	0.140904	0.002716

PRINCIPAL COMPONENT ANALYSIS

11 OBSERVATIONS
2 VARIABLES

SIMPLE STATISTICS

	X11	X17
MEAN	7.29776	5.45455
ST DEV	8.21082	2.33939

COVARIANCES

	X11	X17
X11	67.41757	-12.4703
X17	-12.4703	5.472727

TOTAL VARIANCE=72.89029

	EIGENVALUE	DIFFERENCE	PROPORTION CUMULATIVE
PRIN1	69.8338	66.7772	0.958067
0.95807			
PRIN2	3.0565	.	0.041933
1.00000			

EIGENVECTORS

	PRIN1	PRIN2
X11	0.981742	0.190218
X17	-.190218	0.981742

Regression Model: using the first Principal component of each highly correlated set of variables

DEP VARIABLE: Y

ANALYSIS OF VARIANCE

SOURCE	DF	SUM OF SQUARES	MEAN SQUARE	F VALUE	PROB>F
MODEL	5	2744.60060	548.92012	1.757	0.3408
ERROR	3	937.10162	312.36721		
C TOTAL	8	3681.70222			

ROOT MSE	17.67391	R-SQUARE	0.7455
DEP MEAN	24.25556	ADJ R-SQ	0.3213
C.V.	72.86542		

PARAMETER ESTIMATES

VARIABLE	DF	PARAMETER ESTIMATE	STANDARD ERROR	T FOR H0: PARAMETER=0
INTERCEP	1	303.72064	432.56932	0.702
P1	1	0.04912381	0.02107148	2.331
P2	1	0.01548917	0.01901178	0.815
P3	1	0.04067242	0.06340874	0.641
P4	1	-0.64732832	0.89593575	-0.723
P5	1	-290.92605	439.15510	-0.662

VARIABLE	DF	PROB > |T|
INTERCEP	1	0.5332
P1	1	0.1020
P2	1	0.4749
P3	1	0.5669
P4	1	0.5222
P5	1	0.5550

OBS	ID	ACTUAL	PREDICT VALUE	STD ERR PREDICT	LOWER95% MEAN
1	4.1398	36.0000	36.0000	17.6739	-20.2472
2	29.2134	31.0000	30.4031	17.6639	-25.8124
3	1057.11	64.0000	63.1191	17.6608	6.9137
4	7.66955	48.0000	26.1961	12.3981	-13.2608
5	22.0749	10.0000	26.1133	14.5357	-20.1464
6	40.0765	8.0000	9.2445	8.7823	-18.7051
7	88.4097	6.5000	13.4096	11.7090	-23.8543
8	101.506	6.0000	14.2004	11.3907	-22.0504
9	79.7902	8.8000	-0.3861	15.1309	-48.5401
10	19.8917	.	31.4122	21.2165	-36.1092
11	92.54	.	19.3664	8.4602	-7.5580

OBS	ID	UPPER95% MEAN	LOWER95% PREDICT	UPPER95% PREDICT	RESIDUAL
1	4.1398	92.2472	-43.5456	115.5	3.8E-12
2	29.2134	86.6186	-49.1201	109.9	0.5969
3	1057.11	119.3	-16.3969	142.6	0.8809
4	7.66955	65.6530	-42.5105	94.9027	21.8039
5	22.0749	72.3730	-46.7133	98.9399	-16.1133
6	40.0765	37.1941	-53.5642	72.0532	-1.2445
7	88.4097	50.6734	-54.0615	80.8807	-6.9096
8	101.506	50.4513	-52.7165	81.1174	-8.2004
9	79.7902	47.7679	-74.4304	73.6582	9.1861
10	19.8917	98.9336	-56.4678	119.3	.
11	92.54	46.2909	-42.9928	81.7257	.

OBS	ID	STD ERR RESIDUAL
1	4.1398	1.4E-05
2	29.2134	0.5934
3	1057.11	0.6812
4	7.66955	12.5958
5	22.0749	10.0540
6	40.0765	15.3375
7	88.4097	13.2388
8	101.506	13.5137
9	79.7902	9.1337
10	19.8917	.
11	92.54	.

SUM OF RESIDUALS   1.52323E-12
SUM OF SQUARED RESIDUALS   937.1016
PREDICTED RESID SS (PRESS)   637811.6

Regression Model: using only the first Principal component of the highly correlated set of variables ($x_1, x_2, x_3, x_8, x_9, x_{23}, x_{25}$)

DEP VARIABLE: Y

ANALYSIS OF VARIANCE

SOURCE	DF	SUM OF SQUARES	MEAN SQUARE	F VALUE	PROB>F
MODEL	1	1477.14894	1477.14894	4.690	0.0670
ERROR	7	2204.55328	314.93618		
C TOTAL	8	3681.70222			

ROOT MSE	17.74644	R-SQUARE	0.4012
DEP MEAN	24.25556	ADJ R-SQ	0.3157
C.V.	73.16444		

PARAMETER ESTIMATES

VARIABLE	DF	PARAMETER ESTIMATE	STANDARD ERROR	T FOR H0: PARAMETER=0
INTERCEP	1	17.88125956	6.60725342	2.706
P1	1	0.04011814	0.01852422	2.166

VARIABLE	DF	PROB > |T|
INTERCEP	1	0.0304
P1	1	0.0670

OBS	ID	ACTUAL	PREDICT VALUE	STD ERR PREDICT	LOWER95% MEAN
1	4.1398	36.0000	18.0473	6.5735	2.5035
2	29.2134	31.0000	19.0532	6.3846	3.9559
3	1057.11	64.0000	60.2907	17.6592	18.5330
4	7.66955	48.0000	18.1889	6.5452	2.7119
5	22.0749	10.0000	18.7669	6.4355	3.5492
6	40.0765	8.0000	19.4891	6.3116	4.5643
7	88.4097	6.5000	21.4281	6.0578	7.1035
8	101.506	6.0000	21.9535	6.0102	7.7414
9	79.7902	8.8000	21.0823	6.0942	6.6716
10	19.8917	.	18.6793	6.4516	3.4237
11	92.54	.	21.5938	6.0418	7.3071

OBS	ID	UPPER95% MEAN	LOWER95% PREDICT	UPPER95% PREDICT	RESIDUAL
1	4.1398	33.5912	-26.7030	62.7976	17.9527
2	29.2134	34.1505	-25.5439	63.6504	11.9468
3	1057.11	102.0	1.0903	119.5	3.7093
4	7.66955	33.6660	-26.5382	62.9161	29.8111
5	22.0749	33.9846	-25.8712	63.4049	-8.7669
6	40.0765	34.4138	-25.0500	64.0281	-11.4891
7	88.4097	35.7527	-22.9134	65.7696	-14.9281
8	101.506	36.1655	-22.3518	66.2588	-15.9535
9	79.7902	35.4930	-23.2871	65.4517	-12.2823
10	19.8917	33.9349	-25.9717	63.3303	.
11	92.54	35.8805	-22.7355	65.9231	.

OBS	ID	STD ERR RESIDUAL
1	4.1398	16.4841
2	29.2134	16.5582
3	1057.11	1.7577
4	7.66955	16.4953
5	22.0749	16.5384
6	40.0765	16.5861
7	88.4097	16.6805
8	101.506	16.6977
9	79.7902	16.6672
10	19.8917	.
11	92.54	.

SUM OF RESIDUALS	5.24025E-14
SUM OF SQUARED RESIDUALS	2204.553
PREDICTED RESID SS (PRESS)	145859.2

References

Abramowitz, M. and I. A. Stegun, I.A. (eds.) 1970. <u>Handbook of Mathematical Functions with Formulas, Graphs and Mathematical Tables</u>, U. S. Department of Commerce, National Bureau of Standards, Applied Mathematics Series 55.

Adams, E.N., "Optimizing Preventive Service of Software Products." <u>IBM Journal of Research and Development</u>, June 1984.

Adelson, R.M., "Compound Poisson Distributions." <u>Operational Research Quarterly</u>, V. 17, pp. 73-75, 1966.

AFCCE, <u>A Descriptive Evaluation of Software Sizing Models</u>, Headquarters USAF/Air Force Cost Center, Washington, DC, 1987. NTIS document #A241678.

AGREE (Advisory Group of Electronic Equipment), <u>Reliability of Military Electronic Equipment,</u> Office of the Assistant Secretary of Defense (Research and Engineering), 1957.

Albrecht, A.J., "Measuring Application Development Productivity." <u>Proceedings of the Joint IBM/SHARE/GUIDE Application Development Symposium</u>, pp. 83-92, October 1979.

Albrecht, A.J. and Gaffney, J.E., "Software Function, Source Lines of Code, and Development Effort Prediction: A Software Science Evaluation." <u>IEEE Transactions on Software Engineering</u>, SE-9(6), pp. 639-647, November 1983.

Amstadter, B.L., <u>Reliability Mathematics: Fundamentals, Practices, Procedures</u>, McGraw-Hill, New York, 1971.

Angus, J., Schafer, R.E., Van Den Berg, S. and Rutemiller, H., "Failure-Free Period Life Tests." <u>Technometrics</u>, 27(1), 49-56, 1985.

Aviziensis, A., Grnarov, A. and Arlat, J. "On the Performance of Fault-Tolerance Strategies." <u>Proceedings 10th International Symposium on Fault-Tolerant Computing</u>, pp. 251-253, 1980.

Barbour, G.L., "Failure Modes and Effects Analysis by Matrix Methods." <u>Proceedings, Annual Reliability and Maintainability Symposium</u>, 1977.

Barlow, R.E., and Proschan, F., <u>Journal of the American Statistical Association</u>, V. 62, pp. 548-560, 1967.

Bartholomew, D.J., "Testing for Departure from the Exponential Distribution." _Biometrika_, V. 44, pp. 253-256, 1957.

Basili, V.R. and Hutchens, D.H., "An Empirical Study of a Syntactic Complexity Family." _IEEE Transactions on Software Engineering_, SE-9(6), pp. 664-672, 1983.

Becker, P.W. and Jensen, F., _Design of Systems and Circuits for Maximum Reliability or Maximum Production Yield_, McGraw-Hill, New York, NY, 1977.

Bozoki, G., _SSM User's Guide_, Galorath Associates, Marina del Rey, CA, 1987.

Brocklehurst, S., Chan, P.Y., Littlewood, B. and Snell, "Recalibrating Software Reliability Models." _IEEE Transactions on Software Engineering_, SE-16(4), pp. 458-470, 1990.

Cheung, R.C., "A User-Oriented Software Reliability Model." _IEEE Transactions on Software Engineering_, SE-6(2), pp. 118-125, 1980.

Coulter, N.S., "Software Science and Cognitive Psychology." _IEEE Transactions on Software Engineering_, SE-9(3), 1983.

Cox, D.R. and Smith, W.L., "On the Superposition of Renewal Processes." _Biometrika_, V. 41, 1954.

Crow, L.H, "Reliability Growth Modeling," Army Materiel Systems Analysis Activity Technical Report, No. 55, Aberdeen Proving Ground, Maryland, 1972. NTIS Document #AD747000.

De Marco, T., _Structured Analysis and System Specification_, Yourdon Press, 1978.

Dennis, N. G., "Insight Into Standby Redundancy Via Unreliability", _IEEE Transactions On Reliability_, Vol R-23, No. 5, 1974.

Dhillon, B.S. and Singh, C., _Engineering Reliability: New Techniques and Applications_, John Wiley & Sons, New York, NY, 1981.

DOD-STD-2167A, _Defense System Software Development_, U.S. Department of Defense, Washington, DC, 1988.

Dreger, J.B., _Function Point Analysis_, Prentice Hall, Englewood Cliffs, NJ, 1989.

Duane, J.T., "Learning Curve Approach to Reliability Monitoring." IEEE Transactions on Aerospace, V. 2, pp. 563-566, 1964.

Eckhardt, D.E. and Lee, L.D. "A Theoretical Basis for the Analysis of Multiversion Programming Subject to Coincident Errors." IEEE Transactions on Software Engineering, SE-11(12), 1985.

Epstein, B., "Statistical Techniques in Life Testing." U.S. Department of Commerce, Office of Technical Services Report 171580, pp. 2.24-2.27, 1954. NTIS Document #AD21145.

Epstein, B., "Statistical Techniques in Life Testing," National Technical Information Service, U.S. Department of Commerce, Washington, DC., 1960.

Epstein, B. and Sobel, M., Journal of the American Statistical Association, V. 48, pp. 486-502, 1953.

Feller, W., An Introduction to Probability Theory and its Applications, V. 1, 2nd ed., Wiley, New York, NY, 1957.

Feller, W., An Introduction to Probability Theory and its Applications, V. 2, Wiley, New York, NY, 1966.

Fisher, R.A., Philosophical Transactions of the Royal Society of London A, V. 222, pp. 309-368, 1922.

Fuqua, N.B., Reliability Engineering for Electronic Design, M. Dekker, New York, NY, 1986.

Goddard, P. L. and Davis, R., Automated FMEA Techniques, Final Technical Report, RADC-TR-84-244, AD-A154161, 1984

Goddard, P. L., "Coverage As A Tradeoff Issue In System Architectural Design", Proceedings of the AIAA Computers In Aerospace VII Conference, pp. 761-766, 1989

Goel, A.L. and Okumoto, K., "Time-Dependent Error-Detection Rate Model for Software Reliability and Other Performance Measures." IEEE Transactions on Reliability, R-28(3), pp. 206-211, 1979.

Gremillion, L.L., "Determinants of Program Repair Maintenance Requirements." Communications of the ACM, 27(8), pp. 826-832, 1984.

Grosh, D.L., "A Parallel System of CFR Units is IFR." IEEE Transactions on Reliability, R-31(4), p. 403, 1982.

Grosh, D.L., A Primer of Reliability Theory, John Wiley & Sons, New York, NY, 1989.

Haight, F.A., _Handbook of the Poisson Distribution_, John Wiley & Sons, New York, NY, 1967.

Halstead, M.H., _Elements of Software Science_, Elsevier North Holland, New York, NY, 1977.

Hamer, P.G. and Frewin, G.D., "M.H. Halstead's Software Science--a Critical Examination." _Proceedings 6th International Conference on Software Engineering_, IEE/ACM, 1982.

Hamer, P. G. and Frewin, G.D., "Software Metrics--A Critical Overview." in _The Software Development Process_, State of the Art Report, Series 13, No. 2, Pergamon Infotech, 1985.

Hatley, D.J. and Pirbhai, I.A., _Strategies for Real Time System Specification_, Dorset House Publishing, 1987.

Hecht, H., "Measurement, Estimation, and Prediction of Software Reliability." in _Software Engineering Technology_, 2, Infotech International, Maidenhead, Berkshire, UK, pp. 209-224; also in NASA report CR145135, Jan. 1977.

Hecht, H., "Allocation of Resources for Software Reliability." _Proceedings COMPCON Fall 1981_, Washington, DC, pp. 74-82, 1981.

Humphrey, W.S., _Managing the Software Process_, Addison-Wesley, Reading, MA, 1989.

James, L.E., Angus, J., Bowen, J.B. and McDaniel, J., _Combined HW/SW Reliability Models_, Final Technical Report, RADC-82-68, 1982.

Jelinski, Z. and Moranda, P.B., "Software Reliability Research." (W. Freiberger, Editor), _Statistical Computer Performance Evaluation_, Academic, New York, pp. 465-484, 1972.

Jones, C.L., _Programming Productivity_, McGraw-Hill, New York, NY, 1986.

Kapur, K.C. and Lamberson, L.R., _Reliability in Engineering Design_, John Wiley & Sons, New York, 1977.

Knight, J. C. and Leveson, N.G., "An Experimental Evaluation of the Assumption of Independence in Multi-Version Programming." _IEEE Transactions on Software Engineering_, SE-12(1), pp. 96-109, 1986.

Kopetz, H., _Software Reliability_, Springer-Verlag, New York, pp. 10-11, 1980.

Kozlow, B.A. and Ushakov, I.A., _Reliability Handbook_, Holt, Rinehart, and Winston, Inc., 1970.

Leveson, N. G. and Stolzy, J.L., "Safety Analysis of Ada Programs Using Fault Trees." _IEEE Transactions on Reliability_, R-32(5), pp. 479-240, 1983.

Lévy, P., _Proceedings of the International Congress of Mathematics (Amsterdam)_, V. 3, pp. 314-426, 1954.

Littlewood, B., "MTBF is Meaningless in Software Reliability." Correspondence in _IEEE Transactions on Reliability_, 24(1), p. 82, 1975.

Littlewood, B., "How to Measure Software Reliability and How Not to." _IEEE Transactions on Reliability_, R-28(2), pp. 103-110, 1979a.

Littlewood, B., "Software Reliability Model for Modular Program Structure." _IEEE Transactions on Reliability_, R-28(3), pp. 241-246, 1979b.

Littlewood, B. and Miller, D.R. "Conceptual Modeling of Coincident Failures in Multiversion Software." _IEEE Transactions on Software Engineering_, 15(2), 1989.

Littlewood, B., and Verrall, J.L., "A Bayesian reliability Growth Model for Computer Software." _Journal of the American Statistical Society_, C (Applied Statistics), V. 22, pp. 332-346, 1973.

MacWilliams, W. H., "Reliability of Real Time Control Software Systems." _Record of the 1973 IEEE Symposium on Computer Software Reliability_, pp. 1-6, 1973.

Mallows, C.L., "Some Comments on C_p." _Technometrics_, 15(4), pp. 561-675, November 1973.

McCabe, T.J., "A Complexity Measure." _IEEE Transactions on Software Engineering_, SE-2(4), pp. 308-320, 1976.

MIL-HDBK-217. _Reliability Prediction of Electronic Equipment._

MIL-STD-781. _Reliability Testing for Engineering Development, Qualifications and Production_, U.S. Department of Defense, Washington, DC.

Mills, H.D., "On the Statistical Validation of Computer Programs." FSC-72-6015, IBM Federal Systems Div., Gaithersburg, MD, 1972.

Miyamoto, I., "Software Reliability in On-Line Real Time Environment." _Proceedings of the 1975 International Conference on Reliable Software_, Los Angeles, pp. 195-203, 1975.

Moran, P.A.P., "The Random Division of an Interval. Part II." _Journal of the Royal Statistical Society_, Series B, V. 13, pp. 147-150, 1951.

Moscovitz, F. and McLean, J.B., "Some Reliability Aspects of System Design." _IRE Transactions on Reliability and Quality Control_, PQRQC-8, Sept. 1956.

Musa, J.D., "A Theory of Software Reliability and Its Application." _IEEE Transactions on Software Engineering, SE-1(3)_, pp. 312-327, 1975.

Musa, J.D., "Validity of the Execution Time Theory of Software Reliability." _IEEE Transactions on Reliability, R-28(3)_, pp. 181-191, 1979.

Musa, J.D., Software Reliability Measurement." _Journal of Systems and Software_, 1(3), pp. 223-241, 1980.

Musa, J.D., "A Theory of Software Reliability and Its Application." _IEEE Transactions on Software Engineering_, SE-1(3), 1975.

Musa, J.D., Iannino, A. and Okumoto, K., _Software Reliability: Measurement, Prediction, Application_, McGraw-Hill, New York, 1987.

Musa, J.D., and Okumoto, K., "A Logarithmic Poisson Execution Time Model for Software Reliability Measurement." _Proceedings 7th International Conference of Software Engineering_, IEEE Computer Society, Orlando, pp. 230-238, March 1984.

Musa, J.D., and Okumoto, K., "A Comparison of Time Domains for Software Reliability Models." _Journal of Systems and Software_, 4(4), pp. 277-287, 1984.

Myers, G.J., _The Art of Software Testing_, Wiley, New York, NY, 1979.

Myers, G.J., _Software Reliability: Principles and Practices_, Wiley-Interscience, New York, NY, 1976.

Nelson, E.C., "A Statistical Basis for Software Reliability Assessment." TRW-SS-73-03, March 1973.

Nieuwhof, G.W.E., "An Introduction to Fault Tree Analysis with Emphasis on Failure Rate Evaluation." _Microelectronics and Reliability_, 14, pp. 105-119, 1975.

O'Connor, P.D.T., _Practical Reliability Engineering_, 2nd ed., John Wiley & Sons, Chichester, UK, 1985.

Parzen, E., _Stochastic Processes_, Holden-Day, San Francisco, 1962.

Phillips, D., Ravindran, I. and Solberg, J., _Operations Research_, J. Wiley & Sons, New York, NY, 1976.

Pressman, R.S., _Software Engineering: A Practitioner's Approach_, 1st ed., McGraw-Hill, New York, NY, 1982.

RADC, _RADC Reliability Engineer's Toolkit: An Application-Oriented Guide for the Practicing Reliability Engineer_, Rome Air Development Center, Systems Reliability and Engineering Division, 1988.

Randell, B., "System Structure for Software Fault Tolerance." _IEEE Transactions on Software Engineering_, SE-1(6), pp. 220-231, 1975.

Rau, J.G., _Optimization and Probability in Systems Engineering_, Van Nostrand Reinhold, New York, NY, 1970.

Saaty, T., _Decision Making for Leaders: The Analytical Hierarchy Process for Decisions in a Complex World_, Lifetime Learning Publications, Belmont, CA, 1982.

Sandler, G.H., _System Reliability Engineering_, Prentice-Hall, Englewood Cliffs, NJ, 1963.

Sarje, A. K. and Prasad, E.V., "An Efficient Non-Recursive Algorithm for Computing the Reliability of k-out-of-n Systems." _IEEE Transactions on Reliability_, R-38(2), pp. 234-235, 1989.

Scott, R. K., Gault, J.W. and McAllister, D.F., "Fault-Tolerant Software Reliability Modeling." _IEEE Transactions on Software Engineering_, SE-13(5), pp. 582-592, 1987.

Shen, V.Y, Conte, S.D. and Dunsmore, H.E., "Software Science Revisited: a Critical Analysis of the Theory and Its Empirical Support." _IEEE Transactions on Software Engineering_, SE-9(2), March 1983.

Shooman, M.L., "Operational Testing and Software Reliability Estimation During Program Development." in _Record IEEE_

Symposium on Computer Software Reliability, pp. 51-57, 1973.

Shooman, M.L., Software Engineering: Design, Reliability, and Management, McGraw-Hill, New York, NY, 1983.

Siegrist, K., "Reliability of Systems with Markov Transfer of Control." IEEE Transactions on Software Engineering, SE-14(7), pp. 1049-1053, 1988.

Singpurwalla, N.D. 1985a. "Military Standards for Fixed-Length Tests." Encyclopedia of Statistical Sciences, 5, John Wiley & Sons, New York, NY, pp. 489-490, 1985a.

Singpurwalla, N.D., "Military Standards for Sequential Life Testing." Encyclopedia of Statistical Sciences, 5, John Wiley & Sons, New York, NY, pp. 490-493, 1985b.

Smith, W.L., "On Renewal Theory, Counter Problems, and Quasi-Poisson Processes." Proceedings, Cambridge Philosophical Society, V. 53, pp. 175-193, 1957.

Smith, W.L., "Renewal Theory and its Ramifications." Journal of the Royal Statistical Society, Series B, V. 20, pp. 243-302, 1958a.

Smith, W.L., Addendum, Proceedings, Cambridge Philosophical Society, 54, pp. 305, 1958b.

Souder, W.E. Management Decision Methods for Managers of Engineering and Research, Van Nostrand Reinhold, New York, NY, 1980.

Sunohara, T., Takano, A., Uehara, K. and Ohkawa, T., "Program Complexity Measure for Software Development Management." Proceedings Fifth International Conference on Software Engineering, San Diego, CA, pp. 100-106, 1981.

Takahashi, M. and Kamayachi, Y., "An Empirical Study of a Model for Program Error Prediction." IEEE Transactions on Software Engineering, 15(1), pp. 82-86. 1989.

Thurstone, L.L., The Measurement of Values, University of Chicago Press, Chicago, IL, 1959.

Trachtenberg, M. "The Linear Software Reliability Model and Uniform Testing." IEEE Transactions on Reliability, R-34(1), pp. 8-16, 1985.

von Alven, Willian (ed.), Reliability Engineering, Prentice-Hall, Englewood Cliffs, NJ, 1964.

Volk, W., _Engineering Statistics with a Programmable Calculator_, McGraw-Hill, New York, NY, 1982.

Wald, A. _Sequential Analysis_, Wiley, New York, NY, 1947.

Yamada, S. and Osaki, S., "Reliability Growth Models for Hardware and Software Systems Based on Nonhomogeneous Poisson Processes: A Survey." _Microelectronics and Reliability_, 23(1), pp. 91-112, 1983.

Zipf, G., _The Psycho-Biology of Language: An Introduction to Dynamic Philology_, MIT, Cambridge, MA, 1965.

Part II

Hardware/Software Reliability Assurance and Control

Draft Military Handbook

Rome Laboratory

1. Introduction

1.1 <u>Purpose</u>.   This handbook establishes uniform reliability assurance methods for predicting and estimating the reliability of electronic systems that include software components.   It provides techniques for software reliability that complement the hardware reliability tasks and techniques that appear in MIL-STD-785, MIL-STD-756, MIL-STD-781, and related standards and handbooks.

1.2 <u>Application</u>. This handbook provides both general requirements and specific procedures for predicting and estimating the reliability of systems that contain both hardware and software elements.   Techniques are described for reliability modeling, allocation, prediction, growth modeling/testing, and qualification testing.

2. Applicable Documents

2.1 <u>Military Documents</u>.

MIL-STD-721C	Definition of Terms for Reliability and Maintainability, 12 June 1981
MIL-STD-756B	Reliability Modeling and Prediction, 18 November 1981
MIL-STD-781D	Reliability Testing for Engineering Development, Qualification and Production, 17 October 1987
MIL-STD-785B	Reliability Programs for Systems and Equipment, Development and Production, 15 September 1980
MIL-STD-1521B	Technical Reviews and Audits for Systems, Equipments, and Computer Software, 4 June 1985
MIL-STD-2155	Failure Reporting Analysis and Corrective Action System, 24 July 1985
MIL-HDBK-189	Reliability Growth Management, 13 February 1981
MIL-HDBK-217E	Reliability Prediction of Electronic Equipment, 27 October 1986
MIL-HDBK-781	Reliability Test Methods, Plans, and Environments for Engineering Development, Qualification, and Production, 14 July 1987.
DOD-STD-2167A	Defense System Software Development, 29 February 1988

2.2 <u>Non-Military Documents</u>.

Musa, J.D., Iannino, A. and Okumoto, K., <u>Software Reliability: Measurement, Prediction, Application</u>. McGraw Hill Book Company, New York, NY. 1987.

Friedman, M.A., Tran, P.Y., and Goddard, P.L., <u>Reliability Techniques for Combined Hardware and Software Systems</u>, Final Report, Contract F30602-89-C-0111, Rome Laboratory, Air Force Systems Command, Griffiss Air Force Base, New York. Sept. 1991.

3. Definitions and Symbols

3.1 <u>Definitions of Terms</u>. The definition of all terms used herein are in accordance with the definitions given in MIL-STD-721, except as defined below.

<u>Aggregate</u>. An aggregate is a set of interrelated components. An aggregate can exist at any level of the system structure. The components that comprise the aggregate exist at the next level below the aggregate.

<u>Component</u>. A component is an element at any level of the system structure.

<u>Failure Rate</u>. A failure rate is the rate of failures per unit time.

<u>Frozen Code</u>. Frozen code is program code that is not subject to fault correction or any other alteration.

<u>Functional Profile</u>. A program's functional profile is a description of end-user functions and their probabilities of occurrence.

<u>Hardware Failure</u>. A hardware failure is the inability of a hardware item to perform a required function within specified limits.

<u>Input Space</u>. The input space is the set of all possible input states for a program.

<u>Input State</u>. An input state is the set of values of input variables used by a run.

<u>Input Variable</u>. An input variable is a data item that exists external to a run and is used by the run.

<u>Operational Profile</u>. A program's operational profile is the set of all possible input states with their associated probabilities of occurrence.

<u>Operating System</u>. An operating system is the set of software products that jointly control the system resources and the processes using these resources. As used in this handbook, the term operating system includes both large, multi-user, multi-process operating systems and small real-time executives providing minimal services.

<u>Output State</u>. An output state is the set of values of output variables generated by a run.

Output Variable. An output variable is a data item that exists external to a run and is set by the run.

Per-Fault Hazard Rate. A per-fault hazard rate is the contribution each fault in a program makes to the overall program failure rate, when it is assumed that they contribute equally.

Re-Used Code. Reused code is non-developmental software (NDS) as defined in DOD-STD-2167A, paragraph 3.22. As used in this handbook, re-used code does not include operating systems.

Run. A run is a subdivision of the execution of a program. A run has identifiable input and output variables.

Software Failure. A software failure is a departure of the external results of program operation from program requirements.

Software Fault. A software fault is a missing, extra, or defective instruction or set of related instructions that have caused or can potentially cause a software failure.

Software Metric. A software metric is a measurable characteristic of the software development process or of a work product of the development process.

Software Reliability. Software reliability is the probability of failure-free operation of a computer program for a specified time in a specified environment. In a system context, software reliability is the probability that software will not cause the failure of the system for a specified time under specified conditions.

System Reliability. System reliability is the probability that a system, including all hardware and software subsystems, will perform a required task or mission for a specified time in a specified environment.

Test Case. A test case is an input state for a run, along with the expected output state.

3.2 <u>Abbreviations</u>. Abbreviations used in this document are defined as follows

Cdf	Cumulative Distribution Function
CPU	Central Processing Unit
CSC	Computer Software Component
CSCI	Computer Software Configuration Item
CSU	Computer Software Unit
ETT	Expected Test Time
FMEA	Failure Modes and Effects Analysis
FRACAS	Failure Reporting Analysis and Corrective Action System
HW	Hardware
HWCI	Hardware Configuration Item
KLOC	Kilo (1000) Executable Source Lines of Code
LOC	Executable Source Lines of Code
MIPS	Million Instructions per Second
MTBF	Mean Time Between Failures
NDS	Non-Developmental Software
OS	Operating System
PRST	Probability Ratio Sequential Test
SDD	Software Design Document
SRS	Software Requirements Specification
SW	Software
TAAF	Test, Analyze, and Fix

3.3 <u>Mathematical Symbols</u>.

B   fault reduction factor

C   resource index of computer time

c_1 cost of a failure during system test

c_2 cost of a failure during operational use

c_3 cost per unit of execution time.

D()   total cost

D_1()   total system test failures cost

D_2()   total operation failures cost

D_3()   total system test cost

E{x}   expected value of x

exp[x]   exponential function: e^x

f   linear execution frequency

F   resource index of failure resolution personnel

F()   cumulative distribution function

I   number of object instructions; resource index of failure
            identification personnel; input space

I_i number of object instructions in i-th CSCI

I()   Fisher information

I_s number of inherent source instructions

K   fault exposure ratio

ln x   natural logarithm of x

M   number of operational modes during a mission

m_e cumulative number of failures during system test

N   number of components in an aggregate

p(i)   probability of input state i

Q   mode utilization matrix

R(t)   reliability function

r	resource index (C, I, or F); average instruction execution rate
T	mission phase duration matrix
T'	active time matrix
t	generic time; calendar time since the beginning of system test
t_i	time at which the i-th sequentially active component completes
T	mission duration or other time interval of interest; test duration
U	utilization matrix
u_i	i-th chronologically ordered u-statistic; utilization of the i-th CSCI
$u_{(j)}$	j-th u-statistic when arranged in ascending order of magnitude
V	number of phases in a mission
X	effective operating time matrix
x_i	cumulative execution time at which interval i ends; i-th product/process metric
y	operational life of the system
Y_i	cumulative number of failures through interval i
z	number of intervals
ΔI_s	number of deliverable developed executable source instructions
α	confidence level; producer's risk
β	decrement of failure rate per failure experienced; consumer's risk
β_{high}	upper confidence limit of growth model parameter β
β_{low}	lower confidence limit of growth model parameter β
θ	mean time to failure
θ_0	upper test MTBF
θ_1	lower test MTBF

θ_r	execution time coefficient of resource r usage
$\kappa_{1-\alpha}$	standard normal deviate: $(1-\alpha)$ percentile of a standard normal distribution.
Λ	average aggregate failure rate over an interval
Λ_G	failure rate goal of an aggregate
Λ_P	predicted average aggregate failure rate over an interval
λ	constant failure rate
λ_0	initial failure rate (the software failure rate at the start of system test); reciprocal of lower test MTBF
λ_1	reciprocal of upper test MTBF
λ_F	future failure rate objective
λ_i	failure rate of the i-th software component in an aggregate
λ_{iG}	failure rate goal of the i-th component in an aggregate
λ_P	present failure rate
λ_{iP}	predicted failure rate of the i-th component in an aggregate.
$\lambda(t)$	instantaneous failure rate at time t.
μ_r	failure coefficient of resource r usage
$\mu(t)$	mean value function: expected number of failures experienced by time t
ν_0	expected total failures in infinite time
ξ	failure rate adjustment
τ	cumulative execution time since the beginning of system test
τ_e	cumulative execution time into system test, at which software is actually or hypothetically released
τ_i	cumulative execution time at which i-th failure occurs
τ'	time to failure

τ'_i i-th interfailure time; active time of i-th component

ϕ per-fault hazard rate

ω_0 number of inherent faults (the number of faults in the code at the start of system test)

ω_{0i} number of inherent faults in i-th CSCI

4. General Requirements

Reliability assurance and control of combined hardware and software systems requires implementation of a thorough, integrated set of reliability modeling, allocation, prediction, and test tasks. These tasks allow ongoing evaluation of the reliability of system, subsystem and lower-tier designs. The results of these analyses are used to assess the relative merit of competing design alternatives, to evaluate the reliability progress of the design program, and to measure the final, achieved product reliability through demonstration testing. At each step in the design-evaluate-design process, the figures of merit used to predict product reliability provide a means of establishing a total quality management system to provide ongoing control and refinement of the design process.

Table 4-1 provides a summary of the analysis and test tasks for both hardware and software that provide reliability goals, predictions, and assessments. Figure 4-1 provides a graphical overview of the interrelationships between these tasks. MIL-STD-785 analysis tasks that are important as a part of the design process, but do not directly aid in the calculation of product reliability (e.g., FMEA), have not been included in Table 4-1, Figure 4-1, or the remainder of this handbook. For software reliability tasks, Table 4-1 provides a reference to the appropriate section(s) in this handbook.

4.1 <u>System Reliability Prediction and Estimation Program</u>. The reliability prediction and estimation program for systems which combine both hardware and software elements must be composed of a complementary set of hardware and software tasks for reliability modeling, reliability allocation, reliability prediction, reliability growth testing, and reliability qualification testing. Each of the complementary hardware and software tasks must support system level tasks which combine the results of the individual hardware and software tasks and allow assessment of the overall system reliability performance.

4.1.1 <u>System Modeling</u>. System reliability modeling for hardware and software systems models the dependency between system services and the various hardware elements and their associated software processes. The system model is developed, in general accordance with MIL-STD-756, as an iterative process of decomposing the dependencies within the various system structural elements. As appropriate to the size and complexity of the system being analyzed, the system is first decomposed into a reliability block diagram showing the dependency between the subsystems and the system services required for a given mission or mode of operation.

TABLE 4-1.   Reliability Prediction and Estimation Tasks.

PREDICTION AND ESTIMATION PROGRAM TASK	APPLIES TO		APPLICABLE DOCUMENT OR HANDBOOK SECTION	REMARKS
	HW	SW		
Reliability Modeling	X	X	MIL-STD-785 Task 201, MIL-STD-756, Section 5.1	Reliability modeling for HW/SW systems is presented in Section 5.1 of this handbook
Reliability Allocation	X	X	MIL-STD-785 Task 202 Section 5.2	SW Allocation Procedures are provided in 5.2 of this handbook
Reliability Prediction	X	X	MIL-STD-785 Task 203 MIL-HDBK-217 Section 5.3	Procedures for SW reliability prediction at each phase of SW development are given in 5.3
Environmental Stress Screening	X		MIL-STD-785 Task 301 MIL-STD-2164 DOD-HDBK-344	A SW equivalent of HW stress screening is not defined
Reliability Development/ Growth Testing	X	X	MIL-STD-785 Task 302 MIL-HDBK-189 MIL-STD-1635 Section 5.4	Procedures for use in estimating the time and resource impact of needed SW reliability growth are provided in 5.4
Reliability Qualification Testing	X	X	MIL-STD-785 Task 303 MIL-HDBK-781 Section 5.4	Both hardware and software have exponentially distributed failure rates allowing MIL-HDBK-781 testing to be applied
Production Reliability Acceptance Testing	X		MIL-STD-785 Task 304 MIL-HDBK-781	Software does not require production reliability testing
FRACAS	X	X	MIL-STD-785, Task 104 and Task 105	Effective hardware and software FRACAS programs are needed to deter recurrence of observed fault classes

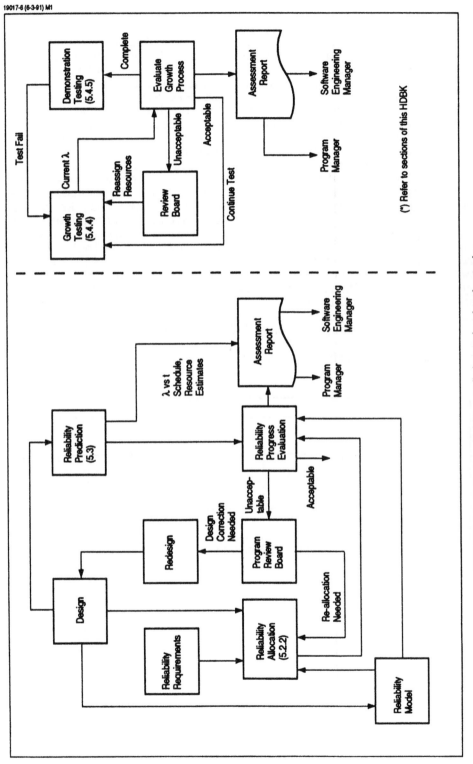

FIGURE 4-1. Software reliability prediction and estimation tasks.

Each of the subsystems is modeled as a series of discrete and redundant hardware and hardware/software elements. This process is continued until the system modeling is detailed enough for individual hardware equipments to be identified, including those hardware elements which host software processes. Detailed models of the individual hardware elements that do not host software can then be developed in accordance with MIL-STD-756. Reliability models for those hardware elements which host software must be developed next. For those cases where redundant equipment for hardware/software elements is supplied, the reliability model developed will depend on the exact method used to implement fault detection and recovery. Section 5.1 provides an overview of some approaches to developing these models. For those cases where a single equipment with software is used, each hardware/software element is decomposed to the model shown in Figure 4-2. As shown in the figure, a single hardware/software element decomposes into a reliability block diagram which consists of a hardware block and a software block in series. The software block of the hardware/software element then decomposes into a set of series software elements: the operating system, re-used software, and newly developed software. At least one, and possibly all of these types of software will exist in a specific model. Since software failure rates are exponential, the failure rates for the software can be added directly to the failure rates for the software. However, the failure rates for the software elements of the system must be expressed with respect to system operating time.

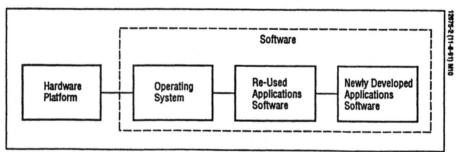

Figure 4-2. Reliability Model for HW/SW Element

4.1.2 <u>System Reliability Allocation</u>. System reliability allocation is the process of allocating the specified system reliability figure(s) of merit (MTBF, MTTF, availability, etc.) to each subsystem or area, hardware element, and hardware/software element in the system. These reliability allocations are based on the system reliability model, which must be developed prior to attempting to allocate figures of merit from the specification to lower tier elements. At the level of the hardware/software elements, reliability allocations are decomposed to apportion the relevant figure(s) of merit between the hardware element and the software which executes on the specific piece of hardware. Any convenient method may be used to balance the allocations to each element of the system so long as achievement of the system reliability requirements are supported. Typically, knowledge of the achievable failure rates for the hardware and software elements of the system will be needed to obtain allocated reliability for each system element which is achievable and still supports the system level reliability requirements. Methods for obtaining reliability estimates for system hardware are well documented and discussed in paragraph 4.2.2 and paragraph 4.2.3, below. Estimates of the software failure rate which is achievable can be obtained using the methods discussed in paragraph 4.3.3 and the procedures provided in section 5 of this handbook.

4.1.3 <u>System Reliability Prediction</u>. System reliability predictions are used to assess overall design progress toward achieving the specified system reliability in accordance with the procedures of MIL-STD-756. Reliability predictions and estimates for the various system hardware elements (section 4.2.3) and software elements (section 4.3.3) are combined using the system model discussed above. The resultant reliability calculation is then compared against the specified system requirement to determine whether the current system design achieves the specified reliability. If the current design fails to achieve the needed system reliability, appropriate corrective action must be implemented.

4.1.4 <u>System Reliability Growth</u>. System reliability growth is caused by a combination of hardware and software reliability growth. The hardware and software growth estimates are combined, using the system reliability model, and used to estimate system reliability growth over time. Projections of hardware reliability growth and software reliability growth are based on different growth curves. Hardware and software growth tests can be conducted separately with the results combined using the system reliability model. In some cases, conducting separate test, analyze, and fix testing may be appropriate since different engineering groups are often assigned to the development of hardware and software elements of the system. However, conducting concurrent hardware and software growth testing is not precluded and may be advantageous in some cases. When both hardware and software reliability growth testing are required on a program, a system level reliability growth test plan discussing all aspects of the planned growth testing and the methods to be used in estimating and reporting system reliability growth should be prepared.

4.1.5 System Reliability Qualification Testing. System reliability qualification testing for hardware/software systems is performed in accordance with the methods of MIL-HDBK-781 and section 5.4 of this handbook. The failure rates for hardware and software are both exponential allowing use of the test methods of MIL-HDBK-781 for a combined test of the hardware and software elements of the system. The test environment to be used can be selected from the standard environments of MIL-HDBK-781 based on the anticipated hardware use environment. Ensuring an appropriate software environment for reliability testing is discussed in paragraph 4.3.6 and section 5.4 of this handbook.

4.1.6 System-Level FRACAS. A system-level FRACAS program that is comprised of the set of tasks needed to evaluate the system reliability being observed on the basis of the hardware and software FRACAS programs should be instituted as a part of the reliability assurance and control program for a combined HW/SW system. The system-level FRACAS activity should support resolution of those problems which cannot readily be assigned to either hardware or software causes. Additionally, a system-level FRACAS activity to track and assess the results of the hardware and software FRACAS activities can provide a resource for ensuring that the results of all observed failures are available for use within system safety programs. MIL-STD-2155 should be used as a guide in developing a system-level FRACAS program specific to the system being developed.

4.2 Hardware Reliability Prediction and Estimation Program. The required tasks and related analysis products for hardware prediction and estimation are described in MIL-STD-785 and the specifications, standards, and handbooks referenced within that standard. Reliability allocation, prediction, and testing techniques for electronic hardware have been thoroughly investigated and have existing procedures documented within the military literature. The addition of software to electronic hardware does not change the expected rate of hardware physical failures. The military standards and handbooks that are in use remain applicable to the design of electronic hardware that provides a platform for software execution.

The specifications, standards, and handbooks that relate to the various hardware reliability prediction and estimation tasks have been presented in Table 4-1. Each of these documents continues to apply in full to systems that contain software in addition to the electronic hardware.

4.2.1 <u>Hardware Reliability Modeling</u>. Reliability modeling for hardware systems is described in Task 201 of MIL-STD-785. Hardware reliability modeling supports system and hardware reliability estimation, and provides a basis for the allocation of reliability goals to individual hardware elements. Reliability modeling for the hardware elements in systems that use both hardware and software is the same as for systems which consist of hardware only. Once system level modeling has decomposed the combined HW/SW system into hardware elements and software elements, the methods of MIL-STD-756 may be used directly to model any individual hardware elements, including those which execute software. Section 4.1.1, above, provides an overview of the system modeling process that results in the decomposition of the system into individual hardware and software elements.

4.2.2 <u>Hardware Reliability Allocation</u>. Reliability allocation for hardware systems is described in MIL-STD-785, Task 202. Allocated reliability goals are assigned to each hardware element and lower-tier indentured item on the basis of a user selected criteria such as criticality or complexity. The system reliability specification value which was allocated between the various subsystems and elements as a part of the system reliability allocation process is further divided into reliability allocations for lower indenture hardware elements. As a general rule, the reliability allocation given to non-developmental hardware is based on the item's previously observed reliability. Reliability allocations internal to non-developmental equipment are not generally needed. Reliability allocations to hardware being designed as a part of the system development process are usually based on a combination of the system requirements, the reliability performance of previous generations of similar equipment, and the overall criticality or complexity of the hardware device. Allocations of reliability goals for lower indenture circuit cards and modules are generally provided for developmental hardware. The allocation of reliability goals to hardware elements proceeds in exactly the same manner for hardware systems that host software processes as for hardware that does not host executable software.

4.2.3 <u>Hardware Reliability Prediction</u>. Hardware reliability predictions are described in MIL-STD-785, Task 203. In order of precedence, hardware reliability predictions are based on 1) known field performance of the same equipment produced during previous production, 2) MIL-STD-781 reliability demonstration test results, 3) reliability test, analyze, and fix (TAAF) or other reliability growth testing results, or 4) MTBF estimates obtained using the procedures of MIL-HDBK-217. Hardware reliability predictions for hardware systems that host software processes proceed in exactly the same manner as the predictions for hardware that does not host software. For hardware which hosts software, however, the hardware prediction results must be combined with the software reliability prediction results using the system model to obtain predictions of the overall system reliability.

4.2.4 <u>Hardware Reliability Growth</u>.   Hardware reliability growth programs are described in MIL-STD-785, Task 302.   Hardware reliability growth programs, in the form of test, analyze and fix testing, are often used to ensure the maturity of newly developed hardware prior to either MIL-STD-781 demonstration testing or release to the field for use. MIL-HDBK-189 provides growth curves and procedures for hardware reliability growth management. These procedures apply directly to the hardware elements of combined hardware and software systems.

4.2.5 <u>Hardware Reliability Qualification Testing</u>.   Hardware reliability qualification testing is described in MIL-STD-785, Task 303. Detailed procedures, including measurement criteria and environmental criteria, for hardware demonstration testing is provided in MIL-HDBK-781.   The testing methods described in MIL-STD-785 and MIL-HDBK-781 apply to all electronic hardware and can be used to test combined hardware and software systems (see paragraph 4.1.5 and paragraph 4.3.6).

4.2.6 <u>Hardware FRACAS</u>. Hardware FRACAS programs are described in MIL-STD-785, Tasks 104 and 105 and in MIL-STD-2155. The procedures of these standards should be applied to all hardware which is a part of a combined hardware and software system.   The hardware FRACAS program for equipment which is a part of a combined hardware and software system needs to be carefully tailored to support the system FRACAS activity, allowing the results of both hardware and software FRACAS activities to be combined.   The hardware FRACAS program is generally established as a standalone program that provides information to the system FRACAS program in recognition that different organizational entities are usually assigned to the hardware and software designs.   The hardware and software FRACAS efforts will need to coordinate with different design teams to resolve ongoing problems and corrective action recommendations. Also, the composition of the failure review boards needed for software failures is likely to be significantly different from that needed for hardware failures.

4.3 <u>Software Reliability Prediction And Estimation Program</u>.   The tasks required for the prediction, evaluation, and estimation of software reliability have been presented in Table 4-1 and Figure 4-1.   The software reliability prediction and estimation tasks comprise three fundamental conceptual tasks: establishment of reliability goals for lower-indenture software elements through modeling and allocation, estimation of software design reliability through the software reliability prediction process, and evaluation of the achieved software reliability through reliability testing. Reliability modeling supports the allocation of reliability requirements to lower-tier software and hardware elements. Reliability modeling also supports assessment of system and software reliability predictions against specified reliability goals at the system level.

One of the most important early program tasks within reliability engineering is the establishment of reliability allocations for lower-tier system elements. Allocation of reliability goals to lower-tier elements allows each part of the design team to target a specific reliability goal for their part of the design so that the design of lower tier elements can proceed without continual reference to system-level requirements. Additionally, the allocated reliability for an individual hardware element or software element provides the design team with a means of assessing the acceptability of their design and serves as a figure of merit to assess the need for corrective action within the design process. The procedures used to establish reliability allocations for software elements are similar to the methods used for the system hardware allocations. However, software reliability allocations recognize the unique character of software execution. Individual software elements can vary in their relative execution times, their degree of concurrency, and their relative complexity and/or criticality. The predominant factor, the one which will be used as the basis for software reliability allocations, will be different for different systems. As a result, several different procedures for software reliability allocation are provided as a part of this handbook. Criteria for selecting among the procedures provided in section 5.2 are discussed in section 4.3.2.

Software reliability prediction is performed at each phase of the software development process. Product/process metrics are collected and used to predict the failure rate that the software will exhibit at the beginning of system test as well as the software reliability growth model parameters. The failure rate prediction is then used along with the reliability growth curve to estimate the duration of, and resources required for, the reliability growth testing, which will be needed to achieve the allocated software reliability. The testing duration and resource requirements are then compared against program schedule and resource plans to evaluate the feasibility of achieving the allocated software reliability. If the allocated software reliability is achievable within planned schedule and resource constraints, no action is necessary. If achieving the allocated reliability will result in an unplanned impact to program schedule and resources, one of three decisions is possible: reassignment of needed resources if the impact is tolerably small, reallocation of software reliability goals if other elements of the system are achieving beyond their allocated requirements by a sufficient margin, or design corrective action. Design corrective actions may include structural changes in the system interrelationships as shown in the reliability modeling. Design changes that result in a more robust design may allow reallocation of system reliability requirements into lower tier software goals that are more achievable. As a part of the software reliability prediction process, a report providing an assessment of the degree of compliance of the software being developed with allocated reliability requirements and the potential program impact of any additional reliability growth testing that may be needed should be provided to the program and software engineering managers to ensure that any program impacts are identified and controlled. Procedures for software reliability prediction are provided within this handbook as a part of section 5.3. An overview and discussion of the software reliability prediction process is provided in paragraph 4.3.3.

Software reliability evaluation testing consists of reliability growth testing, used to continuously evaluate and improve the reliability of the software product, and reliability qualification testing, used to certify for acceptance the final achieved software reliability. Software reliability growth testing is a process of operation (test), failure occurrence, fault isolation, and software modification to eliminate recurrence of the same and similar failures. This continuous test, analyze, and fix procedure is coupled with an ongoing evaluation of the software reliability for rate of growth and current value. The software reliability growth testing continues until the software failure rate has achieved its allocated requirements. Once the reliability growth testing indicates that the software has achieved the needed maturity, the software can be subjected to reliability qualification testing either for just the software element or as an integral part of a combined hardware/software system. Reliability qualification testing for software is based on the statistical test plans of MIL-STD-781. Both hardware and software have constraints that must be placed on their test environment to ensure that the testing adequately simulates field usage. An overview and discussion of software reliability growth and qualification testing is provided in paragraph 4.3.5 and paragraph 4.3.6 of this handbook. Procedures for evaluating software reliability growth and selecting appropriate input environments are provided in section 5.4.

4.3.1 <u>Software Reliability Modeling</u>. Reliability modeling of system software elements is similar in approach to the modeling performed for the overall system and for the hardware elements. Combining software failure rates to calculate an overall failure rate for the software introduces, complexity not normally associated with combining hardware failure rates. As shown previously in Figure 4-2, the executing software can be decomposed into up to three separate types of software elements; the operating system (OS), re-used application software, and newly developed application software. The operating system or executive is unique in that it operates continuously, on an interruptive basis with the application program, monitoring system operation and providing control of and access to processor resources for all executing processes. Thus, the failure rate of the OS is conveniently measured in failures per machine operating hour which is directly compatible with hardware failure rates. When the OS being used is a purchased product, the software vendor can supply a failure rate for use in assessing system reliability models. Re-used application software is modeled as a separate software elements because its failure rate is usually much lower than the failure rate for newly developed application software. The failure rate for re-used software should be obtained from previous use(s) of the software. Care should be used to ensure that the failure rate for re-used code obtained from a previous use is either expressed in or converted to a rate expressed in failures per system operating hour for compatibility with hardware failure rates. Software execution proceeds either sequentially or concurrently, depending on the system design. Systems with a single processing element that must execute all software activate the various software elements sequentially. Systems with multiple processors execute software concurrently. Sequentially executing software elements must have their failure rates weighted by the amount of execution time they require as a part of calculating a failure rate for the system software. Additional complexity may be added by the changing relationship between execution time for each lower-tier software element and the mission phase of the system. As the system enters different modes of operation, different software elements will be required to execute more of the time. Section 5.1 of this handbook provides procedures for calculating top-level software failure rates for both sequential (Procedure 5.1.2.5-1) and concurrent (Procedure 5.1.2.5-2) software execution. Procedure 5.1.2.5-3 provides step-by-step guidance in calculating software reliability under the changing conditions of multi-mode mission scenarios.

4.3.2 **Software Reliability Allocation**.   Software reliability allocation, the establishment of reliability goals for individual software elements based on a top-level reliability requirement for all software, is a crucial early program activity that establishes the criteria for evaluating the achieved reliability of elements of the design.   As shown in Table 4-2, five initial allocation procedures and a reallocation procedure are provided in section 5.2 of this handbook. These procedures allow allocations to be made based on the type of execution expected--sequential or concurrent-- or on the basis of utilization, complexity, or criticality.

Two equal-apportionment allocation procedures have been provided. Procedure 5.2.3-1 provides equal apportionment between software elements for sequentially executing software. Procedure 5.2.3-2 provides equal apportionment among software elements for concurrently executing software.   These equal apportionment allocation procedures are designed for use during proposals and early design phases when very little is known about the relative sizes, complexity, or criticality of the software being designed. Two allocation procedures--criticality, and complexity--are provided for allocation among the various software elements in a design once the top-level software design is available.

TABLE 4-2.   Software Reliability Allocation Procedures.

Procedure #	Procedure Name	Use Description
5.2.3-1	Equal apportionment applied to sequential software components	Use early in the SW development process when the software components are executed sequentially
5.2.3-2	Equal apportionment applied to concurrent software components	Use early in the SW development process and the software components are executed concurrently
5.2.3-3	Allocation based on achievable failure rates	Use when CSCI utilization varies significantly
5.2.3-4	Allocation based on criticality factors	Use when the criticality factors of the software components are known
5.2.3-5	Allocation based on complexity factors	Use when the complexity factors of the software components are known
5.2.3-6	Re-allocation based on predicted failure rates	Use to re-balance the SW reliability allocations

A re-allocation procedure, Procedure 5.2.2-6, is provided to allow balancing allocated values as more software design information becomes available. Re-allocation between the various software elements of a design is expected to be required early in the design process as the software design develops.

4.3.3 Software Reliability Prediction. Software reliability prediction is performed to help forecast, in conjunction with the software reliability growth model, the reliability the end-user will experience when the software is released. The predicted reliability provides the developer with a customer-oriented view of software quality. Reliability prediction allows reliability to become an integral part of the software design process. It provides a quantitative basis for design tradeoffs and helps identify and rank problem areas. It also assists in the evaluation of choices between designs, development technologies, and processes. Software reliability prediction provides a uniform basis for proposal preparation and evaluation and is useful for helping determine the feasibility of proposed reliability requirements.

Software reliability predictions are made during the software
development phases that precede system test, and are available in
time to feed back into the software development process. The
predictions are based on measurable characteristics of the software
development process and the products produced by that process.
Figure 4-3 shows the software reliability prediction process.
Product/process metrics are collected and used to predict the
initial failure rate and fault content. From these quantities, the
reliability growth model parameters are predicted, then the growth
model is used to obtain estimates of the test time and resources
needed to meet reliability objectives. Up through the requirements
analysis phase, the software reliability prediction is made on the
basis of gross characteristics of the software such as estimated
size and processor speed. During the preliminary design phase
through the CSCI testing phase, product/process metrics are used
for prediction. As development proceeds, more and more metrics
become available, and metrics that were available before are
updated. The predictions become more accurate as system test is
approached. Once system test begins, the metrics are no longer
needed for prediction, because actual failure data can be used to
statistically estimate the values of the growth model parameters.

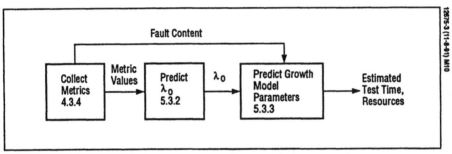

Figure 4-3. Software Reliability Prediction Procedure

Since the failure rate of the software changes over time as the software is modified to correct faults, the prediction procedures contained in section 5.3 provide values for the parameters of the software reliability growth model. The growth model can be used to forecast what the failure rate $\lambda(\tau)$ will be at any time τ into system test. Conversely, the growth model can be used to forecast when a particular failure rate objective will be reached. The amount of execution time to reach an objective can be translated into calendar time for schedule and resource estimates. Reliability progress is evaluated as a part of the prediction process. An Assessment Report detailing the reliability progress to date against established goals and potential schedule and resource impacts should be prepared and delivered to the Program Manager and Software Engineering Manager. If the reported progress is unacceptable, a Program Review Board can be informed. The board can then determine whether design correction or re-allocation is needed to meet the specified reliability requirements in a timely, cost-effective manner.

4.3.4 <u>Software Metrics Collection</u>. Software metrics are measurable characteristics of the software development process and the products of that process. The specific objective of collecting the metrics described here is to allow software reliability to be predicted during the software life cycle phases preceding system test. Table 4-3 provides a mapping between the software metrics and the phases during which they are used in the prediction process. These metrics are not available all at once. Different metrics become available as each life cycle phase concludes. Metrics that were previously available become updated as work products evolve.

The metrics are simple, objective, and compatible with the software development framework described in DOD-STD-2167A. The metrics are numbered 1 through 13. Depending on the development phase (proposal through CSCI testing) during which the prediction is made, some subset of the metrics will be available. The metrics available during each phase enter into a software reliability prediction model associated with that phase, as described in section 5.3. Most of the metrics are normalized based on lines of code. The metrics are collected separately for each Computer Software Configuration Item (CSCI). In addition to the metrics, failure rate prediction requires knowledge of the processor speed of the target machine.

<u>Metric #1</u> is the number of errors in the Software Requirements Specification (SRS). Error counting begins when the SRS is placed under configuration control. Usually, the number of errors will keep increasing monotonically throughout development, as errors are uncovered. Thus, the metric always lags behind its final value.

Table 4-3 - Software reliability metrics by program phase

Metrics / Phase		Proposal/Pre-contractual and Requirements Analysis phase (Procedure 5.3.2-1)	Preliminary Design phase (Procedure 5.3.2-2)	Detailed Design phase (Procedure 5.3.2-3)	Coding and CSU Testing (Procedure 5.3.2-4)	CSC integration and testing and CSCI testing (Procedure 5.3.2-5)
No.	Description					
13	Executable lines of code	X	X	X	X	X
1	Errors in SRS		X	X	X	X
2	Requirements statements in SRS		X	X	X	X
3	Pages in SRS		X	X	X	X
4	Man-months for Requirements Analysis		X	X	X	X
5	Requirements changes after baseline		X	X	X	X
6	Errors in Preliminary Design Document			X	X	X
7	Number of CSCs			X	X	X
8	CSUs in design structure			X	X	X
9	Pages in SDD			X	X	X
10	Man-months for Preliminary Design			X	X	X
11	Times a CSU is unit-tested					X
12	Defects identified through walkthroughs and reviews					X

Metric #2 is the number of requirements statements ("shalls") in the SRS.

Metric #3 is the number of pages in the SRS. Writing style will account for a small, unavoidable, variation in this metric.

Metric #4 is the effort expended, in man-months, on the requirements analysis phase. Once the requirements analysis phase is completed, this metric will not change.

Metric #5 is the number of changes (corrections and modifications) to the SRS after it has been placed under configuration control. This metric will increase monotonically throughout development.

Metric #6 is the number of errors in preliminary design documents, a number that can be expected to grow throughout development.

Metric #7 is the number of Computer Software Components (CSCs) in the software structure. The CSCs may all be at one level in the structure, or there may be high- and low-level CSCs. This metric will generally not change after preliminary design is complete.

Metric #8 is the number of Computer Software Units (CSUs) in the design structure. Generally, Ada packages will reside at this level in the design hierarchy. This metric will not ordinarily change after preliminary design is complete.

Metric #9 is the number of pages in the Software Design Documents (SDDs). This metric is subject to some variation resulting from writing style and the use of tables and figures. This metric will increase or decrease to some extent throughout development as the SDD changes.

Metric #10 is the number of man-months expended for preliminary design. This number will not change after preliminary design is complete.

Metric #11 is the average number of times a unit is tested by the programmer during CSU testing. The metric will not change after CSU testing is complete.

Metric #12 is the sum of the number of design errors identified after the SDD has been placed under configuration control, the number of design errors identified as the result of internal reviews, and the number of faults found through code reviews and related inspections. This metric becomes available after the coding and CSU testing phase. The metric will increase, to some extent, as time goes on.

Metric #13 is the total number of executable lines of source code. Data declarations and assembler/compiler directives are not included in this count. This metric is needed for converting fault

density to fault content and for normalizing metrics #1-#10 and
#12. The purpose of normalization is to cancel out the effect on
metric values that derive solely from size. Estimates of software
size must be used until the code is actually written. An estimate
is usually available in the proposal stage of the project because
software size is an input to software cost models. After the code
is written, the program size will be known but may change to some
extent as the code is modified to correct faults.

Since the values of most of the metrics change as development
proceeds, the latest updated values should always be used when
making a prediction. The predictions will tend to become more and
more accurate as the metrics from each successive phase become
available and as the values are updated to more closely reflect the
characteristics of the final design and implementation.

The metrics for each CSCI should be carefully recorded on a data
collection worksheet.

4.3.5 <u>Software Reliability Growth Testing</u>. Software reliability
growth testing takes place during the system test phase, after the
software has been fully integrated. During growth testing, the
software is executed in an environment that emulates the way the
software will be used in the field. In particular, input is
randomly selected from the software's operational profile. An
operational profile associates each input state or end-user
function with a probability of occurrence. Testing according to
the operational profile is efficient, because it reveals those
faults that the user is most likely to encounter in use, those
faults that contribute most to the program failure rate. When a
failure is observed, the execution time--among other information--
is recorded. The observed failure times are used as input to a
statistical estimation technique that determines the parameters of
the software reliability growth model. This way, the current
reliability can be measured and the future reliability can be
forecast. Figure 4-4 depicts an idealized software reliability
growth curve.

A program that is not running cannot fail. Thus, the growth model
selected expresses its basic results with respect to execution
time. Since project managers and software engineers think in terms
of calendar time, the growth model contains a component that
addresses the relationship between execution time and calendar time
by focusing on resource usage rates. Three primary resources are
involved in system test: failure identification personnel, failure
resolution personnel, and computer time. Failure identification
personnel are the testers, the people who run test cases and detect
the occurrence of failures. Failure resolution personnel are the
debuggers, the people who isolate and remove the faults that cause
the failures. The expenditure of failure identification personnel

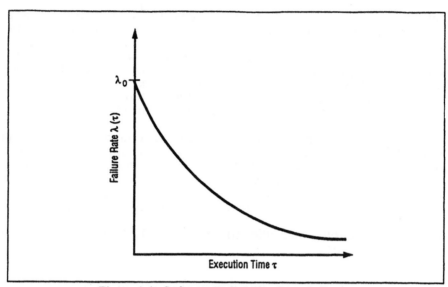

Figure 4-4. Software Reliability Growth Curve

resource and failure resolution resource are each modeled as having a cost per unit of execution time and a cost per failure experienced. At any time, one of the three resources will be the limiting resource that determines the ratio of calendar time to execution time. Testing can only be accelerated by adding more of the limiting resource. Except for overtime, the available amounts of the personnel resources are fixed during the extent of the system test period, because of the long lead times required for training.

In addition to reliability assessment, another benefit of growth testing is that the debugging activity after each failure occurrence will result in fault removal. Debugging is imperfect: The occurrence of one failure does not guarantee the immediate removal of one fault. Sometimes new faults are inadvertently introduced during the repair activity. Sometimes multiple, related faults are removed at once. Sometimes the causative fault behind a failure is not found. Over the long run, the reliability of reasonably maintainable software improves as growth testing continues.

Section 5.4 of this handbook provides a detailed discussion and specific procedures for software reliability growth testing.

4.3.6 <u>Software Reliability Qualification Testing</u>. Reliability qualification testing is performed toward the end of system test. Its purpose is to prove with a specified statistical confidence that the software meets the stated reliability requirement. Software reliability qualification testing, like growth testing, is performed using inputs randomly selected in accordance with the operational profile the software will experience in field use.

During demonstration testing, however, the code is frozen (just as it would be between releases). Any failures that occur are merely recorded; no software repair activity takes place.

Frozen code subjected to inputs randomly selected from a stationary (non-changing) operational profile exhibits a constant failure rate. This implies that the interfailure times are exponentially distributed. The exponential model is currently employed for complex, maintained hardware systems that do not have redundancy. When software is embedded in such systems, the overall failure rate is a constant that is the sum of the hardware and software failure rates. The exponential model is applicable to the software product alone and to the combined hardware/software system.

Three types of qualification tests are described in section 5.4: fixed-duration test, sequential test, and failure-free execution period test. Each type of test has advantages and disadvantages, as summarized in Table 4-4.

TABLE 4-4. Software Reliability Qualification Test Types.

Test Type	Advantages	Disadvantages
Fixed-Duration	Total test time is known in advance. An estimate can be made of true failure rate.	Takes longer than sequential test on average.
Sequential	Accepts very low failure rates and rejects very high failure rates quickly. Shorter test times on average than the other types.	Total test duration is undetermined; maximum duration must be planned for.
Failure-Free Execution Interval	Will accept very quickly if true failure rate is much better than required.	Can take a long time if true failure rate is close to that required

4.3.7 Software FRACAS. A software Failure Reporting and Corrective Action System (FRACAS) is an efficient closed-loop management tool established to identify and correct deficiencies in software. The software FRACAS program must be carefully tailored to support providing the information required by the system level FRACAS program. Software FRACAS is based on the systematic reporting and analysis of software failures during testing. Software FRACAS includes documented procedures for reporting failures, analyzing failures to determine their root causes, and establishing effective corrective action to prevent future recurrence of the failure. MIL-STD-2155 provides specific FRACAS procedures which can be applied to both software and hardware FRACAS programs. As a part of the program, each failure must be documented and reported, with sufficient information to identify the software element involved, the symptoms of the failure, input and other conditions preceding the failure, and, for the purposes of software reliability growth modeling, the cumulative execution time at the moment of failure. The failure should be verified, if possible, by repeating the circumstances that led to it. All files and other pertinent data must be preserved. The "root cause" of the software failure in the traditional FRACAS sense is a fault. Corrective action requires a change to the software code. On formal concurrence of the adequacy of the corrective action, the failure report is closed out.

Software FRACAS should be augmented by the establishment of a "defect prevention" program. In a defect prevention program, not only is the fault removed from the code but attention is also focused on the root cause of the fault, how it got there in the first place. A fault in the code may be the result of a problem in interpersonal communications, lack of training, a management problem, inadequate methodology, or another reason. Seeking out and eliminating the root cause of the fault modifies the development process to completely eliminate the cause and prevent a whole class of related faults. If that cannot be done, then the objective is to at least advance the time at which such faults are detected.

After the fault is isolated and removed, information about the fault should be fed back to the programmers themselves, who establish and categorize the root cause of the fault. This is called the "causal analysis." Corrective action includes not only the removal of the immediate fault on hand but modification to the development process to eliminate the recurrence of the class of similar faults. Often, just making programmers aware of the root cause will discourage recurrence.

5. Detailed Requirements

5.1 <u>Hardware/Software System Reliability Modeling.</u> Reliability modeling of combined hardware and software systems is analogous to reliability modeling of purely hardware systems. The failure rates for both hardware and software are treated as constant. Reliability block diagrams of system elements are developed and employed. Individual hardware platforms and the software assigned to those platforms are independent of other hardware/software platforms. Reliability block diagrams that accurately portray the interrelationship between the hardware platforms and the software executing on the platforms are developed and used in estimating reliability figures of merit. For complex structures, state diagrams are developed to accurately portray the unique interrelationships of the structure being modeled.

This section provides the techniques applicable to the reliability modeling of combined hardware and software systems. For series systems, the process is straightforward. For complex, redundant systems, an abbreviated overview of the system modeling process is provided. Because these complex models are unique to the system being modeled, detailed procedures for developing these complex models cannot be provided. The overview provided is used to help the analyst identify those system properties which are unique to redundant combined hardware and software systems. The majority of this section is dedicated to describing the development of software failure rates that are a composite of the multiple processes that may be executing during any time period. MIL-STD-756 provides detailed modeling procedures for hardware systems. For hardware/software systems, this standard is still applicable to many reliability modeling tasks.

Two types of models are developed for combined hardware/software systems: a basic or logistics reliability model and an operational reliability model.

5.1.1 <u>Basic Reliability Model.</u> A basic reliability model for a hardware/software system can be prepared in accordance with MIL-STD-756, Task 101. However, the resultant is two reliability models; one for the software and one for the hardware elements of the system. Both models can be used to assess the logistics requirements of the system being developed. The basic hardware reliability model consists of all hardware elements of the system in series so that the overall logistics support requirements for spares, maintenance personnel, training, etc, can be readily assessed based on the failure rates of the equipment. This model is the same for hardware only systems as it is for hardware/software systems. For combined hardware/software systems, a basic software reliability model is also developed. The basic software reliability model is created in the same way as the basic hardware reliability model. All software elements, regardless of which hardware platform they execute on, are modeled in series. The failure rates of the software elements, weighted appropriately for execution frequency (see the material in paragraph 5.1.2.6) are added together to produce an overall estimate of the mean time between observed software failures. This failure rate, together with estimates of the rate at which functionality extensions will be made to the fielded system, is used to determine the software maintenance requirements. For hardware/software systems, the results of the basic software reliability model can be used to estimate the number and types of equipment that must be supplied when a software maintenance facility is required as a part of the contractual effort.

5.1.2 **Mission Reliability Model.** A mission reliability model, in accordance with MIL-STD-756, Task 102 and this handbook can be developed for combined hardware/software systems. The mission reliability model is then used to support allocations of system requirements to individual hardware and software elements of the system and to support assessment of the compliance of the overall system to specified reliability requirements. The methods employed in the development and assessment of the mission reliability models closely follow those of MIL-STD-756 with some extensions as discussed in subsequent paragraphs. The modeling of software failure rates is not addressed in MIL-STD-756.

Reliability modeling methods used to model combined HW/SW systems for the purposes of reliability estimation and allocation need to accurately assess the interdependence between individual software elements, the hardware platforms on which these software elements execute, and the services provided by the system being analyzed. Additionally, the methods used need to be based on and compatible with modern system engineering methods. This results in a modeling procedure which consists of six steps; 1) Development of a system FMEA, 2) Development of the top level reliability model based on the system FMEA results, 3) Development of detailed reliability block diagrams and models based on the top level reliability model, 4) Modeling the combined hardware/software elements of the system, 5) Development of hardware models and appropriate hardware failure rates, and 6) Use of the appropriate software failure rate modeling and calculation procedures of this handbook to predict software failure rate. The reliability model(s) developed using these steps can then be used to estimate the reliability of the system being analyzed.

System reliability modeling is based on system Failure Modes and Effects Analysis (FMEA), a bottom-up reliability analysis technique that provides a mapping between failures and their impact on system services. These FMEAs need not always be a formal analysis since the results are expressed in the reliability model block diagrams. A system-level adaptation of Matrix FMEA techniques which results in a compact readily usable display of the needed FMEA information is used to support the development of system reliability models.

Estimation of system reliability characteristics is based on the reliability block diagrams and Markov state diagrams developed from the system FMEA and the individual hardware and software component failure rates. Estimation techniques for hardware reliability and maintainability characteristics are well known and can be applied to the hardware portions of combined hardware/software systems. Software reliability characteristics can be estimated using the procedures provided in this handbook. For redundant, fault tolerant systems, software recovery characteristics are system design and implementation dependent. These recovery characteristics will need to be estimated on a case by case basis in conjunction with performance modeling and estimation.

Complex, redundant systems and system elements are modeled using state diagrams to accurately portray the possible operational and non-operational states. In general, these state diagrams will be complex enough to require access to automated tools for solution. They are not, strictly speaking, intractable. However, the labor required to manually determine a specific closed form solution for a state diagram that has been developed to model a specific design being analyzed is usually prohibitive. Automated solutions of these state diagrams are possible both analytically and through simulation. The use of automated tools to support complex modeling is highly recommended. However, the user of automated reliability modeling tools will need to determine whether or not the numerical accuracy needed for their specific situation is supported. Analytic solutions to complex diagrams often require the solution of a transition matrix with potentially significant losses in numerical accuracy due to the multiple arithmetic operations compounded by the accuracy limitations of the processing platform used. Monte Carlo solutions to state diagrams can result in both numerical inaccuracy due to the methods employed and may involve substantial cost for multiple program runs. The costs associated with Monte Carlo solutions rise dramatically as the accuracy demanded increases.

Software maintainability, the time required to isolate and correct a fault in the design, is not used in the reliability modeling and allocation discussed in this section. Software maintenance is expected to proceed in parallel with ongoing system operation following a software failure. Thus, the time required to re-establish system operation following a software failure is used as the repair or recovery rate in the modeling of software elements of combined HW/SW elements. Software maintenance will result in a software failure rate that is not constant over time due to the software corrections being implemented. However, for the purposes of modeling and allocation of combined hardware and software systems, an assumption of constant software failure rate during any operational period (i.e., between software fixes) is justified.

5.1.2.1 System FMEA Development. Reliability modeling of combined HW/SW systems, whether for reliability allocation or estimating purposes, is approached on a functional service basis using a matrix FMEA approach. The resultant FMEA can then be used to develop a HW/SW system reliability block diagram of independent elements. The individual series/parallel elements of the reliability block diagram can then be modeled. Non-redundant systems can be modeled as series strings of hardware and HW/SW system elements.

Development of a system FMEA to support creation of reliability models for use in reliability estimation and allocation begins with the use of the functional decomposition that has been developed as a part of the system engineering process. For small or relatively simple system structures, system functional analysis may have been omitted as a formal procedure. If the system level functional decomposition is not available, the reliability engineer may find it necessary to recreate this analysis using Data Flow Diagrams. The functional decomposition of the system is used to identify the hardware configuration items (HWCIs), the computer software configuration items (CSCIs) along with the processing provided by these CSCIs, and the allocation of CSCIs to various HWCIs within the system. The analyst can then begin to create the system level FMEA that will support reliability modeling of the combined HW and SW system.

The system-level FMEA, shown diagrammatically in Figure 5-1, is a mapping of the hardware and software components of the system onto the system services provided. To create the FMEA, the analyst first constructs a matrix with each of the hardware CIs and their associated software CSCIs or CSCs as appropriate along the vertical axis. The horizontal axis is formed by the system services or outputs of the system grouped in convenient ways that support the desired analysis. A grouping of system services by system operating mode often supports development of the various models required by the system specification. The HWCIs and CSCIs (CSCs) are then mapped onto the system services or outputs based on the impact on system services caused by the failure of each hardware and software element. In performing this mapping, the analyst will need to assess the impact of failure of both hardware platforms and software elements. The failure impact of software elements will need to be examined in depth based on the data flow that has been established for the system design. Similarly, the failure of hardware platforms will need to be examined for its impact on software-provided services using the data flow diagrams for the system software resident on the hardware platform.

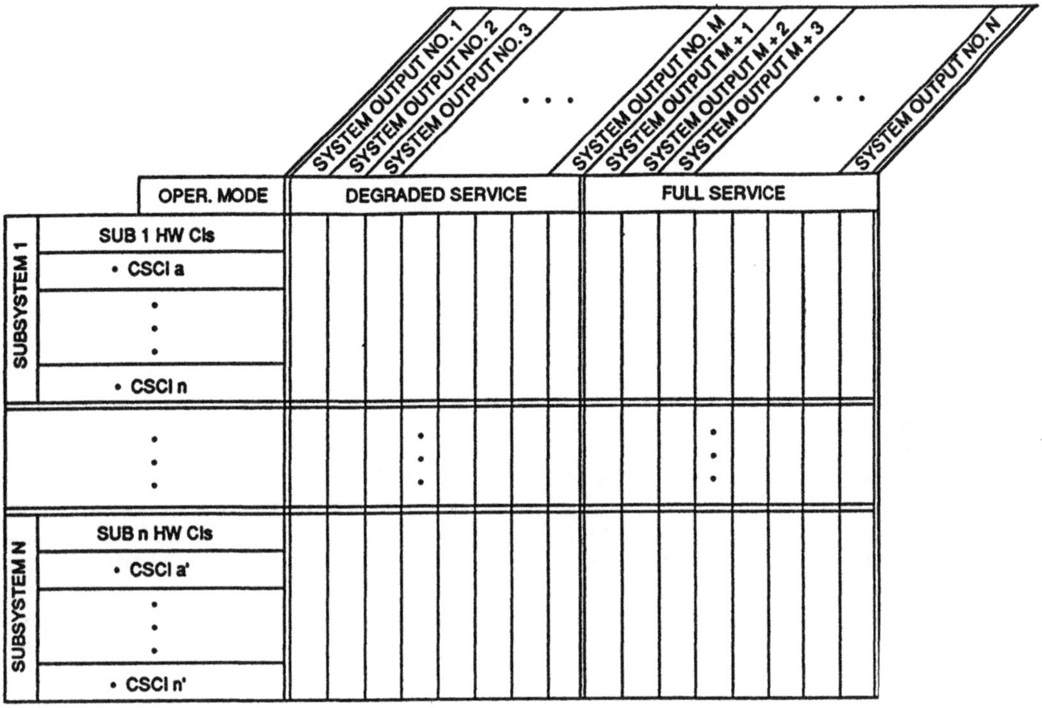

Figure 5-1. Example of System Level Functional FMEA

Once the system level FMEA has been completed, the analyst can examine the hardware and software that are required for any particular mode or set of system services. A reliability model for these services can then be developed.

5.1.2.2 **System-Level Reliability Model Development**. The system level reliability model, expressed as a reliability block diagram for combined HW/SW systems is developed based the methods of MIL-STD-756 and the system FMEA, using a procedure that is analogous to that used for purely hardware systems. The FMEA results are used to determine which hardware and software elements are required to provide a set of system services required by the system mission or mode being modeled. The analyst then proceeds to develop a

reliability block diagram that consists of a set of series blocks
for each of the independent HW/SW subsystems or elements that must
be operational to provide the services being modeled. At the system
level of modeling, separation of the hardware and software elements
in the system is not needed. For small systems and equipment,
"system" level modeling as a separate activity may not be required.
For these small systems, the methods discussed below under
development of detailed reliability models may be directly applied.

5.1.2.3 <u>Developing Detailed Reliability Models.</u> The system level
reliability models which have been developed are then further
decomposed to produce reliability models, expressed as reliability
block diagrams, of increasing detail. These block diagrams are
developed in accordance with the methods of MIL-STD-756. The
decomposition process is stopped when the reliability model block
diagrams are sufficiently detailed to show all hardware and
combined hardware/software elements of the system as single blocks.
The reliability analyst must use care in assessing the level of
detail required by the system being analyzed. The detailed block
diagrams must allow separation of hardware and software elements as
a next step. However, the block diagrams must not be so detailed
prior to the separation of the hardware and software elements that
hardware and software interdependencies for redundant structures
are lost from the model(s).

5.1.2.4 <u>Reliability Modeling of Hardware/Software Elements.</u> Once
the detailed reliability models are complete, the reliability
analyst must further decompose those system elements which contain
hardware which hosts executing software. For the purposes of
reliability modeling, software includes firmware - executable code
stored in read only memory. Decomposition of series elements which
contain hardware and software is straightforward. Modeling of
complex, redundant systems with recovery, is more difficult and
requires a highly skilled analyst.

5.1.2.4.1 <u>Modeling Series Hardware/Software Elements.</u> Series
hardware/software elements are modeled as a series string
consisting of the hardware platform and the software which executes
on that platform as shown in Figure 4-2 and discussed in paragraph
4.1.1. As shown in that figure, the software further decomposes
into three elements; the operating system, re-used software, and
newly developed software.

Failure rates for operating systems or executives can usually be
obtained from the supplier of the operating system or executive.
Failure rates obtained from the operating system supplier are
usually quoted in the number of outages caused over some period of
time (e.g., a year). Failure rates for operating systems are
generally quoted with respect to system operating time because the
operating system is active at all times when the computer is

powered and ready for processing. The reliability analyst will need to convert the failure rate given to failures per hour for compatibility with hardware failure rates. Operating system failure rates can be substantial and should not be ignored. Operating systems for mainframe computers can be very large in size and are often very complex and difficult to completely debug. Smaller computers, including single board processor applications, sometimes use real-time executives which can still contribute substantially to the overall software failure rate. Failure rates for re-used code can be obtained from applications where the code was previously used. These failure rates should generally be much lower than the failure rates for newly developed code. The availability of this data depends on the completeness of organizational record keeping and the amount of code modification that has been necessary to allow the code re-use. If the failure rate for re-used code is available in terms compatible with conversion to failures per system operating hour, the failure rate can generally be used directly in the reliability modeling. If the failure rate for re-used code is known in failures per CPU operating period (second, minute, hour, etc), the failure rate will have to be converted to failures per system operating hour using the methods discussed in paragraph 5.1.2.6.

Estimates of the failure rate for newly developed software are obtained using the prediction procedures provided in section 5.3 of this handbook. The failure rate estimates produced by these procedures is provided in failures per CPU operating second for each software element being developed. These failure rates must then be combined as discussed in paragraph 5.1.2.6 to account for the specific software topology and timing. Additionally, the resultant software failure rate must be converted to a system operating hour form as discussed in paragraph 5.1.2.6.

5.1.2.4.2 Modeling   Redundant   Hardware/Software   Elements. Reliability models of redundant HW/SW elements are significantly more complex than reliability models of series hardware/software elements. The addition of redundancy introduces complexity associated with the ability of the hardware and software to correctly respond to failure events. Reliability modeling of redundant HW/SW elements with hot standby and automatic switchover capability significantly increases the complexity required to properly account for system behavior. Of necessity, this discussion of modeling redundant hardware/software elements will focus on the state diagrams which are used to accurately assess the behavior of these complex systems. This discussion is designed to assist an experienced reliability analyst to determine the information which will need to be included in the state diagrams developed for the system being analyzed.

5.1.2.4.2.1   Redundant Hardware Models.   A general model for hardware redundancy using identical equipment is shown in Figure 5-2. As shown in the figure, redundant system elements transition to the next higher state upon the occurrence of any hardware failure. Hardware repairs transition the system element model to the next lower (numerically) state. The system is a closed form semi-Markov process that can be solved for the appropriate reliability measures using conventional methods. Closed-form solutions for the reliability measures of interest for this type of model under most common repair restrictions, types of standby, etc., are available in the technical literature.

The model shown in Figure 5-2 provides an upper bound on the reliability of redundant hardware only systems. Estimation of the expected reliability of hardware systems requires that the fault tolerance employed in the redundancy be included in the model. For cold standby systems, where backup elements are not powered and thus immune to failure occurrence, the model of Figure 5-2 provides a reasonable estimate if the transition rates shown from each success state to the next higher number state are adjusted to account for the constant number of elements in operation (m units). However, for hot standby systems with automatic switchover, the model of Figure 5-2 significantly overstates the reliability achieved by the redundant hardware elements. Failures in the fault detection mechanisms that may lead to latent faults in backup equipment, as well as failures in fault detection, fault isolation, and fault recovery mechanisms that may lead to an inability to activate redundant system elements and resume system services in response to primary element failures, are not included in the model shown in the figure.

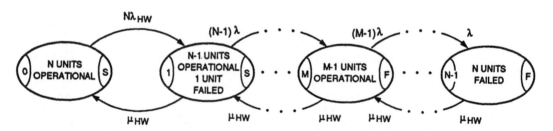

Figure 5-2. General Hardware Redundancy Model: M Required of N Supplied Identical Elements

Figure 5-3 is a simplified reliability model for a hardware system employing hot standby, and automatic switchover with one of two identical elements required. The model accounts for failures in the fault detection, isolation, and recovery mechanisms. The concept of three types of "coverage" is introduced as a part of the model. Fault detection coverage (Cd) is the probability of detecting a fault given that a fault has occurred. Fault Isolation coverage (Ci) is the probability that a fault will be correctly isolated to the recoverable interface (level at which redundancy is available) given that a fault has occurred and been detected. Fault recovery coverage (Cr) is the probability that the redundant structure will recover system services given that a fault has occurred, been detected, and correctly isolated. The model shown in Figure 2-5 is a simplified model since it does not separately consider the possible impact of transient failures. The model also assumes that fault detection coverage (Cd) is the same for both the primary element and the backup element. In practice, there may be different levels of fault detection coverage between primary and backup equipments due to a difference in test exposure intensity.

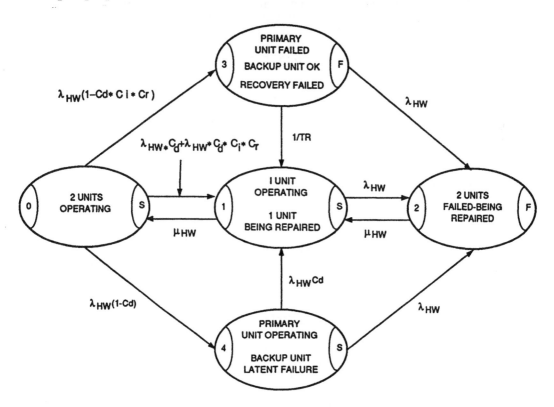

Figure 5-3. Hardware Reliability Model for 1:2 Identical Elements Hot Standby with Automatic Switchover

As shown in the state diagram of Figure 5-3, the structure can transition from the full up state (1) to one of three states. The structure transitions to state 1 whenever a hardware failure occurs in the primary element that is correctly detected, isolated, and recovered from. Similarly, a detected failure in the backup element results in a transition from state 0 to state 1. The structure transitions from state 0 to state 4 when a failure occurs in the backup equipment which is not detectable. Failures in the primary hardware element that cannot be correctly detected, isolated, or recovered from result in a transition from state 0 to state 3. State 3 is a system state to account for the failure time accrued during manual intervention by system operations or maintenance personnel to restore lost system services. Transitions from states 1, 3, and 4 to state 2 are caused by a hardware failure occurring prior to repair of the first failure which occurred in the system structure.

In actual practice, the model to be used will need to be based on the fault tolerant characteristics of the design being analyzed. Models that incorporate system fault behavior, such as shown in Figure 5-3, do not specifically include SW as a part of the model. However, the system or structure control processing, a software based functionality, determines the model structure to account for system behavior under fault conditions.

The reliability estimates which result from the use of system reliability models that account for fault detection, isolation, and recovery are less optimistic than estimates from reliability models based only on the quantity of hardware supplied and required. The reliability of the system structure being modeled is usually very sensitive to the total fault coverage provided by the system design. System designs that feature well-designed fault detection and isolation coupled with rapid and effective recovery of system services avoid most sudden losses of system services due to undetected latent failures in backup equipment or due to the inability of backup equipment to successfully restore system services when failures to the primary equipment occur. Similarly, models of HW/SW systems that include SW as well as the fault tolerance characteristics of the system design are sensitive to the overall effectiveness of the fault detection, isolation, and recovery provided by the hardware and software designs.

5.1.2.4.2.2 Redundant HW/SW Models. Inclusion of software into hardware reliability redundancy models further increases the complexity of the models. As in the hardware-only reliability models, accurate modeling of system behavior requires that fault coverage (Cd, Ci, Cr) be included into the model. Similarly, software fault coverage and the impact of long persistence faults must be included in the system models where appropriate. This results in each model of redundant HW/SW elements being uniquely tailored to the design being analyzed.

5.1.2.4.2.2.1 Cold Standby Systems. Redundant hardware/software systems that use cold standby techniques to provide fault tolerance can be modeled without undue difficulty as long as automatic switchover and startup schemes are not used in the design.   In general, only the hardware and software failure rates for the HW/SW elements need to be considered in developing the reliability model. For designs that use manual restoration of system services through the activation of an unpowered backup unit, an adaptation of the reliability model shown in Figure 5-4 can be used to estimate the reliability of the redundant structure. As shown in the figure, structure state transitions are caused by either hardware or software failures. Hardware failures cause a transition to a state with one less hardware element and commencement of repair actions on the failed element if repair is allowed. The reliability model of Figure 5-4 does not allow latent failures in the backup element to be modeled.   The model assumes that failures of unpowered elements are impossible. Similarly, problems in recovering system services are not modeled since the recovery of system services must be directly managed by the system operator. Software failures result in system recovery using the same processing hardware and a restart of the failed software. Both repairable and non-repairable systems are allowed to have software restarted to enable recovery from software failures. Inclusion of the transition path allowing recovery from software failures is optional for non-repairable systems. The existence or lack of this transition path will depend on how the equipment is operationally employed.

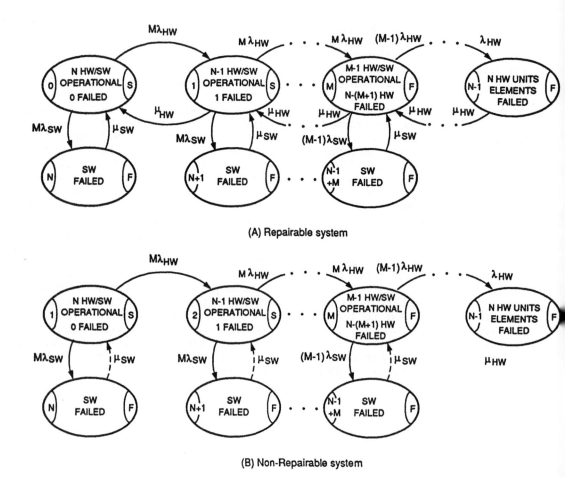

Figure 5-4. HW/SW Reliability Model: M Required of N Supplied Identical Elements, Cold Standby

5.1.2.2.2.2.2   Hot Standby Systems. Reliability modeling of hot standby HW/SW structures requires consideration of hardware failure rates, software failure rates, hardware fault detection, isolation, and recovery coverage, software failure detection, isolation, and recovery coverage, hardware repair rates and software restart/recovery rates. The effect of long persistence software failures on the reliability achieved by hot standby redundant structures is included in the software fault coverage estimates for recovery coverage (Cr). Depending on the system design being modeled, all or most of these parameters will be used to help identify states and/or transition rates between structure states. The exact state diagrams that result from an FMEA of the HW/SW redundant structure will depend on the design being evaluated. An example of a reliability model for a very simple redundant structure is discussed below.

Figure 5-5 presents a simplified state diagram for a HW/SW structure with one of two identical elements required. The model shown is for a hot standby system with automatic switchover. In modeling this structure, five parameters of interest are recognized. The model states depend on primary HW platform state (operational or failed), primary SW state (operational or failed), backup hardware platform state, backup software state, and recovery status. Recovery status is defined to have two states, successful or failed. A successful recovery indicates that the structure has successfully transitioned from primary equipment to the backup equipment after failure of either the primary hardware or software. Alternatively, successful recovery can indicate that a failure in a backup equipment was successfully detected, allowing repair of the backup equipment to commence. A failed recovery indicates that either recovery from primary to backup equipment has failed or that a failure has occurred in the backup equipment which has not been detected.

Since there are five parameters of interest, each of which has two possible values, a total of 32 possible states would be expected. However, some of the 32 possible states cannot exist in practice. Also, some of the states that can exist are functional duplicates that can be merged. For example, a state with a hardware failure in the primary equipment and operational software in the primary equipment can by shown to be one of the 32 possible states. However, the state is impossible because software cannot be operational on a failed hardware platform. The two states that can exist for (1) a failed backup equipment with successful recovery and (2) a failed primary equipment with successful recovery can be shown to be functionally equivalent since successful recovery implies that whichever hardware remains operational has been assigned to primary processing as a part of the recovery process.

12675-9 (11-8-91) M10

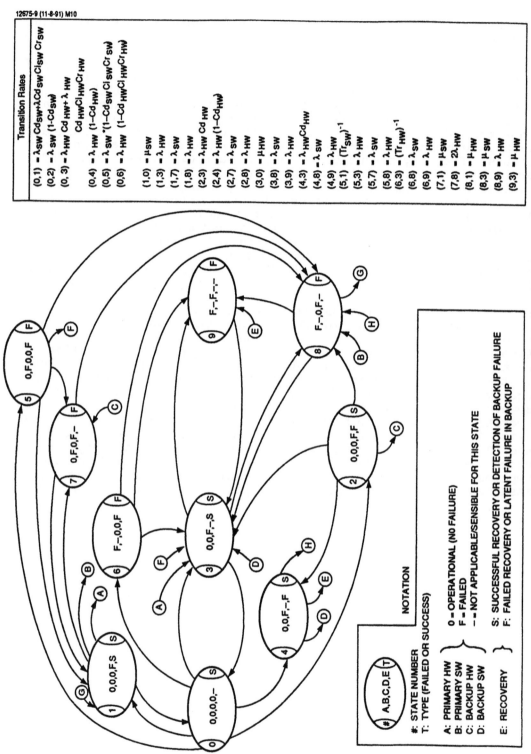

Transition Rates

(0,1) — $\lambda_{SW}\,Cd_{SW} \cdot \lambda\,Cd\,{}_{SW}\,Cl_{SW}\,Cr\,{}_{SW}$
(0,2) — $\lambda\,{}_{SW}\,(1-Cd_{SW})$
(0,3) — $\lambda\,{}_{HW}\,Cd\,{}_{HW} + \lambda\,{}_{HW}$
     $Cd\,{}_{HW}Cl\,{}_{HW}Cr\,{}_{HW}$
(0,4) — $\lambda\,{}_{HW}\,(1-Cd\,{}_{HW})$
(0,5) — $\lambda\,{}_{SW}\,{}^*(1-Cd_{SW}\,Cl\,{}_{SW}Cr\,{}_{SW})$
(0,6) — $\lambda\,{}_{HW}\,(1-Cd\,{}_{HW}Cl\,{}_{HW}Cr\,{}_{HW})$

(1,0) — μ_{SW}
(1,3) — $\lambda\,{}_{HW}$
(1,7) — $\lambda\,{}_{SW}$
(1,8) — $\lambda\,{}_{HW}$
(2,3) — $\lambda\,{}_{HW}\,Cd\,{}_{HW}$
(2,4) — $\lambda\,{}_{HW}\,(1-Cd_{HW})$
(2,7) — $\lambda\,{}_{SW}$
(2,8) — $\lambda\,{}_{HW}$
(3,0) — μ_{HW}
(3,8) — $\lambda\,{}_{SW}$
(3,9) — $\lambda\,{}_{HW}$
(4,3) — $\lambda\,{}_{HW}Cd_{HW}$
(4,8) — $\lambda\,{}_{SW}$
(4,9) — $\lambda\,{}_{HW}$
(5,1) — $(T_{SW})^{-1}$
(5,3) — $\lambda\,{}_{HW}$
(5,7) — $\lambda\,{}_{SW}$
(5,8) — $\lambda\,{}_{HW}$
(6,3) — $(T_{HW})^{-1}$
(6,8) — $\lambda\,{}_{SW}$
(6,9) — $\lambda\,{}_{HW}$
(7,1) — μ_{SW}
(7,8) — $2\lambda\,{}_{HW}$
(8,1) — μ_{HW}
(8,3) — μ_{SW}
(8,9) — $\lambda\,{}_{HW}$
(9,3) — μ_{HW}

NOTATION

(# A,B,C,D,E T)

\#: STATE NUMBER
T: TYPE (FAILED OR SUCCESS)

A: PRIMARY HW
B: PRIMARY SW
C: BACKUP HW
D: BACKUP SW
E: RECOVERY

0 – OPERATIONAL (NO FAILURE)
F – FAILED
– – NOT APPLICABLE/SENSIBLE FOR THIS STATE

S: SUCCESSFUL RECOVERY OR DETECTION OF BACKUP FAILURE
F: FAILED RECOVERY OR LATENT FAILURE IN BACKUP

Figure 5-5. Simplified State Diagram for 1:2, Hot Standby, HW/SW System

For the model of Figure 5-5, a total of ten states result, with the following definitions:

State 0: Success State - Fully Operational State

State 1: Success State - Backup has a detected SW failure which is being recovered from.

State 2: Success State - System is operational with a latent SW failure in the backup element.

State 3: Success State - System is operational with a detected hardware failure in the backup element.

State 4: Success State - System operational with a latent HW failure in the backup element.

State 5: Failed State - Primary SW has failed, recovery to the backup HW and SW has not been successful. System operations intervention will be required to restore system operation on either HW platform.

State 6: Failed State - Primary HW has failed. The recovery process has failed. Either incorrect detection, isolation, or incomplete recovery has occurred. Manual intervention by the system operator will be required to restore system services on the backup equipment.

State 7: Failed State - Software failures have occurred on both primary and backup system elements.

State 8: Failed State - The primary HW and backup SW have failed. Both elements are down, recovery is not possible without manual intervention by the system operator and/or maintenance personnel.

State 9: Failed State - Both hardware elements have failed.

As shown in Figure 5-5, transitions between states occur due to either failures in the hardware or software or due to the status of the recovery process. Using state diagrams that model the impact of hardware, software, and fault coverage for both hardware and software failures results in more accurate assessment of the potential reliability of redundant systems. Also, accurate models that reflect the system design decisions which have been made provide a basis for evaluating the reliability demands of candidate architectural approaches early in the design process.

5.1.2.5 Hardware Failure and Repair Rates. Individual hardware components which are identified as blocks on the detailed reliability block diagrams should be decomposed into detailed internal models of the hardware device using the methods MIL-STD-756 where appropriate.

Hardware failure rates for use in combined HW/SW models should be obtained from the same sources as those traditionally used for hardware only reliability models. In service, field, reliability records are the best estimators of expected hardware failure rates. When field reliability records are not available, reliability test results are the next best estimator of expected hardware reliability performance. When neither field nor test reliability records are available, MIL-HDBK-217 is the preferred reference for obtaining component level failure rates that can be used to predict hardware reliability performance. When MIL-HDBK-217 predictions cannot be applied due to lack of equipment definition, the reliability performance of the previous generation of similar equipment can be used as an estimate of the lower bound for the expected reliability of current generation equipment.

5.1.2.6 Software Failure Rates. Determining software failure rates for use in combined hardware/software models requires that the software being analyzed be treated as a subsystem. A software subsystem can be viewed as a hierarchy. The hierarchy consists of Computer Software Configuration Items (CSCIs), Computer Software Components (CSCs), and so on, as described in DOD-STD-2167A. Because of the different names for items at different levels, two generic names will be used in the following discussion to represent software items at adjacent levels. The first generic name is "component." A component is an item at any level in the system hierarchy. The second generic name is "aggregate." An aggregate is an item composed of an interrelated set of components. An aggregate exists at one level higher in the system hierarchy than its components. For example, an aggregate of CSCIs can be a software subsystem. The terms CSCI, CSC, and so on refer to the static structure of software, and are designated for the purpose of configuration management. In modeling the reliability of software, the dynamic (run-time) relationship among the software elements is what is important.

The software components that comprise an aggregate will be related to one another in two ways: a particular timing configuration and a particular reliability topology.

Timing configuration concerns when it is that the various components are active and inactive during a period of interest. Reliability topology concerns the number of components in the aggregate that can fail before the aggregate fails.

5.1.2.6.1   <u>Timing Configurations</u>.   Several different timing configurations are possible. The major timing relationships among software components are "concurrent" and "sequential." Components will be termed concurrent if they are active simultaneously. The components are sequential if they are active one after the other. It is also possible for component active times to overlap, resulting in a hybrid concurrent/sequential timing configuration.

Concurrently active software components are found in aggregates that are serviced by more than one CPU, for example, in a multiprocessing system or a distributed system.

5.1.2.6.2   <u>Reliability Topology</u>.   Reliability topology is the relationship between the failure of individual components to the failure of the aggregate.   Generally, software components are related in a "series" topology, meaning that the failure of one component results in the failure of the aggregate. Software fault tolerance techniques can result in aggregates that can survive the failure of one or more components.   Software fault tolerance consists of a new, very controversial, set of techniques which are not covered by this handbook.

5.1.2.6.3 <u>Notation</u>. Capital letters will be used to refer to the aggregate item and lowercase letters to refer to the component item. The average aggregate failure rate will be denoted Λ, and the aggregate reliability function will be denoted $R(t)$.   The component failure rate is denoted λ, or λ_k for the k-th component.

5.1.2.6.4 <u>Software Failure Rate Adjustment</u>. A failure rate is the rate of failures with respect to time. A computer program's failure rate can be expressed with respect to three different time frames of reference: execution time, system operating time, and calendar time. Execution time is CPU time; it only advances when the program is executing instructions. System operating advances whenever the hardware/software system as a whole is operating. Calendar time, short periods of which are called wall-clock time, is always advancing.

The ratio of a CSCI's execution time to system operating time is the CSCI's utilization u_i.   The utilization can exceed 100% if copies of the software run on multiple CPUs reading different input streams. The CSCI's execution-time failure rate is multiplied by the CSCI's utilization to obtain the system-operating-time failure rate.

A program can only fail when it is running. The failures uncover faults, and the removal of the faults results in reliability growth. Thus, software reliability growth curves are based on cumulative execution time and express a single program's failure rate in terms of execution time. For scheduling purposes, execution time can be converted to calendar time in light of resource constraints.

An execution-time failure rate is sensitive to processor speed: The execution-time failure rate is always linearly proportional to the processor speed. If the failure rate λ for a software component was measured on or predicted for a processor with average instruction rate of g_1 instructions per second, and the target machine's processor has average instruction rate g_2, then the failure rate should be adjusted to:

$$\lambda^* = \frac{g_2}{g_1}\lambda \tag{1}$$

For example, using a software reliability growth model, the execution-time failure rate of a program is estimated at 0.00004 failures per CPU hour. Growth testing is performed on a machine with a performance rating of 3 MIPS (millions of instructions per second). The target machine is a faster model that runs at 5 MIPS. The adjusted failure rate is $\lambda^* = (5{,}000{,}000 / 3{,}000{,}000)\,(0.00004) = 0.000067$.

In general, a CSCI's utilization will simultaneously decrease in proportion to the increase in processor speed.

During the operation of a system, programs may not operate continuously. For example, some of the programs may time-share a single CPU. Also, multiple CPUs may be present, allowing program executions to overlap. In order to combine the failure rates of the various programs with one another to arrive at an overall software failure rate, it is first necessary to translate all the program failure rates into a common time frame of reference. This frame of reference is system operating time, the same time frame used to express hardware failure rates.

If the programs are in a series configuration, then the (average) failure rate is simply the sum of the system-operating-time failure rates of the individual CSCIs. This result can be derived as follows. Suppose there are N CSCIs that run during the time period T. Let λ_i be the execution-time failure rate for the i-th CSCI. Let $\mu(T)$ be the expected number of failures during that period.

The expected number of failures contributed by the i-th CSCI is $\lambda_i u_i T$. Thus

$$\mu(T) = \sum \lambda_i u_i T \tag{2}$$

The overall failure rate is

$$\Lambda = \frac{\mu(T)}{T} = \sum \lambda_i u_i \tag{3}$$

The sum $\Sigma \lambda_i u_i$ is seen to be the sum of the CSCIs' system-operating-time failure rates.

5.1.2.6.5 <u>SW Reliability Combination Models</u>. The solution for the reliability of an aggregate of series components 1, ..., N is calculated by first determining the average failure rate

$$\Lambda = \frac{\displaystyle\sum_{k=1}^{N} \lambda_k \tau'_k}{T} \tag{4}$$

where λ_k is the failure rate of the i-th component and τ_i' is the amount of time component i is active during period [0,T].

Procedure 5.1.2.6.5-1 through Procedure 5.1.2.6.5-3, below provide specific solutions for modeling the failure rate of software which is sequentially active, concurrently active, and for mission software where the activation times are indeterminate.

Procedure 5.1.2.6.5-1 - Sequentially Active Software Model.

In this situation, components 1 through N are active one after the other. The time t_k is the point at which component k finishes and component (k+1) is activated.

The mission time T will lie between the times t_i and t_{i+1}. The average failure rate is

$$\Lambda = \frac{\sum_{j=1}^{i} \lambda_j (t_j - t_{j-1}) + \lambda_{i+1}(T - t_i)}{T} \tag{5}$$

Sometimes the components are not active consecutively; a time period during which no component is active can be represented by a pseudocomponent whose failure rate is zero. If a component is active intermittently, that is, for several piecewise continuous periods, then a pseudocomponent can be created for each such period. All pseudocomponents created for a particular component will have the same failure rate as that component.

Steps

A. Determine the failure rate and stopping time of each component.

B. For a particular time T of interest, use the formula

$$\Lambda = \left[\sum_{j=1}^{i} \lambda_j (t_j - t_{j-1}) + \lambda_{i+1}(T - t_i) \right] / T \tag{6}$$

to determine the average failure rate.

Example

Suppose that there are four sequentially active components, whose characteristics are provided in Table 5-1. Find R(100).

TABLE 5-1.   Series Sequential Example

Component i	Start Time	End time t_i	Failure Rate λ_i
1	0	45	3×10^{-5}
2	45	200	6×10^{-5}
3	200	300	2×10^{-5}
4	300	800	8×10^{-5}

The average failure rate is calculated by

$$\Lambda = \left[\sum_{j=1}^{i} \lambda_j (t_j - t_{j-1} + \lambda_{i+1}(T-t_i)) \right] / T \tag{7}$$

$$= \frac{(45-0)(3 \times 10^{-5}) + (100-45)(6 \times 10^{-5})}{100} = 0.0000465$$

The reliability at time 100 is obtained as

$$R(100) = \exp[-\Lambda(100)] = \exp[-(0.0000465)(100)] = 0.995 \tag{8}$$

Procedure 5.1.2.6.5-2 - Concurrently Active Software Model.

If throughout a time interval, components 1, ..., N are concurrently (simultaneously) active, then the average failure rate is

$$\Lambda = \sum_{k=1}^{N} \lambda_k \qquad (9)$$

If all components have the same failure rate λ, the aggregate failure rate will be $\Lambda = N\lambda$.

Steps

A.   Start with the component failure rates λ_k.

B.   Use the formula

$$\Lambda = \sum_{k=1}^{N} \lambda_k \qquad (10)$$

to determine the average failure rate for the aggregate.

Example

Suppose that there are three series components that function concurrently. The first component has a failure rate of 1×10^{-5}, the second a failure rate of 4×10^{-4}, and the third has a failure rate of 3×10^{-5}. Find the aggregate failure rate.

The aggregate failure rate is the sum of the three failure rates:

$$\Lambda = \sum_{k=1}^{3} \lambda_k = (1\times10^{-5}) + (4\times10^{-4}) + (3\times10^{-5}) = 0.00044 \qquad (11)$$

Procedure 5.1.2.6.5-3 - Mission Oriented Software Combination
Model.

In many practical cases, the exact component starting and stopping
times are unknown or nondeterministic. As long as the failure rate
λ_k and total active time τ'_k for each component k are known, the
average failure rate, and hence the reliability, can be obtained.

A mission-oriented system is described by means of a mission
profile and consists of V consecutive time periods, called phases.
During each phase the mission has to accomplish a specified task.
An example of a space vehicle's mission phases is ground operation,
launch, and orbit. Furthermore, at any point in time the system is
in one of M possible operational modes. The effective operating
time X_j for the j-th operational mode is given by

$$X_j = \sum_{i=1}^{V} t_i q_{ij} , \quad j=1,2,...,M \tag{12}$$

where t_i is the duration of the i-th mission phase and q_{ij} is the
fraction of time the j-th mode is utilized during that phase.

Suppose there are N components in the aggregate. Let u_{jk} be the
utilization ("duty cycle") of component k during operating mode j.
Then the amount of time component k is active during the mission is

$$\tau'_k = \sum_{j=1}^{V} X_j u_{jk} , \quad k=1,2,...,N \tag{13}$$

In matrix notation, the foregoing equations are

$$X = TQ; \quad T' = XU \tag{14}$$

Let λ_k be the failure rate of the k-th component. The (average)
failure rate over the mission can be calculated as

$$\Lambda = \frac{\sum_{k=1}^{N} \lambda_k \tau'_k}{\text{mission duration}} \tag{15}$$

Steps

A. From the mission profile, form the matrices T and Q. T is a
    row matrix of the durations t_1, t_2, ..., t_N of the mission
    phases, where V is the number of mission phases. Q is an SxM
    matrix whose elements q_{ij} are the fraction of time the j-th
    mode is utilized during the i-th phase, where M is the number
    of operational modes.

B. Compute the row matrix X by

$$X = TQ \tag{16}$$

The elements x_1, x_2, ..., x_M are the effective operating times
for each operational mode.

C. Form the MxN matrix U, whose elements u_{jk} are the utilization
    of component k during mode j.

D. Compute the row matrix T' by

$$T' = XU \tag{17}$$

These are the active times τ'_i for the components.

E. Denote the failure rates of the components as λ_1, λ_2, ...,
    λ_N.

F. Calculate the average failure rate over the mission by
    applying the formula

$$\Lambda = \frac{\sum_{k=1}^{N} \lambda_k \tau'_k}{\text{mission duration}} \tag{18}$$

Example

A mission has V = 8 phases. The names and durations are given by
Table 5-2.

TABLE 5-2. Mission Phases

Phase Number i	Phase Name	Duration t_i (hours)
1	Start-Up	0.1
2	Taxi	0.1
3	Climb	0.2
4	Loiter	1.0
5	Attack	0.3
6	Return	0.2
7	Land	0.1
8	Shutdown	0.2

During the mission, there are M=4 operational modes (see Table 5-3).

TABLE 5-3. Operational Modes

Operational Mode j	Mode Name
1	Idle
2	Scan
3	Track
4	Maintenance

Suppose the mode utilization is

$$Q = \begin{bmatrix} 1.0 & 0 & 0 & 0 \\ 1.0 & 0 & 0 & 0 \\ 0.5 & 0.5 & 0 & 0 \\ 0 & 0.8 & 0.2 & 0 \\ 0 & 0.33 & 0.67 & 0 \\ 0.5 & 0.5 & 0 & 0 \\ 1.0 & 0 & 0 & 0 \\ 0 & 0 & 0 & 1.0 \end{bmatrix} \qquad (19)$$

From Table 5-2, the phase durations are

$$T = [0.1\ 0.1\ 0.2\ 1.0\ 0.3\ 0.2\ 0.1\ 0.2] \qquad (20)$$

Then the effective operating times are computed as

$$X = TQ = [0.5\ 1.1\ 0.4\ 0.2] \qquad (21)$$

and summarized in Table 5-4.

TABLE 5-4.   Effective Operating Time in Modes

Operational Mode j	Mode Name	Effective Time X_1
1	Idle	0.5
2	Scan	1.1
3	Track	0.4
4	Maintenance	0.2

TABLE 5-5.   Software Components

S/W Component k	Name	Failure Rate λ_k (10^{-6}/hr)
1	Exec	50.0
2	Test	10.0
3	Scan	100.0
4	Track	100.0
5	Calibrate	10.0

Suppose that there are N = 5 software components (see Table 5-5). Suppose that the software component utilization is

$$U = \begin{bmatrix} 0.05 & 0.75 & 0.05 & 0.05 & 0.1 \\ 0.05 & 0.05 & 0.9 & 0 & 0 \\ 0.05 & 0.05 & 0 & 0.9 & 0 \\ 0.2 & 0.4 & 0 & 0 & 0.4 \end{bmatrix} \qquad (22)$$

Then the amount of time each component is active is given by the elements of

$$T' = XU = [0.1 \ \ 0.5 \ \ 1.0 \ \ 0.4 \ \ 0.1] \qquad (23)$$

summarized in Table 5-6.

TABLE 5-6.   Software Component Execution Times

Software Module k	Component Name	Active Time τ'_k (hr)
1	Exec	0.1
2	Test	0.5
3	Scan	1.0
4	Track	0.4
5	Calibrate	0.1

From Table 5-2, the mission time is found by summing the phase durations, yielding 2.2 hours. The average failure rate is

$$\Lambda = \frac{\displaystyle\sum_{k=1}^{5} \lambda_k \tau'_k}{2} \cdot 2 \qquad (24)$$

$$= [(0.1)(50.0 \times 10^{-6}) + (0.5)(10.0 \times 10^{-6}) + (1.0)(100.0 \times 10^{-6})$$

$$+ (0.4)(100.0 \times 10^{-6}) + (0.1)(10.0 \times 10^{-6})] \ / \ 2.2 \approx 68 \times 10^{-6}$$

5.2 <u>Reliability Allocation</u>. The purpose of reliability allocation is to translate specified system level reliability requirements into specific reliability objectives for each subsystem and lower-tier element. Allocating specified system- level reliability figures of merit to lower-tier elements supports the use of multiple design teams working on different parts of the developing design and is crucial in allowing effective reliability control of subcontractor design efforts. At all stages of the reliability allocation process, the requirements apportioned to the various design elements must build up to the required system reliability. Additionally, the individual allocations must be achievable.

5.2.1 <u>System Reliability Allocation</u>. Reliability allocations for hardware/software systems can be started as soon as the system reliability models have been created. The initial value allocated to the system itself should either be the specified values for the various reliability figures of merit for the system, or a set of reliability values which are marginally more difficult to achieve than the specified values. Reliability values that are slightly more aggressive than the required values are sometimes allocated to the system to allow for later system functionality growth and to allow those parts of the system which cannot achieve their allocated values to be given some additional reliability margin later in the design process. The apportionment of reliability values between the various subsystems and elements can be made on the basis of complexity, criticality, estimated achievable reliability, or any other factor considered appropriate by the analyst making the allocation. The procedures provided under paragraph 5.2.3 for allocation of software failure rates can be applied to both hardware and system elements so long as the user recognizes that these elements usually operate concurrently.

System-level allocations are successively decomposed using the reliability model(s) developed until each hardware and hardware/software component has been apportioned an appropriate set of reliability measures. The allocation process is then continued for the hardware and the hardware/software elements within the system.

5.2.2 <u>Hardware Reliability Allocation</u>. The allocation of reliability values to lower tier indentures of hardware elements is a continuation of the allocation process begun at the system level. The hardware reliability models are used to successively apportion the required reliability measures between the various individual pieces of hardware and from the hardware equipment level to the various internal elements. For existing hardware items, the reliability allocation used should be the reliability performance of previous production equipment. Reliability allocations to internal elements of existing hardware are not usually performed. For new development hardware, allocations to internal elements (power supplies, circuit cards) should be made.

5.2.3 <u>Software Reliability Allocation</u>. This section provides the procedures used to allocate the appropriate reliability goal to lower-level software components, in order to achieve the reliability goal of the software system. These software components are assumed to be in series, that is, each individual component must succeed for the system to succeed.

The terminology used in this section is the same as in section 5.1.

Figure 5-1 shows the appropriate procedures used in different scenarios to allocate the failure rate goals to software components. Once predicted failure rates for the software components are known, Procedure 5.2.3-5 is used to re-allocate an appropriate failure rate goal to each software component.

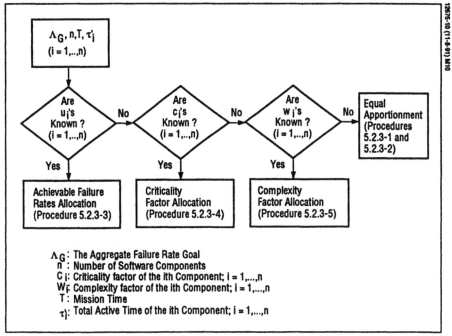

Figure 5-6. Reliability Allocation Procedures

Procedure 5.2.3-1 - Equal apportionment applied to sequential software components.

This procedure is used to allocate a failure rate goal to each individual software component when the components are executed sequentially. This procedure should be used when only Λ_G, the failure rate goal of the software aggregate, and N, the number of software components in the aggregate, are known. The aggregate's failure rate goal is either specified in the requirements or is the result of an allocation performed at a higher level in the system hierarchy.

Steps

A. Determine Λ_G, the failure rate goal for the software aggregate

B. Determine N, the number of software components in the aggregate

C. For each software component, assign the failure rate goal

$$\lambda_{iG} = \Lambda_G \qquad\qquad i=1,2,\ldots,N$$

Example

A software aggregate is required to have a maximum of $\Lambda_G = 0.05$ failures per hour. The aggregate consists of N = 5 software components that are executed one after another, that is, the five components run sequentially. All components must succeed for the system to succeed (this is a series system).

Then, using the equal apportionment technique, the failure rate goal for the i-th software component is assigned to be

$$\lambda_{iG} = \Lambda_G = 0.05 \qquad\qquad i=1,2,\ldots,5$$

Procedure 5.2.3-2 - Equal apportionment applied to concurrent software components.

This procedure is used to allocate the appropriate failure rate goal to each individual software component, when the components are executed concurrently. Λ_G, the failure rate of the software aggregate, and N, the number of software components in the aggregate, are needed for this procedure.

Steps

A. Determine Λ_G, the failure rate goal for the software aggregate

B. Determine N, the number of software components in the aggregate

C. For each software component, assign the failure rate goal to be

$$\lambda_{iG} = \Lambda_G \; / \; N \qquad\qquad i=1,2,\ldots,N$$

Example

A software aggregate has a failure rate goal of $\Lambda_G = 0.05$ failures per hour. The aggregate consists of $N = 5$ software components, which are in series and executed concurrently.

Then, the allocated failure rate goal of each of the 5 software components is

$$\begin{aligned}
\lambda_{iG} &= \Lambda_G \; / \; N \\
&= 0.05 \; / \; 5 \\
&= 0.01 \qquad\qquad i = 1,2,\ldots,5
\end{aligned}$$

Procedure 5.2.3-3 - Allocation Based on Achievable Failure Rates

Allocation Based on Achievable Failure Rates uses each CSCI's utilization (see 5.1.2.6.4). The utilization governs the growth rate a CSCI can be expected to experience during system test. All things being equal, the greater a CSCI's utilization, the faster its reliability will grow during system test.

The method starts out by forecasting each CSCI's initial failure rate as a function of predicted size, processor speed, and industry average figures for fault density and fault exposure ratio. Then the reliability growth model parameter β, the decrement in failure rate (with respect to execution time) per failure occurrence, is predicted. Next, it is determined how much growth each CSCI can be expected to achieve during system test. The growth is described by the softwre reliability growth model. From the growth model, each CSCI's failure rate at release is predicted, taking into account that CSCI's utilization. These predicted at-release failure rates provide relative weights, which are used to apportion the overall software failure rate goal Λ_G among the CSCIs.

Using the Proposal/Pre-Contractual Stage software reliability prediction equation, the i-th CSCI's initial failure rate λ_{0i} (with respect to execution time) is obtained:

$$\lambda_0 = r_i \cdot K \cdot \omega_{0i} / I_i \qquad (25)$$

where r_i is the host processor speed (average number of instructions executed per second), K is the fault exposure ratio (use 4.20×10^{-7}), ω_{0i} is the CSCI's fault content (use the number of developed lines of source code in the CSCI times 0.006), and I_i is the number of object instructions in the CSCI (number of source lines of code times the code expansion ratio (see Table 5-10) [4.5 for Ada]). It is thus assumed that each CSCI is developed by a mature, reproducible software development process that produces code with the approximate industry average of 6 faults per KLOC. Note that, in this model, the initial failure rate is primarily a function of fault density, as opposed to size or number of faults.

The software reliability growth model is employed to forecast the failure rate (with respect to system operating time) $\lambda_i(t)$ each CSCI will exhibit after t system operating time units of system test. Each CSCI's utilization u_i is that CSCI's ratio of execution time to system operating time. The growth model provides the formula

$$\lambda_i(t) = \lambda_0 \cdot \exp\left[-\beta_i \cdot t \cdot u_i\right] \cdot u_i \qquad (26)$$

For each CSCI the parameter β_i can be computed from

$$\beta = B \cdot \frac{\lambda_{0i}}{\omega_{0i}} \qquad (27)$$

(Use 0.955 for the fault reduction factor B). If the CSCIs are not integrated with one another all at once, but through a series of incremental builds, each CSCI can have its own value of t.

A relative failure rate weight w_i can now be associated with each CSCI. The weight is computed from the formula

$$w_i = \frac{\lambda_i(t)}{\sum \lambda_i(t)} \qquad (28)$$

Finally, the failure rate goal (with respect to system operating time) λ_{Ai} to be allocated to the i-th CSCI is

$$\lambda_{Ai} = \Lambda_G \cdot w_i \qquad (29)$$

If desired, this failure rate can be expressed in terms of execution time by dividing by u_i.

The allocation works with failure rates expressed with respect to system operating time. Note that changing to a faster (slower) processor does not affect a system-operating-time failure rate; the reduction (increase) in the utilization is exactly offset by a proportionate increase (decrease) in the execution time failure rate. Therefore, the allocation obtained from this method does not need to be changed if the hardware platform changes to a faster or slower processor.

Steps

A. Predict each CSCI's initial failure rate (with respect to the CSCI's execution time) using the formula

$$\lambda_{0i} = r_i \cdot K \cdot \omega_0 / I_i \qquad (30)$$

where r_i is the host processor speed (average number of instructions executed per unit time), $K = 4.20 \times 10^{-7}$, ω_0 is the fault content (lines of developed source code times 6), and I_i is the number of object instructions (number of source lines of code in the CSCI times the code expansion ratio of the programming language (4.5 for Ada).

B.   Let t the number of system operating time units to be expended in system test.   Compute each CSCI's failure rate at release (with respect to system operating time) by the formula

$$\lambda_i(t) = \lambda_{0i} \exp[-\beta \cdot u_i] \cdot u_i \tag{31}$$

where

$$\beta = B \cdot \frac{\lambda_0}{\omega_0} \tag{32}$$

Use 0.955 for the fault reduction factor B.

C.   Calculate each CSCI's relative failure rate weight by the formula

$$w_i = \frac{\lambda_i(t)}{\sum \lambda_i(t)} \tag{33}$$

D.   Calculate the failure rate $\lambda_{Ai} = \Lambda_G \times w_i$.

Example

A software subsystem consists of three CSCIs.   The first CSCI, hosted on a 3-MIPS processor, is predicted to contain ΔI_{S1} = 10,200 lines of newly developed Ada source code and 2,000 lines of reused Ada source code, for a total of 12,200 lines of source code.   The second CSCI, hosted on 4- MIPS processor, is predicted to consist of ΔI_{S2} = 20,000 lines of Ada source code, all newly developed.   The third CSCI, hosted on a 4-MIPS processor, is predicted to consist of ΔI_{S3} = 45,000 lines of newly developed Ada source code.   Since the code expansion ratio for Ada is 4.5 object instructions per source line of code, the number of object instructions are I_1 = 54,900; I_2 = 90,000; and I_3 = 202,500.

The first CSCI has a utilization factor of 20%; the second CSCI, 20%, and the third, 40%.   The failure rate goal for the software subsystem is Λ_G = 0.00005 failures per system operating second. Table 5.7 summarizes these figures.

TABLE 5.7.   CSCI Characteristics

CSCI i	ΔI_{si}	I_i	r_i	u_i
1	10,200	54,900	3,000,000	0.2
2	20,000	90,000	4,000,000	0.2
3	45,000	202,500	4,000,000	0.4

The predicted fault contents ω_{01}, ω_{02}, and ω_{03} are

$$\omega_{01} = \Delta I_{S1} \times 0.006 = 10,200 \times 0.006 \approx 61$$

$$\omega_{02} = \Delta I_{S2} \times 0.006 = 20,000 \times 0.006 = 120 \qquad (34)$$

$$\omega_{03} = \Delta I_{S3} \times 0.006 = 45,000 \times 0.006 = 270$$

The initial failure rates λ_{01}, λ_{02}, and λ_{03} are

$$\lambda_{01} = r_1 \times K \times \omega_{01} / I_1 = (3 \times 10^6)(4.20 \times 10^{-7})(61) / (54,900) = 0.0014$$

$$\lambda_{02} = r_2 \times K \times \omega_{02} / I_2 = (4 \times 10^6)(4.20 \times 10^{-7})(120) / (90,000) = 0.00224$$

$$\lambda_{03} = r_3 \times K \times \omega_{03} / I_3 = (4 \times 10^6)(4.20 \times 10^{-7})(270) / (202,500) = 0.00224$$

$$(35)$$

The software reliability growth model parameters β_1, β_2, and β_3 are

$$\beta_1 = B \times \lambda_{01} / \omega_{01} = (0.955)(0.0014) / (61) = 0.0000219$$

$$\beta_2 = B \times \lambda_{02} / \omega_{02} = (0.955)(0.00224) / (120) = 0.0000178 \qquad (36)$$

$$\beta_3 = B \times \lambda_{03} / \omega_{03} = (0.955)(0.00224) / (270) = 0.0000079$$

Table 5-8 summarizes.

TABLE 5-8.   Growth Model Quantities

CSCI i	ω_{0i}	λ_{0i} per system operating second	β_i per system operating second
1	61	0.0014	0.0000219
2	120	0.00224	0.0000178
3	270	0.00224	0.0000079

The number of hours system test is expected to last is 250. Thus,

$$t = 250 \text{ hr} \times \frac{3600 \text{ sec}}{1 \text{ hr}} = 900,000 \text{ sec} \tag{37}$$

The failure rates (with respect to system operating time) at the end of the 900,000-second system test period are predicted to be

$\lambda_1(900,000) = \lambda_{01}\exp[-t\cdot\beta_1\cdot u_1]\cdot u_1 = 0.0014\exp[-(0.0000219)(900,000)$

$\lambda_2(900,000) = \lambda_{02}\exp[-t\cdot\beta_2\cdot u_2]\cdot u_2 = 0.00224\exp[-(0.0000178)(900,000$

$\lambda_3(900,000) = \lambda_{03}\exp[-t\cdot\beta_3\cdot u_3]\cdot u_3 = 0.00224\exp[-(0.0000079(900,000)$

$$\tag{38}$$

The sum of the failure rates is

$$\sum_1^3 \lambda_i(900,000) = 5.9393847 \times 10^{-5} \tag{39}$$

The computed failure rates weights are

$$w_1 = \lambda_1(900,000)/5.9393847 \times 10^{-5} = 0.0915011$$

$$w_2 = \lambda_2(900,000)/5.9393847 \times 10^{-5} = 0.0306235 \tag{40}$$

$$w_3 = \lambda_3(900,000)/5.9393847 \times 10^{-5} = 0.8778752$$

The allocated failure rates (with respect to system operating time) are computed by multiplying the system failure rate goal ($\Lambda_G = 0.00005$ failures per system operating second) by each of the weights w_1, w_2, and w_3:

$$\lambda_{G1} = \Lambda_G \times w_1 = 0.00005 \times 0.0915011 = 4.575055 \times 10^{-6}$$

$$\lambda_{G2} = \Lambda_G \times w_2 = 0.00005 \times 0.0306235 = 1.531175 \times 10^{-6} \qquad (41)$$

$$\lambda_{G3} = \Lambda_G \times w_3 = 0.00005 \times 0.8778752 = 4.389376 \times 10^{-5}$$

Procedure 5.2.3-4 - Allocation based on criticality factors.

The following procedure is used to allocate the appropriate value to the failure rate of each software component in an aggregate, provided that the criticality factor of each component is known.

A CSCI's criticality refers to the degree to which the reliability and/or safety of the system as a whole is dependent on the proper functioning of the CSCI. Furthermore, gradations of safety hazards translate into gradations of criticality. The greater the criticality, the lower the failure rate that should be allocated.

A criticality factor c_i should be assigned to each CSCI. The more critical the i-th component is, the lower the value that should be assigned to c_i.

Steps

A. Determine Λ_G, the failure rate goal of the software aggregate

B. Determine N, the number of software components in the aggregate

C. For each i-th component, i = 1, 2, ..., N, determine its criticality factor c_i.

D. Determine τ'_i, the total active time of the i-th component, i = 1, 2, ..., N. Determine T, the mission time of the aggregate.

E. Compute the failure rate adjustment ξ:

$$\xi = \frac{\sum_{i=1}^{N} c_i \, \tau'_i}{T} \qquad (42)$$

F. Then, the allocated failure rate of the i-th component is

$$\lambda_{iG} = \Lambda_G \cdot c_i \, / \, \xi$$

(Dividing by ξ makes the allocated component failure rates build up to the aggregate failure rate goal.)

Example

Suppose a software aggregate consisting of N = 3 software components is to be developed. Assume the failure rate goal of the aggregate is Λ_G = 0.002 failures per hour. Suppose that the mission time is T = 4 hours. Furthermore, the criticality factors and the total active time of the software components are:

$$
\begin{array}{ll}
c_1 = 4, & \tau'_1 = 2 \text{ hours} \\
c_2 = 2, & \tau'_2 = 1 \text{ hour} \\
c_3 = 1, & \tau'_3 = 2 \text{ hours}
\end{array}
$$

(Note: In this example, since c_3 has the smallest value, it indicates that the third component of this software aggregate is the most critical.)

Compute ξ:

$$
\xi = \frac{\sum_{i=1}^{3} c_i \tau'_i}{T} \tag{43}
$$

$$
= \frac{(4)(2) + (2)(1) + (1)(2)}{4}
$$

$$
= 3
$$

Then, the failure rate goals of the software components are

$$
\begin{aligned}
\lambda_1 &= \Lambda_G \cdot c_1 / \xi \\
&= (0.002)(4) / 3 \\
&= 0.0027 \text{ failures/hour}
\end{aligned}
$$

$$
\begin{aligned}
\lambda_2 &= \Lambda_G \cdot c_2 / \xi \\
&= (0.002)(2) / 3 \\
&= 0.0013 \text{ failures/hour}
\end{aligned}
$$

$$
\begin{aligned}
\lambda_3 &= \Lambda_G \cdot c_3 / \xi \\
&= (0.002)(1) / 3 \\
&= 0.00067 \text{ failures/hour}
\end{aligned}
$$

Procedure 5.2.3-5 - Allocation based on complexity factors.

The following procedure is used to allocate the failure rate goal to each software component in an aggregate, based on the complexity of the components.

Complexity refers to how complicated the problem to be solved is and how intricate the program structure is expected to be (prevalence of branches and loops. Sophisticated measures of complexity (such as "cyclomatic numbers") have been proposed, but these measures have been found to often be highly correlated with the number of lines of code. Predictions of the number of lines of code are often available early on (because the predictions are used as input to scheduling and costing models). The greater the complexity, the more effort required to achieve a particular failure rate goal. Thus, CSCIs with higher complexity should be assigned higher failure rate goals.

The complexity factor w_i associated with the i-th component can be based on predicted lines of code or the estimated value of another software complexity measure. Raw lines of code or other complexity figures are not directly usable. A raw figure must be transformed into a complexity factor that has the property that it is linearly proportional to the achievable failure rate: If the complexity factor doubles, for example, the failure rate goal should be twice as high.

Steps

A. Determine Λ_G, the failure rate goal of the software aggregate

B. Determine N, the number of software components in the aggregate

C. For each component i, i = 1,2,...,N, determine its complexity factor w_i.

D. Determine τ'_i, the total active time of the i-th component, i = 1,2,..., N. Determine T, the mission time of the aggregate

E. Compute ξ:

$$\xi = \frac{\sum_{i=1}^{N} w_i \tau'_i}{T} \tag{44}$$

G. Then, the allocated failure rate of the i-th component is

$$\lambda_{1G} = \Lambda_G \cdot w_1 \, / \, \xi$$

Example

A software aggregate consisting of N = 4 software components is to be developed. The failure rate goal of the aggregate is Λ_G = 0.006 failures per hour. The mission time is T = 3 hours. Furthermore, the complexity factors and the total active time of the software components are:

$w_1 = 4$,	$t_1 = 2$ hours
$w_2 = 2$,	$t_2 = 1$ hour
$w_3 = 3$,	$t_3 = 3$ hours
$w_4 = 1$,	$t_4 = 2$ hours

Compute ξ:

$$\xi = \frac{\sum_{i=1}^{4} w_i \, \tau_i'}{T} \tag{45}$$

$$= \frac{(4)\,(2) + (2)\,(1) + (3)\,(3) + (1)\,(2)}{3}$$

$$= 7$$

Then, the failure rate goals of the software components are

$$\begin{aligned}
\lambda_{1G} &= \Lambda_G \cdot w_1 \, / \, \xi \\
&= (0.006)(4)/7 \\
&= 0.0034 \text{ failures/hour}
\end{aligned}$$

$$\begin{aligned}
\lambda_{2G} &= \Lambda_G \cdot w_2 \, / \, \xi \\
&= (0.006)(2) \, / \, 7 \\
&= 0.0017 \text{ failures/hour}
\end{aligned}$$

$$\begin{aligned}
\lambda_{3G} &= \Lambda_G \cdot w_3 \, / \, \xi \\
&= (0.006)(3) \, / \, 7 \\
&= 0.0026 \text{ failures/hour}
\end{aligned}$$

$$\begin{aligned}
\lambda_{4G} &= \Lambda_G \cdot w_4 \, / \, \xi \\
&= (0.006)(1) \, / \, 7 \\
&= 0.0009 \text{ failures/hour}
\end{aligned}$$

Procedure 5.2.3-6 - Re-allocation based on predicted failure rates.

Once failure rate predictions become available for the components, the allocations can be revised. If the predicted failure rate of the aggregate is equal to or better than the goal, the components are re-allocated a failure rate based on the ratio of the predicted failure rate of the component to the predicted failure rate of the aggregate. The failure rate "goal" is expressed in terms of the failure rate at release. The predicted failure rates at release are obtained by using the appropriate software reliability prediction model and then a software reliability growth model. If the new failure rate goal of a particular component is lower than its predicted failure rate, it may be possible to take some resources from that component and use the resources to help other components reach their respective goals. If the predicted failure rate of the aggregate falls short of the goal, then actions such as re-design or resource re-allocation need to be considered.

Steps

A. Using the procedures in section 5.3, predict the failure rates the N components will have at release:

$$\lambda_{1P}, \lambda_{2P}, \ldots, \lambda_{NP} \tag{46}$$

The P stands for "predicted."

B. Combine the predicted component failure rates to obtain a predicted failure rate for the aggregate:

$$\Lambda_P = \frac{\sum_{i=1}^{N} \lambda_{iP} \tau_i'}{T} \tag{47}$$

C. If $\Lambda_P \leq \Lambda_G$, then the failure rates are re-allocated using the formula

$$\lambda_i = \frac{\lambda_{iP}}{\Lambda_P} \cdot \Lambda_G , \qquad i=1,2,\ldots,N \tag{48}$$

If $\Lambda_P > \Lambda_G$, then it is likely that the failure rate goal will not be met, and management action is required.

Example

A software aggregate consisting of N = 3 software components is to be developed with the failure rate goal of Λ_G = 0.008 failures per hour. The total active times of the software components are

$$t_1 = 2 \text{ hours}$$
$$t_2 = 3 \text{ hours}$$
$$t_3 = 1 \text{ hour}$$

After the detailed design phase, the predicted failure rates of the software components are

$$\lambda_{1P} = 0.5 \text{ failures/hour}$$
$$\lambda_{2P} = 0.9 \text{ failures/hour}$$
$$\lambda_{3P} = 0.2 \text{ failures/hour}$$

Compute ξ:

$$\Lambda_P = \frac{\sum_{i=1}^{3} \lambda_{iP} \tau'_i}{T} \tag{49}$$

$$= \frac{(0.5)(2) + (0.9)(3) + (0.2)(1)}{6} = 0.65$$

The predicted failure rate of the aggregate is less than its failure rate goal Λ_G = 0.8. Therefore, the re-allocated failure rate goals of the software components are

$$\lambda_{1G} = \lambda_{1P} \cdot \Lambda_G / \Lambda_P$$
$$= (0.5)(0.008)/(0.65)$$
$$= 0.0062 \text{ failures/hour}$$

$$\lambda_{2G} = \lambda_{2P} \cdot \Lambda_G / \Lambda_P$$
$$= (0.9)(0.008)/(0.65)$$
$$= 0.011 \text{ failures/hour}$$

$$\lambda_{3G} = \lambda_{3P} \cdot \Lambda_G / \Lambda_P$$
$$= (0.2)(0.008)/(0.65)$$
$$= 0.0025 \text{ failures/hour}$$

5.2.4 <u>Hardware/Software Allocations.</u> Once the hardware/software elements of the system have been allocated a set of reliability goals, these allocations must be apportioned between the hardware platform and the executing software. To apportion the allocated reliability measures between the hardware and software, the analyst should first determine if the actual reliability of any of the elements of the hardware/software combination is known. The hardware element may be an existing design with proven reliability. Any re-used software elements should have a known reliability. Commercially available operating system software failure rates can be obtained from the software vendor. Prior to apportioning the allocated reliability values to the hardware platform or software elements, those elements with known reliability should be assigned a set of allocated values that reflect their known reliability performance. These allocations should be subtracted from the hardware/software total allocations. The remaining elements can then be apportioned a set of reliability goals based on criticality, complexity, achievable failure rate, or such other factors as the analyst may deem appropriate to the system being developed. Hardware elements of hardware/software combinations which have allocations that need to be further developed should be treated in exactly the same way as purely hardware elements. Allocations to lower tier software elements should be treated as described in paragraph 5.2.5, below.

5.2.5 <u>Software Reliability Allocation.</u> Allocations to lower tier elements of newly developed software can be based on estimated achievable values, complexity, criticality, or equal apportionment. Procedures are provided for each type of allocation for sequentially operating and concurrently operating software. The allocation procedures assume that the software elements are in series, that is, each individual component must succeed for the system to succeed.

Figure 5-6 shows the appropriate procedure to use in different scenarios to allocate failure rate goals to the software components. Procedure 5.2.4-6 can be used to re-allocate failure rates if reallocation becomes necessary.

5.3 <u>Prediction</u>. Reliability prediction is useful in a number of ways. A prediction methodology provides a uniform, reproducible basis for evaluating potential reliability during the early stages of a project. Predictions assist in evaluating the feasibility of proposed reliability requirements and provide a rational basis for design and allocation decisions. Predictions that fall short of requirements at any level signal the need for both management and technical attention. In some cases a shortfall in reliability may be offset by the use of fault tolerance techniques. For hardware, adding redundancy will often result in increased reliability. Software fault tolerance techniques, such as N-version programming and recovery blocks, are controversial but may be effective in some cases.

Hardware reliability prediction, as documented in MIL-HDBK-217 and related publications, provides a constant failure rate figure for the "inherent reliability" of the product, the estimated reliability attainable when all design and production problems have been worked out. A hardware reliability growth model is used to monitor product reliability in the period during which the observed reliability advances toward the inherent reliability.

Software reliability prediction provides an estimate of the software failure rate at the start of system test. A software reliability growth model covers the period after the prediction, as reliability improves as the result of testing and debugging.

Hardware and software reliability predictions, when adjusted by their respective growth models to coincide with the same point in time, can be combined to obtain a prediction of the overall system reliability.

Table 5-9 shows which software reliability prediction procedure to use during each DOD-STD-2167A software development life cycle phase. When system test begins, actual failure data can be used to statistically estimate the growth model parameters (see 5.4.4).

5.3.1 **Hardware Reliability Prediction**. Hardware reliability prediction is a process of quantitatively assessing an equipment design. Standards have been established for techniques and data sources so that hardware reliability predictions may be applied and interpreted uniformly. MIL-HDBK-217 contains methods for predicting the failure rates of electronic and electromechanical components. Prediction is based on a part's quality, environmental stress, complexity, and other factors. Other references are available that address non-electronic parts. The final outcome of a prediction is a constant failure rate that can be combined with other failure rates in a system model.

TABLE 5-9. Prediction Procedures by Phase

Phase	Procedure
Proposal and Pre-contractual	5.3.2-1
Requirements Analysis	5.3.2-1
Preliminary Design	5.3.2-2
Detailed Design	5.3.2-3
Coding and CSU Testing	5.3.2-4
CSC Integration and Testing	5.3.2-5
CSCI Testing	5.3.2-5

5.3.2 <u>Software Reliability Prediction</u>. Figure 5-2 summarizes the software reliability prediction procedure.

Metrics are collected, and the values of the metrics used to predict the initial failure rate λ_0 and fault content as well as the parameters of the software reliability growth model.

A software failure occurs when program output (such as printouts, displays, commands, and control) deviates from that dictated by the requirements and causes the system to fail. In general, a program will fail on some inputs and not on others. The input state (the values of the input variables) determines the path through the program. A program generally will contain faults. A software fault is a missing, extra, or defective instruction or set of related instructions. Every time a fault is encountered, a failure may occur. Some faults are data-dependent and will only cause a failure when program variables have certain values. The chief determinant of software failure rate is the fault density, the number of faults per 1000 lines of executable source code (KLOC). The fault content or density, however, does not take into account the program usage, which inputs and functions the customer will emphasize.

At any point in time, an executing computer program exhibits a constant failure rate λ, provided that the code is frozen and the operational profile is stationary. A constant failure rate implies an exponential time-to-failure distribution; therefore, the reliability--the probability that the program executes without failure for a period of time τ'--is given by

$$R(\tau') = \exp[-\lambda\tau'] \tag{50}$$

The reliability of a piece of software will change as the software is tested and repair activity takes place. Consequently, a software reliability prediction must be associated with a particular point in time. The earliest point in time that it makes sense to talk about the reliability of the software per se is when the software is fully integrated and is executed in an environment that is representative of its operational use. This point is the start of system test and is designated $\tau = 0$. For any later point in time, τ indicates the cumulative execution time since the start of system test.

The failure rate will vary over time. The failure rate at the instant τ is denoted $\lambda(\tau)$. When the program code is frozen, the software will exhibit a constant failure rate $\lambda = \lambda(\tau)$. The failure rate predicted is the initial failure rate $\lambda_0 = \lambda(0)$, the failure rate the software is expected to exhibit at the beginning of system test ($\tau = 0$). The prediction procedures in this section (5.3.2) provide λ_0. The procedures in section 5.3.3 employ the software reliability growth model to estimate additional quantities, such as the schedule and resource impact to achieve a failure rate objective.

<u>Procedure 5.3.2-1 - Proposal/pre-contractual and requirements
analysis phase prediction</u>. This section shows how to predict
software reliability before product/process metrics are
available. It is assumed that the only thing known about the
hypothetical program is a prediction of its size and the
processor speed.

The failure rate of the software is a function of the number of
faults it contains, the size of the program, and the processor
speed. The number of faults is determined by multiplying the
number of developed executable source instructions by the fault
density. "Developed" excludes re-used code that is already
debugged. "Executable" excludes data declarations and compiler
directives. For fault density at the start of system test, a
value of 6 faults per 1000 source instructions, based on an
average of a series of industry studies, is recommended.

Technically, the failure rate of the software is also a function
of the operational profile, but in practice the operational
profile has little effect on the initial failure rate. The
reason is that at the start of system test the faults tend to be
fairly evenly distributed throughout the code. Later on, as
growth testing proceeds, inequities in fault density start to
appear, and the operational profile becomes more of a factor in
affecting the failure rate.

The measurement of processor speed is complicated by the fact
that each instruction takes a different amount of time, depending
on the nature of the operation and where the operands reside. A
unit such as "million instructions per second" (MIPS) implies an
average taken over some arbitrary mix of instructions. The best
way to determine the average instruction rate, denoted r, is
through benchmarking, using an application program and
environment representative of the program whose reliability is
being predicted. Second best, a "MIPS rating" can be obtained
from the computer vendor.

To predict the initial failure rate λ_0, the failure rate at the start of system test, requires the estimated size of the program and the processor speed. The formula for initial failure rate is

$$\lambda_0 = K \cdot r \cdot \omega_0 / I \qquad (51)$$

where r is the processor speed, ω_0 is the number of faults in the program, and I is the number of object instructions. The quantity K is called the "fault exposure ratio." It accounts for data dependency and program structure. Methods exist for obtaining K from historical data. The value recommended for use here is

$$K = 4.20 \times 10^{-7} \qquad (52)$$

which is the average value obtained in a series of industry studies.

Steps

A. Determine the processor speed, r, in instructions per second.

B. To compute the number of object instructions I, take the number of executable lines of code and multiply by the code expansion ratio, supplied in Table 5-10.

TABLE 5-10.   Code Expansion Ratios

Programming Language	Expansion Ratio
Assembler	1
Macro Assembler	1.5
C	2.5
COBOL	3
FORTRAN	3
JOVIAL	3
Ada	4.5

C. Estimate the fault content from

$$\omega_0 = \frac{6}{1000} \cdot \Delta I_s \qquad (53)$$

The quantity ΔI_s is the number of developed executable source lines of code (excludes re-used code).

D. Calculate the initial failure rate as

$$\lambda_0 = K \cdot r \cdot \omega_0 / I \qquad (54)$$

Example

A 20,000-line Ada program is to be developed. It will execute on a 2-MIPS machine. What failure rate can be expected at the beginning of system test?

The number of object instructions is calculated by multiplying the 20,000 executable lines of source code by the code expansion ratio for Ada, 4.5, to yield

$$I = (20{,}000 \text{ source lines}) \left(4.5\frac{\text{object instructions}}{\text{source line}}\right) \qquad (55)$$

$$= 90{,}000 \text{ object instructions}$$

The fault content is predicted as

$$\omega_0 = 6 \cdot \Delta I_s = (20{,}000 \text{ LOC}) \times$$

$$\left(\frac{6 \text{ faults}}{1000 \text{ LOC}}\right) = 120 \text{ faults} \qquad (56)$$

The initial failure rate is then computed by

$$\lambda_0 = r \cdot \omega_0 \cdot K / I$$

$$= \left(\frac{2{,}000{,}000 \text{ instructions}}{\text{second}}\right)$$

$$\times (120 \text{ faults}) \qquad (57)$$

$$\times \left(4.20 \times 10^{-7} \frac{\text{failures}}{\text{fault}}\right)$$

$$/ 90{,}000 \text{ instructions} = 0.00111888 \text{ failures per second}$$

The prediction technique presented so far relies on the new program's predicted size and processor speed. Beginning with the requirements analysis phase of software development, product/process metrics become available. These metrics can be used in conjunction with empirically obtained prediction models to provide better predictions. In order to determine the software reliability growth model parameters (see section 5.3.3), the value of ω_0 needs to be retained for use during later phases. If the projected number of developed executable source lines of code changes, the value of ω_0 should be updated.

Procedure 5.3.2-2 - Preliminary design phase prediction.

This procedure is used to find the best estimate of the initial software failure rate λ_0 (the number of failures per hour at the beginning of the system test), based on the product/process characteristics that are available at the end of the software requirements analysis phase.

Steps

A. Obtain values for the variables in the following list:

x_1: number of errors in the requirements specifications (SRS)
x_2: number of requirements statements in the SRS
x_3: pages in the SRS
x_4: number of man-months for requirements analysis
x_5: number of requirements changes after SRS has been placed under configuration control
x_{13}: number of executable lines of code (LOCs)

See 4.2 for details on these metrics.

B. Determine the average instruction rate, r, of the target machine in instructions per second of the target machine. This rate can be obtained through benchmarking or from vendor specifications.

C. Normalize all variables in the list above based on kilo lines of code (KLOC), by assigning

$$x_i \leftarrow \frac{x_i}{x_{13}} \times 1000 \quad , \quad i = 1,2,3,4,5 \tag{58}$$

D. Compute the software metrics composite based rate

$$\lambda_b = 0.0085x_1 + 0.9949x_2 + 0.1007x_3 - 0.0001x_4$$
$$+ 0.0005x_5 \tag{59}$$

E. Calculate the predicted initial software failure rate as

$$\lambda_0 = (c_1 + c_2 * \lambda_b) * \Lambda \qquad (60)$$

where $c_1 = 0.0668$, $c_2 = 0.0002$ and $\Lambda = r/3,000,000$.

(Note that, theoretically, the above formulas may yield a negative value for the predicted software failure rate. This can only happen, however, in the implausible case that the value of x_4 [number of person-months expended in the requirements analysis phase] exceeds 2.7 million, and the values of all other variables are zero.)

Example

An Ada program comprised of approximately $x_{13} = 30,000$ executable lines of code is to be developed. After the requirements analysis phase, $x_1 = 25$ errors have been found in the requirements documents, which consist of $x_2 = 740$ requirements statements. The requirements specification of this program has $x_3 = 140$ pages. Furthermore, it took $x_4 = 5$ man-months to complete the requirements analysis. There are $x_5 = 25$ changes in the requirements documents after being placed under configuration control. The program will be run by a 6-MIPS machine.

The predicted failure rate that the software exhibits at the beginning of the system test is computed as follows:

A. Normalize the variables:

$x_1 = (x_1/x_{13}) * 1000 = (25/30000) * 1000 = 0.83$

$x_2 = (x_2/x_{13}) * 1000 = (740/30000) * 1000 = 24.67$

$x_3 = (x_3/x_{13}) * 1000 = (140/30000) * 1000 = 4.67$

$x_4 = (x_4/x_{13}) * 1000 = (5/30000) * 1000 = 0.17$

$x_5 = (x_5/x_{13}) * 1000 = (25/30000) * 1000 = 0.83$

B. Compute the software metrics composite based rate

$\lambda_b = 0.0085x_1 + 0.9949x_2 + 0.1007x_3 - 0.0001x_4 + 0.0005x_5$

$= (0.0085)(0.83) + (0.9949)(24.67) + (0.1007)(4.67) - (0.0001)(0.17) + (0.0005)(0.83)$

$= 25.02$

C.   Then, after the requirements analysis phase, the predicted initial software failure rate is

$$\lambda_0 = (c_1 + c_2 * \lambda_b) * \Lambda$$
$$= (0.0668 + (0.0002)(25.02)) * (6,000,000/3,000,000)$$
$$= 0.144$$

That is, the predicted number of software failures per hour at the start of system testing, for a 6-MIPS machine, is 0.144.

Procedure 5.3.2-3 - Detailed design phase prediction.

During the preliminary design phase, as more information about the software becomes available, the variables $x_1,...,x_5$ should be updated.   The procedure in 5.3.2-2 can be used throughout the preliminary design phase to obtain more accurate predictions for the initial software failure rate.

Once the preliminary design phase is completed, however, the procedure in this section must be used instead of that in 5.3.2 to compute the predicted initial software failure rate.

Steps

A.   Update the values variables $x_1,...,x_5,x_{13}$.

B.   Collect the values for the following software metrics:

   x_6: number of errors in the preliminary design documents
   x_7: number of Computer Software Components (CSCs)
   x_8: number of CSUs (Ada packages) in the design structure
   x_9: number of pages in the Design documents (SDDs)
   x_{10}: number of man-months for preliminary design

C.   Determine the average instruction rate, r, in instructions per second, of the target machine. This can be determined through benchmarking or from the computer vendor.

D.   Normalize all variables $x_1,...,x_{10}$ based on KLOCs, by assigning

$$x_i \leftarrow \frac{x_i}{x_{13}} \times 1000 \qquad i = 1,...,10 \tag{61}$$

E.   Compute the software metric composite based rate

$$\lambda_b = 0.0069x_1 + 0.7959x_2 + 0.08x_3 - 0.0003x_4$$
$$+ 0.0003x_5 + 0.0001x_6 + 0.0043x_7 \tag{62}$$
$$+ 0.0128x_8 + 0.6x_9 + 0.0028x_{10}$$

F.   Finally, compute the new predicted software failure rate

$$\lambda_0 = (c_1 + c_2 * \lambda_b) * \Lambda \qquad\qquad (63)$$

where $c_1 = 0.0663$, $c_2 = 0.0001$ and $\Lambda = r / 3,000,000$.

(Note that, theoretically, the above formulas could yield a negative value for the predicted software failure rate.   A negative result is implausible, however, since the formulas only result in a non-positive predicted software failure rate if (1) the value of x_4 (number of man-months in the requirements analysis phase) is greater than 2.7 million and (2) the values of all other variables are zero.)

Example

The preliminary design phase for the Ada program described in the example in 5.3.2 is completed.   The updated values of variables $x_1, \ldots, x_5$ are as follows:

    $x_1 = 35$
    $x_2 = 740$
    $x_3 = 140$
    $x_4 = 5$
    $x_5 = 60$

The size of the program (number of executable lines of code) is re-estimated to be 40,000 (i.e., $x_{13} = 40000$).   The following values of the software metrics associated with the preliminary design are observed:

    $x_6 = 14$
    $x_7 = 19$
    $x_8 = 120$
    $x_9 = 939$
    $x_{10} = 5$

Then, based on the above procedure, the new predicted initial software failure rate (if run on a 6-MIPS machine; i.e., $r = 6,000,000$) is computed as follows:

A.   Normalize the variables:

    $x_1 = (x_1/x_{13})*1000 = (35/40000)*1000 = 0.875$

    $x_2 = (x_2/x_{13})*1000 = (740/40000)*1000 = 18.5$

    $x_3 = (x_3/x_{13})*1000 = (140/40000)*1000 = 3.5$

    $x_4 = (x_4/x_{13})*1000 = (5/40000)*1000 = 0.125$

x_5 = $(x_5/x_{13})*1000$ = $(60/40000)*1000$ = 1.5

x_6 = $(x_6/x_{13})*1000$ = $(14/40000)*1000$ = 0.35

x_7 = $(x_7/x_{13})*1000$ = $(19/40000)*1000$ = 0.475

x_8 = $(x_8/x_{13})*1000$ = $(120/40000)*1000$ = 3

x_9 = $(x_9/x_{13})*1000$ = $(939/40000)*1000$ = 23.475

x_{10} = $(x_{10}/x_{13})*1000$ = $(5/40000)*1000$ = 0.125

B. Compute the software metric composite based rate:

λ_b = $0.0069x_1$ + $0.7959x_2$ + $0.08x_3$ − $0.0003x_4$ + $0.0003x_5$ + $0.0001x_6$ + $0.0043x_7$ + $0.0128x_8$ + $0.6x_9$ + $0.0028x_{10}$

   = (0.0069)(0.875) + (0.7959)(18.5) + (0.08)(3.5) −
     (0.0003)(0.125) + (0.0003)(1.5) + (0.0001)(0.35) +
     (0.0043)(0.475) + (0.0128)(3) + (0.6)(23.475) +
     (0.0028)(0.125)

   = 29.14

C. Then, the predicted initial software failure rate is

λ_0 = $(c_1 + c_2*\lambda_b)$ * Λ
     = (0.0663 + (0.0001)(29.14)) * (6,000,000 / 3,000,000)
     = 0.138

That is, the Ada program described in the examples in 5.3.2 is predicted to have 0.138 failures per hour at the beginning of the system test for a 6-MIPS machine.   This is the predicted initial failure rate based on the values of software metrics collected after the preliminary design phase.

<u>Procedure 5.3.2-4 - Coding and CSU testing phase prediction</u>.

After the detailed design phase has been completed, the initial software failure rate is re-estimated based on the updated values of the variables $x_1, \ldots, x_{10}$ as follows:

<u>Steps</u>

A.   Update the values of all variables $x_1, \ldots, x_{10}$

B.   Repeat steps C, D, E, and F of procedure 5.3.2-3 to compute λ_0, the initial software failure rate.

Procedure 5.3.2-5 - CSC integration and testing and CSCI testing phase prediction.

The following procedure is used to determine the values of λ_0, the software failure rate after the CSU testing phase.

Steps

A. Update the data for variables $x_1, x_2, x_3, x_8, x_9, x_{13}$.

B. Collect the data for the following software characteristics:

   x_{11}: number of defects identified through walkthroughs and reviews
   x_{12}: number of times a CSU is unit-tested.

C. Determine the average instruction rate, r, in instructions per second, of the target machine. This rate can be obtained from benchmarking or from vendor specifications.

D. Normalize variables x_1, x_2, x_3, x_8, x_9, x_{11}, x_{12}, based on KLOCs, by assigning

$$x_i \leftarrow \frac{x_i}{x_{13}} \times 1000 \qquad i = 1,2,3,8,9,11,12 \tag{64}$$

E. Compute the software metric composite based rate

$$\lambda_b = 0.0069x_1 + 0.7955x_2 + 0.08x_3 + 0.0128x_8$$
$$+ 0.6x_9 + 0.032x_{11} + 0.0084x_{12} \tag{65}$$

F. Finally, compute the new predicted software failure rate

$$\lambda_0 = (c_1 + c_2 * \lambda_b) * \Lambda \tag{66}$$

where $c_1 = 0.066$, $c_2 = 0.0001$ and $\Lambda = r/3,000,000$.

Example

After the coding and CSU testing phase for the Ada program introduced in the example of (5.3.2) has been completed, the new predicted software failure rate is computed as follows:

The updated values of variables x_1, x_2, x_3, x_8, and x_9 are 60, 740, 140, 120, 970 respectively. Also, the size of the program (number of executable lines of codes) is re-estimated to be 45514 (i.e., x_{13} = 45514). Furthermore, there are x_{11} = 200 defects identified through walkthroughs and reviews. Finally, assume that each CSU is tested once during the CSU test phase (x_{12} = 1).

Then the new predicted initial software failure rate (if it is run on a 6-MIPS machine) is obtained as follows:

A. Normalize the variables:

x_1 = (x_1/x_{13})*1000 = (60/45514)*1000 = 1.318

x_2 = (x_2/x_{13})*1000 = (740/45514)*1000 = 16.259

x_3 = (x_3/x_{13})*1000 = (140/45514)*1000 = 3.076

x_8 = (x_8/x_{13})*1000 = (120/45514)*1000 = 2.637

x_9 = (x_9/x_{13})*1000 = (970/45514)*1000 = 21.312

x_{11} = (x_{11}/x_{13})*1000 = (200/45514)*1000 = 4.394

B. Compute the value of the software metric composite based rate

λ_b = 0.0069x_1 + 0.7955x_2 + 0.08x_3 + 0.0128x_8 + 0.6x_9 + 0.032x_{11} + 0.0084x_{12}

= (0.0069)(1.318) + (0.7955)(16.259) + (0.08)(3.076) + (0.0128)(2.637) + (0.6)(21.312) + (0.032)(4.394) + (0.0084)(1)

= 26.16

C. Then, the predicted initial software failure rate is computed as

λ_0 = $(c_1 + c_2*\lambda_b)$ * Λ
   = (0.066 + (0.0001)(26.16)) * (6,000,000/3,000,000)
   = 0.137

That is, after the coding and CSU test phase, the Ada program described in the examples in (5.3.2), is predicted to have 0.137 failures per hour at the beginning of the system test, if the processor speed is 6 MIPS.

5.3.3 <u>Use of Predictions for Project Planning and Control</u>.   The failure rate predicted by the prediction techniques in section 5.3.2 is λ_0, the failure rate at the start of system test.   To determine the failure rate at τ execution time units into system test, the software reliability growth model (see section 5.4) is employed.   The growth model parameters are β and v_0.   The parameter β is the (expected) decrement in failure rate per failure occurrence.   The parameter v_0 is the "total failures": the number of failures that must be experienced to uncover and remove all faults.   They are obtained from the predicted values of the initial failure rate λ_0 and fault content ω_0.   The fault content is obtained by multiplying the number of developed executable lines of code by the fault density. Based on a series of industry studies, the average fault density at the start of system test is 6 faults per 1000 lines of code.   The relationships are

$$\beta = B\frac{\lambda_0}{\omega_0}$$

$$(67)$$

$$v_0 = \frac{\omega_0}{B}$$

where B is the "fault reduction factor."   The value B = 0.955, the average of a series of industry studies, should be used. Using the predicted reliability, time-adjusted by the growth model, provides a continuous customer-oriented assessment of what reliability the end-user will experience if the software is released at a given future date.   Early on in the life cycle, some, perhaps crude, prediction will be available (Procedure 5.3.2-1).   This prediction will be updated as pre-system-test metrics become available (Procedure 5.3.2-2 through Procedure 5.3.2-5), and will become even more accurate as the system test phase gets underway and the growth model parameters can be statistically estimated.

Reliability planning and management are facilitated by use of the software reliability growth model, which can be inverted in different ways to derive various quantities of interest.   The earliest time for which a reliability prediction is made is the start of system test because, before integration, the system the user will work with does not really exist yet.   The start of system test is designated time $\tau = 0$.   With that origin, τ denotes the cumulative amount of execution time expended in system test.   During this phase, the software is subjected to the environment it will experience in operational use.   A software reliability growth model (see 5.4.4) describes the decline in the software failure rate that occurs during the system growth phase as the number of faults in the code declines. Let $\lambda(\tau)$ be the instantaneous failure rate at time τ.   The failure rate at the start of system test is denoted $\lambda_0 \equiv \lambda(0)$.

The relationship between calendar time, denoted t, and execution time, denoted τ, during system test, is governed by whichever resource is limiting: failure identification personnel (testers), failure resolution personnel (debuggers), or computer time. The method for mapping execution time to calendar time is detailed in Procedure 5.4.4-4.

Reliability objectives should be set for λ_0 and for later points in system test. Throughout development, starting at the proposal /pre-contractual stage, the values of λ_0 and the growth model parameters should be predicted. The growth model should be employed to compare the predicted failure rate values with the failure rate objectives. If there is a significant discrepancy, then resources can be re-allocated, the system design can be modified, and the reliability re-allocated as necessary to achieve the anticipated reliability growth.

The software reliability growth model, once its parameters are determined, provides one-to-one mappings between any two of the following quantities: execution time, calendar time, failure rate, and expected cumulative number of failures.

<u>Procedure 5.3.3-1 - Forecasting failure rate versus execution</u>
<u>time</u>.

The growth model can be used to forecast the failure rate the software will exhibit at τ execution time units into system test. The formula is

$$\lambda(\tau) = \beta v_0 \exp[-\beta\tau] \qquad (68)$$

The function

$$\ln\lambda(\tau) = \ln\beta v_0 - \beta\tau \qquad (69)$$

will plot as a straight line on semi-log paper. If the software code is frozen at time τ, the software will exhibit a constant failure rate $\lambda = \lambda(\tau)$. The reliability function is then $R(\tau') = \exp[-\lambda\tau']$, where τ' is execution time measured from the present.

<u>Procedure 5.3.3-2 - Forecasting cumulative failures versus</u>
<u>execution time</u>.

The expected cumulative number of software failures that will be experienced in system test up to time τ is given by

$$\mu(\tau) = v_0(1-\exp[-\beta\tau]) \qquad (70)$$

<u>Procedure 5.3.3-3 - Forecasting when a reliability objective will
be met</u>.

The growth model can answer many useful planning questions.   For
example,   when   will   a   failure   rate   requirement   or   some
intermediate failure rate objective λ_F be met?   From the growth
model, the number of failures that must be experienced to reach
that objective is

$$\mu = v_0\left(1 - \frac{\lambda_F}{\lambda_0}\right)$$ (71)

where v_0 is one of the two parameters of the software reliability
growth model.

The amount of execution time to meet that failure rate objective
is

$$\tau = \frac{1}{\beta} \ln\frac{\lambda_0}{\lambda_F}$$ (72)

where β is the other growth model parameter.

<u>Steps</u>

A.   Predict or estimate the software reliability growth model
parameters β and v_0.

B.   Predict or estimate the initial failure rate λ_0.   Note that

$$\lambda_0 = \beta v_0$$ (73)

C.   Determine a failure rate objective λ_F.

D.   Determine the expected number of software failures that must
be experienced from the relationship

$$\mu = v_0\left(1 - \frac{\lambda_F}{\lambda_0}\right)$$ (74)

E.   Determine the amount of execution time to reach λ_F as

$$\tau = \frac{1}{\beta} \ln\left(\frac{\lambda_F}{\lambda_0}\right)$$ (75)

Example

Suppose that the initial failure rate has been predicted to be λ_0 = 18 failures per CPU hour.   The software reliability growth model parameters have been predicted at v_0 = 139 and

$$\beta = \frac{\lambda_0}{v_0} = \frac{18}{139} \tag{76}$$

The expected number of failures that must be experienced to reach λ_F = 1 is

$$\mu = v_0\left(1 - \frac{\lambda_F}{\lambda_0}\right) = 139\left(1 - \frac{1}{18}\right) \approx 131 \tag{77}$$

The execution time required is

$$\tau = \frac{1}{18/139} \ln\frac{1}{18} \approx 22.317 \text{ CPU hours} \tag{78}$$

<u>Procedure 5.3.3-4 - Additional failures and execution time to reach a reliability objective</u>.

The growth model can also estimate the incremental number of failures or amount of execution time to get from a present failure rate λ_P to a failure rate objective λ_F. The additional number of failures that must be experienced to go from λ_P to λ_F is

$$\Delta\mu = \frac{1}{\beta}(\lambda_P - \lambda_F) \tag{79}$$

The additional execution time $\Delta\tau$ that is required to reach the failure rate objective is

$$\Delta\tau = \frac{1}{\beta}\ln\frac{\lambda_P}{\lambda_F} \tag{80}$$

<u>Steps</u>

A.   Start with a present failure rate λ_P and a failure rate objective λ_F.

B.   Determine the software reliability growth model parameter β.

C.   Obtain the additional number of failures that must be experienced to go from failure rate λ_P down to failure rate λ_F, apply the formula

$$\Delta\mu = \frac{1}{\beta}(\lambda_P - \lambda_F) \tag{81}$$

D.   To determine the additional amount of execution time to reach λ_F, apply the formula

$$\Delta\tau = \frac{1}{\beta}\ln\frac{\lambda_P}{\lambda_F} \tag{82}$$

<u>Example</u>

Suppose that the present failure rate is $\lambda_P = 22$ failures per hour and an intermediate failure rate objective is $\lambda_F = 8$ failures per hour. The software reliability growth model parameter β has been estimated at 0.6.

A.   Obtain the additional number of failures that must be experienced to get from the present failure rate λ_P to the future failure rate objective λ_F:

$$\Delta\mu = \frac{1}{\beta}(\lambda_P - \lambda_F) = \frac{1}{0.6}(22-8) \approx 23 \qquad (83)$$

B.   Obtain the additional execution time to get from λ_P to λ_F through the formula

$$\Delta\tau = \frac{1}{\beta}\ln\frac{\lambda_P}{\lambda_F} = \frac{1}{0.6}\ln\frac{22}{8} \approx 1.686 \qquad (84)$$

Project management generally thinks in terms of calendar time (t) rather than execution time (τ).   Determining the relationship between the two is described in Procedure 5.4.4-4.   The quantities derived from the prediction and growth models feed back into the software development process to provide systematic planning for and control of reliability achievement as a function of calendar time.   Project management can set intermediate reliability goals based on the predicted reliability figure and growth rate.   If later predictions show that an intermediate goal is not likely to be met, management can re-allocate resources based on comparison between the planned and assessed reliability figures.

An important schedule determinant once the software is in system test is the ratio between execution time and calendar time.   This ratio is determined by the limiting resource.   The resources involved in system test are failure identification personnel, who perform the testing; failure resolution personnel, who debug the programs; and computer time.

If too many failures are experienced, the failure resolution personnel will become backlogged with debug work, holding up testing.   If setting up test cases and analyzing the output for failures takes a long time, then the failure identification personnel are the limiting resource.   If one category of personnel is the limiting resource, then overtime may be an appropriate solution.   The important thing is that the management decisions are based on the achievable reliability, which enforces a customer orientation.

Procedure 5.3.3-5 - Optimum release time.

The software reliability growth model can be used to determine the optimum release time for minimizing overall cost. Each failure during development entails a cost c_1. Each failure in operational use entails a cost c_2 (the failure costs can be broken out by failure severity category). Additionally, there is a cost c_3 for each time unit of system test. The total cost of system test can be computed as follows: If the software is hypothetically released at time τ_e, the cost attributed to system test failures is

$$D_1(\tau_e) = c_1 \cdot \mu(\tau_e) \tag{85}$$

The cost incurred by failures during operation is

$$D_2(\tau_e) = y \cdot \lambda(\tau_e) \cdot c_2 \tag{86}$$

where y is the number of time units of operation. The cost incurred by system test is

$$D_3(\tau_e) = \tau_e \cdot c_3 \tag{87}$$

The total cost when the software is released at time τ_e is the sum of the three costs:

$$D(\tau_e) = D_1(\tau_e) + D_2(\tau_e) + D_3(\tau_e) \tag{88}$$

The optimum time to release the software, from a pure cost point of view, is found by minimizing the function $D(\tau_e)$:

$$(\tau_e)_{min} = \frac{\ln \dfrac{yc_2\beta^2 v_0 - c_1\beta v_0}{c_3}}{\beta} \tag{89}$$

Steps

A. Based on labor, overhead, and related expenses, determine the cost per failure c_1 for failures that occur during system test, as well as the cost per unit of execution time, c_3.

B. Based on program maintenance, service impact, and related expenses, determine the cost per failure c_2 for failures that occur during operational use. Determine the operational life of the system, y.

C. From prediction or from growth testing, determine the software growth model parameters β and v_0.

D. Compute the minimum-cost release time as

$$\tau_e = \frac{\ln\frac{y c_2 \beta^2 v_0 - c_1 \beta v_0}{c_3}}{\beta} \qquad (90)$$

Example

Suppose that the cost of a failure during system test is $c_1 = \$1000$, and that the cost of a failure during operation is $\$6000$. Each day of system test costs $\$4500$. The growth model parameters are

$$\beta = 0.002, \ v_0 = 120 \qquad (91)$$

Using the day as the unit of time, the minimum-cost release point is

$$\tau_e = \frac{\ln\frac{y c_2 \beta^2 v_0 - c_1 \beta v_0}{c_3}}{\beta}$$

$$= \frac{\ln\frac{(1825)(6000)(0.002)^2(120) - (1000)(0.002)(120)}{4500}}{0.002} \qquad (92)$$

$$= 54 \text{ days}$$

5.4   Growth and Demonstration Testing.   Reliability growth testing is performed to assess current reliability, identify and eliminate faults, and forecast future reliability.   The reliability figures are compared with intermediate reliability objectives to measure progress so that resources can be directed to achieve the reliability goals in a timely and cost-effective manner.   Whenever a failure occurs, corrective action is undertaken to remove the cause.   For hardware, growth testing is the process of testing the equipment under both natural and induced environmental conditions to discover latent failure modes and mechanisms to ensure that all performance, design, and environmental problems have been resolved.   Hardware reliability growth measurement is addressed in MIL-HDBK-189.   Hardware reliability demonstration is addressed by MIL-HDBK-781.

Reliability demonstration is employed toward the end of the growth testing period to prove that a specific reliability level has been achieved.   During a demonstration test, the software code is frozen, just as it would be in field use.

Other than repair policy, software growth testing and demonstration testing are performed under the same conditions as field use: The environment in which the software executes must emulate what the software will experience in field use, and the environmental conditions must be maintained throughout the test period.

5.4.1 Software Operational Profile.   The software execution environment includes the hardware platform, the operating system software, the system generation parameters, the workload, and the operational profile.

An input state is a set of input variable values for a particular run.   Each input variable has a declared data type--a range and ordering of permissible values.   The set of all possible input states for a program is the input space.   Each input state is a point in the input space.   An operational profile is a function p that associates a probability $p(i)$ with each point i in an input space I.   Since the points in the input space are mutually exclusive and exhaustive, all the probabilities must add up to one:

$$\sum_{i \in I} p(i) = 1 \qquad\qquad (93)$$

Example

To illustrate these definitions, consider a program with three input variables.   Each is of data type Boolean, meaning that it has two possible values: TRUE or FALSE. The input space has eight points: (FALSE,FALSE,FALSE), (FALSE,FALSE,TRUE), (FALSE,TRUE,FALSE), (FALSE,TRUE,TRUE), (TRUE,FALSE,FALSE), (TRUE,FALSE,TRUE), (TRUE,TRUE,FALSE), (TRUE,TRUE,TRUE). Letting T stand for TRUE and F for FALSE, an operational profile for the program might look like:

$$p(FFF) = 0.1$$

$$p(FFT) = 0.2$$

$$p(FTF) = 0.1$$

$$p(FTT) = 0.3$$

$$p(TFF) = 0.025$$

$$p(TFT) = 0.2$$

$$p(TTF) = 0.025$$

$$p(TTT) = 0.05$$

(94)

The distribution of input states is thus established by the operational profile. The concept of operational profile formalizes what is meant by a consistent input environment.

During growth and demonstration testing the operational profile must be kept stationary: The p(i)'s must not change. The input states chosen for test cases must form a random sample from the input state in accordance with the distribution of input states that the operational profile specifies.

It is generally not practical to fully express or specify an operational profile, because the number of input states for even a simple program can be enormous. As an example, if a program has three input variables, each of which is a 32-bit integer, the number of distinct input states is

$$2^{32} \cdot 2^{32} \cdot 2^{32} = 2^{96} \approx 7.9 \times 10^{28} \qquad (95)$$

Generally, in practical situations, the software usage is expressed in terms of end-user-oriented functions. For example, it might be specified that the usage of the software is 40% user function A, 45% user function B, and 15% user function C. This is called a "functional profile." Once the operational profile is established, a procedure for selecting a random sample of input states is required, so that test cases can be generated for growth testing and demonstration testing. Random input-state selection is recommended for selecting the input states during testing.

5.4.2 <u>Random Input-State Selection</u>. During growth testing and demonstration testing, the software must be exercised with inputs randomly selected from a specified operational profile or, more commonly, from a specified functional profile. The methods described here can be followed for either an operational profile or a functional profile, but will be presented in terms of the more common functional profile. The first step is to associate each end-user function with a subinterval of the real interval [0,1] whose size is equal to the input state's probability of selection p(i).

<u>Example</u>

Suppose that there are only three possible end-user functions, ADD, UPDATE, and DELETE. The functional profile says that an ADD occurs 28% of the time, an UPDATE occurs 11% of the time, and a DELETE occurs 61% of the time. The ADD end-user function should be associated with the real interval [0,0.28]; the UPDATE function should be associated with the real interval [0.28,0.39]; and DELETE should be associated with the real interval [0.39,1.0].

The next step is, for each test case needed, to generate a random number in the interval [0,1]. Any number of short computer or programmable calculator programs are available that can generate random or pseudorandom numbers in that range.

Three test cases are needed. Three random numbers in the interval [0,1] are generated. The numbers are 0.7621, 0.5713, and 0.1499. Since the first random number, 0.7621, lies in the subinterval [0.39,1], the first test case is a DELETE. Since the second random number, 0.5713, also lies in the subinterval [0.39,1], the second test case is also a DELETE. Since the third random number, 0.1499, lies in the subinterval [0,0.28], the third test case is an ADD.

Testing efficiency of testing can be increased by recognizing "equivalence classes." An equivalence class is a set of input states such that if a run with one input state results in a failure, then a run with any other of the input states would also result in a failure. Conversely, if the program would succeed on a run with one input state in the class, then it would also succeed on any other input state in the class. Once an equivalence class is identified, only one representative input state from the class needs to be tested; if a run starting from the representative input state results in success, then it can be concluded that runs starting from all members of the class would result in success. If a run starting from the representative input state results in failure, then it can be concluded that runs starting from all members of the class would fail.

The input states that are members of an equivalence class are removed from the operational profile and replaced by their one representative input state. The probability associated with the representative input state is assigned the sum of the probabilities of the members of the equivalence class.

Since the probability of selection of the representative of an equivalence class is a sum, it can be relatively large compared to individual input states. The equivalence class representative input will likely be selected more than once during testing. After the first selection, the test case does not have to be re-run, only the results from the original run recounted.

5.4.3 <u>Multiple Copies</u>.   The time on test during growth or demonstration testing can be accumulated on more than one copy of the software.   The copies can run simultaneously to accelerate testing.   This procedure can be especially helpful in testing when the reliability requirement is very high.   Because the total amount of calendar time on test is reduced, the use of multiple copies can provide economic and scheduling advantages. To retain the statistical integrity of the test, certain precautions must be carefully followed.

Each copy must have its own separate data areas, both in main memory and secondary storage, to prevent cross-contamination. Each copy must use independently selected test inputs.   The test inputs are selected randomly from the same operational profile. The time on test at any point in calendar time is the execution time accumulated on all versions.   When one copy fails, it alone is recovered and restarted.   If the processors on which the copies are running are of differing speed, the contributions to total time on test must be adjusted.   For example, if the target processor in the operational environment has a speed of three million instructions per second (MIPS), and the three test processors run at 4 MIPS, 2 MIPS, and 3 MIPS, respectively, then the first test processor's cumulative execution time must be multiplied by 4/3, the second processor's time must be multiplied by 2/3, and the third test processor's time requires no adjustment.

Each copy should execute a set of test cases selected independently from the same operational profile.   When a failure occurs on one copy, the cumulative execution time accumulated on all copies is recorded.   When the program is repaired, all copies must be changed so as to remain identical.

5.4.4 <u>Software Reliability Growth Modeling/Testing</u>.   Reliability growth for software is the positive improvement of software reliability over time, accomplished through the systematic removal of software faults.   The rate at which the reliability grows depends on how fast faults can be uncovered and removed.   A software reliability growth model allows project management to track the progress of the software's reliability through statistical inference and to make projections to future milestones. If the assessed growth falls short of the planned growth, management will have sufficient notice to develop new strategies, such as the re-assignment of resources to attack identified problem areas, adjustment of the project time frame, and re-examination of the feasibility or validity of requirements.

Measuring and projecting software reliability growth requires the use of an appropriate software reliability model that describes the variation of software reliability with time. The parameters of the model can be obtained either from prediction, which is performed during the period preceding system test, or from estimation, which is performed during system test. Parameter estimation is based on the times at which failures occur.

The Basic Execution Time Model, originated by John Musa, views the phenomenon of software failure as a Nonhomogeneous Poisson Process (NHPP). The counting process $\{M(\tau), \tau \geq 0\}$ represents the cumulative number of software failures in the execution time interval $[0,\tau)$. The Greek letter tau, τ, is used for execution time to distinguish it from calendar time, t. Execution time is the failure-inducing stress for software. The model also has a "calendar time component" that relates τ to t. The mean value function is the expected cumulative number of failures in the interval:

$$\mu(\tau) \equiv E\{M(\tau)\} \qquad (96)$$

The failure rate can be defined as the execution time derivative of the mean value function:

$$\lambda(\tau) \equiv \frac{d\mu(\tau)}{d\tau} \qquad (97)$$

When the program code is frozen and subjected to a stationary operational profile, the software is modeled as having a constant failure rate

$$\lambda(\tau) = \lambda, \ \tau \geq 0 \qquad (98)$$

resulting in a (homogeneous) Poisson process. The probability that the software will execute for execution time τ' measured from the present is given by the reliability function

$$R(\tau') = \exp[-\lambda\tau'] \qquad (99)$$

In the Basic Execution Time Model, ν_0 is the total number of failures that would have to occur to uncover all faults. These faults include ω_0 faults that were present at the start of system test--called "inherent faults"--plus any faults that might be inadvertently introduced into the program as the result of fault correction activity.

Not every failure results in exactly one fault being removed from the program code.   Sometimes additional faults are discovered from code reading, when a failure reveals a whole class of closely related faults.   And sometimes the fault that caused a failure is not found, or a new fault is introduced.   In the model, the net number of faults removed per failure is called the "fault reduction factor," denoted B.   The fault reduction factor is related to the inherent faults and total failures by

$$B = \frac{\omega_0}{\nu_0} \qquad (100)$$

The initial failure rate, the one at the start of system test, is denoted λ_0.   The contribution of each fault to the overall program failure rate is called the "per-fault hazard rate," denoted ϕ.   The per-fault hazard rate is related to the initial failure rate and the inherent number of faults by

$$\phi = \frac{\lambda_0}{\omega_0} \qquad (101)$$

It is called a "hazard rate" (called also force of mortality [FOM]) because a fault is considered to have a finite lifetime: If testing is continued long enough, the fault will be discovered and subject to correction.

The failure rate is expected to improve as time goes on, as faults are removed from the code.   Since B faults are removed per failure occurrence, the failure rate declines by $\beta = B\phi$ upon each failure.   If μ is the expected number of failures at time τ, then the overall program failure rate is

$$\lambda(\mu) = \beta(\nu_0 - \mu) \qquad (102)$$

or

$$\lambda(\tau) = \beta[v_0 - \mu(\tau)] \tag{103}$$

Since

$$\lambda(\tau) \equiv \frac{d\mu(\tau)}{d\tau} \tag{104}$$

it must be the case that

$$\frac{d\mu(\tau)}{d\tau} + \phi B\mu(\tau) = \phi v_0 \tag{105}$$

The solution to this differential equation provides the mean value function

$$\mu(\tau) = v_0(1 - \exp[-\beta\tau]) \tag{106}$$

The parameters β and v_0 can be determined by prediction or estimation.   Prediction procedures depend on the software development phase in which the prediction is made (see 5.3).

Procedure 5.4.4-1 - Point estimation of model parameters.

Estimation establishes values for the Basic Execution Time Model parameters β and v_0 based on the history of software failure during system test. The method of maximum likelihood estimation chooses the values of β and v_0 that maximize the likelihood of obtaining the failure times that were in fact observed.

Once system test begins, the cumulative execution times

$$\tau_1, \tau_2, \ldots, \tau_{m_e} \tag{107}$$

at which failures occur are recorded. The quantity m_e is the cumulative number of failures. The time at which the parameters are estimated is denoted τ_e and may or may not coincide with the time τ_{m_e} of the last failure. This "time censoring" is taken into account in the estimation equations.

The maximum likelihood estimate of β is obtained as the solution to

$$\frac{m_e}{\beta} - \frac{m_e \tau_e}{\exp(\beta \tau_e) - 1} - \sum_{i=1}^{m_e} \tau_i = 0 \tag{108}$$

and then v_0 is given by

$$v_0 = \frac{m_e}{1 - \exp[-\beta \tau_e]} \tag{109}$$

rounded to the nearest integer.

Steps

A. Upon the occurrence of each software failure, the failure identification personnel record the cumulative execution time, in CPU seconds since the start of system testing. The execution time can be obtained from the operating system's accounting facility, or the program can be instrumented to provide this information. Collect these failure times into a table and denote the ordered failure times as

$$\tau_1, \tau_2, \ldots \tag{110}$$

B. To assess the current failure rate and reliability of the software, follow these steps:

   i. Record the current cumulative execution time, in CPU seconds since the start of system testing. Denote this time τ_e.

   ii. Record the cumulative number of failures that have occurred since the start of system testing. Denote this count m_e.

   iii. Using the knowns--m_e, τ_e, and

$$\tau_1, \tau_2, \, \ldots, \tau_{m_e} \tag{111}$$

   --solve the following equation for the unknown parameter β:

$$\frac{m_e}{\beta} - \frac{m_e \tau_e}{\exp[\beta \tau_e] - 1} - \sum_{i=1}^{m_e} \tau_i = 0 \tag{112}$$

   The equation is best solved using a root-finding procedure on a computer or programmable calculator. The remaining parameter of the model, v_0, is found by substituting β into the formula

$$v_0 = \frac{m_e}{1 - \exp[\beta \tau_e]} \tag{113}$$

   and rounding v_0 to the nearest integer.

iv. With the point estimates obtained for β and v_0, the failure rate of the software is given by

$$\lambda = \beta v_0 \exp[-\beta\tau_e] \qquad (114)$$

and the reliability function is

$$R(\tau') = \exp[-\lambda\tau'] \qquad (115)$$

where τ' is execution time measured from the present.

Example

In this example, there are seven software failures, so $m_e = 7$. The current cumulative execution time is $t_e = 445$. The software failure times are presented in Table 5-11.

TABLE 5-11.   Example Failure Times

FAILURE NUMBER i	CPU SECONDS τ_i
1	5
2	35
3	144
4	229
5	342
6	353
7	441

To estimate the parameter β, the following equation is solved:

$$\frac{m_e}{\beta} - \frac{m_e\tau_e}{\exp[\beta\tau_e]-1} - \sum_{i=1}^{m_e}\tau_i = 0 \qquad (116)$$

The sum term is

$$\sum_{i=1}^{7} \tau_i = (5+35+144+229+342+353+441) = 1549 \qquad (117)$$

yielding

$$\frac{7}{\beta} - \frac{(7)\,(445)}{\exp[\beta\,(445)]-1} - 1549 = 0 \qquad (118)$$

The solution $\beta=7.3\times10^{-5}$ is obtained.   Several methods for solving equations can be found in any text on numerical analysis.   The solution here was obtained using the method of "bisection," which involves repeatedly halving the interval containing the root of the relevant function.   The value for v_0 is found as

$$v_0 = \frac{7}{1-\exp[-(7.35\times10^{-5})\,(445)]} \approx 217.54 \qquad (119)$$

which, rounded to the nearest integer, gives $v_0=218$.

The failure rate of the software is obtained as

$$\lambda(\tau_e) = \beta v_0 \exp[-\beta\tau_e]$$
$$= (7.3\times10^{-5})\,(217.54)\exp[-(7.3\times10^{-5})\,(217.54)] \approx 0.016 \qquad (120)$$

The reliability function is obtained as

$$R(\tau') = \exp[-\lambda\tau'] = \exp[-0.016\tau'] \qquad (121)$$

Procedure 5.4.4-2 - Confidence intervals.

The degree of uncertainty present in the point estimates of β and v_0 can be expressed through the use of confidence intervals. To determine confidence intervals, compute the "Fisher information"

$$I(\beta) = m_\theta \left\{ \frac{1}{\beta^2} - \frac{\tau_\theta^2 \exp[\beta\tau_\theta]}{([\exp[\beta\tau_\theta]-1)^2} \right\} \qquad (122)$$

Then a $100(1-\alpha)\%$ confidence interval for β is

$$\beta \pm \frac{\kappa_{1-\alpha/2}}{\sqrt{I(\beta)}} \qquad (123)$$

where $\kappa_{1-\alpha/2}$ is the corresponding normal deviate. To obtain a $100(1-\alpha)\%$ confidence interval for v_0, the high and low confidence limits for β are substituted into the equation for v_0.

Steps

A. Compute the "Fisher information" from

$$I(\beta) = m_\theta \left\{ \frac{1}{\beta^2} - \frac{\tau_\theta^2 \exp[\beta\tau_\theta]}{([\exp[\beta\tau_\theta]-1)^2} \right\} \qquad (124)$$

B. Choose a confidence level, α. Find the corresponding normal deviate $\kappa_{1-\alpha/2}$. Table 5-12 shows the normal deviate values for selected values of α. More-extensive tables can be found in many statistics textbooks.

TABLE 5-12.   Normal Deviates

α	$\kappa_{1-\alpha/2}$
0.001	3.29
0.002	3.09
0.01	2.58
0.02	2.33
0.05	1.96
0.10	1.64
0.20	1.28

C. To find the lower limit of a 100(1-α)% confidence interval for β, substitute the point estimate for β into the formula

$$\beta_{low} = \beta - \frac{\kappa_{1-\alpha/2}}{\sqrt{I(\beta)}} \tag{125}$$

To find the upper limit, use

$$\beta_{high} = \beta + \frac{\kappa_{1-\alpha/2}}{\sqrt{I(\beta)}} \tag{126}$$

To find the same confidence interval for v_0, substitute β_{low} and then β_{high} into

$$v_0 = \frac{m_e}{1-\exp[\beta\tau_e]} \tag{127}$$

Example

Suppose that there were $m_e = 19$ software failures during the interval through time $\tau_e = 150.0$ and that β was estimated to be .04. Then, the "Fisher information" is

$$I(.04) = I(\beta) = m_e \left\{ \frac{1}{\beta^2} - \frac{\tau_e^2 \exp[\beta\tau_e]}{([\exp[\beta\tau_e]-1)^2} \right\} \tag{128}$$

$$= (19)\left(\frac{1}{(19)^2} - \frac{(150.0)^2\exp[(.04)(150.0)]}{\{\exp[(.04)(150.0)]-1\}^2} \right) = 10810.06$$

For a 95% confidence interval, α = 0.05 and $\kappa_{1-\alpha/2} = 1.96$. Thus

$$\beta_{low} = \beta - \frac{\kappa_{1-\alpha/2}}{\sqrt{I(\beta)}}$$
$$= 0.04 - 1.96/\sqrt{10810.06} \approx 0.02 \tag{129}$$

$$\beta_{high} = \beta + \frac{\kappa_{1-\alpha/2}}{\sqrt{I(\beta)}}$$
$$= 0.04 + 1.96/\sqrt{10810.06} \approx 0.06$$

Procedure 5.4.4-3 - Grouped data.

Sometimes it is more convenient to work with the number of failures that occurred over execution time intervals rather than with failure times. Suppose the failure data is grouped into z intervals, with interval i ending at cumulative execution time x_i. The duration of interval i is then $x_i - x_{i-1}$, with $x_0 \equiv 0$. Let the number of failures in interval i be denoted y_i' and the cumulative number of failures through interval i be denoted y_i. The total test time is x_z, and the cumulative number of failures for the test is y_z. The maximum likelihood estimate for β is given by solving the following equation for β:

$$\sum_{i=1}^{z} \frac{y_i'(x_i \exp[-\beta x_i] - x_{i-1} \exp[-\beta x_{i-1}])}{\exp[-\beta x_{i-1}] - \exp[-\beta x_i]} - \frac{y_z x_z}{\exp[\beta x_z] - 1} = 0 \qquad (130)$$

The maximum likelihood estimator for v_0 is then given by

$$v_0 = \frac{y_z}{1 - \exp[-\beta x_z]} \qquad (131)$$

rounded to the nearest integer. In this case

$$I(\beta) = \frac{y_z x_z^2 \exp[\beta x_z]}{(\exp[\beta x_z] - 1)^2}$$

$$- \sum_{i=1}^{z} \frac{y_i'(x_i - x_{i-1})^2 \exp[-\beta(x_i + x_{i-1})]}{(\exp[-\beta x_{i-1}] - \exp[-\beta x_i])^2} \qquad (132)$$

can be used in the same way as for ungrouped failures to construct confidence intervals for β and v_0.

Steps

A. Divide the execution time since the start of system testing into p intervals. Denote the cumulative execution time at the end of the i-th interval as x_i.

B. Count the number of software failures that occurred in each interval i. Denote the count for interval i as y_i'. Denote the cumulative number of failures through interval i as y_i.

C.   Using the knowns--z;

$$
\begin{aligned}
y_1, \ y_2, \ \ldots, \ y_z; \\
y_1', \ y_2', \ \ldots, \ y_z'; \\
x_1, \ x_2, \ \ldots, \ x_z
\end{aligned}
\tag{133}
$$

--solve for the unknown parameter β:

$$
\sum_{l=1}^{z} \frac{y_l' \left(x_l \exp[-\beta x_l] - x_{l-1} \exp[-\beta x_{l-1}] \right)}{\exp[-\beta x_{l-1}] - \exp[-\beta x_l]} \\
- \frac{y_z x_z}{\exp[\beta x_z] - 1} = 0
\tag{134}
$$

To find the value of the parameter v_0, substitute the estimate found for β into the formula

$$
v_0 = \frac{y_z}{1 - \exp[-\beta x_z]}
\tag{135}
$$

Example

In this example, there are four intervals, so $z = 4$. The total test time is $x_p = 55$. The total number of failures is $y_z = 12$. The failure data appears in Table 5-13.

TABLE 5-13.   Example of Grouped Failures

Interval Number l	Ending Time x_l	Number of Failures y_l'	Cumulative Number of Failures y_l
1	15	4	4
2	25	3	7
3	35	3	10
4	55	2	12

The solution to the equation is $\beta = 0.022$. The parameter v_0 is found to be

$$
v_0 = \frac{y_z}{1 - \exp[-\beta x_z]} = \frac{12}{1 - \exp[-0.022(55)]} \approx 17.1
\tag{136}
$$

which, rounded to the nearest integer, is 17.

Procedure 5.4.4-4 - Calendar time modeling.

The relationship between cumulative execution time τ and cumulative calendar time t is determined from the "calendar time component" of the Basic Execution Time Model. The calendar time component takes into account the constraints involved in applying test and repair resources to the software development project. The rate of testing is constrained by failure identification personnel (test team), failure resolution personnel (debuggers), and available computer time. Because of long lead times for training and computer procurement, the model assumes that the quantities of those resources are constant throughout the system test period.

The subscript r is an index that indicates the particular resource involved:

$\quad\quad\quad$ I = failure identification personnel

$\quad\quad\quad$ F = failure resolution personnel

$\quad\quad\quad$ C = computer time

Let θ_r be the amount of resource r required per unit of execution time, and let μ_r be the amount of resource r required per failure experienced. Note that $\theta_F=0$ since failure resolution personnel only address failures. The expected resource requirement χ_r is

$$\chi_r = \theta_r\tau + \mu_r\mu(\tau) \quad\quad\quad\quad (137)$$

where τ is cumulative execution time. Then the change in resource usage per unit of execution time is

$$\frac{\partial \chi_r}{\partial \tau} = \theta_r + \mu_r\lambda \quad\quad\quad\quad (138)$$

If P_r is the available quantity of resource r that is available and ρ_r is its utilization, then $P_r\rho_r$ represents the effective amount of resource r that is available. Then

$$\frac{dt_r}{d\tau} = \frac{1}{P_r\rho_r}\frac{\partial \chi_r}{\partial \tau} \qu\quad\quad\quad (139)$$

Note that $\rho_I=1$, because failure identification personnel can be fully utilized. At any point in execution time, one resource will be limiting, the one that yields the maximum derivative of calendar time with respect to execution time:

$$\frac{dt}{d\tau} = \max_r \left(\frac{dt_r}{d\tau}\right) \tag{140}$$

The testing phase can be divided into segments. During each segment, exactly one of the resources C, F, or I will be limiting. Each segment will exhibit its own calendar-to-execution time ratio t/τ. To find the potential transition points (in terms of failure rate values) between resource-limited segments, compute

$$\lambda_{rs} = \frac{P_s \rho_s \theta_r - P_r \rho_r \theta_s}{P_r \rho_r \mu_s - P_s \rho_s \mu_r} \ , \qquad r \neq s \tag{141}$$

for each pair of resources. To find the limiting resource within each segment, calculate

$$\max_r \left(\frac{dt}{d\tau}\right) = \max_r \left\{\frac{1}{P_r \rho_r} [\theta_r + \mu_r \lambda(\tau)]\right\} \tag{142}$$

for an arbitrary choice of λ within each segment.

If the boundaries of a resource-limited segment are λ_1 and λ_2, the expected number of failures during the segment is

$$\Delta\mu = \nu_0 \frac{\lambda_1 - \lambda_2}{\lambda_0} \tag{143}$$

while the execution time interval is

$$\Delta\tau = \frac{\nu_0}{\lambda_0} \ln\frac{\lambda_1}{\lambda_0} \tag{144}$$

The calendar time increment during the segment is

$$\Delta t_r = \frac{1}{P_r \rho_r \beta} \left[\theta_r \ln\frac{\lambda_1}{\lambda_2} + \mu_r(\lambda_1 - \lambda_2)\right] \tag{145}$$

Confidence limits are obtained by substituting the high and low endpoints of the confidence interval for β.

Typically, three resource-limited segments occur:

> $[0, \lambda_{FI}]$: Failures occur frequently. The limiting resource is failure resolution personnel. Testing has to be stopped to allow the debugging team to catch up.

> $[\lambda_{FI}, \lambda_{IC}]$: Intervals between failures lengthen. The test team becomes the bottleneck, as the team can only make test runs and evaluate the results so fast.

> $[\lambda_{IC}, \ldots]$: Interfailure times become very long. Only the computing capacity limits how fast testing can be accomplished.

The total increment of calendar time over the three segments is given by

$$\Delta t = \Delta t_F + \Delta t_I + \Delta t_C \tag{146}$$

Steps

A. For each resource--computer time (C), failure resolution personnel (F), and failure identification personnel (I)--determine resource quantity:

> P_I: available identification personnel (person-hours)

> P_F: available failure resolution personnel (person-hours)

> P_C: available CPU time (CPU hours)

B. For each resource r, determine the utilization fraction ρ_r.

C. Determine the amount of each resource expended per failure:

> I_C: computer time (CPU hours per failure)

> I_F: failure resolution personnel (person-hours per failure)

> I_I: failure identification personnel (person-hours per failure)

D.   Determine the amount of each resource expended per CPU hour:

θ_C: computer resource expenditure (=1)

θ_F: failure resolution personnel (=0)

θ_I: failure identification personnel

E.   Compute the potential transition points (in terms of failure rate) between resources by applying the following formula with the combinations r=I, s=F; r=I, s=C; and r=F, s=C:

$$\lambda_{rs} = \frac{P_s \rho_s \theta_r - P_r \rho_r \theta_s}{P_r \rho_r \mu_s - P_s \rho_s \mu_r}, \quad r \neq s \tag{147}$$

Disregard any λ_{rs} that is negative. Put the potential transition points in descending order. Determine which resource is limited in the interval between each pair of successive transition points by choosing an arbitrary λ in each interval and determining the resource r for which the following expression is maximized:

$$\frac{dt_r}{d\tau} = \frac{1}{P_r \rho_r}(\theta_r + \mu_r \lambda) \tag{148}$$

F.   To determine the incremental calendar time, in hours, between two execution times, τ_1 and τ_2, that lie within the same resource-limited period, calculate

$$\Delta t_r = \frac{1}{P_r \rho_r \beta}\left\{\theta_r \ln\left[\frac{\lambda(\tau_1)}{\lambda(\tau_2)}\right] + \mu_r [\lambda(\tau_1) - \lambda(\tau_2)]\right\} \tag{149}$$

where r is the limiting resource in that interval. For two points that lie in different intervals, sum the incremental calendar time incurred in each intervening interval.

Example

Suppose that the calendar time component parameters are

$\theta_C = 1.5$; $\theta_I = 3.0$; $\theta_F = 1.0$; $\mu_C = 2.0$; $\mu_F = 6.5$; $\mu_I = 2.0$;

$\rho_C = 1.0$; $\rho_I = 1.0$; $\rho_F = 1.0$; $\tag{150}$

$P_F = 200$; $P_I = 300$; $P_C = 250$

Then, from

$$\lambda_{rs} = \frac{P_s\rho_s\theta_r - P_r\rho_r\theta_s}{P_r\rho_r\mu_r - P_s\rho_s\mu_r} \quad , \quad r \neq s \tag{151}$$

the potential transition points are found to be

$$\lambda_{IC} = \frac{(2540)(1.0)(3.0) - (300)(1.0)(1.5)}{(300)(1.0)(2.0) - (250)(1.0)(2.0)} = 3.0 \tag{152}$$

$$\lambda_{IF} = \frac{(200)(1.0)(3.0) - (300)(1.0)(1.0)}{(300)(1.0)(6.5) - (200)(1.0)(2.0)} \approx 0.19 \tag{153}$$

$$\lambda_{FC} = \frac{(250)(1.0)(1.0) - (200)(1.0)(1.5)}{(200)(1.0)(2.0) - (250)(1.0)(6.5)} \approx 0.04 \tag{154}$$

The intervals are thus (3,0.19), (0.19,0.04), and (0.04,0). The next step is to find out which resource is limiting in each of these intervals. For resource I,

$$\frac{dt_I}{d\tau} = \frac{1}{P_I\rho_I}(\theta_I\mu_I\lambda) = 0.003(3.0 + 2.0\lambda) \tag{155}$$

For resource C,

$$\frac{dt_C}{d\tau} = \frac{1}{P_C\rho_C}(\theta_I + \mu_I\lambda) = 0.004(1.5 + 2.0\lambda) \tag{156}$$

And for resource F it gives

$$\frac{dt_F}{d\tau} = \frac{1}{P_F\rho_F}(\theta_I + \mu_I\lambda) = 0.005(1.0 + 6.5\lambda) \tag{157}$$

Table 5-14 summarizes the results of the calculations.

TABLE 5-14.   Execution Time Derivatives

Interval	Arbitrary λ	$dt_I / d\tau$	$dt_C / d\tau$	$dt_F / d\tau$
(3.0,0.19)	2.0	0.021	0.022	0.07
(0.19,0.04)	0.1	0.0096	0.0068	0.00825
(0.04,0.0)	0.02	0.00912	0.00616	0.00565

In the first row, the maximum value for $dt_r/d\tau$ is from resource F; for the second and third rows it is from resource I. Therefore, in the interval (3.0,0.19), the limiting resource is failure resolution personnel and, during the interval (0.19,0.04), it is failure identification personnel.

Suppose now that the Basic Execution Time Model parameters are $\beta = 0.001$, and $v_0 = 200$. Then the time-dependent failure rate of the software is

$$\lambda(\tau) = \beta v_0 \exp[-\beta\tau]$$

$$= (0.02)(200)\exp[-(0.02)\tau] = 4.0\exp[-0.02\tau] \qquad (158)$$

To find the calendar time increment from $\tau=69$ to $\tau=184$, compute the failure rate at those points: $\lambda(69)\approx0.101$ and $\lambda(184)\approx1.006$. The failure rate interval (1.006,0.19) is in a failure resolution personnel limited period, and the failure rate interval (0.19,0.101) is in a failure identification personnel limited period. The total calendar time over the failure rate interval (1.006,0.101) is the sum of the increments over the two intervals (1.006,0.19) and (0.19,0.101). The calendar time increment over each resource limited segment is

$$\Delta t_x = \frac{1}{P_x \rho_x \beta}\left\{\theta_x \ln\left[\frac{\lambda(\tau_1)}{\lambda(\tau_2)}\right] + \mu_x[\lambda(\tau_1) - \lambda(\tau_2)]\right\} \qquad (159)$$

For the first interval, the calendar time increment is given by

$$\Delta t_F = \frac{1}{(200)(1.0)(0.003)}$$

$$\times\left[(1.0)\left(\ln\frac{1.006}{0.19}\right) + (6.5)(1.006-0.19)\right] \qquad (160)$$

$$\approx 11.62$$

For the second interval, the calendar time increment is

$$\Delta t_F = \frac{1}{(1.0)(1.0)(0.003)}\left[(0)\ln\left(\frac{0.19}{0.101}\right)+(6.5)(0.19-0.101)\right] \approx 192.83 \qquad (161)$$

Thus, the total calendar time increment is

$$\Delta t = \Delta t_F + \Delta t_I = 11.62 + 192.83 = 204.45 \qquad (162)$$

hours.

Procedure 5.4.4-5 - Goodness-of-fit/recalibration.

When the growth tester uses the Basic Execution Time Model or some other time-domain software reliability model, it is not sufficient to blindly apply the model. The tester should monitor how well the model is fitting the failure data. If the model is 6not fitting well, then the user should switch to an alternative model and/or parameter estimation technique. Another option is to employ a technique known as adaptive reliability modeling or recalibration. This technique uses the data on the historical performance of the software reliability model on the program in question to modify the model itself. The accuracy of recalibrated models has been shown generally to be better than that of the original model.

The parameters β and v_0 are estimated on the basis of the first (i-1) failures and used to evaluate

$$\lambda(\tau) = \beta v_0 \exp[-\beta\tau] \tag{163}$$

The estimated cumulative distribution function (Cdf) is then

$$\hat{F}_i(\tau') = 1 - \exp[-\lambda(\tau_{m_\bullet})\tau'] \tag{164}$$

where τ_{me} is the cumulative execution time to the end of the growth test, $\lambda(\tau_{me})$ is the failure intensity at that time, and τ' is execution time measured from the present. When the i-th failure--and thus the interfailure time τ'_i between the (i-1)st and i-the failure--is later observed, the probability integral transform

$$u_i = \hat{F}_i(\tau'_i) \tag{165}$$

is recorded. Each failure results in another u_i. The probability integral transform implies that the u_i's should look like a random sample from a U(0,1) distribution, if the sequence of one-step-ahead predictions was good. The accuracy of the model with respect to the particular program can be gauged by drawing a u-plot. In a u-plot the sample Cdf of the u_i's is visually compared with the Cdf of the uniform distribution over (0,1). Let m be the number of u_i's. To create a u-plot the m u_i's are put in ascending order

$$u_{(1)} \leq u_{(2)} \leq \cdots \leq u_{(m)} \tag{166}$$

and then the points

$$(u_{(1)}, 1/(m+1)), \ (u_{(2)}, 2/(m+1)), \ \ldots, \ (u_{(m)}, m/(m+1)) \qquad (167)$$

are plotted.   The line of unit slope (uniform Cdf) is also plotted on the same graph, for comparison.

Furthermore, the u-plot can be employed to recalibrate the software reliability model.   The recalibrated model corrects systematic bias or noisiness that the model is experiencing when being used on a particular program.   The recalibration takes place by applying a function $G^*(\cdot)$ to the estimated Cdf.   The function $G^*(\cdot)$ is expressed as

$$G_i^*[\hat{F}_i(\tau')] = \frac{\hat{F}_i(\tau') + j[u_{(j+1)} + u_{(j)}] - u_{(j)}}{(m+1)[u_{(j+1)} + u_{(j)}]}, \quad u_{(j)} \le \hat{F}_i(\tau') \le u_{(j+1)} \qquad (168)$$

where m is the number of u_i's and, for convenience, $u_{(0)} \equiv 0$ and $u_{(m+1)} \equiv 1$.

To perform the recalibration the user applies the transformation

$$\hat{F}_i^*(\tau') = G_i^*[\hat{F}_i(\tau')] \qquad (169)$$

Steps

A.   Upon the i-th software failure, use the Basic Execution Time Model to estimate the failure rate based on the software failures

$$\tau_1, \ \tau_2, \ \ldots, \ \tau_i \qquad (170)$$

The estimated cumulative distribution function is

$$\hat{F}_i = 1 - \hat{R}_i(\tau') = 1 - \exp[-\hat{\lambda}\tau'] \qquad (171)$$

When failure number (i+1) occurs, record

$$u_i = \hat{F}_i(\tau_{i+1} - \tau_i) \qquad (172)$$

B.   To form a u-plot, put the sequence $\{u_i\}$ into ascending order.   Denote the ordered u values as

$$u_{(1)}, \ u_{(2)}, \ \ldots, \ u_{(m)} \qquad (173)$$

C. Plot the points

$$(u_{(1)}, 1/(m+1)), \ (u_{(2)}, 2/(m+1)), \ \ldots, \ (u_{(m)}, m/(m+1)) \quad \textbf{(174)}$$

If the points mostly lie above the line, the model is producing pessimistic estimates of the failure rate. If the points mostly lie below the line, the model is producing pessimistic estimates.   If the points are spread out both above and below the line, the problem is noisiness. The bias or noisiness can be corrected by recalibration.

D. Correct the value cumulative distribution function by

substituting it into the formula

$$\frac{\hat{F}_i(\tau') + j[u_{(j+1)} + u_{(j)}] - u_{(j)}}{(m+1)[u_{(j+1)} + u_{(j)}]}, \quad u_{(j)} \le \hat{F}_i(\tau') \le u_{(j+1)} \quad \textbf{(175)}$$

to obtain a recalibrated value.

Example

The estimated failure rate after the m software failures is $\lambda = 0.27$.   The estimated cumulative distribution function is thus

$$\hat{F}_7(\tau') = 1 - \exp[-0.27\tau'] \quad \textbf{(176)}$$

Suppose further that the ordered u sequence is

$$\begin{gathered} u_{(1)} = 0.03, u_{(2)} = 0.06, u_{(3)} = 0.12, \\ u_{(4)} = 0.59, u_{(5)} = 0.8, u_{(6)} = 0.86, \\ u_{(7)} = 0.92 \end{gathered} \quad \textbf{(177)}$$

It is desired to recalibrate

$$\hat{F}_7(6.35) = 0.82 \quad \textbf{(178)}$$

Since

$$u_{(5)} \le 0.82 \le u_{(6)} \quad \textbf{(179)}$$

the recalibrated value is

$$\frac{0.82+5(0.86+0.8)-0.8}{7(0.8+0.86)} \approx 0.72 \tag{180}$$

Since

$$\hat{R}_i(\tau') \equiv 1-\hat{P}_i(\tau') \tag{181}$$

the reliability is estimated to be 1−0.72=0.28.

5.4.5   <u>Software Reliability Demonstration</u>.   The purpose of reliability demonstration testing is to prove, with a stated degree of statistical confidence, that the system or the software product meets the specified reliability requirement.

An executing program can be modeled as having a constant failure rate when its code is frozen and it is being subjected to inputs randomly selected from a stationary operational profile.   An operational profile associates each possible input state with a probability of selection.   A "stationary" operational profile means that those probabilities stay the same throughout the test period.   The best operational profile to use is the one the program will experience out in the field, because then the program's failure behavior will be representative of what the end-user would experience if the program were released.

The constant failure rate model is also applicable to types of hardware addressed in MIL-HDBK-217, "Reliability Prediction of Electronic Equipment."   In general, the following types of hardware are modeled by a constant failure rate: (1) parts that are in their "useful life" period, which is after burn-in but before wearout; (2) assemblages of those parts, when in a series reliability configuration; and (3) complex, maintained equipment that does not have redundancy.   When software runs concurrently and in series with such hardware, the overall failure rate will be a constant that is the sum of the constant hardware failure rate and the constant software failure rate.   In the remainder of this section, the item under test will be referred to as "software," but the term should be understood as applying to both software products and to combined hardware/software systems in which the hardware can be modeled by a constant failure rate.

Let λ be the true failure rate of the software.   It is unknown. In designing a demonstration test, two failure rates, λ_0 and λ_1, must be specified ($\lambda_0 < \lambda_1$).   A good test plan will reject, with high probability, software with a true failure rate that approaches λ_1.   A good test plan will accept, with high probability, software with a true failure rate that approaches λ_0.

Relying on the results of the demonstration test for making an accept/reject decision entails two basic risks.   First, if good software happens to perform poorly (fails too many times during the test), then it could be rejected.   Conversely, if, by chance, a bad piece of software performs well during the test, bad software could be accepted.   These two risks must be specified in advance as parameters to the test.   The "producer's risk" is the probability of rejecting software with a true failure rate equal to λ_0.   The "consumer's risk" is the probability of accepting software with a true failure rate equal to λ_1.

Three types of demonstration test are recommended for software: fixed duration test, failure-free execution interval test, and sequential test.

A fixed duration test is used when the amount of test time and cost must be known in advance. A fixed duration test provides demonstrated failure rate to a desired confidence level.

A sequential test will accept software that has a failure rate much lower than λ_0 and reject software that has a failure rate much higher than λ_1 more quickly than a fixed duration test having similar parameters. However, the total test time may vary significantly according to the true failure rate.

A failure-free execution interval test will accept software that has a failure rate lower than λ_0 more quickly than a fixed duration test.

Producer's and consumer's risks usually range from 10% (low risk) to 30% (high risk). The lower the risks, the longer the test.

The ratio

$$d = \frac{\lambda_1}{\lambda_0} \qquad\qquad (182)$$

is called the "discrimination ratio." The discrimination ratio establishes the power of the demonstration test in distinguishing between reliable and unreliable items.   The lower the discrimination ratio, the more test time required.   The simultaneous execution of multiple copies will allow a lower discrimination ratio or save test time. Some low failure rates may be impossible to demonstrate without using multiple copies.

The standard fixed duration and sequential test plans defined in MIL-HDBK-781 can be used for software because these plans assume a constant failure rate (exponential time-to-failure distribution). These test plans are parameterized in terms of mean time between failures (MTBF).

If it is assumed that the program cannot be perfect (fault-free), then the MTBF θ will always exist. The MTBF is the reciprocal of the failure rate:

$$\theta = \frac{1}{\lambda} \qquad\qquad (183)$$

The higher the MTBF the greater the software reliability. In the terminology of MIL-STD-781D, the "lower test MTBF" is $\theta_1 = 1 / \lambda_1$. The "upper test MTBF" is $\theta_0 = 1 / \lambda_0$. To use the tests, one must specify α, β, and d. The tabulated values of the decision risks are 10%, 20%, and 30%. The available values for d are 1.5, 2.0, and 3.0. Not all combinations appear. The MIL-HDBK-781 table provides the test duration (as a multiple of θ_0 and as a multiple of θ_1), the range of number of failures for which a reject decision should be made and that for which an accept decision should be made.

MIL-HDBK-781D also tabulates sequential test plans, called PRST (probability ratio sequential test) plans.

In a failure-free execution period test, the software is given T time units to achieve a failure-free interval of t time units. In the most stringent version of this test, t = T; the software must get through the test with zero failures. In the zero-failure test, the discrimination ratio will be $\ln \beta / \ln (1-\alpha)$ and the test time will be $t = T = -\ln \beta / \lambda_1 = -\ln (1 - \alpha) / \lambda_0$. For lower discrimination ratios, tests can be designed in which t < T. Since β is small, the test time will tend to be just a little longer than θ_1.

The parameters of the test are the α and β risks, λ_0, and λ_1. Table 5-13 provides test plans for various combinations of α, β, and d. The test time T is obtained by dividing either column 4 by λ_1 or dividing column 5 by λ_0. Once T is obtained, the duration t of the failure-free interval is obtained by multiplying column 6 by T. The expected test time (ETT) depends on what the true failure rate is. The true failure rate is not known. The expected test time when the true failure rate is λ_1 is obtained by multiplying column 7 by T. The expected test time when the true failure rate is λ_0 is obtained by multiplying column 8 by T.

Before the test, clear definitions must be established as to what constitutes satisfactory operation and what constitutes failure. The definitions need to be agreed to by both the producer and the consumer.

The software environment must emulate the field operating conditions. These include the operating system version and the versions of other system software with which the application will interact, system parameter settings, workload (transactions per second, for example), as well as the operational profile. To maintain the statistical integrity of the test, each failure must be statistically independent of the rest. Thus, when a failure occurs, any corrupted files or databases must be restored and the software restarted.

For the purposes of demonstration testing, only one software failure can occur per run. A software failure is the sum total of the program behavior that resulted in a system failure. This contrasts with growth testing, where every discrepancy between

TABLE 5-15. Failure-Free Execution Interval Test Plans

1	2	3	4	5	6	7	8
α	β	d	λ_1 T	λ_0 T	t/T	ETT/T λ_1	ETT/T λ_0
.10	.10	2.442	63.308	25.925	.10	.88	.43
.10	.10	2.814	38.581	13.710	.15	.84	.45
.20	.20	1.793	54.330	30.301	.10	.84	.52
.20	.20	1.968	32.618	16.574	.15	.81	.53
.20	.20	2.147	22.445	10.454	.20	.78	.54
.20	.20	2.338	16.640	7.117	.25	.76	.55
.20	.20	2.547	12.927	5.075	.30	.73	.56
.20	.20	2.779	10.365	3.730	.35	.71	.58
.20	.20	3.052	8.501	2.785	.40	.68	.59
.30	.30	1.438	48.707	33.871	.10	.80	.59
.30	.30	1.695	14.361	8.473	.25	.74	.61
.30	.30	1.995	7.088	3.553	.40	.68	.62
.30	.30	2.454	4.086	1.665	.55	.62	.63
.30	.30	3.059	2.526	.826	.70	.58	.66

the actual values of output variables and their required values
is counted as a separate failure, if caused by a different fault.

Procedure 5.4.5-1 - Demonstration test.

Steps

A. Obtain the specification of the lower test MTBF θ_1, an unacceptable value.

B. Obtain the consumer's risk, the probability of accepting software whose true MTBF is θ_1.

C. Obtain the value of the upper test MTBF θ. This is the goal the producer attempted to achieve.

D. Obtain the producer's risk, the probability of rejecting software whose true MTBF is θ_0.

E. Calculate the discrimination ratio as θ_0/θ_1.

F. Choose a tabulated MIL-HDBK-781 fixed length or sequential test plan, or choose a failure-free execution interval test plan from Table 5-13.

Example 1 - Fixed-length test plan

The customer specifies the lower test MTBF θ_1 as 500 hours. The producer's and consumer's risks are set at 20%.   The reliability goal for the software was specified as 750 hours. Design a fixed duration test.

A. The discrimination ratio is calculated at 750 / 500 = 1.5.

B. Using MIL-HDBK-781 Test Plan XID, the duration of the test is provided as 21.5 × 500 hours = 10,750 hours. The acceptable number of failures is provided as 17 or fewer.

Example 2 - PRST test plan

The customer specifies the lower test MTBF θ_1 as 600 hours. The producer's and consumer's risks are set at 10%. The reliability goal for the software was specified as 1200 hours. Design a PRST test plan.

The discrimination ratio is calculated as 1200 / 600 = 2.0. Using MIL-HDBK-781 Test Plan IIID, the minimum time to accept decision is 4.40 × 600 hours = 2640 hours. The expected time to an accept decision (assuming a true MTBF equal to θ_0) is 10.2 × 600 hours = 6120 hours. The maximum time to reach an accept decision (assuming a true MTBF equal to λ_1) is 20.6 × 600 hours = 4120 hours.

Example 3 - Failure-free execution interval test plan

The customer specifies λ_1 as 0.0001 failures/hour. The producer's and consumer's risks are set at 30%. The reliability goal for the software was specified as λ_0 = 0.00005 failures/hour.

The discrimination ratio is calculated as 0.0001/0.00005 = 2.0. Entering Table 5-15 at α=.30 (column 1), β=.30 (column 2), and d=1.995 (column 3) provides $\lambda_1 T$ = 7.008 (column 4), or T = 70.08 hours. Since t/T = .40 (column 6), t = 28.032. The software thus has 80.08 (80 hours, 4 minutes, 48 seconds) hours to achieve a failure-free execution period of 28.032 hours (28 hours, 1 minute, 55.2 seconds).

5.5   Defect Prevention.

MIL–STD–785 includes requirements for the establishment of Program Reviews (PR), Task 103; a Failure Reporting and Corrective Action System (FRACAS) Task 104; and a Failure Review Board (FRB) Task 105. The scope and intent of these tasks make them applicable to combined hardware/software systems. Current implementation of these tasks on hardware, however, tend to emphasize defect detection with relatively minor attention given to promoting process understanding and improvement. The guidelines offered here provide a much more aggressive process–oriented, attention–to–detail, approach to these tasks with the ultimate aim of defect prevention through continuous process improvement. Although the guidance is focused on software, the approach, with appropriate modification, is equally applicable to the hardware.

Simply stated, defect prevention is the process of improving the quality and reliability of the product by preventing the introduction of defects. The defect prevention process can be implemented with little change in the resources needed for conventional FRACAS, FRB and PR tasks. Implementing a defect prevention program requires extensive use of project teams as well as management commitment and advocates to support the process until it becomes firmly established. Defect prevention consists of four basic elements which are similar in nature and intent to the FRACAS, FRB and PR tasks, but with a much greater focus on improving the processes used during software development. The basic elements of defect prevention include the use of:

A.   Causal analysis teams to identify root causes of defects and to generate recommended action items to prevent such defects in the future.

B.   Action teams to implement the recommended preventive actions and to facilitate communications among different functional groups in the organization.

C.   Process reviews to increase the development teams knowledge of key process steps as well as an awareness of quality and reliability issues and goals in each stage of the development.

D.   Fault data collection, processing and monitoring system to facilitate communication of the status of problem areas and progress in their resolution.

5.5.1 Causal Analysis

The purpose of causal analysis is to learn from the errors made in the past by identifying the root causes of defects and recommending action items to prevent recurrence in the future. Simply preventing those defects which have been detected however, is too narrow a goal. When a number of defects of a given type are found, it is likely that more of the same are present or likely to be introduced, but as yet are undetected. It is the underlying process which must be corrected in order to promote extinction of the sources of defects. The action items usually involve process changes, enhancement to existing tools, improved communication, more tailored education and training requirements, new or improved documentation or enhancements in the product design itself. Causal analysis team meetings are periodically conducted during a specific development phase or at the end of a major work stage within a particular phase. Team members should be comprised of the developers who created the software because they are in the best position to identify root causes. To provide guidance in identifying root causes the following checklist of questions and root cause categorization scheme is provided. For each fault uncovered, the following basic questions can be posed.

A.   How was the error introduced?

B.   At what development stage or process step was the fault created? At what stage was the fault detected?

C.   What specific activity contributed to the fault?

D.   Is it likely that similar fault types are present in the product but as yet remain undetected?

E.   What activity could have advanced the time at which the fault was detected?

F.   What category does the root cause of the fault fall in and how can the fault be prevented in the future?

G.   Why? Why? Why? Why? Why? (ask 5 whys)

Examples of a root cause classification scheme and various types of preventive actions is provided in Table 5-16.

Table 5-16. Defect Root Cause Categories

Root Cause Category	Failure/Defect Circumstances	Root Cause Determination and Types of Preventive Action
Oversight	Failure to consider all cases and conditions of the problem. Lack of thoroughness or omission of an important detail. Lack of time due to schedule pressure or difficulty in running complete manual check.	What was overlooked? Why was it overlooked? Types of Preventive Action Reminders or warnings in checklists or common error lists. Use of automatic checkers. On-Line availability of product design documentation.
Education and Training	Failure in understanding of the product or process or the external environment. Misunderstanding of the specification requirements or of the mission in which the program is to operate.	What specifically was not understood? Why was it not understood? Types of Preventive Action Seminars and classes related to the product and/or process. Tutorials on hardware/software interface requirements. Improved process documentation.
Communication	Failure to receive correct or complete information. Failure to receive updated information on changes made to the software.	What was not communicated? Why was it not communicated? Types of Preventive Action On-Line failure reporting and preventive action tracking system. Process review team participation.
Transcription	Mistakes in copying code or inputting data. Misspelling of variable name. Error-prone procedures.	What procedure was being used? What is wrong with the procedure? Types of Preventive Action Use of spelling checker. Use of automated tools for configuration management. Team participation. Change in procedure.

5.5.2 Process Review

Process review team meetings are held at the beginning of each major development stage (e.g., Requirements Analysis, Preliminary Design, Detailed Design, Coding and CSU Testing) to prepare the development team for the work to be done. The process review meeting serves as the primary means of feedback for the Defect Prevention Process. Emphasis is placed on the technical aspects of the development process and on quality and reliability issues. Review team activities generally should include:

A.   A complete description of the objectives and purpose of the work stage and of the process to be used such as the procedures, tools, common error lists, design checklists, validation, and test methods, including a review of change activity and the reliability analysis results from previous stages.

B.   Review of the inputs (e.g., specification requirements, hardware/software interfaces of the design, change activity implemented, reliability goals and the major activities and responsibilities needed to produce the required outputs.

C.   Identification of critical items and potential problems that can affect quality and reliability.

The use of process review teams at each stage of the development process encourages the development teams to view the process as a living and dynamic process that is being constantly improved. Process changes which come about through the Defect Prevention Program and their relationship to quality and reliability issues can thus be thoroughly understood by all members of the development team.

5.5.3 Process Action Team

Action teams act upon and implement the preventive actions recommended by the causal analysis teams. Team hierarchical structure and composition is highly dependent on the complexity and nature of both the product and process and the unique needs of the organizations. Action teams can be either local or at a higher level. Local action teams can be comprised of members representatives of different cross-functional groups who must work together and who face common problems in developing the product. Higher level action teams act upon those action items that cannot be handled at the local level such as those that may span several functional areas or may involve commitment of resources. Team members can be representative of various disciplines such as design, test, documentation or training. A common element however, is that the members should be highly dedicated and motivated to improve the processes in which they are involved. The action team maintains a data base to track all new action items, to monitor progress in resolving open action items and to ensure closure of the items with a definitive preventive action. The action items are valuated and prioritized by the action team so that those with the greatest potential payoff are acted upon first. Analyses of the failure/fault data are also performed to, for example, rank problems having the highest frequency of occurrence or those which potentially have a large impact on reliability. Cost to fix the problems must also be considered in prioritizing action items.

5.5.4 Failure Reporting Database

The failures and defects found during code inspections and test should be documented in a data base for use by the causal analysis, process review and action teams. Failure/fault reporting and data base management procedures should be developed which provide unique identification and complete traceability of failure/fault discovery incidents as well as ease of communication to all team members. An example of the data elements which should be collected is as follows:

A. Failure/defect report number
B. Activity or work center where defect was discovered
C. Identification of component, module which contained the defect
D. Description of symptom created by the defect
E. Description of defect
F. Action recommended to prevent the defect
G. Activity where defect was injected
H. Failure priority (see Appendix C MIL-STD-2167A)
I. Execution Time-To-Failure
J. Causal analysis required (yes or no)
K. Causal Analysis Date and Report number if applicable
L. Root Cause Category (Oversight, Education, Transcription, etc.)
M. Description of preventive action taken by action team.
N. Preventive action implementation and problem report closure date

Printed and bound by CPI Group (UK) Ltd, Croydon, CR0 4YY

03/10/2024

01040333-0008